Emerging Trends, Threats, and Opportunities in International Marketing

Emerging Trends, Threats, and Opportunities in International Marketing

What Executives Need to Know

Michael R. Czinkota, Ilkka A. Ronkainen,
and Masaaki Kotabe

business**expert**
Press

First published in 2009 by
Business Expert Press, LLC
222 East 46th Street, New York, NY 10017
www.businessexpertpress.com

ISBN-13: 978-1-60649-035-8 (paperback)
ISBN-10: 1-60649-035-4 (paperback)

ISBN-13: 978-1-60649-036-5 (e-book)
ISBN-10: 1-60649-036-2 (e-book)

DOI 10.4128/9781606490365

A publication in the Business Expert Press International Business
collection

Collection ISSN: 1948-2752 (print)
Collection ISSN: 1948-2760 (electronic)

Cover design by Artistic Group—Monroe, NY
Interior design by Scribe, Inc.

First edition: October 2009

10 9 8 7 6 5 4 3 2 1

Printed in the United States of America.

To Ilona and Margaret, MRC

To Susan, Sanna, and Alex, IAR

To Sylvia, MK

Abstract

The context of international business has evolved over the years and has always reflected the climate of the time. Three major changes that have taken place in the last decade or so should be noted. *First*, the landscape of the global economy changed drastically in the last decade or so. The Asian and Latin American financial crises, the further expansion of the European Union (EU), and the emergence of BRIC (Brazil, Russia, India, and China) as economic powerhouses have occurred during this period. And most recently, the global financial and economic crisis caused primarily by the U.S. subprime mortgage loan crisis since late 2008 is ravaging the integrity of the global economy with unprecedented severity.

Second, the explosive growth of information technology tools, including the Internet and electronic commerce (e-commerce), has had a significant effect on the way we do business internationally. On one hand, everyone seems to agree that business transactions will be faster and more global early on. And it is very true. As a result, the nature of the global supply chain and global trade as managed by multinational firms has fundamentally changed. However, on the other hand, the more deeply we have examined this issue, the more convinced we have become that certain things would not change or could even become more local as a result of globalization that the Internet and e-commerce bestow on us.

Third, it is an underlying human tendency to desire to be different when there are economic and political forces of convergence (often referred to as globalization). When the globalization argument (and movement) became fashionable in the 1980s and 1990s, many of us believed that globalization would make global business easier. Doing business beyond national borders, indeed, has become easier, but this does not necessarily mean that customers want the same products in countries around the world. For example, many more peoples around the world than ever before are trying to emphasize cultural and ethnic differences as well as accepting those differences. Just think about many new countries being born as well as regional unifications taking place at the same time.

Indeed, these global changes we have observed in recent years are more than extraordinary. As a result, business practitioners are facing enormous challenges to cope with those changes in an uncertain world.

This book is constitutes a timely compilation of work addressing marketing in an uncertain world, competition from emerging and reemerging markets, global sourcing, and meeting old and new global challenges.

Keywords

Globalization, global trends, exporting, trade policy, corporate strategy, strategic alliances, global sourcing, global supply chain, outsourcing, competitive advantage, emerging markets, regional transformation, terrorism

Contents

Preface

The recent changes in the climate of the time mandates that firms adjust to a new world in which to compete and thrive. This book constitutes a timely compilation of work addressing doing business in an uncertain world, competition from emerging and reemerging markets, global sourcing, and the meeting of old and new global challenges. These themes are briefly described below.

I. Marketing in an Uncertain World

The global business environment has undergone enormous changes within the last decade and in particular in the last two years. The markets around the world have become truly interconnected as a result of a confluence of four forces: (a) saturated domestic markets forcing companies to look for market opportunities abroad, (b) emerging markets and an increased number of formidable competitors from those emerging markets that have added to the nature of global competition, (c) increased global cooperation among companies to spread out the risk of enormous investment requirements, particularly in high-tech industries, and (d) the rise of IT that has helped reduce the geographical and political boundaries of international business. The extent of global interconnectedness has touched everybody's central nerves as the subprime mortgage loan problems in the United States have suddenly caused the worst global recession in many decades, ushering in an era of unprecedented uncertainty.

The first section analyzes the implications of these shifts and trends in the global business environment. Chapter 1 highlights the linkages between international marketing and freedom, positioning the marketing field as a key change agent in times of global adjustments. In chapter 2, a global group of policy makers, business executives, and academic experts participate in the development of a 10-year research agenda for international marketers. Chapter 3 highlights the limited influence marketers have in today's policy debates and offers opportunities for a greater role of marketing. Chapter 4 explains how export promotion has changed over time and how marketers can enhance their firm's international activities while staying within the constraints of global trade agreements. Chapter 5 explores the gradual change in the manufacturing position of industrialized nations, warning about further shifts in this sector away from leading economies.

II. Competition From (Re)emerging Markets

Country competitiveness is neither fixed nor stable. The dominant feature of the global economy is the rapid change in the relative status of various countries' economic output. In 1830, China and India alone accounted for about 60% of the manufactured output of the world. Since then, the share of the world manufacturing output produced by the 20 or so countries that are today known as the rich industrial economies moved from about 30% in 1830 to almost 80% by 1913. In the 1980s, the U.S. economy was characterized as "floundering" or even "declining," and many pundits predicted that Asia, led by Japan, would become the leading regional economy in the 21st century. Then the 1997–1999 Asian financial crisis changed the economic milieu of the world. Since the September 11, 2001, terrorist attacks, the U.S. economy has grown faster than that of any other developed country at an annual rate of 3–4% for much of the first decade of the 21st century—that is, until the U.S. subprime mortgage crisis triggered a severe global recession in 2008. In the past 20 years, however, China's real annual gross domestic product (GDP) growth rate has averaged 9.5% a year, while India's has been 5.7%, compared to the average 3% GDP growth in the United States. Accordingly, an increasing number of competitors are also expected to originate from those emerging economies. A few notable recent changes attest to the globalization of the markets. First, Germany overtook the United States as the largest exporting country for the first time. Second, China surged to become the second largest exporting country, surpassing Japan. Third, Mexico has emerged as one of the major exporting countries. Clearly, the milieu of the world economy has changed significantly.

As a result, over the next two decades, the markets that hold the greatest potential for dramatic increases in U.S. exports are not the traditional trading partners in Europe and Japan, which now account for the overwhelming bulk of the international trade of the United States. But they will be those big emerging markets (BEMs). Already, there are signs that in the future the biggest trade headache for the United States may be not Japan but China and India. China's trade surplus with the United States ballooned from $86 billion in 2000 to $162 billion in 2004; it had already surpassed Japan's trade surplus position with the United States by 2000. India has increasingly become a hotbed as sources of IT, communications, software development, and call centers—particularly for many U.S. multinationals. Russia is extremely rich in natural resources, including oil and natural gas, that are dwindling in the rest of the world; has gradually warmed up to international commerce; and will potentially become a major trading nation. These major emerging economies, among others, are likely to reshape the nature of global competition in the next decade.

Chapter 6 discusses the opportunities offered by volatile conditions, with particular advantages accruing to the flexibility and responsiveness of smaller firms. Chapter 7 analyzes the foreign market entry strategies of firms originating from Brazil, Chile, and Mexico. Those companies tend to use two-pronged strategies vis-à-vis their competitors by emphasizing cost leadership strategy when entering the developed country markets and while employing differentiation strategy when entering other developing/emerging markets. Chapter 8 further examines the nature of alliances those Latin American companies pursue with companies from developed countries. It explains the strategic objectives of these Latin American companies, their partnership structures, and their satisfaction in collaborating with companies from developed countries. Chapter 9 highlights how marketing has supported, and on occasion even initiated, the social and economic shifts that have occurred in the European member nations of the former Soviet Empire. Chapter 10 examines the consumers in different East Asian countries—namely, Japan, South Korea, and China—and addresses the importance of not overgeneralizing about their consumption characteristics. Globalization does not necessarily mean that the markets have become similar. Companies need to tailor country-specific strategies to target consumers in these countries; however, young generations are found to demonstrate similarities that allow for standardized strategies across national boundaries. Practical marketing strategies to tackle the Asian markets also are discussed.

III. Global Sourcing and Supply Chain Management

Global sourcing and supply chain management have played a critical role in the growth and development of world trade and in the integration of business operations on a worldwide scale. In fact, the level of world trade in goods and, to some extent, services depends to a significant degree on the availability of economical and reliable international transportation services. We can distinguish among three waves of global sourcing. The first wave, starting in the mid-1980s and continuing to this day, was primarily focused on international sourcing of manufacturing activities. Large manufacturing firms were increasingly spreading their operations across the world and began to use suppliers from a variety of countries to exploit so-called best-in-world sources. Supply chains, as a consequence, became more global and also much more complicated in nature. A second wave started to occur in the early 1990s, when firms decided to start getting rid of their IT departments that had, over time, grown to a substantial size. International sourcing mostly involved labor-intensive programming activities, which due to their relatively standardized nature could be sourced from locations like India with relative ease. IT itself had turned into more and more of a commodity, and many firms started to show little interest in developing new information systems in-house. In recent years we have seen the rise of business process outsourcing (BPO) in what has become known as the offshoring movement. The object has now broadened from just IT services to a range of other services, including those in accounting, human resources management, finance, sales, and after-sales, such as call centers. India is still a primary target country and has now produced a range of strong local business process providers such as Infosys and Wipro from India, but competition from elsewhere is on the rise. It is this third wave of BPO that is now generating so much noise and so many media headlines.

In its early years, global sourcing was examined mostly from in-house development and procurement perspectives, and in the last decade, research focus has shifted to "outsourcing" activities. Along with this shift from an internal to an external focus on global sourcing, many researchers and business practitioners have applied a core competency argument to justify increased levels of outsourcing activities on a global basis. Chapter 11 discusses that no such consensus exists in reality as to the effect of outsourcing and explores potential limitations and negative consequences of outsourcing strategy on a global scale. Chapter 12, with a dynamic perspective of outsourcing strategy and its performance implications, provides a theoretical argument on an optimal degree of outsourcing and explores ways in which developments in e-commerce are linked to changing outsourcing levels. Chapter 13 specifically focuses on outsourcing of services activities and addresses such questions as what types of service activities are conducive to outsourcing, what factors are important in selecting suppliers for outsourcing service activities, and how service outsourcing strategy affects firm performance.

Chapter 14 longitudinally analyzes three cases of major consumer electronics manufacturers—Emerson Radio from the United States, Japan's Sony, and Philips from the Netherlands—to understand the dynamic process related to their sourcing strategies. An evolutionary stage model is developed relating outsourcing to competence development inside the firm and shows that a vicious cycle may emerge. The evolutionary stage model helps managers understand for which activities and under which conditions outsourcing across borders is not a viable option. Chapter 15 explores a market potential for offshore IT and BPO. Although Eastern Europe lags far behind more prominent locations, including India, Ireland, Malaysia, and the Philippines, it may change soon, as demand for offshoring among Western European companies has risen rapidly, with Eastern Europe emerging as a favorite destination. Finally, Chapter 16 describes the maturing nature of service outsourcing relationships between service providers and customers. Outsourcing could eventually resemble a utility computing model, with services purchased a la carte without costly up-front investments and enlightened outsourcing customers rigorously managing their outcomes, not their inputs.

IV. Meeting Old and New Global Challenges

The fourth section is mainly about reconciliation of the irreconcilable. Finding opportunity in conflict and dissent is one of the most substantial opportunities offered by and to international business. This chapter highlights how, instead of walking away or discontinuing operations, business executives can make a difference by developing new approaches and finding new solutions.

Chapters 17 and 18 open up the room for dissent by exploring how firms can address the standardization/adaptation issue in new ways. There is also a focus on how to bring outsiders into the tent, making firms head in a common direction. Chapter 19 explores the impact of terrorism on global corporate activity. A key emphasis rests with the need and ability of corporations to prepare for friction and disruption in the global marketplace and the particularly crucial role played by marketers in assessing risk and developing new strategies. Chapters 20–22 further discuss how management needs to initiate a corporate readiness for change, with special attention to shifts in globalization and their impact on corporate activities.

Contributors

Martijn Allessie is a consultant in McKinsey's Amsterdam office.

Maria Cecilia Coutinho de Arruda is with Fundação Getúlio Vargas, São Paulo, Brazil.

Preet S. Aulakh is Pierre Lassonde Chair Professor in International Business at Schulich School of Business, York University. He received his PhD from the University of Texas at Austin. His research interests include international technology licensing, firm strategies in emerging markets, and foreign entry modes.

Wendy M. Becker is a principal in McKinsey's London office.

Andrew Cainey is a senior executive advisor for Booz Allen in Greater China. He works with both local and multinational financial institutions on all aspects of strategy, organization, and capability-building in China, Korea, and the rest of Asia.

Marla Capozzi is a consultant in McKinsey's Boston office.

Bhaskar Chakravorti is a principal in McKinsey's Boston office.

Vinay Couto is a vice president with Booz Allen Hamilton in Chicago. He advises companies across multiple industries on BPO sourcing strategies and assists those clients in running outsourcing programs.

Michael R. Czinkota is a professor at the McDonough School of Business of Georgetown University in Washington, DC, and at the University of Birmingham in the United Kingdom, where he teaches international business and marketing.

Claudiu V. Dimofte is assistant professor of marketing at the McDonough School of Business, Georgetown University.

Ashok Divakaran is a principal with Booz Allen Hamilton in Chicago. He specializes in the development of strategies for large-scale organizational transformation, with a focus on outsourcing, offshoring, and shared services.

Renee Dye is a consultant in McKinsey's Atlanta office.

Vanessa M. Freeman is a consultant in McKinsey's London office.

Walter Greene is with The University of Texas–Pan American.

Klaus-Peter Gushurst is a Booz & Company senior partner based in Munich and a member of the firm's global board of directors. He specializes in strategy, turnaround and restructuring, and corporate management, primarily in the financial-services and automotive industries.

Ronald Haddock is a vice president of Booz Allen in Greater China. He works with auto and industrial companies from around the world on strategies for growth and operational effectiveness in the Asia Pacific markets.

Detlev Hoch is a director in McKinsey's Düsseldorf office.

Crystal Jiang is an assistant professor of strategy and international business at Bryant University. She received her PhD from Temple University.

Johny K. Johansson is McCrane/Shaker professor of international business and marketing, McDonough School of Business, Georgetown University.

Sonia Ketkar is assistant professor at the College of Business and Economics, Towson University, Towson, Maryland.

Gary Knight is with Florida State University.

Masaaki Kotabe is the Washburn Chair Professor of International Business and Marketing and the director of research at the Institute of Global Management Studies at the Fox School of Business, Temple University.

Michal Kwiecinski, a consultant in the operations practice, is based in McKinsey's Warsaw office.

Michael J. Mol is an associate professor in strategic management at Warwick Business School in the United Kingdom.

Janet Y. Murray is E. Desmond Lee Professor for Developing Women Leaders and Entrepreneurs in International Business and professor of marketing at the College of Business Administration, University of Missouri–St Louis.

Peter Peters, a principal in the global IT practice, is based in McKinsey's Düsseldorf office.

Ilkka A. Ronkainen is a professor of international business and marketing, McDonough School of Business, Georgetown University, and a docent of international marketing, Helsinki School of Economics.

Roberto J. Santillán-Salgado is with ITESM, Monterrey, Mexico.

Olivier Sibony is a director in McKinsey's Paris office.

Ivan de Souza is a Booz & Company senior partner. A member of the firm's global board of directors, he oversees the firm's Latin America business. He specializes in strategy, marketing, and organization services for financial institutions and conglomerates.

Reiner Springer is with Wirschaftsuniuersitat Wien, Vienna, Austria.

Hildy Teegen is the dean at the Moore School of Business, University of South Carolina–Columbia. She received her PhD from the University of Texas at Austin. Her research focuses on international alliances, marketing strategy, and negotiation, particularly in Latin America.

Carrie Thompson is a consultant in McKinsey's Atlanta office.

Edward Tse is Booz Allen Hamilton's managing partner for Greater China. He advises multinational and local clients on strategy, organizations, and operations.

Vanessa Wallace is a Booz & Company partner and leads the financial-services practice in Asia, Austrailia, and New Zealand. She specializes in strategy, postmerger integration, and restructuring in retail banking, wealth management, insurance, and the public sector.

PART I

Marketing in an Uncertain World

CHAPTER 1

Freedom and International Marketing

Janis Joplin's Candidacy as Patron of the Field

Michael R. Czinkota

Some Background

Patrons have been anointed to watch over guilds, professions, or special intentions. St. Valentine watches over lovers and florists, Hippocrates looks after physicians and their patients, and Her Majesty the Queen is the Patron of the Royal Society for the Arts. Having a patron appears to be particularly useful under conditions where a field and its adherents are under scrutiny or even under fire, or when the results of an undertaking can go either way. The patron is either expected to extend some measure of protection or provide that special "nudge" from above that hopefully tilts the eventual outcome in the right direction.

Given the Janus-like face of international marketing, often beneficial but also known to be controversial, it seems only appropriate to search for a patron to obtain guidance for the future of the profession and to bring distinction upon a discipline that all too often has had to fight for recognition and acceptance.

Finding the Candidate

Searching for patron candidates is not easy. In spite of today's rampant globalization, many people want nothing to do with things international, much less with marketing. Others haven't made a contribution that deserves such honorific recognition.

That rapidly slims the eligible listing, and brings us to Janis Joplin. She has lots of patron support going for her. She was a great communicator and her songs are famous for their outreach even more than three decades after her death. She is from America—the cradle of marketing as a scholarly discipline. She was an interpreter of modern international marketing issues at their inception. She sang of key international brand thinking—her lyrics praised the glory of Porsches when Corvettes were cool, but she implored the Lord to buy her a Mercedes-Benz. In another international marketing song titled "Me and Bobby McGee," Joplin sang about the *bandanna*, Hindi for "ties and bonds," which are the core focus of the marketing discipline. She sang about the "shared secrets of my soul," an early reference to customer relationship management. But Joplin is at her most powerful when she sings,

> Freedom's just another word for nothin' left to lose
> Nothin', it ain't nothin', honey, if it ain't free
> And feeling good was easy Lord, when he sang the blues
> And feeling good was good enough for me
> Good enough for me and my Bobby McGee. (Kristofferson, 1969)

In her concern for freedom, she has an ability to reach out across generations, which leads to her continued broad global appeal today. Millions of fans are still singing these lines. Today, when the issue of freedom has surged to the forefront in the thinking of many, let us do some thinking about its meaning in an international marketing context.

An Analysis

Let us briefly think back to the environment of the early 1970s when "Me and Bobby McGee" entered the world. The Western world in particular was reaching far beyond globalization, exploring the universe through regular Apollo landings on the moon. Back on earth, there was economic turmoil. The dollar had begun to depreciate sharply. Global trade volume was about $200 billion per year, poised to take off and reach about $8,300 billion in 2003 (International Monetary Fund, 2004).

In the global financial sector, the gold window had already been closed to everyone but central banks. In light of seemingly large trade deficits, which then amounted to $5 billion per year, the U.S. government would soon abandon the gold standard altogether and replace it gradually with freely floating currencies that would adjust to market demand and supply. Terrorism was introduced on a global scale during that time. In Germany, the Bader Meinhof Gang was laying bombs and shooting at police, and for the first time, the modern Olympics were disrupted by the murder of a country's delegation when members of the Black September organization took over the quarters of Israeli athletes. These years laid the groundwork for the globalization trends to follow over the next 30 years.

The Issue of Freedom

Back to the lyrics and Joplin's preoccupation with freedom. You may ask what this has to do with international marketing, particularly in light of the fact that trade between far-flung peoples has existed for millennia (just think of the Silk Road or the Spice Caravans). Well, that is true, but in modern times, international marketing, just like the term *freedom*, has had many links with the United States. Consider why the Pilgrims came to American shores—to be free from persecution. Look at the U.S. Constitution, which, in its preamble, refers to "securing the Blessing of Liberty." Americans have had a special affinity for the term *freedom*, just as, in his time, the Yankee trader had been of world repute.

Second, freedom is about options. If there is no alternative, there is no freedom, only a predestined path taken without conscious decision or the possibility to exercise one's virtue. Having a true alternative provides the opportunity to decide, to exercise virtue. In the blaze of the klieg lights, it is easy to make the "right" decision. That is not an exercise in virtue, because real alternatives are effectively removed. The real selection among alternatives takes place in the darkness of night when nobody is looking and when there is a good chance of getting away with things.

The focus and aim of international marketing is on crossing borders to provide more than one selection for customers, letting them pick among the variety offered in order to attain the greatest possible satisfaction. International marketing does so in all corners of the globe, the glamorous ones—often called the Elizabeth Arden circuit of London–Paris–Rome—as well as in the small and remote ones where the efforts are not seen by others. By operating in the limelight but also well outside of it, international marketing offers the freedom to exercise virtue—be it in decisions of pricing, supplying, or purchasing.

By providing choices, international marketing also helps with decision making in general. It participates in shaping environments, if the participants are allowed actual choices (Johansson, 1990). That's where the linkage to freedom becomes very evident, because the claims of freedom do not always match reality. An analysis of market thinking can quite easily provide the acid test here. I like going to countries where stuff is owned by "the people"—things like parks, steel plants, or television studios. I like to suggest to individuals (usually state-sponsored guides) who proudly show off these achievements of freedom that they sell their share. As we discuss this issue, typically several things happen. First, the box they all live in is pointed out: "Nobody has ever done that!" Then, the demand limitation is highlighted: "We are unaware of a buyer." Finally, the real supply constraints emerge: "I couldn't because they wouldn't let me." By then, understanding typically begins to emerge about the difference between purported and actual freedom.

Freedom and international marketing are linked in many more ways. Freedom is typically recognized by specific rights and privileges in order to be meaningful. When John F. Kennedy wanted to make life better in America, he focused on the freedom of consumers. He formulated the individual's right to safety, to be heard, to be informed, and to choose—rights that continue to play key roles worldwide when international marketers branch out today.

Another key dimension of freedom is not to be hemmed in, allowing people to be able to work outside of the box. For most activities, the box tends to be the result of the borders that define a nation. That is usually where government policy ends and where citizenship encounters its limits. But that is a mere point of transition for international marketing.

The discipline depends on the understanding of how to successfully cross national borders, what the differences are once the crossing is done, and how to reconcile profitably any conflicts resulting from variances and inconsistencies in rules and expectations.

Concurrently, international marketing contains the freedom of almost unlimited growth potential. Activities confined to domestic borders will likely soon run into limits of expansion. With international market opportunities, the limits to growth are reached far less quickly. Different families of products can extend the life of goods or services for a long time. Instead of restrictions, the international marketing paradigm encourages the stripping away of restraints; instead of limitations, there is the pointing out of opportunity. Being passionate about international markets can open one's eyes to the prospects of freedom.

Freedom also means not being forced to do something one does not want to do. In the words of Hayek, freedom is the absence of force (Hayek, 1971). In today's times, many speak about migration pressures that force people to move from their rural homes into urban areas or from their developing countries into industrialized ones. Industrialized nations, in turn, speak about immigration pressure. For both sides, little if any freedom is involved here. The individuals who do the moving would much rather stay home but cannot afford to do so due to economic exigencies. The recipient countries might not want to welcome the migrants but do so in response to political and humanitarian pressures. Both sides are losing or have lost their freedom. International marketing may have been part of what triggers some of these migrations, but it also can be instrumental in stemming the tide. It can provide the economic opportunity at home for individuals so that they need not migrate. It can let individuals become productive contributors to the global economy and, in an organized, proud, and supraterranean fashion, remove sensitive political points of friction.

The chapter of world history written in the late part of the 20th century has been most instrumental in showing us how markets, market forces, and the recognition of demand and supply have directly affected human rights and the extent of freedom. That was the time when the long-standing rivalry between socialism and market orientation was resolved. With all humility and gratefulness, one can now make the following conclusion: markets were right! In country after country, markets have demonstrated typically greater efficiency and effectiveness in their ability to better satisfy the needs of people. International marketing has been instrumental in stimulating these newly emerging market forces.

When the Iron Curtain disintegrated, Central and Eastern Europe very rapidly joined the community of market-oriented nations. All too often, these important political shifts in the latter part of the 20th century are ascribed simply to an overwhelming desire for democracy. To a large degree, however, the key demand for change was aimed at perestroika, a fundamental reform of the Soviet-style economy through increased availability of food, housing, and consumer goods; in other words, an increase in choice and market alternatives (Theroux & George, 1989). In spite of complaints about the slowness of change, the insufficiency of wealth redistribution, and the inequities inherent in societal upheavals, a large majority of participants in all these market-oriented changes seem to be better off now than they were before. Without the transition provided by international marketing, these changes would not have come about that swiftly.

The Cost of All This Freedom

Another big issue raised in the context of freedom is its cost. One keeps hearing about the large segment of the world population that is poor and therefore supposedly excluded from any international marketing efforts; the World Bank's president calls them the 3 billion $2-a-day poor (Wolfensohn, 2001). One can also see them as an attractive $6 billion-a-day opportunity for firms who may have valuable exchanges to offer. Consider the surprising (for some) effects of exchanging surpluses through international marketing:

> One really big surprise of the postwar era has been that historic enemies such as Germany and France, or Japan and the United States have not had the remotest threat of war (between them) since 1945. Why should they? Anything Japan has that we want we can buy, and on very easy credit terms, so why fight for it? Why should the Japanese fight the United States and lose all those profitable markets? France and Germany, linked intimately through

marketing and the European Union, are now each other's largest trading partners. Closed systems build huge armies and waste their substance on guns and troops; open systems spend their money on new machine tools to crank out Barbie dolls or some such trivia. Their bright young people figure out how to tool the machines, not how to fire the latest missile. For some reason, they not only get rich fast but also lose interest in military adventures. Japan, that peculiar superpower without superguns, confounds everyone simply because no one has ever seen a major world power that got that way by selling you to death, not shooting you to death. In short, if you trade a lot with someone, why fight? The logical answer—you don't—is perhaps the best news mankind has had in millennia. (Farmer, 1987)

So international marketing provides us with the opportunity to acquire resources from someone else without force. International marketing, therefore, is also crucial in contributing to freedom from war and, at the same time, assuring additional choice for consumption.

The Rising Cost of Freedom

We are finding that the cost of freedom seems to be increasing lately. Terms like *free trade* or *free choice* have been misleading since they all come with a price, which international marketers pay in terms of preparing their shipments, scrutinizing their customers, and conforming to government regulations of tariffs or taxes. They pay for it when subsidies are reduced and markets are opened further, resulting in more intense competition.

Now prices are going up when international marketers have to file special paperwork or comply with security guidelines, which slow down the flow of merchandise. Every time a shipment is delayed, international transactions are less profitable and the subsequent business dealings become less competitive. Customers talk about unmet expectations and domestic firms point to the vagaries of international markets.

We all are paying a higher price due to global terrorism, which has permeated the global marketplace. In most instances, terrorism is not an outgrowth of choice but rather the lack of it. Terrorists may succeed in reducing the freedom of others but not in increasing their own. The principal choices played out between those exercising terrorism and those exposed to it are those consistent with economic theory of return on investment. When terrorists select targets in response to governmental implementation of antiterrorism policies, the harder targets are likely to motivate them to go for easier ones. Increased protection of past targets may result in attacks on new and unexpected targets that are more likely to succeed. Similarly, if terrorists can no longer enter a country, they may attack that country's symbols and representatives abroad. If embassies are then more secured and fortified, terrorists may attack that nation's individuals and companies.

Who is typically most affected by terrorist acts? Attacks aimed at businesses, such as the infamous bombings of U.S. franchises abroad, do not bring big MNCs to their knees. The local participants, the local employees, the local investors, and the local customers are affected most. Who can protect themselves against such attacks and who can afford to protect targets? Only the more wealthy countries and companies can. They have the choice of where to place their funds, with whom to trade, and whether to hold the enemy at bay through a security bubble created via exports, a franchise, or a wholly owned subsidiary. The poor players do not have any choices and their alternatives are not improved by any gruesome act. The local firms, the nations with economies in development, and the poor customers continue to be out there, exposed to further acts of terrorism without the ability to influence events.

But international marketing can enable the disenfranchised to develop alternatives. As suggested by Prahalad and Hammond (2002), multinational firms can invest in the world's poorest markets and increase their own revenue while reducing poverty. With support from shareholders and the benefit of good governance, marketers can, and should, continue in their role as social change agents. It should be kept in mind that international marketing has value maximization at its heart. If it is worthwhile to fulfill the needs of large segments of people, even at low margins, then it will be done.

Value and Freedom

Implicit in raising the cost consideration is also the question of value. In a global setting, freedom can take on many dimensions. It would appear then that there are likely to be differences in valences of freedom across borders. Privileges and obligations that are near and dear to one may well be cheap and easily disposed of by others. The views of Western society may differ from those views of other parts of the world. Such differences then account for misunderstandings, surprises, and long-term conflicts. It is therefore important to consider ways we can harmonize values or at least get a shared view and understanding of values.

There are two value dimensions at work here, both of them highly relevant to international marketing. One of them refers to the macro dimension and may also be circumscribed as the international values and virtues of a market economy. It is important to understand the value here because it offers, quite subtly, a mechanism of checks and balances. In a world that no longer has the political adversity and restraint of the second half of the 20th century, the existence of a neutral and effective mechanism for this role is necessary and crucial.

The unheralded underpinnings of what is being "sold" to the world in a market economy setting are fourfold. First, there is an interaction between supply and demand that is driven by reasonably free market forces. Second, this interaction permits the price mechanism to work, which provides indications as to where investments are likely to be most profitable. Third, investors, who provide resources to the economy, will find these resources to be steered to productive and efficient uses and receive the opportunity to earn profits and to keep these profits. Fourth, in return for high compensation, the nonowner managerial class provides the absentee owners or shareholders with their best efforts to preserve and increase stakeholder benefits.

The keys to making this macro dimension work are governmental, managerial, and corporate virtue, vision, and veracity. Unless the world can believe in what firms and their managers say and do, it will be difficult to forge a global commitment between those doing the marketing and the ones being marketed to. It is therefore of vital interest to the proponents of freedom and international marketing to ensure that corruption, bribery, lack of transparency, and poor governance are exposed for their negative effects in any setting or society. The main remedy will be the collaboration of the global policy community in agreeing on what constitutes transgressions and swift punishment of the culprits involved. In order to avoid an abuse of such regulations as nontariff barriers, rigid standards emanating from an agreement supervised by the World Trade Organization are in everyone's interest (Czinkota, Ronkainen, & Donath, 2004).

A second and perhaps even more crucial issue is the value system we use in making choices. Some years ago, the Mars Climate Orbiter missions failed spectacularly as a result of the use of different values by the mission navigation teams. One team was using metric units and the other used the English system of measurement. This mistake caused the orbiter to get too close to the atmosphere, where it was destroyed ("NASA's Metric Confusion," 1999).

There are major differences among what people value around the world. Contrasts include togetherness next to individuality, cooperation next to competition, modesty next to assertiveness, and self-effacement next to self-actualization (Hofstede, 1998). Often, global differences in value systems are what keep us apart and what frequently result in spectacularly destructive differences. How we value a life, for example, can be crucial in terms of how we treat individuals. What value we place on family, work, leisure time, or progress has a substantial effect on how we see and evaluate each other.

Cultural studies tell us that there are major differences between, and even within, nations. International marketing, through its linkages via goods, services, ideas, and communications, can achieve important assimilation of value systems. On the consumer side, new products have attained international appeal and encouraged similar activities around the world, where many of us wear denim, dance the same dances, and eat pizza and sushi (Marquardt & Reynolds, 1994). It has been claimed that local product offerings help define people and provide identity and that it is the local idiosyncrasies that make people beautiful (Johansson, 2004). Some offer the persistence of the specific breakfast habits of the English and the French as evidence of immutability in the face of globalization (de Mooij, 1998). It is worth remembering that values as key manifestations of culture are learned, not genetically implanted. As life's experiences grow more international and more similar, so do values. Therefore, every time marketing forges a new linkage in thinking, new progress is made in shaping greater commonality in values.

There is another value aspect to consider. In today's times, many people are growing uncertain about the issue of values in general. Old providers of values who were societal pillars, such as teachers, soldiers, and even churchmen, have, through their behavior, sown doubt on their personal rectitude. Institutions such as government or universities have suffered from a similar growth of public doubt in their credibility. In such an era of uncertainty, it is important to have some anchors on which one can rely and platforms to which one can rally. Freedom provides such an opportunity—philosophers in their vernacular call the term a "hurrah" word (Cranston, 1953). International marketing, in turn, aims to achieve the "feeling good" part of Joplin's song—another hurrah experience— and it does so by bringing new resources and opportunities to consumers.

Overall, international marketing's interaction with the issue of values may eventually become the field's greatest gift to the world. Its participation in aligning global values may make it easier for countries, companies, and individuals to build bridges between them.

On the business side, Raymond Vernon developed an international product cycle (IPC) theory to look at the production, technology, and cost of production and to formulate predictions about their country of production (Vernon, 1966). In the years since this economic theory was formulated, many things have changed. The innovators, which Vernon saw primarily in the United States, have now emerged around the world; manufacturers have been joined by service providers in the international market; and the entire process has been gaining speed. But the fundamentals still apply. Those countries that follow the innovators most closely are the ones that participate rapidly in new developments and are consequently catching up. Here is another opportunity for international marketing to contribute to value assimilation. When a German firm moves from Hungary to Romania, the move represents a success story for both Romania and Hungary. It means that in Hungary the wages have risen to such a degree and the comparative advantage differential has shrunk by such a measure that it is no longer sufficiently attractive to maintain the investment of the firm. That means Hungary has caught up—come closer—to the level of the economy of Germany. It also means that Romania has become more productive and represents now a viable alternative for an investment decision. The result is that both Hungary and Romania are better off than before.

But just like with Sherlock Holmes's evidence of the dog that did not bark, a lack of response to IPC should give rise to questions. The logical consequence of the IPC theory should have led economic expansion into an increasing number of developing nations. In some regions, this has occurred. There has been the entry and subsequent movement of plants from Germany to Central and Eastern Europe. There have been U.S. plants going from Mexico to Brazil. Japanese plants have shifted from Korea to Vietnam. But for the past decades, we have failed to see any significant thrust of international markets into Africa. Since the withdrawal of British and French forces two generations ago, most of these nations have not been able to develop a successful domestic economic environment by themselves. If change is to come, international marketers, with their desire to create new customers and suppliers and bring about relief and freedom from extremes of hunger, sickness, and intolerance, will need to be a key part of it (Samli, 2003).

Facing the Music

How does all that match with today's discontent so forcefully expressed by the antiglobalists in their opposition to international marketing? Many claim that never before in history has there been so much evidence about such a strong opposition movement to globalization—pointing to the demonstrations in Genoa, Washington, DC, and Seattle.

Perhaps those making such claims are sadly mistaken. In looking at other "globalizers" in world history, such as the Vikings, the Mongols, the Tatars, and the Romans, there probably was both intellectual and physical opposition (or do we really believe that everybody enjoyed Genghis Khan?). But protest was never allowed to become very vocal, or to engage in repeated, large demonstrations or widespread pamphleteering. Due to rather harsh policies of dealing with the opposition, very few records of such resistance are available today. Consequently, comparisons with past intensity are difficult to make. It would appear that it is perhaps even more difficult to find comparable examples of benign exercise of power.

Take as an example the instance when a superpower like the United States decides to bury nuclear waste within its own borders rather than foisting it upon the territory of its hapless opposition abroad. Indeed, power structures and networks are subject to shifts, but for now the timing of the how and when looks favorable for the United States.

The news is good for international marketing. The discipline is so closely aligned with freedom that one can call it essential for freedom. It is the freedom Thomas Aquinas saw as the means to human excellence and happiness (Weigel, 2001). There is much reciprocal causality. Freedom has caused and facilitated international marketing; international marketing is a key pillar of the cause of freedom. Here we have identified 12 linkages between international marketing and freedom. In the art and science of fingerprint analysis, it is generally accepted that the presence of 12 points of agreement during a comparison indicates that the items compared are the same (Interpol, 2004).

With hard work, and at a price, international marketing offers a road leading to growth, peace, and the emergence of values that will let humankind be more human and more kind to each other.

In the matter of Janis Joplin's candidacy for patron of international marketing, you be the judge. Just listen closely to the music and to your heart and let your mind decide.

References

Cranston, M. (1953). *Freedom*. New York: Basic Books.

Czinkota, M. R., Ronkainen, I., & Donath, B. (2004). *Mastering global markets: Strategies for today's trade globalist*. Cincinnati, OH: Thomson.

de Mooij, M. (1998). *Global marketing and advertising: Understanding cultural paradoxes*. Thousand Oaks, CA: Sage.

Farmer, R. N. (1987, October). Would you want your granddaughter to marry a Taiwanese marketing man? *Journal of Marketing, 51*, 114–115.

Hayek, F. V. (1971). *Die verfassung der freiheit*. Tuebingen: Mohr Siebeck.

Hofstede, G. (1998). Foreword. In M. de Mooij, *Global marketing and advertising* (p. xiii). Thousand Oaks, CA: Sage.

International Monetary Fund. (2004). *International financial statistics*. Washington, DC: Author.

Interpol. (2004). *Method for fingerprint identification*. European Expert Group on Fingerprint Identification. Retrieved January 24, 2004, from http://www .interpol.int/public/Forensic/fingerprints/WorkingParties/IEEGFI/ieegfi.asp

Johansson, J. K. (1990). *Marketing, free choice and the new international order*. Washington, DC: Georgetown University Press.

Johansson, J. K. (2004). *In your face: How American marketing excess fuels anti-Americanism*. Upper Saddle River, NJ: Pearson.

Kristofferson, K. (1969). *Me and Bobby McGee* [Recorded by J. Joplin]. On *Pearl* [CD]. New York: Sony Records. (1971)

Marquardt, M., & Reynolds, A. (1994). *The global learning organization*. Burr Ridge, IL: Irwin.

NASA's metric confusion causes Mars orbiter loss. (1999). Retrieved from http:// www.cnn.com/TECH/space/9909/30/mars.metric/

Prahalad, C. K., & Hammond, A. (2002, November/December). *Serving the world's poor, profitably*. Harvard Business Review, pp. 48–57.

Samli, C. (2003). *Entering and succeeding in emerging countries: Marketing to the forgotten majority*. Cincinnati, OH: Thomson.

Theroux, E., & George, A. L. (1989). *Joint ventures in the Soviet Union: Law and practice* (Revised edition). Washington, DC: Baker & McKenzie.

Vernon, R. (1966, March). International investment and international trade in the product cycle. *Quarterly Journal of Economics, 80,* 190–207.

Weigel, G. (2001, December 1). *Two ideas of freedom*. Washington, DC: Ethics and Public Policy Center.

Wolfensohn, J. (2001, August). Address at the Opportunity International Australia's Annual Corporate Dinner, Sydney.

CHAPTER 2

A Forecast of Globalization, International Business, and Trade

Report From a Delphi Study

Michael R. Czinkota and Ilkka A. Ronkainen

Introduction

The importance and the impact of international business has become a fact accepted by practitioners, policy makers, and academics alike. Globalization ranks high on the strategic agenda of executives as they seek to exploit commonalities and leverage resources across borders. Governments and legislatures have dramatically increased their debate and involvement in international trade and investment issues, and universities have adjusted their business curricula and research to address international business issues (Kwok & Arpan, 2002).

A unifying conclusion drawn by all observers of the international business scene is that international business causes many changes but is itself also the subject of major transformations. As a result, it is important to anticipate such changes and to adapt to them by formulating new paradigms (Dunning, 1995).

Most frequently, investigations by the academic community have questioned the relevance of current international business research activities in universities and mapped out issues to be researched in the future

(Buckley, 2002). There has also been encouragement for research to have more of an international focus. However, analyses indicate that on average still only about 1 in 20 articles in the top management journals can be considered international (Werner & Brouthers, 2002).

Several characteristics are common to all these studies. One is their primary focus on one country only when investigating a global phenomenon. Even though change in international business is driven by the interaction of the business, policy, and academic communities, past research typically queries only one group of these players. As a consequence, the insights provided are limited to the views of the one group investigated and do not reflect the important and possibly different perspectives of the two groups that might be left out.

This dearth of coverage is particularly noticeable with regards to the policy community, whose views are only rarely investigated by international business scholars. Policy concerns continue to be woefully underrepresented. Czinkota (2000) found the policy orientation by authors to range between 2.4% and 5.2% in key journals, and Schlegelmilch (2003) reports that over a 10-year period, only 5.8% of the articles published in the *Journal of International Marketing* focused on legal and public policy aspects. The situation differs little in reverse. A 20-year analysis of the *Journal of Public Policy and Marketing* showed that only 11% of policy articles focused on multinational policy makers. "Policy watch" articles had a 0% international focus (Sprott & Miyazaki, 2002).

A final key characteristic of past research is the fact that virtually none of these studies reflected any interaction between the business, policy, and research communities on the subject of trends and changes. Such interaction, however, is imperative in order to obtain a reasonably accurate and calibrated forecast of impending metamorphoses.

Research Usefulness

This chapter presents an assessment of changes in the international business field, and it does so with a broader perspective than earlier research. On a general level, the material presented here lends some specificity to the amorphous issue of globalization, which is bandied about by so many, and helps readers to build their understanding of the present and of future scenarios. More specifically, this should help policy makers to refocus on the forest rather than just look at the trees. Since they have to work under daily pressures that can cause the long term to often be defined as "next week," the findings presented here can help anticipate the emergence of longer-term frictions and uncover the opportunities for alliances. The insights may be suggestive of some areas in need of future negations and enhance the ability of individuals to harmonize policy and business objectives.

On the managerial side, this work can suggest input for the formulation of long-term strategy. The insights provided by corporate colleagues, paired with the concerns of those in government, can offer a broadened perspective of challenges and opportunities by highlighting potential alternatives. An additional breadth of view is suggested by the input from key global locations rather than just one geographic region. Therefore, distant cultural and locational peculiarities, which ordinarily might not rise to the attention of managers, can now be incorporated into the understanding of business phenomena.

Academics can use this research to identify new opportunities for high research "pay-offs." By receiving an early alert about global concerns, shifts, and responses, they are not confined in their research to simply respond to local business input but can assume a leadership role with the conduct of anticipatory work. Furthermore, the forecast presented here can serve as a basis for the futurity work of other international business researchers, offering them a benchmark for comparison with their results. On the service side, the findings presented here may better arm academics to advise students in their career objectives and placement activities, to develop outreach programs to firms, and to position their programs within the business and policy communities. In the area of teaching, the findings can help doctoral students to identify desirable topics for their research. In addition, individual issues can be highlighted in the classroom to serve as the basis for further projections or as defining parameters for project assignments that are future oriented yet maintain a close relevance with the business and policy communities.

Research Approach

Various approaches can establish how pertinent constituents view the future. A broad-based content analysis of the current literature can examine trends

(Naisbitt, 1990; Wheeler, 1988). However, this approach is very resource intensive and, due to language limitations, possibly biased by the perceptions and interpretations of U.S.-based analysts. Due to progress in technology, it might also be possible to accumulate information via a keyword search in various search engines. However, a key constraint here is the fact that the helpful computerized search engines tend to pick up only a small portion of actual work and are heavily biased toward English-language publications (Czinkota, 2000). In addition, neither approach benefits from any interaction between policy makers, business leaders, and academics, and they are, by their very nature, focused on what was or, at best, what is.

A second alternative is the interview method, which allows for in-depth questioning. This approach is often used by well-connected organizations to obtain large quantities of input. Yet, as the example of the World Economic Forum (2003) shows, many participants in such surveys are self-selected and do not interact with each other in their responses. The latter flaw can be remedied by convening a group of experts at one location and facilitating their interaction over an extended period to secure in-depth assessment. However, in order to be meaningful, such an approach requires the invitation of carefully identified and stratified experts reflecting different types of insights and different parts of the world. Financial and time constraints make this approach unfeasible.

It might also be useful to employ a market-driven analysis. Here, one could employ the cumulative insights of a vast number of inputs stimulated by a profit motive. The hypothesis is that when there are transactions in support of certain plans and activities, those transactions will leave a signature in the information space (Poindexter, 2003). If one could provide a market mechanism to the public where anyone can buy or sell contracts with predicted outcomes, the price of such contracts would then be a key indicator for the probability of such outcomes (Wolfers & Zitzewitz, 2003). An effort of this nature by the U.S. Defense Advances Research Projects Agency (DARPA) attempted to gather information in the field of global terrorism. However, there was substantial public outcry and political rejection of this approach.

This study uses the Delphi technique, which integrates the judgment of a number of experts who cannot come together physically, but also facilitates feedback, debate, and comment. The overall objective of this technique is to achieve consensus among a diverse group of participants. Past studies using such an approach have typically accumulated groups of up to 30 experts based on the finding that larger groups create few additional ideas and limit the in-depth exploration of the ones generated (Delbeq, Van De Ven, & Gustalson, 1975). For the success of such a study, it is critical to secure the participation of the right kinds of experts, who understand the issues, have a vision, and represent a substantial variety of viewpoints. A research council composed of one leader each in the international policy, business, and academic communities, all of them with more than 20 years of experience in their fields and very well connected to their global counterparts, identified possible participants in the study. The selection criteria were an active career in international business for at least 10 years, a leadership role within the participant's professional setting, a global vision beyond local and temporary concerns, and accessibility and willingness to engage in intellectual dialogue.

A list of 45 global experts with 15 each in the policy, business, and research fields was developed. Of these, 33 were contacted and stratified to ensure that there were 11 representatives each from the three geographic areas chosen. The business leaders approached were typically either corporate presidents or vice-presidents for international operations. At the policy level, the representatives were current or former members of the legislative and executive branches of government. The academic participants were professors and program directors specializing in international business. Although most of the experts invited to join the panel participated in the first round, duties, travel, illness, and time constraints eliminated some of them in the second and third rounds. Twenty-five experts participated in the study, a quite acceptable number of participants and well below the maximum number of 30 that Delbeq et al. (1975) recommended. The profile of the participants in Table 2.1 indicates the number, type, location, and range of titles of the panelists contributing to this research.

The Delphi started out with an open-ended questionnaire asking for "the identification of international business dimensions subject to change in the next 10 years." In addition, respondents were requested to "highlight the corporate and policy responses to these changes." Issues and

Table 2.1. Delphi Responses

	America	Europe	Asia	TOTAL
Business community	5	3	3	11
Policy community	4	3	2	9
Academic community	2	2	1	5
TOTAL	11	8	6	25
Range of titles				
Business community	Chairman, member of the board, president, executive vice president, partner			
Policy community	Ambassador, director general, executive director, director, assistant secretary, senior strategist			
Academic community	Rector, chaired professor, professor			

responses were to be rated for their impact on a 10-point scale, ranging from very low to very high. This first round resulted in 36 pages of issues and trends. In most instances, respondents provided ratings for an issue or trend heading and then added substantial comments that elaborated on that dimension. Based on these replies, the research council devised issue categories into which the various comments were grouped. In addition, predicted changes were linked with specific corporate responses. This consolidation of comments served to eliminate overlaps and made the wealth of information more amenable for evaluation and discussion in the subsequent rounds.

In the second iteration of the Delphi, the panelists were presented with these categories and comments and were asked to elaborate on the statements and to indicate the level of their agreement or disagreement. In addition, the respondents were asked to rate the impact such a change would have on corporations and policy makers. Both of these assessments were made using a 10-point rating scale. In the first two rounds, experts in a specific industry or sector were likely to expound on changes particular to their interests. The other panelists were able to express their agreements or disagreements with these views in the subsequent rounds, leading to the gradual building of consensus. The third and final round focused on those statements for which there continued to be disagreement between the panelists.

Policy Concerns

The first strand of inquiry focused on upcoming policy concerns. While the range of issues addressed was very broad, key topics emerged on which consensus could be achieved. This list and rank order are shown in Table 2.2.

Globalization

Globalization will continue. However, globalization issues increasingly will be understood to go far beyond the economic dimension and will be much broader than "Americanization." We define globalization as "the increase in the frequency and duration of linkages between countries leading to similarities in activities of individuals, practices of companies, and policies of governments" (Czinkota, 2002). One key question will be whether it is possible to accept globalization and its linkages but reject some of its resulting implications. For example, if one discusses trade relations, must human rights, environmental commitments, and conservation of culture necessarily be part of such discussions? Similarly, do open trade relations with the outside require a country to simultaneously adhere to a market economy inside the nation? Clearly there are interactions between all these dimensions, some of them more direct than

Table 2.2. Policy Concerns

Issue	Scale value[a]
Globalization	100
Markets and governance	98
Environment	95
Security	76
Trade and investment negotiations	74
Legal concerns and capital markets	69
Religious conflict	66

[a]Scale values were determined by multiplying the measures of an event/issue or region with its impact on international business, based on individual responses. The result was then standardized on a scale ranging from 1 (lowest) to 100 (highest).

others. The question is where to draw the boundaries between international linkages and national sovereignty.

Historically, great companies have used global coordination to gain the benefits of multinationality, such as learning, standardization, and innovation transfer. At the same time, significant efforts were expended on offering local goods and services, as well as securing inputs from and producing in countries providing the most cost-efficient base (Ghemawat, 2003). However, in a swinging back of the pendulum, many discern an increasing movement away from the Porterian global strategy with the development of a major regional or even local focus. Global expertise and best practices can still be leveraged; however, a main emphasis on local adaptation and implementation is becoming key to success.

Governments will continue to be confronted with redistribution issues in regard to income and retirement. Rather than increase direct taxation on domestic activities, it will be easier to impose new burdens on trade to raise revenue, especially in areas such as e-business. Concurrently, worldwide overcapacities will require structural change and encourage incentives for the creation of new markets. It can be expected that plant-closing regulations will become easier.

Highly developed nations may have to change the implicit commitments made to their citizens. Over the past 50 years, an unwritten agreement has promised a healthy birth, an education-filled adolescence, an employed adult life, and a comfortable retirement, all of it in a reasonably safe environment. Emerging and developing nations never raised such expectations for their citizens. In an era of cross-border flow of technology, knowledge, products, and people, a new global environment may no longer permit such exalted promises. Rather than the emergence of health, comfort, and safety around the globe, compromises—and to some degree, losses—of past achievements may have to be accepted. Rearguard actions may delay the global harmonization of expectations at an enormous cost, but they cannot eliminate the direction of reality.

At the same time, globalization and global corporations can be seen as a powerful force for positive social change. Public-private sector partnerships will provide a crucial impetus for improved economic conditions. Some say that, together with nongovernmental organizations, local and state governments, and communities, global corporations can build the commercial infrastructure and bring prosperity to the developing world (Prahalad & Hart, 2002).

Markets and Governance

A worldwide push for more corporate transparency and accountability is emerging. Quick, ongoing, and public action by ndustrialized nations against nefarious business practices is essential for world acceptance of globalization and market forces. The proponents of market-based systems are "selling" the world on two key approaches to doing business. One benefit of market forces results from the interplay of supply and demand:rather than having to rely on government actions, price signals indicate the effectiveness of economic activities. Competition works—if practiced responsibly and with a respect for profitability and private property. In exchange for the chance to earn profits, investors provide resources to the most productive and efficient uses.

The second comprises managerial and corporate virtue, vision, and veracity. Unless the world can have trust in what firms and their managers say and do, it will be impossible to forge a global commitment between those doing the marketing and the ones being marketed to. It is therefore of vital interest to the proponents of globalization to ensure that corruption, bribery, lack of transparency, and the misleading of stakeholders are exposed for the damage they cause. The main remedy is an early identification of transgressions and the collaboration of the global policy community in administering swift punishment of the culprits involved.

In order to avoid an abuse of regulations such or as nontariff barriers, public and transparent standards—established in a World Trade Organization or equivalent international accord—are in everybody's interest. National public authorities will then have the crucial role of enforcing such rigid standards. Concurrently, there will be much closer supervision of managers by boards of outside directors or even international boards of stakeholders. Countries that consider offering safe havens from such supervision will then become financial outcasts as well.

The Environment

Environmental standards will tighten as a result of corporate compliance rather than significant new regulations. Business will discover new market opportunities for friendlier technologies. More selectivity among environmental issues will permit those companies that lead on them to win an advantage in the market place. Governments will directly support the emergence of new technology with measures such as tax incentives and fuel standards. There will be an increase in coordination efforts between governments, perhaps through international agreements administered by the United Nations. The European Union's (EU) concern with the environment will remain high, but other issues such as competitiveness will take on a larger role. For example, even though the ability to offer a more attractive region to live and work in may present a serious competitive advantage, the successful establishment of such a position brand may take too long to warrant the investment.

Environmental disagreements may lead to new tensions between the EU, Japan, and the United States. A general reluctance of the United States to follow may lead to regional standards that differ substantially from each other. There will be increased political pressure in multilateral institutions such as the World Trade Organization (WTO) to forge agreement on standards. Eventually, significant compromises for the sake of new international agreements will bring the United States into the fold.

There will be a push led by the United States for the liberalization of trade in genetically modified organisms (GMO), either through the WTO or bilateral agreements. It might occur that the two major trading blocs will begin to carve up the world into pro and con nations regarding GMOs—akin to the political orientation of the cold war days. There is likely to be more development and testing of GMOs. However, unless specific and significant deleterious effects are identified, the productivity and efficiency of GMOs will win out because they have science, business, and free trade on their side.

Security

Concern with terrorism has long been present in international business. What is new is its ubiquity, proximity, randomness, and widespread visualization. After the 9/11 attacks, the awareness has much increased, as have the countermeasures. Terrorism, defined as "the systematic threat or use of violence to attain a political goal or communicate a political message through fear, coercion, or intimidation of particular persons or the general public" (Alexander, Valton, & Wilkinson, 1979, p. 4) will increasingly affect international business. Consistent with economic theory, when governments implement antiterrorism policies, terrorists will respond. The protection of vulnerable targets, such as civil aviation or embassies in high-threat countries, is likely to motivate terrorists to substitute easier targets for those less accessible (Crenshaw, 2001). Increased protection may result in attacks on new and unexpected targets, which are more likely to succeed (Sandier, Enders, & Lapan, 1991). If terrorists can no longer enter a country, they may attack that country's symbols and representatives abroad. If the embassies are then more secured and fortified, terrorists may attack that nation's individuals, companies, or tourists.

This problem needs to be of concern to all. International enterprises need to be accessible to their customers, and most potential targets cannot be hardened enough to prevent an attack. Hotels will continue to let their guests drive up close; fast food stores will let their customers come in freely; houses of worship will be open to visitors. Even if one wanted to provide full security, there are neither enough resources nor return on investment benefits to do so. As a result, all activities around the globe will remain subject to terrorism's major aim: to spread insecurity, increase perceived risk, and alarm the population.

Specific corporate repercussions in response to terrorism, anticipated by the Delphi participants, focused primarily on a reduction in international spending and investment by firms, which was estimated to decline in some locations to a level of 62% of pre-9/11 values. Investment was seen as migrating to less risky countries, making the capital required for investment in riskier nations more expensive. In turn, a portion of that risky investment is not productive because it needs to support antiterrorism measures, therefore further raising the cost of capital and increasing the transaction cost of international business. These cost increases do not come as a stable upward trend but rather come in waves, which set a higher plateau of costs. Furthermore, there was an anticipation of less expatriate personnel transfers in support of local operations and a reduction of technology transfer. Combined, these changes are likely to trigger a downward spiral of competitiveness in those countries that are already under pressure from or vulnerable to terrorist threats.

If there is ever to be safety, terrorism will need to be addressed at its roots. The causes need to be removed, and there needs to be a clear understanding of what happens after an attack. A drastic response and overwhelming power by themselves will deter only over time. The most important outcome of greater security will be a growing willingness of companies to invest in regions that once were insecure. Emerging nations will benefit most from peace and tranquillity, since their investments provide the largest relative proportion of jobs, income, and poverty alleviation.

The United States is likely to take a unilateral approach to security issues. Export controls and import review measures will be on the increase and have a significant effect on trade flows. A key effort will aim to reduce the proliferation of dual-use technology. U.S. attempts at harmonization will try to contain any major divergences of competitiveness due to security measures. Even though the playing of the security card will work best in bilateral relations, the United States will be willing to make use of the WTO as an organizing forum for coordinating talks.

All these efforts and commitments on behalf of security demand a vision of how the U.S. relationship with the world should be 10 years from now. What should be the worldwide standing of future generations of individual Americans? This eventual outcome will determine whether current policies, activities, efforts, and expenditures are worth it. One indicator for safety is the "Travel Warning" Web site of the U.S. Department of State. There one finds admonitions for 28 countries regarding where not to go and what not to do. Visitors are counseled to avoid crowds, demonstrations, and areas where Americans generally congregate; to keep a low profile; and to blend in and avoid showing that you are an American. So where should we be in 10 years? Perhaps by then a travel advisory from the State Department might recommend, "As a traveler, you are advised to carry identification of being a U.S. citizen with you at all times. Wear an American flag pin to let everyone know that you are an American. This way, you will carry an umbrella of respect, safety, and security. Remember, you represent your country. We wish you success in your travels." Such an outcome might truly help bring peace to the world. After all, if Americans are secure, others will be as well.

Trade and Investment Negotiations

For the next few years, global trade negotiations are not likely to succeed. The differences between 147 member nations in the WTO are too great to be bridged in traditional ways. Some say that nations can be differentiated between those that feed the world, those that fight in the world, and those that provide the funding for all the feeding and fighting. Such a trichotomy, however, seems to be oriented along the problems of yesteryear. From the perspective of national and corporate strategy, funding, feeding, and fighting are symptoms reflecting the needs of the moment. More long term is a division of countries and firms into four categories of economic contribution: those who grow, those who make, those who create, and those who coordinate. Each category has very distinct needs, concerns, and desires when it comes to trade and investment. For some, the purity of their agricultural production is paramount. Others require a focus on skills and manufacturing employment. Innovators insist on the protection of intellectual property rights—especially in emerging markets such as China.

Initially, this wide disparity of goals will act as a damper to negotiations and reduce the simplification of trade and investment flows. There will appear to be too much contradiction to achieve closer cooperation, leading to quite substantial delays in any international agreement. However, over time, a better understanding of trade-off capabilities between national or bloc objectives, as well as the pressure emanating from new bilateral and regional negotiations (such as those between the United States and the Central American Common Market), will reinvigorate the activities of multilateral institutions. To some degree, the search for differences and disagreements will be replaced by the identification of commonalities. At the same time, even the bigger countries will accept the necessity to prioritize their agendas once they realize that they cannot win every time. Smaller countries within trading blocs may have to find common interests to have their voices heard.

Religious Conflict

It will be important to recognize the danger of ongoing religious conflict and to work on its diminution. Governments will need to devote substantial resources to reduce religious tensions between and within countries. In part, this will take place through a rechanneling of religious fervor. Even though there will be a decline of religious overtones in international transactions, there will be a greater effort to understand and incorporate religion when appropriate. Other efforts will have to ensure the constitutional right of religious freedom, even in countries that are less broadly focused. There will be a search for symbolic opportunities that help open minds on all sides. Education and information will be key—largely supported by socially responsible actions of corporations. These in turn are driven by a desire to continue involvement within Muslim markets, particularly due to their growth potential and opportunities in the consumer goods sector.

Corporate Strategies

The second focus of our panel concentrated on corporate strategies over the next decade. Table 2.3 highlights the top areas of consensus.

Cultural Sensitivity and Education

The concept of culture has been understood by corporations, but the implementation of this understanding has not necessarily been successful.

Table 2.3. Corporate Strategies

Issue	Scale value[a]
Outsourcing	99
Mass customization	97
Bundling	90
New revenue streams	86
Knowledge transfer	84
Branding policies	82

[a]Scale values were determined by multiplying the measures of an event/issue or region with its impact on international business, based on individual responses. The result was then standardized on a scale ranging from 1 (lowest) to 100 (highest).

An overdrawn focus on the bottom line has given way to a greater appreciation of differences among employees of multinational corporations. Our panelists agreed that the dimension of humanity will take on a new and more enhanced role in the corporate world.

It was suggested that rather than offering lip service, board of directors of both large and midsized international firms will increasingly have a global composition. Cultural training of staff and a growing role of long-term oriented human resource management were predicted. Such improvements are seen as essential if corporate culture and decision-making processes are to incorporate different local approaches and management styles and if firms are to attract the best of worldwide talent.

In a world of change, new expectations were also placed on the performance of the higher education sector. A formidable need for administering national transition was seen. Universities have internationalized over time but have not kept pace with globalization and the transformation of world relations. For many years, foreign language training was the main international activity on campus. Over time, culture was added and international studies departments were formed. Policy concerns led to programs in international diplomacy. More recently, global marketing and management courses produced the now highly competitive international business programs. In all instances, however, little has been done to deal with the conflicts and problems of transition management.

The new mandate for institutions of higher learning is still to develop leaders well grounded in functional skills; however, they need a knowledge of international affairs and a sensitivity to diversity of beliefs and social forces. They must know about the impact of culture and the workings of legal institutions. They need to have a sense of history and appreciation of ethics. They have to administer crowd control, guard national treasures, and provide for public health. They will need to have an understanding of logistics and be experts at liaison with groups ranging from local zealots to representatives of international organizations. They will need to learn a dose of market-based thinking but also be understanding of clashing religious beliefs and the importance of family ties. Above all, they need to communicate well, convey a sense of hope, and be able to initiate a joint national purpose.

It will not be easy to pull together all the necessary capabilities to teach conciliation. Fortunately, there is a vast array of technology to collect knowledge and to disseminate it. Institutions will be able to contact individuals at virtually any place in the world to obtain their insights. They can place at their disposal tools that permit them to explain their views in the best possible way. They can provide for data transfer, group interaction, live views, and taped lectures. They can then use the same technology to reach out to the world and let a wide variety of students learn.

New thinking in academia must pool the best knowledge, the most spirited desire for change, and the deepest experience in implementation. Matching such resources with the most talented students from around the world will give new meaning to the term "elite." Such global learning centers need to be linked to centers of power and maintain insights into both business and policy processes. The occasional physical presence of key decision makers from legislative, military, and judicial organizations will help. Other than that, such programs will be footloose around the world. While it may help to be part of an existing organization, close relations with like-minded partners can provide the opportunity for a coalition of many countries and institutions to teach each other how to do things better in the future.

Outsourcing

An increasing portion of high-end, high-value added services will be sourced from countries with highly skilled, low-cost labor. The internationalization of the back office functions of multinational corporations will continue to grow. However, even sophisticated services will quickly move to low-cost locations. To remain competitive, firms in developed economies must change their strategy to focus on their ability to manage, coordinate, and define the interfaces between suppliers and customers. The challenge will be to effectively qualify the workers in the emerging markets to carry out their tasks but to stay ahead of them in the ability to take on global coordination.

More manufacturing jobs will move to emerging markets. Firms will face the challenge to retain first-mover advantages through continued innovation. When cost pressures force firms to source globally, some will locate their own plants abroad, while others will outsource the needed inputs. Sourcing from abroad through independent suppliers on a contractual basis will have long-term consequences on the processes, competence, and capabilities of firms. In comparing the outsourcing networks of Japanese and U.S. companies, there is key concern that U.S. companies will gradually sever their value chain. In search of cost efficiency, they will increase their dependence on foreign suppliers for products that become technologically more sophisticated. The creation of new technology is a gradual and painstaking learning process of continual adjustment and refinement as new productive methods are tested and adapted in light of a company's accumulated experience. Thus, overreliance on acquisitions and new technologies from other firms may not result in the same sustainable competitive advantage available through internal development. The manufacturing shift abroad may, therefore, eradicate current technology, design, and process advantages possessed by U.S. firms, placing them and the country at further future disadvantage (Kotabe, 1999). As one panelist put it, "It helps to develop and hang on to the blueprints."

Increased Differentiation of Buyers

The tailoring of products to narrow customer groups will be a mainstream element for many years to come. The less tangible products are (i.e., the higher their service-based composition), the more customization will take place. Seen in reverse, the more tangible the product, the more expensive customization will be due to increased logistics cost. However, technological progress will present individualized production as an eventual end goal, especially if the price premium of customization can be contained. Firms will aim to adjust products to the needs of the single customer—initially in the business-to-business sector and, over time, in consumer goods industries.

New cross-selling efforts can then emerge based on customer lifestyle trends. A better understanding of the underlying needs and desires of customers will offer major new opportunities. For example, a supplier receiving orders for a variety of ornithology books from a customer may be able to discern the verge of a substantial lifestyle change by the individual. The company can then develop a series of offers to assist the customer—going far beyond selling him an additional set of binoculars. Rather, the story line of "finding the new self" can be accompanied by offering a lower-priced (perhaps even used) car, different types of insurance, new destinations for holidays, and participation in nongovernmental recycling organizations.

Cost containment will remain at the heart of being globally competitive. The marketing challenge will be not just to develop new goods and services but also to find ways to affect the peripheral cost. Offering a better product is good, but reducing manufacturing costs, logistics expenses, and after-sales costs will be instrumental for success.

Bundling

Firms will increasingly bundle goods, services, technology, and financing to achieve a competitive advantage. Such bundling tends to increase profits by allowing firms to introduce and sell, at a reduced price, products that may otherwise not be in demand. Customers often look beyond the product and expect a package.

It is through such bundling that manufacturers can gain specific advantages not available to their competitors abroad. Consider one example from the automotive industry: airbags, the global positioning system, and a telephone in a car are no longer anything special. Yet by bundling all these components together, car manufacturers have been able to develop an entire new set of passenger assistance services that can even independently notify emergency services in case of an accident. Such combinations of available products, technology, and networks can lead to an entire new plateau of customer satisfaction.

Revenue Restreaming

Pressures of consumer behavior will have a major impact on the revenue streams of corporations. One particular problem will be consumer payment for the use of intellectual property. Companies will continue seek payment from illicit property transfers, but these efforts will often be rearguard actions sometime marked by Pyrrhic victories, where the very achievement of victory leads to failure.

When technology has turned against them, the firm will need to find new revenue streams by adjusting their product or refining its service. For example, the music industry will continue to suffer from substantial decreases in sales. New revenue streams will be instrumental to the survival of the industry. One alternative will be the sale of music portions in direct response to customer desires. By interacting directly yet impersonally with individuals and billing for incremental amounts, music can be sold to personalize telephone rings, doorbells, or even dog whistles and car horns. Finding a new riverbed of revenue flows will be much more important than trying to stop the gradual trickling of streams into the sand.

Knowledge Transfer

Corporations have recognized the importance of the creation and the use of knowledge. Multinational firms understand that only through an efficient dissemination of knowledge and processes leading to the organizational absorption of this knowledge can the firm learn and set itself apart from the competition. They will also learn that accumulated knowledge, if readily accessible and searchable, can become a new source of revenue. Ironically, this will mean that better corporate knowledge management will lead to higher societal knowledge cost.

Technological progress can be seen as an inverted pyramid, with more of it growing on top every day. Increasingly, there will be limits to the implementation of this capability. How to program their video recorders will remain a major secret for most consumers in the near future. Consumers increasingly will ignore superior technology for the sake of technological compatibility and comfort. It will therefore be imperative to offer innovation with an "irresistible functionality," so that consumers do not even think about exercising an opt-out path. Achieving such a stage requires a move from what is technically possible to what is highly desired by consumers. Traditional knowledge generation has had a consumer focus only in its second or third generation. An increasing emphasis on investors and implementers is likely to concentrate innovations more on consumer needs.

There will be more knowledge flow in the business-to-business markets and within corporations. Firms and governments are likely to seek intelligent applications and levers to increase control over their employees, customers, and citizens.

Branding Policies

There has been a growing emergence of the personalization of international business. For example, reports have been made of American tourists not being able to use their American Express cards. Less public but nonetheless important have been actions by nations such as Nigeria and Indonesia aimed at reducing their reliance on the dollar as a reserve currency and substituting the Euro and the Yen instead. Most visible, of course, have been the actions taken against American icons abroad, such as the defacing of fast food franchises or the introduction of "Mecca Cola."

In response, multinational firms increasingly will be shifting to a new tri-branding strategy. There will be the continuity of the global brand, which is known widely and continues to have its adherents, and there will also be the "American" brand, both to satisfy a large and wealthy constituency as well as to provide a country-linked experience to customers abroad. In addition, there will be the increased emergence of the local brand, reflecting the desire of individuals to set themselves apart, to remember their roots, and to return to "the good old days." Such branding policy, even though designed to separate products in the minds of the customers, does not reflect ownership issues, however. For example, in Hungary's cell phone industry, an early leader has been Westel, owned by U.S. telephony firms. The gradually emerging competition was very successful with its "Pannon" brand, which highlighted the ancient Hungarian name of Pannonia. However, the actual ownership of the brand was far from being Hungarian. At the same time, local brands will allow country managers of multinationals a new entrepreneurial freedom that they may not enjoy in managing global brands.

Emerging countries' companies will be pushing into global markets by establishing their own brands or by acquiring famous global brands. Chinese brands such as Haier and Huawei are becoming part of many markets' key brands, while brands such as Murray have been bought by Chinese investors.

Conclusions and Discussion

This research provided an overview of what a global panel of knowledgeable experts believes to be the most important and relevant issues in international business and trade over the next decade. What makes the results particularly interesting is the unusual nexus of insight between the business, policy, and academic communities on a global level. While some of the issues presented here are already at the early stage of public recognition, many of the dimensions addressed seem to have escaped wide attention so far. The findings provided here can help guide academicians in both their research and teaching efforts. Rather than being trapped in providing a description of state-of-the-art of business practices, the forecasts presented here may enable researchers to carry out normative and prescriptive work. While sectoral and regional specialists will develop their own insights from the findings presented here, there are several overarching implications for business executives, policy makers, and academics.

Firms will continue their globalization efforts in two significant parallel ways: they will pursue economies of scale through standardization and the ability to leverage resources (such as knowledge) across borders. At the same time, they are concentrating their manufacturing or contracting in low-cost countries such as China and India. Globalization will result in significant internal changes, especially in terms of the efficiency of organizational learning to detect both commonalities and differences and in terms of securing the best talent worldwide. Policy makers will have to acknowledge the ever-increasing differences in the agenda of countries, which will make multilateralism challenging. Bilateral free-trade agreements, for example, may be necessary to restart the WTO process, and non-payoff-based leadership by some countries may be necessary to bring others into the fold in areas such as environmental protection. Academic institutions need to broaden their curricula to create leaders of international change both for nation building and for dealing with political and market transitions.

Of course, one may wonder about the accuracy and reliability of Delphi studies. The Delphi technique was originally applied by the Rand Corporation for business forecasting purposes. Over time, it has gained substantial acceptance across disciplines. It is used as a research tool in the fields of library and information science (Buckley, 1995), in the medical disciplines (Linstone & Turoff, 1975), and in multicountry studies of communications in Europe (www.feiea.org.uk, 2003). Those experienced with the Delphi technique report that "the method produces useful results which are accepted and supported by the majority of the expert community" (Fraunhofer Institut, 1998). Even actuaries have used the technique to forecast economic conditions (Society of Actuaries, 1999). In the business field, the technique has been rated highly by some as a systematic thinking tool but has also been challenged in its ability to serve as an identifier of strategic issues (Schoemaker, 1993). Such ambivalence may be understandable in an era in which high-powered quantification of business analyses is desired and admired by many. However, we believe that the study of business remains a social science and is heavily dependent on the in-depth thoughts, evaluation, vision, and imagination of individuals. Their informed consensus is more likely to indicate future directions than the opinions of many uninformed survey participants.

To evaluate the accuracy of the Delphi technique for forecasting in the international business arena, we scrutinized three major Delphi studies carried out in the field (Czinkota, 1986; Czinkota & Ronkainen, 1992, 1997). In the 1986 study, a total of 17 key forecasts were made, of which 14 were deemed accurate 5 years later. In spite of this 82% "hit-rate," however, the panel did not foresee one key, world-altering event: namely, the collapse of the Iron Curtain. It may well be, however, that this failure to foresee was a function of the fact that this particular study drew only on experts from one country. Input on a global level might at least have raised the possibility of such an event. In the 1992 study, which did use a global panel, a total of 40 key predictions were made, which, by 1997 turned out to be accurate on 32 dimensions, or 80%. All inaccuracies, however, were in the form of overstatements of speed rather than issue—that is, the issues raised were on point, but transformations had been anticipated to take place more quickly.

Finally, the 1997 study offered 6 years later an accuracy level of 65% of its 69 predictions. Again, a major world-altering event and its consequences had not been predicted: the attacks of September 11, 2001. However, the imminence of these events was apparently missed even by the major intelligence agencies around the world.

Overall, the average predictive accuracy in the three studies comes to 76%, which makes the Delphi method a powerful forecasting tool. Of course, the key to the usefulness of this type of research will remain the selection of the participants, since their level of knowledge and degree of enthusiasm in participating in such a research venture will vitally affect the quality of the output.

A few comments are appropriate regarding the execution of this research. In order to make use of available technology and to reduce the time delays inherent in the Delphi process, we chose to use the Internet and e-mail to conduct this study. Given the widespread availability of this technology in our regions of scrutiny, we expected that the requirement of participants to have Internet access would not be a major intervening variable shaping the outcome of this study. The diversity of results and the effort necessary to achieve consensus confirms this expectation. However, there were some surprising "e-mail effects" encountered in this study. First, there was a struggle for the e-mailed Delphi materials to get the attention of the participants. Even with advance alerts, repeat mailings, and follow-up requests, it was more difficult than ever before to reach the top of the mail heap. Similarly, the return of the Delphi responses was much slower than expected. It may well be that the decision makers pursued by the study might be inundated with e-mails and have much less effective ways of prioritizing both incoming and outgoing materials than with regular "snail" mail.

We also found that the quantity of materials is perceived to be larger with e-mail. Just as television is said to add many pounds to a person, so apparently does e-mail to data. Due to the interactive format of the Delphi method, which includes arguments and counterarguments, materials accumulate quite rapidly. Apparently, a number of respondents were working on-screen with the study data. Given the formatting limitations of e-mail, the materials then appeared much more voluminous than they would have on paper, leading to a series of complaints from participants who felt overwhelmed. Our conclusion from this experience is that we should perhaps learn from our students, who are beginning to limit their e-mails in many of their personal interactions and are again returning to writing with pen and paper. Next time, we will probably go back to using regular old-fashioned mail service.

References

Alexander, Y., Valton, D., & Wilkinson, P. (1979). *Terrorism: Theory and practice.* Boulder, CO: Westview Press.

Buckley, C. (1995). Delphi: A methodology for preferences more than predictions. *Library Management, 7,* 16–19.

Buckley, P. J. (2002). Is the international business research agenda running out of steam? *Journal of International Business Studies, 13*(2), 365–373.

Crenshaw, M. (2001). Terrorism. In N. Smelser & P. Bates (Eds.), *International encyclopedia of the social & behavioral sciences* (pp. 15,604–15,606). Amsterdam: Elsevier.

Czinkota, M. R. (1986). International trade and business in the late 1980s: An integrated U.S. perspective. *Journal of International Business Studies, 77*(1), 127–134.

Czinkota, M. R. (2000). The policy gap in international marketing. *Journal of International Marketing, 8*(1), 99–111.

Czinkota, M. R. (2002). *Georgetown globalization project.* Washington, DC: Georgetown University McDonough School of Business.

Czinkota, M. R., & Ronkainen, I. A. (1992, January/February). Global marketing 2000: A marketing survival guide. *Marketing Management,* pp. 37–40

Czinkota, M. R., & Ronkainen, I. A. (1997). International business and trade in the next decade: Report from a Delphi study. *Journal of International Business Studies, 28*(4), 827–844.

Delbeq, A., Van De Ven, A. H., & Gustafson, D. H. (1975). *Group techniques for program planning,* Glenview, IL: Scott Foresman.

Dunning, J. H. (1995). Reappraising the eclectic paradigm in an age of alliance capitalism. *Journal of International Business Studies, 26*(3), 461–491.

Federation of European Internal Editors Associations. (2003). *The Delphi Study.* Retrieved October 7, 2003, from http://www.feiea.org.uk

Fraunhofer Institut. (1998). *Second German Delphi Study.* Retrieved October 7, 2003 from http:// www.isi.fhg.de

Ghemawat, P. (2003). The forgotten strategy. *Harvard Business Review, 81*(11), 76–84.

Kotabe, M. (1999). Efficiency vs. effectiveness orientation of global sourcing strategy: A comparison of U.S. and Japanese multinational companies. *Academy of Management Executive, 12*(4), 107–119.

Kwok, C. C. Y., & Arpan, J. S. (2002). Internationalizing the business school: A global survey in 2000. *Journal of International Business Studies, 33*(3), 571–581.

Linstone, A., & Turoff, M. (1975). *The Delphi method: Techniques and applications.* Reading, MA: Addison Wesley.

Naisbitt, J. (1990). *Megatrends*. New York: Morrow.

Poindexter, J. M. (2003). *Letter of resignation in Anthony Tether, Director, DARPA. 12 August 2003*. Retrieved September 1, 2003, from http://www.washingtonpost.com/wpsrv/nation/transcripts/poindexterletter.pdf

Prahalad. C. K., & Hart, S. L. (2002). The fortune at the bottom of the pyramid. *Strategy and Business, 8*(1), 35–47.

Sandler, T., Enders, W., & Lapan, H. E. (1991, February). Economic analysis can help fight international terrorism. *Challenge*, pp. 10–18.

Schlegelmilch, B. (2003). The anatomy of an international marketing journal. *Journal of International Marketing, 11*(1), 2–7.

Schoemaker, P. J. H. (1993). Multiple scenario development: Its conceptual and behavioral foundation. *Strategic Management Journal, 14*, 193–213.

Society of Actuaries. (1999). *Final report of the 1999 Delphi study*. Retrieved October 7, 2003, from http://www.soa.org

Sprott, D. E., & Miyazaki, A. D. (2002). Two decades of contributions to marketing and public policy: An analysis of research. *Journal of Public Policy and Marketing, 21*(1), 105–125.

Werner, S., & Brouthers, L. E. (2002). How international is management? *Journal of International Business Studies, 33*(3), 583–591.

Wheeler, D. R. (1988). Content analysis: An analytical technique for international market research. *International Marketing Review, 4*, 34–40.

Wolfers, J., & Zitzewitz, E. (2003, July 31). The furor over terrorism futures. *The Washington Post*, p. A19.

World Economic Forum. (2003). *Global competitiveness programme*. Retrieved August 1, 2003, from http://www.weforum.org

CHAPTER 3

The Policy Gap in International Marketing

Michael R. Czinkota

All nations have policies that affect international marketing. These policies may be publicly pronounced or kept secret, they may be disjointed or coordinated, influence international marketers directly or indirectly, and they may be applied consciously or determined by a laissez-faire attitude. Whenever governments regulate, stimulate, direct, protect, or neglect activities that influence the flow of trade and investment across national borders, international marketing is affected.

It could be argued that with the diminishing role of government in the economy, the role and importance of public policy and its intervention in the international marketplace is on the decline. However, such an argument neglects several key aspects of the interaction between policy and international marketing. First, even a reduction in government involvement precipitates international marketing repercussions. For example, less discretionary power by national governments due to more transparent and harmonized regulations by the World Trade Organization (WTO), may force the international firm to develop and pursue new marketing strategies. Second, even though governments have reduced their involvement in their domestic economies, new election results in Europe, global problems in the international financial sector, and ongoing discussions of a "third way" of economic policy may reverse this trend. Third, the effects of globalization cause many governments to actively search for new ways to exercise sovereignty over international trade and investment. For example, Vernon (1992) claims that "governments are exhibiting extraordinary ingenuity in devising new ways to buffer vulnerable industries against competition." Others have discussed the growing importance of the so-called technical track of trade policy (Finger, 1993), and have posited that "the most insidious forms of trade protection take the form of trade quotas or trade prohibitions that come at the end of administrative reviews" (Cumby & Moran, 1994, p. 3). Fourth, governments at all levels are becoming more activist about specific aspects of international trade that they perceive as important for economic, competitive, or ethical reasons. When Massachusetts introduced a penalty of 10% on state contract bids from companies known to be dealing with Myanmar, the international marketing activities of Apple Computer, Eastman Kodak, and Hewlett-Packard were curtailed (Lely-veld, 1998). When government decisions legalized gray market activities, many firms were forced to redesign their global product and price segmentation strategies (Chaudhry & Walsh, 1995). When the WTO strengthened intellectual property rights (IPR), international marketers encountered a host of new licensing and franchising opportunities (Contractor & Kundu, 1998). Overall, nation-states continue to define, implement, and enforce specific national interests through sovereign power over their territory. Therefore, policy considerations are not just applicable but central to the international marketer (Kobrin, 1992).

Policy Integration in International Marketing

Early international marketing work was a practical extension of the international trade field. Books dealing with an international theme focused mainly on the "how to" aspects, covering issues such as export and import mechanics, financing, and documentation. Over time, the field developed a comparative marketing approach, looking at similarities and differences between consumers, institutions, and environments in different markets. Bartels' *Comparative Marketing: Wholesaling in Fifteen Countries* (1963) may serve as an example.

By 1965 Fayerweather had developed an approach to international marketing that explicitly recognized the importance of the policy dimension. He highlighted the variations between countries arising from differences in basic systems of society and the distortions of international trade patterns by nationalistic government policies. Since then, authors writing on marketing on a domestic level have reiterated the essential role of policy within the marketing framework. Kotler, in an assessment of marketing thought, argues forcefully "that marketing executives need to acquire skills and understandings of political and public opinion forces in their efforts" (Kotler, 1988). Shelby Hunt, in a similar statement, explains that one of the guiding values in his research has been "the belief that marketing should devote more attention to the broader societal issues that have come to be called 'macromarketing'" (Hunt, 1988). However, in the international marketing field, most textbooks have not embraced the policy dimension. Even though all existing international marketing books make some references to governmental institutions and activities, only a few reflect the integral role that governmental policies play for the international marketer.

The situation is not much different for academic journals. A review was conducted of the policy orientation of two key journals which, based on their stated editorial objectives, are squarely positioned in the international marketing field. These were the *Journal of International Marketing (JIM)* in the United States and the *European Journal of Marketing (EJM)* in the United Kingdom. The results indicated that in *JIM* 5.2% of all its authors (or 10 of 192 authors from its 1993 foundation until 1997) addressed policy issues in their writings. In *EJM* an even lower proportion of writers focused on policy, with only 2.4% (or 21 of all 874 authors from 1987 to 1997) doing so. These results are consonant with earlier findings of a very low policy orientation of the articles in the *Journal of International Business Studies* (Inkpen & Beamish, 1994).

The range of policy topics addressed was quite limited as well. Articles incorporating policy issues typically covered changes in the regulatory environment of one country and their effect on international marketers, bilateral trade relations, exporting, and export promotion. Issues such as antidumping, antitrust, or the effects of multilateral policy changes on international marketing received hardly any article space.

Some Areas for Policy Work in International Marketing

The market effects of the environment and its institutions are clearly within the domain of marketing. Therefore, international marketers should develop research designs which incorporate the public policy dimension.

An analysis of policy actions and scenarios permits the researcher to evaluate developments and repercussions early on, well before corporate practice has begun to reflect the policy change. Therefore, rather than being only descriptive, as is often the case in business research, international marketing policy work can be predictive and prescriptive. Such an outcome would not only strengthen the value of individual research, but could also make a major contribution to the further establishment and acceptance of the international marketing research domain.

Policy work in international marketing can take two different approaches. One is reactive to policy decisions, where the international marketer determines new ways of responding to policy decisions already taken. A second focus can be on ways in which the international marketer can influence policy decisions and perhaps even help shape the policy framework. The next two sections address both of these approaches.

International Marketing Responses to Policy Market Integration

Market Integrations

Market integrations take place around the world, but are currently most clearly seen in the European Union. By facilitating transactions across borders, encouraging the intra-European flow of factors of production, and introducing a common currency, European integration offers new opportunities and challenges to the international marketing field. Corporations will have to revisit their segmentation strategies, particularly in light of increased price comparability and merchandise mobility between adjoining markets. Researchers can help corporations to either keep their strategy and change tactics, or to change strategies altogether. For example, firms can retain their established geographic segmentation approaches by adjusting their product mix, strengthening their degree of channel control, or by introducing measures which inhibit price transparency and restrict trade flows. Alternatively, firms can develop new segmentation strategies which define markets based on a nongeographic criteria and differentiate between segments with targeted communication efforts and a high degree of customer specific responsiveness.

It will be important to measure consumer reaction to policy changes. Will consumers take advantage of increased product mobility and price transparency by obtaining their products in a variety of geographic markets? For example, if car manufacturers continue to segment by geographic region, will German consumers travel to France to obtain lower priced German cars? If so, can one link geographic distance and product category with consumer search behavior and determine, for instance, that consumers will travel only 50 kilometers for perfume, but up to 200 kilometers for a car? A better understanding of change in deeply ingrained local product preferences may well rejuvenate the "country of origin" research thrust.

Transitions from Planned to Market Economies

The dissolution of command economies has produced policy shifts in many nations. These transitions offer major new market opportunities for firms, but also confront them with a host of new rules, regulations, and institutions. New forms of partnering are emerging, often untested and designed to accommodate political rather than economic concerns. Firms in these markets are less able to use sophisticated marketing tools and customers lag behind in their understanding of marketing. How should corporations react to feelings of collectivism which remain strong, to nationalistic urges which reemerge, or to governmental suspicions toward corporate communications? How can international marketing assist in achieving a smooth transition rather than abrupt changes? Are the shifting conditions in Eastern Europe perhaps fertile breeding ground for marketing postmodernism (Brown, 1997)?

Environmental and Social Policies

Environmental and social policies have gained greater prominence worldwide, but their roles and emphases differ by markets. Global communications between markets can highlight questionable corporate practices within markets and lead to global repercussions of perceived local missteps. Could this lead to similar labor regulations on a global level? What then will happen to the current competitive advantage of less industrialized nations? How will these changes affect the sourcing and location decisions of international firms?

Tighter international treaty constraints reduce the ability of governments to influence trade flows. Some governments attempt to regain their power by developing new regulations under the guise of domestic policy imperatives such as health, human rights, or animal protection. Obscure developments in labeling policies, for example, can have major effects on international marketers. Labels such as "caught without dolphin protection" or "manufactured by child labor" may dramatically affect marketing outcomes. Environmental regulations also lead to the emergence of global reverse logistics systems and a new "postmortem" stage in the product life cycle, where firms may have terminated a product, but due to environmental policies, are faced with continued costs.

Improved IPR Protection

Multilateral negotiations in the Uruguay Round have strengthened global IPR. In consequence, firms need to be less concerned about losing their competitive edge when taking their knowledge abroad. This IPR protection can open up new entry modes to the global firm. For example, IPR protection may increase the role of franchising and licensing in international markets and speed up technology transfer around the world. The length of the global product life cycle may be affected, since there is now less of a rationale to leave some markets behind when introducing new products. Finally, how can such protection be further strengthened for copyright issues and business processes?

Lower Tariffs

Past negotiations and the continuing implementation of trade agreements have substantially reduced the level of tariffs worldwide. Theories on foreign direct investment (FDI), have postulated that the circumvention of tariff barriers serves as one key motivator for FDI. Are reduced and disappearing tariffs perhaps a harbinger for increased exports and a decrease in circumvention-motivated investment flows? Will there be an increase in FDI incentives by state and national governments in order to maintain FDI inflows? If there are dramatic increases in exports, how will these shifts affect the capacity of global logistics systems?

Development of Dumping Regulations

World Trade Organization rules have increased the use of antidumping regulations. In the 1980s, only a few industrialized nations conducted the bulk of antidumping investigations, but today this tool is used by a rapidly growing number of countries, many of them in the less industrialized category (Czinkota & Kotabe, 1997). How will this increase in governmental action affect the pricing and roll-out strategies of firms? For example, the use of forward pricing, where firms determine their allocation of fixed costs based on, often very optimistic, projections of future global market demand, may be substantially restricted. Fears of antidumping actions may slow down the global roll-out of products, since firms may wish to avoid public discussions of price differentials in various regions and prefer to use price skimming in high-end markets. The quest for rapid gains of market share may then give way to a more gradual increase in market penetration.

Trade Sanctions

There is a growing trend toward the use of trade sanctions at the national and regional level in the United States. As a result, corporations are faced with greater uncertainty in their market activities abroad and may even need to abandon markets if forced to do so by governmental entities. Apart from forgone market opportunities, these developments may also reduce the perception of reliability of U.S. firms by their trading partners. How do such changes in perceptions affect the international marketing success of U.S. firms? Should corporations change their market selection criteria because of distant threats of possible sanctions? How can one quantify the cost of such sanctions, which are often seen as "free" by legislators?

Export Controls

Even though the demise of the Iron Curtain has reduced the political divide between nations, export controls of specific products and technologies continue to be important national policy-making tools. Such controls are now mainly applied to very high technology industries but are also regularly expanded to encompass low technology in instances of regional conflict. How do such controls affect the market penetration strategies of corporations? What costs do safeguard measures for satellite launches in China, for example, impose on firms? Does an uneven enforcement of such controls on a global level affect the market share of firms from different countries? Can some nations use their laxness of export control enforcement as a tool to enhance the global competitiveness of their firms? How can export controls remain effective in an era of high global availability of technology and the increased ease of knowledge transfer through new means of communication? How can firms protect themselves from violating the law when the composite of individual components can result in the eventual production of a controlled product? How can a new control policy be more surgical in terms of precision, more swift in terms of timing, and yet less onerous on firms?

Currency Volatility

By adopting floating currency regimes, governments have posed new challenges for their firms and trading partners. With the growing volatility of currencies, the development of a sound marketing plan no longer is enough. Long term currency exchange risks must be incorporated into international planning, investment, and sourcing strategies. How can international marketing researchers assist corporations to swiftly and nimbly develop location, manufacturing, sourcing, and market servicing strategies which react to rapid currency shifts? What role can or will countertrade play in mitigating such risks? How can market share be preserved during periods of high currency volatility? Should corporations abandon their customers when shifts in currency values lead to (possibly) temporary declines in profitability?

These are just a few areas in which policy actions affect international marketers, and where additional research work would be fruitful. Table 3.1 summarizes this incomplete listing of policy actions and their actual or potential effects on international marketing practice. Naturally, this listing is subject to the dynamics of the policy process and international marketing activities, and deserves to be revisited and expanded over time.

Table 3.1. Selected Policy Actions Affecting International Marketing

Policy actions	International marketing effects
Market integration	Reimportation of goods
	Redesign of segmentation strategies
Transitions from planned to market economies	New markets and customers
	New rules and institutions
	Increase in joint ventures
Environmental and social policies	Development of labeling strategies
	Emergence of reverse logistics
	Postmortem product life cycle stage
Improved IPR protection	Increased licensing activities
Lower tariffs	More exports instead of FDI
Development of dumping regulations	Abandonment of forward pricing
	Weakening of market share strategy
Trade sanctions	Closing of markets
	Perception of decreased reliability
	Problems at the state and local level
Export controls	High cost of safeguard measures
	Risk of inadvertent violations
Currency volatility	Expanded corporate planning
	Revival of countertrade

Yet these policy issues may yield fruitful results for the international marketing researcher and they deserve to be incorporated appropriately into the design of research projects.

International Marketing's Shaping of Public Policy

The cause-effect direction between international marketing and public policy does not only go one way. When policies are formulated, policy makers need to rely on the input from area experts. In international negotiation fora, policy makers are the principals with a seat at the table, but they are supported by the staff, advisors, and specialists sitting behind them. In many instances these back chairs are crowded by engineers, chemists, physicists, and physicians. Additional advice is rendered by representatives of trade associations and corporate lobbyists. However, only rarely does one see an international marketing expert occupying one of those seats. In consequence, international marketing issues are often insufficiently reflected in the formulation of policy and are only discovered long afterward when it comes to policy implementation. At that time, of course, major changes in policy thrust become very difficult to achieve.

International marketing academics are, or should be, the guardians that separate fact from fiction in policy discussions. Not by weight of office, but qualified by expertise and thoughtfulness, and by offering knowledge rather than emotions, international marketers are the indirect guarantors of and guides toward free and open markets. Often, however, their lack of input and impact has resulted in public apathy, ignorance, and missteps in trade policy. Here are some suggestions how international marketers may assist in shaping public policy.

Terminology

The use of terms of art in the international marketing field can have major effects. Devised when international marketing issues where the concern of only a few experts, these terms can be misunderstood in an era of general public scrutiny. In the United States, for example, the failure—since 1994—to gain approval for "fast track" legislation, which would expose any trade deal negotiated by the administration to a simple Congressional up or down vote rather than to a plethora of amendments, has gravely undermined the ability of the U.S. president to conduct trade talks. The reason for the failure lies at least in part with terminology. Fast Track has a connotation of rushing things through without concern for bystanders. Similarly, the issue of "most favored nation" (MFN) treatment of trade relations with China has led every spring to contentious policy debates when it was questioned why China should be so favored. Also consider the perception of consumers when governments label activities as "dumping."

Marketing efforts can clarify the meaning of terminology, and, when necessary, work to alter the terminology to change the parameters of the debate. Consider the perception effect of changing "Fast Track" to "Trade Negotiation Support," or "dumping" to "Low Consumer Prices." New terms might well trigger a significant change of policy. That such approaches can work has been shown by the diligent and successful efforts to rename MFN into "normal trade relations" (NTR). This clarification that MFN treatment does not involve any special favors for China has much reduced the acerbity of annual debate about U.S.-Chinese trade relations.

Definition

The power of definitions should not be underestimated. Definitions determine domains and many subsequent policy reactions. For example, the definition of markets and their size will affect how governments evaluate the effectiveness of their regulations. The definition of competition can play a determining role in antitrust actions. Defining the role and need for privacy in the context of international data transmissions can have a major effect on encryption and data regulation policies. Definition can also have a major impact on standards. For example, when evaluated, the members of many professions have long been held to the standards of the average professional in their geographic home area. In light of the globalization of services, international marketers can and should redefine the reference points for such standards. By playing a key role in arriving at specific definitions, international marketers can become crucial players in shaping those policy actions which derive from such definitions.

Holism

In an increasingly specialized world, many experts apply only the narrowest of approaches. The use of experts may then provide many aspects of trees, but not a perspective of the forest. International marketers can help shape policy debates by contributing a holistic perspective of linkages between policy repercussions. For example, a reduction in steel imports due to quotas may result in more comfort and profit for the domestic steel industry. It will also result in more costly automobiles, a reduction in domestic automobile purchases, fewer automobile exports due to higher steel prices, and a further reduction in exports to those nations which can no longer export their steel due to foreign quotas. In addition, the jobs of workers in the automotive sector are at risk—with their job losses perhaps exceeding the gains achieved in the steel sector.

Information

It often appears as if academics assume that everyone is aware of the benefits of free trade. But not all are concerned or have had the benefit of insightful academic training in the international marketing field. It is necessary to develop concise, cogent, and easily understood information on why, for example, a reduction of barriers to international marketing is important. A well researched, precise explanation on why trade disputes and the resulting sanctions, such as the current banana, beef, and genetically altered food crises, which produce only lose-lose effects, could have a powerful impact on the worldwide reconsideration of such policy measures. The work by Czinkota (1987) on a cost of protection index, and by Hufbauer and Elliott (1994) on the cost of protection may serve as example.

Dissemination

Once a well researched explanation is developed, it needs to be disseminated widely to motivate adversely affected individuals to take action. Even an excellent piece of work may matter little if it does not reach an audience that can effect change. Researchers should therefore consider carefully which medium has the most direct and indirect impact on policy makers.

Increasing the Policy Orientation in International Marketing

In addition to businesses and consumers, policy makers play a major role in shaping international marketing activities. They are often the gatekeepers of international marketing opportunities and they can introduce major international marketing challenges.

On the managerial side, international marketing executives experience the rising impact of, if not conflict with, policy. Firms continue to seek access to a greater number of markets in order to remain competitive. In doing so, corporate strategic processes increasingly tend to plan outside of national and geographic boundaries. Such global corporate expansion means the addition of more government players, each one of which is able to exercise individual sovereignty. At the same time that managers integrate markets across borders, they are exposed to strong political pressures toward fragmentation (Kobrin, 1992). International marketing executives will have to incorporate these policy pressures as a core component into their strategic plans.

One key approach to an increased policy orientation in international marketing practice will consist of making policy issues a dedicated responsibility that maintains awareness of policy initiatives and also participates in the policy process itself. Whether this is done via a government affairs office or through consultants matters little, as long as the policy advocacy is represented internally at the corporate planning stage.

Firms should also ensure a greater degree of participation of international marketing representatives in meetings that discuss and determine international policy. Even though the technical delegates may be best equipped to discuss intricate details, the international marketing expert can make important contributions in terms of the marketing capabilities and needs of the corporation and its customers, and offer insights through the building of coalitions. Larger corporations and trade associations in particular may wish to post permanent observers at organizations such as the WTO, the European Commission, and at large gatherings of nongovernmental organizations (NGOs).

On the academic side, international marketing work, which ignores policy implications, runs the risk of having its findings reflect the inherent instability of a two-legged chair. Therefore, some policy perspective should be considered for all work in international marketing. Within some international marketing programs, it might even make sense to develop a major policy focus. Such a concentration might well become a key differentiating variable for program visibility and prominence. Here is a "wish list" of activities that might be useful in increasing the policy orientation of researchers in international marketing.

For a general increase in policy orientation, the editors and reviewers of journals are powerful forces. If they were to highlight the importance of a policy orientation, researchers would certainly listen. For example, review sheets for submissions in international marketing could devote a line to the extent to which an article addresses the policy dimension. Article abstracts could incorporate policy implications and article titles could reflect policy orientation.

For purposes of specialization in the policy aspects of international marketing, faculty members, department chairs, and tenure and promotion committees on campus may wish to include the policy dimension when assessing the impact of a colleague's work. Policy level work is time consuming and risky. Therefore, there is a built-in disincentive and bias against policy oriented work. As Shelby Hunt so aptly stated, "Young professionals find it easier to make their mark with micro level work" (1998). The impact of meaningful policy work, however, can be very significant and long-term if it leads to shifts in policy direction. After all, most policy makers are very interested in good information that helps them do the right thing. The proof in the pudding was offered by a research symposium specifically directed at the international trade policy makers in the U.S. government. This meeting, which brought together the leading international researchers on export promotion, was attended by a standing-room-only audience and resulted in a book that, judging by ongoing feedback, continues to be read and used by policy makers in the United States and Europe (Cavusgil & Czinkota, 1990).

Specialization might also require a fine-tuning of some PhD programs. One could encourage joint ventures between international marketers and faculty members in the fields of political science and political economy. Shared grants and joint appointments may be helpful in furthering issue synergism over departmental isolationism.

It might be helpful if academics were more exposed to the policy process and learned about policy issues. Technology has become the great geographic equalizer here. International marketers in any location can derive policy information from the Web sites of the WTO (www.wto .org), the Organization for Economic Cooperation and Development (www.oecd.org), government offices such as the Office of the U.S. Trade Representative (www.ustr.org), or the International Trade Administration (www.ita.doc.gov), and of local trade and investment development agencies. International marketing researchers need to scrutinize the agenda and activities at international negotiations, read the testimony at congressional hearings, and perhaps even offer to testify themselves if they have insights to contribute. They should also not shy away from condensing and simplifying research findings and distributing them through editorials, which often offer the quickest access to policy makers. Only by clearly reflecting the policy issues and subsequent policy changes that research findings indicate, can one expect policy makers to pay attention. Policy makers need research insights, just as international marketers need them. Subtle hints or slight intonations will not bring out the hidden gem and will only deprive international marketers of the opportunity to contribute through their work to a more prosperous, safer, and more responsive international marketplace. If academics can deliver the goods to policy makers, their journals will be read, and their work will have an impact.

References

Bartels, R. (1963). *Comparative marketing: Wholesaling in fifteen countries*. Homewood, IL: Richard D. Irwin.

Brown, S. (1997). Marketing science in a postmodern world. *European Journal of Marketing, 31*(3/4), 167–182.

Cavusgil, S. T., & Czinkota, M. R. (Eds.). (1990). *International perspectives on trade promotion and assistance*. Westport, CT: Greenwood Press.

Chaudhry, P. E., & Walsh, M. G. (1995). Managing the gray market in the European union: The case of the pharmaceutical industry. *Journal of International Marketing, 3*(3), 11–33.

Contractor, F. J., & Kundu, S. K. (1998). Franchising versus company-run operations: Modal choice in the global hotel sector. *Journal of International Marketing, 6*(2), 28–53.

Cumby, R. E., & Moran, T. H. (Fall, 1994). *Testing models of the trade policy process: The case of anti-dumping in the Uruguay Round*. Mimeo, Georgetown University, School of Foreign Service.

Czinkota, M. R. (1987). *Development of a protection cost index*. U.S. Department of Commerce. Washington DC: U.S. Government Printing Office.

Czinkota, M. R., & Kotabe, M. (Summer 1997). A marketing perspective of the U.S. international trade commission's antidumping actions: An empirical inquiry. *Journal of World Business, 32*, 169–187.

Fayerweather, J. (1965). *International marketing*. Englewood Cliffs, NJ: Prentice Hall.

Finger, M. J. (1993). *Antidumping: How it works and who gets hurt*. Ann Arbor: University of Michigan Press.

Hufbauer, G. C., & Eliott, K. A. (1994). *Measuring the cost of protection in the United States*. Washington DC: Institute for International Economics.

Hunt, S. (1988). Letter to Robert Bartels. In R. Bartels, *The history of marketing thought* (3rd ed., pp. 272–273). Columbus, OH: Publishing Horizons.

Hunt S. (May 29, 1998). Personal discussion. Norfolk, VA.

Inkpen, A. C., & Beamish, P. W. (1994). An analysis of twenty-five years of research in the journal of international business studies. *Journal of International Business Studies, 25*(4), 703–713.

Kobrin, S. J. (December 1992). International business as international politics. In A. Rugman & W. Stanbury (Eds.), *Global perspective: Internationalizing management education.* Centre for International Business Studies: University of British Columbia. 205–235

Kotler, P. (1988). Letter to Robert Bartels. In R. Bartels, *The history of marketing thought* (3rd ed., pp. 255–257). Columbus, OH: Publishing Horizons.

Lelyveld, M. (May 1, 1998). Industry group takes Massachusetts to court over Myanmar sanctions. *The Journal of Commerce,* p. 3A.

Vernon, R. (December 10, 1992). *Ascendancy of the private sector in developing countries: Trend or pendulum?* Washington DC: International Finance Corporation.

CHAPTER 4

Export Promotion

A Framework for Finding Opportunity in Change

Michael R. Czinkota

Introduction

Exports represent one of many market expansion alternatives. The fact that the new customers live in another country, however, has motivated governments to devise policy instruments designed to encourage exports, particularly those of small- and medium-sized firms.

Exports are seen as special because they can affect currency values and fiscal and monetary policies. Economic theory sees them as a key balancing beam of international economic performance. Exports also shape the public perception of the competitiveness of a nation and determine (at least in the long run) the level of imports that a country can afford. Therefore, exports are crucial for the degree of choice and quality of life experienced by consumers. The impact of exporting has been tantalizing during the past 30 years, when the value of world exports of goods and services rose from US$200 billion to US$7.6 trillion, and the growth rate of exports has consistently exceeded average domestic growth rates (WTO, 2002).

For the firm, exports offer the opportunity for economies of scale. With a broader market reach and many customers abroad, a firm can produce more, and, particularly in the manufacturing sector, do so more efficiently. As a result, exporting can lead to lower costs and higher profits both at home and abroad. Exporting also means market diversification, and provides stability by not making the firm overly dependent on any particular market. Exporting lets the firm learn from the competition, makes it sensitive to different demand structures, and makes its managers appreciate and cope with diverse cultural environments.

Research in the United States has shown that exporters of all sizes and industries outperform their strictly domestic counterparts—they grow more than twice as fast in sales and earn significantly higher returns on equity and assets (Taylor & Henisz, 1994). Workers also benefit from export activities. Exporting firms of all sizes pay significantly higher wages than nonexporters, and workplace stability is significantly greater for exporting plants (Business America, 1996; Richardson & Rindal, 1996).

Successful exporting is therefore often proof of a firm's special talents that enable it to prosper in spite of higher transaction costs. Such a display of economic strength of the firm is, on an aggregate level, also a manifestation of the economic success and security of a nation.

Traditional Export Promotion

One could expect in a market-driven economy, that exports will take place on their own and that export profitability would be a suitable reward for the successful exporter. Nonetheless, most governments maintain an export policy which regulates, stimulates, directs, and protects exports (Czinkota, 2000). The following are key reasons for this intervention:

- Dealing with market barriers abroad
- Bridging market gaps
- Alleviating a trade deficit

Governments have developed various approaches toward export promotion. One focuses on knowledge transfer to enable greater competence within firms. Here, governments offer either export service programs or market development programs. Service programs typically consist of seminars for potential exporters, export counseling, and "how to export" handbooks. Market development programs provide sales leads to local firms, offer participation in foreign trade shows, preparation of market analyses, and export newsletters. Within each category, program efforts can provide informational knowledge (of the how to nature) or experiential knowledge, which provides hands-on exposure.

A second export promotion approach deals with direct or indirect subsidization of export activities. For example, low-cost export financing can produce an attractive and competitive offer, particularly for large sales that are paid over time, such as airplanes or power plants. Exports are also supported by lower tax rates for export earnings and favorable insurance rates. The overall focus of these subsidized activities is to increase the profitability of exporting to the firm, either by reducing the risks or by increasing the rewards.

A third approach to export promotion consists of reducing governmental red tape for exporters. For instance, the requirements for multiple export licenses or permits issued by various government agencies and the imposition of technology export controls constitute impediments to exporting which the government can remove, thus stimulating an increase in exports. Similarly, the reduction of antitrust concerns in the export arena has led to the formation of (export) trading firms, which are able to share facilities and expertise without the threat of government intervention.

Changes in the Export Promotion Environment

The trade environment has changed and with it the need for and capabilities of export promotion. Several rounds of trade negotiations have successfully lowered barriers to exports. High tariffs have been reduced. Nontariff barriers have been identified and, in many instances, have been lowered. Market gaps continue, with many firms still highly reluctant or not able to participate in exporting.

The regulatory aspects of the trade environment have also changed. Decades ago governments were virtually unrestrained in their export promotion activities. Today, international accords are very restrictive when it comes to such government intervention.

The North American Free Trade Agreement (NAFTA), for example, sharply limits the extent to which governments can encourage their exports, and provides for very specific and rapid remedies when violations are suspected.

Most importantly, the World Trade Organization (WTO) has taken a much closer look at export promotion activities, identified trade distorting practices, and devised rules that permit the countervailing of prohibited export promotion practices. These WTO rules are particularly opposed to export subsidization.

Export Promotion—Dead End or Crossroads?

New thinking needs to clarify the purpose of export promotion, and a new business environment enables and requires a new approach. Export promotion must be seen as offering the latest approaches and the most recent tools to bring efficiency and effectiveness to an important component of governmental policy aimed at international business.

Every day, new firms are beginning to learn about the international market and are running into barriers to international trade. For example, in any given year, 15% of U.S. exporters will stop exporting, while 10% of nonexporters will enter the global market (Bernard & Jensen, 1997). The most critical juncture for firms is when they begin or cease exporting, which is where export promotion has its greatest impact.

Export promotion may also be critical in countries that wish to open their markets further to world trade. In order to "sell" such a policy to different constituents, some of which may be negatively affected by more openness to the world, countries may be able to use export promotion as a compensatory tool in their public diplomacy. With sufficient backing for exports, legislators, unions, and industry leaders may then become supporters of trade expansion policies, or, at least, reduce their opposition (Czinkota, 2001).

Determinants of Export Performance

An Inward Look

The key determinant of export performance is the increased competitiveness of firms. Ironically, this means that rather than through international negotiations, it is mostly through down to earth domestic measures that firms receive their greatest opportunity to be a part of the export playing field. Export promotion must, then have a decidedly inward-looking component, which makes the production of goods and services cheaper, faster, and better. It has to permit domestic producers to measure levels of competitiveness by benchmarking their performance compared to firms in other nations, and allow them to correct weaknesses.

Concurrent with such an inward look, governmental efforts also need to pay heed to the financial environment, particularly the variations in exchange rates. There is little benefit to the development of competitive products if, due to currency gyrations, carefully developed business plans fall apart and entire markets disappear. Therefore, global collaboration to find a financial architecture, which, although flexible, does offer some stability to firms with a reasonably foreseeable international financial outcome, is an important second pillar of the international launching pad.

A Key Limitation

Export promotion will always only comprise a small fraction of any national budget and directly support only a minute portion of exports. It cannot be the role of export promotion to directly support all export activities. Rather, export promotion needs to initiate activities, to blaze trails with new approaches and experimentation, and to highlight new ways of overcoming hurdles. Perhaps one should characterize export promotion funds as the venture capital of international economic activity. Export promotion should not be placing the safe bet—why have government compete against market forces? Such a perspective may make it difficult to evaluate export promotion activities with traditional return on investment criteria. However, it develops an entire new focus and burden on export promotion efforts—concentrating a large portion of them "outside the box."

Some Program Considerations

Here are some considerations for policy makers interested in structuring effective export promotion programs.

Captive Export Trade

What has not received sufficient attention are intrafirm trade and other captive exports. The relationship between multinational firms and their subsidiaries have a major impact on their internal trading activities, which, in turn, greatly affect export performance.

In the United States, over 25% of overall exports are from U.S. multinationals to their affiliates. An additional 10% of U.S. exports come from foreign affiliates in the United States sending products to their parent firms (Zeile, 1999). Furthermore, many firms are likely to have developed long-term supplier relationships, which lead to a large set of "captive" exports. This extent of linked trade relations is similar in many other countries.

With almost one half of exports so affected, export promotion needs to address several new dimensions of these relationship-influenced exports. Key questions are, How can these intrafirm flows be identified and segmented into specific niches? What promotional tools can be brought to bear to specifically assist in increasing these captive export flows? Are there investment promotion strategies that can influence the corporate strategic sourcing choice? How can the affiliates of foreign multinationals be made part of a domestic export promotion effort?

Demand-Oriented Focus

Traditionally, export promotion has aimed to please the local customer, the constituent—the exporting firm. Given the intent to increase exports, however, it may make sense to devote promotional funds to develop a better understanding of the actual buyer of exports, namely the customer abroad. Any promotion of exports will fall short if no one in the market is buying.

Such a demand-oriented customer focus would require substantial research activities abroad. Findings could tell us about the weaknesses of export activities. In what areas does an industry or firm need to improve its export product or export processes? How can it be more responsive to changing demand patterns? For example, is better/faster/safer transportation required? How can transport-tracking systems be linked to facilitate better global supply chain management? A better understanding and meeting of such customer-driven needs can help propel the potential exporter to become the winning bidder.

Making Accidents Happen

Many firms become exporters by accident. Managers often receive unsolicited orders over the transom from abroad, and then have to make a choice as to whether or not to fill them. Such unsolicited orders have been found to account for more than half of all cases of export initiation by small and medium sized firms in the United States. Due to the growth of corporate Web sites, firms can become unplanned participants in the international market even more often. For example, customers from abroad can visit a Web site and place an international order. Of course, a firm can choose to ignore foreign interest and lose out on new markets. Alternatively, it can find itself unexpectedly an exporter. In the service area, specialty retailers such as bookstores and fitness equipment are examples of firms that have become international this way.

Export promotion can focus on such unsolicited orders and try to ensure that more of them reach a firm. Key questions are, In which ways can the offering of a firm be disseminated globally so that interested parties can learn about the existence of a product? How can such parties then be guided in order to make easy, unsolicited inquiries about such product? How can both the buyer and seller exchange information and develop a trust level to such a degree that order placement and order fulfillment becomes possible?

Using and Disseminating New Technologies

It is assumed by many that the emergence of electronic commerce has opened up new opportunities to exporters. While this may be true conceptually, the actual understanding and use of e-commerce lags far behind its potential. For example, in the United States most e-tailers do not accept orders from outside their home market. More than 55% of U.S. Web merchants do not even ship to Canada (Putzger, 2000). What a lost potential!

Of key importance are also the content within and the approach to the technology. Export Web site content must be available appropriately to help exports. Apart from content translation, one also needs content localization. For example, sentences in Japanese need to be formal, whereas an informal tone may be more appropriate for the United States.

Length of text plays a role—a page of English may need up to two pages in German. Also, users may read in different directions (e.g., left to right and right to left) (MacLeod, 2000).

The supply chain dimension also needs to be incorporated into e-commerce approaches. Domestically, there is a good understanding that companies are embedded in linkages with direct and indirect suppliers and customers. Internationally, however, most Web sites still represent companies rather than networks, thus, missing out on an important cooperative perspective (Wilkinson et al., 2000).

Finally, there is the issue of technology power, which can both help and hurt the exporter. For example, the availability of e-mail can inform more customers more quickly about new opportunities. However, it also brings new risks to firms. Today, one complaint can easily be shared with millions of customers via e-mail (Makihara, 2001).

Export promotion endeavors have a rich choice of activities with this new technology. The use of electronic commerce in international marketing can redefine traditional trade shows and missions, alter payment structure and flows, and recast distribution and customer complaint systems, to name but a few. It is here where the greatest potential lies for export promotion to become a venture capital tool of innovation and creativity.

A Resource-Sharing Paradigm

In today's rapidly changing business environment, few resources are permanently needed. A shift is moving us all from "possession" to "usage." Jobs are only held temporarily, cars are leased rather than purchased, and stocks are acquired through mutual funds rather than purchased directly. In the new millennium, ownership has become less important, giving way to the use of things.

In an export context, this shift is giving rise to a resource-sharing paradigm. Companies have more opportunities to collaborate by, for example, sharing warehousing, transportation, or even assembly facilities abroad, thus, making exports easier and cheaper. Governments can encourage such export collaboration and alliances within or even across their borders in order to make their firms more competitive. For example, an accumulation and subsequent sharing of benchmarking information on industry specific performance dimensions can make a major difference in letting firms learn how and where to compete. One successful performance example for other export promotion organizations to emulate is the automotive equipment benchmarking already offered by the International Trade Centre in Geneva, Switzerland. It provides comparative performance data across countries and firms for one global industry and informs firms about their strengths and weaknesses. Such collaborative opportunities also apply to all the government agencies that usually provide a nation's far-flung export promotion effort. For example, one could envision boundary-spanning joint activities between a trade or commerce ministry, an international insurance or financing agency and a transportation ministry. Such an effort could result in more streamlined government efforts that provide more export assistance in a more efficient way.

Other alternatives include risk-sharing opportunities between governments and exporters, approaches that are already used in the foreign direct investment promotion field (Mudambi, 1999). Actual financial exposure of government to its own advice might also reduce the frequency with which export promotion counseling reflects the wishful thinking of government policy rather than economic reality.

Conclusion

Export promotion must take new approaches to remain viable. The new business environment calls for new strategies. The focus of export promotion can no longer be on subsidization.

Much of export promotion has to become domestically oriented, aiming to develop a competitive platform that permits a successful launch of exports. Even though, perhaps accompanied by too little political credit from the export community, the streamlining of regulations, the tight focusing of export controls, and the development of infrastructure and information systems can be crucial in enhancing the competitive capability of firms. In an era of globalization, many nations may have only the export promotion card to play in support of their firms.

It is also important to recognize the limits of export promotion efforts. They should be seen as a supplement, and not as a substitute for market forces. Therefore, export promotion expenditures should be evaluated using criteria such as innovativeness, identification and use of new technology, and the filling of temporary market gaps.

Finally, exports need to be seen from a spirit of international collaboration—after all, every export has to be someone else's import. Export promotion needs to recognize the nexus between trade and investment, as well as the links between economic and national security. Economic strength of firms, after all, on an aggregate level, manifests the economic success and security of a nation.

Note

For an extensive research treatment of the issue discussed in this chapter, see Czinkota, M. R. (2002). National export promotion. In M. Kotabe & P. S. Aulakh (Eds.), *Emerging issues in international business research*. Northampton, MA: Elgar Publishing.

References

Bernard, A. B., & Jensen, J. B. (1997). *Exceptional exporter performance: Cause, effect or both?* Pittsburgh, PA: Census Research Data Center, Carnegie Mellon University.

Business America. (1996, September). *117*(9), 9.

Czinkota, M. R. (2000). The policy gap in international marketing. *Journal of International Marketing, 8*(1), 99–111.

Czinkota, M. R. (2001, July 8). Trade authority requires export promotion. *Journal of Commerce*. Retrieved March 15, 2003, from http://www.joc.com

MacLeod, M. (2000). Language barriers. *Supply Management, 5*(14), 37–38.

Makihara, M. (2001). Co-Chairman of the Annual Meeting of the World Economic Forum, Davos, Switzerland. Retrieved March 15, 2003, from http://www.worldeconomicforum.org

Mudambi, R. (1999). Multinational investment attraction: Prinicipal-agent consideration. *International Journal of the Economics of Business, 6* (1), 65–79.

Putzger, I. (2000). On-line and international. *Journal of Commerce Weekly, 11*, 13–19, 27–28.

Richardson, J. D., & Rindal, K. (1996). *Why exports matter: More!* Washington, DC: The Institute for International Economics and the Manufacturing Institute.

Taylor, C., & Henisz, W. (1994). *U.S. manufacturers in the global marketplace*. Report 1058, the Conference Board.

Wilkinson, I. F., Mattson, L. G., & Easton, G. (2000). International competitiveness and trade promotion policy from a network perspective. *Journal of
World Business, 35*(3), 275–299.

World Trade Organization. (2002). *International trade statistics.* Retrieved February 13, 2002, from http://www.wto.org

Zeile, W. J. (1999). Foreign direct investment in the United States. *Survey of Current Business, August, 79*(8), 21–44.

CHAPTER 5

An Analysis of the Global Position of U.S. Manufacturing

Michael R. Czinkota

Since 1975 the United States has been importing more than export-ing, therefore running a continuous current account deficit. Exhibit 5.1 shows the U.S. current account balance over the past 32 years. While there have always been ups and downs, since the early 1990s the growth of the deficit has been rapid and major. On a global level, U.S. imports are necessarily some other country's exports. The U.S. current account deficit is matched by bilateral current account surpluses of other nations. At $103 billion, China had the largest current account surplus with the United States in 2002, followed by Japan with $70 billion, Canada with $50 billion, and Germany with $36 billion.

Exhibit 5.2 breaks the current account down into its components: merchandise trade, services trade, investment income, and net unilateral transfers. Merchandise trade not only is the largest factor but also con-tributes the most to the deficit. In 2002, services trade had a surplus of over $49 billion; investment income ran at a deficit of $5 billion; while net unilateral transfers resulted in a deficit of $56 billion.

Exhibit 5.3 shows that U.S. merchandise exports have been constantly rising. However, since the mid-1990s, these increases have remained far

This article is based on the author's testimony to the Congress of the United States, 108th Congress, First Session, House of Representatives, Committee on Small Business on April 9, 2003.

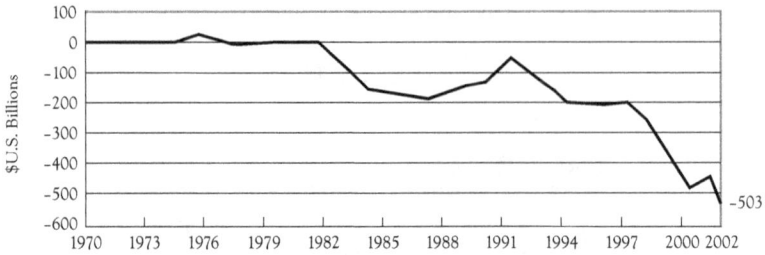

Exhibit 5.1. U.S. Current Account Balance, 1970–2002

Source: Bureau of Economic Analysis (BEA), 2003.

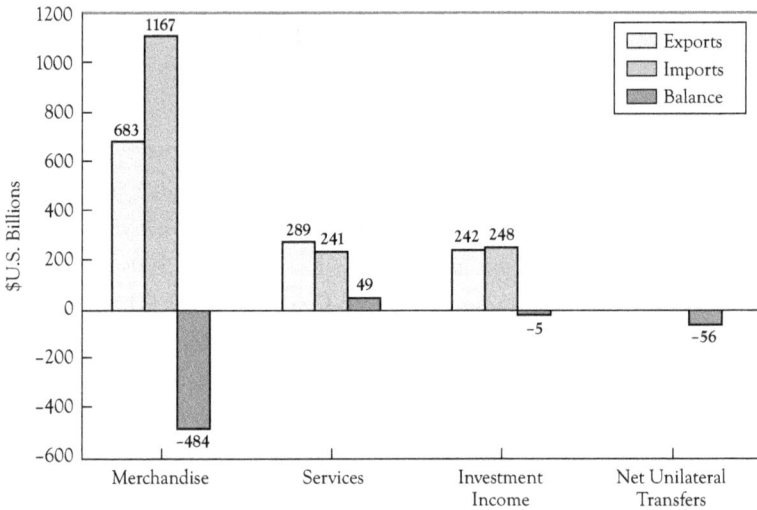

Exhibit 5.2. U.S. Current Account Components, 2002

Source: BEA, 2003.

below the increases in merchandise imports. Therefore, the gap between imports and exports has been growing rapidly.

Exhibit 5.4 breaks overall merchandise trade down into its components: manufactured goods, mineral fuels, agricultural goods, and the catchall category of "other." For both U.S. exports and imports, manufactured goods play a key role. Eighty-one percent of merchandise exports are manufactured goods, as are almost 84% of imports.

Exhibit 5.5 focuses on manufactures trade. While there have been deficits over the decades, these were quite stable in their size during the 1980s and into the early 1990s. However, from 1992 on, the growth of

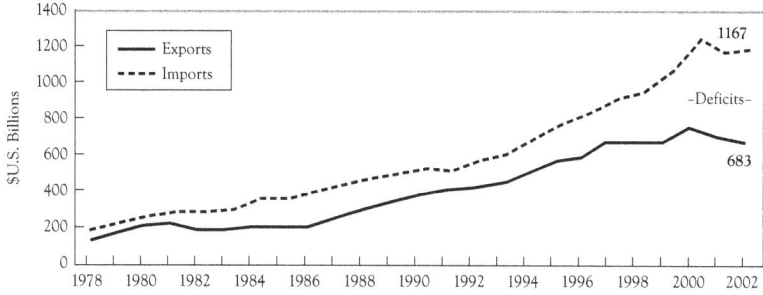

Exhibit 5.3. U.S. Merchandise Exports, Imports, and Deficits, 1978–2002

Source: BEA, 2003.

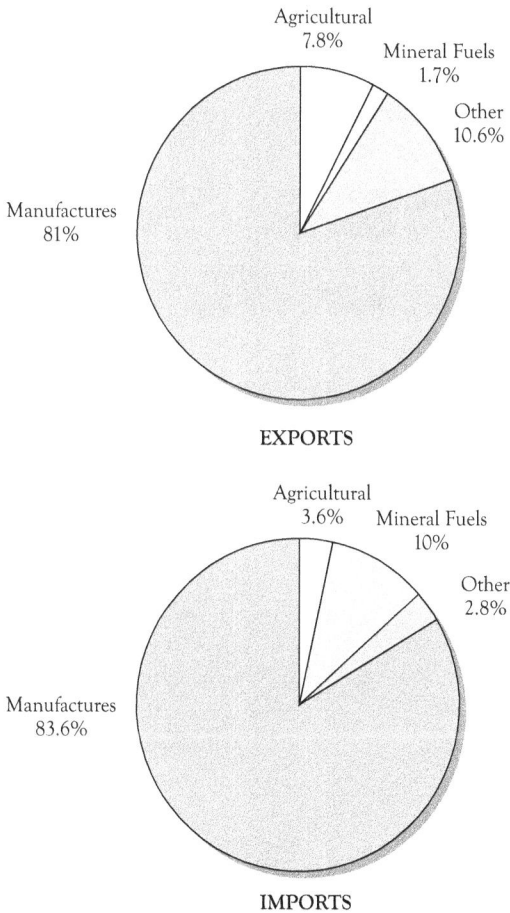

Exhibit 5.4. Composition of U.S. Merchandise Trade, 2002

Source: Census, 2003.

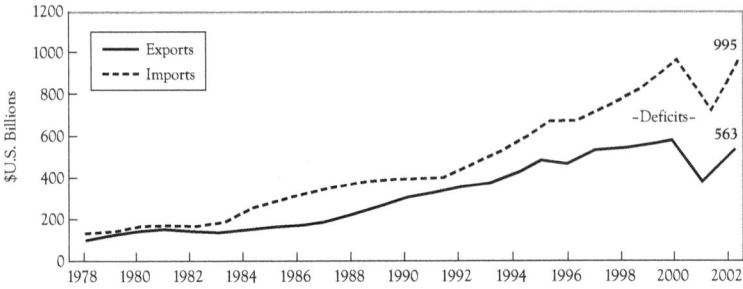

Exhibit 5.5. U.S. Manufactures Exports, Imports, and Deficits, 1978–2002

Source: Census, 2003.

imports in manufactured goods has been much steeper than the growth of exports, leading to a widening manufactures trade deficit.

Exhibit 5.6 indicates the top surplus and deficit countries in U.S. manufactures trade. While there are substantial manufactures surpluses with the Netherlands, Australia, and Belgium, these are dwarfed by manufactures deficits with Mexico, Germany, Japan, and China. In 2002 U.S. bilateral manufactures trade with China alone was $103 billion in deficit.

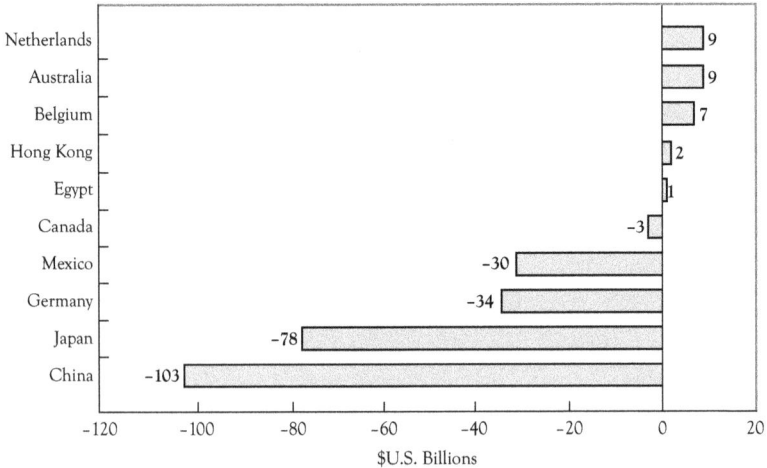

Exhibit 5.6. Key Manufactures Trade Imbalances for Top Surplus and Deficit Countries, 2002

Source: Census, 2003.

Looking at the key manufactures trade imbalances by type of commodity, Exhibit 5.7 shows that in 2002, there were large U.S. surpluses in airplanes and parts, wood manufactures, scientific instruments, and chemicals. Yet these surpluses were far outweighed by deficits in industries such as furniture, toys and games, televisions and VCRs, and apparel. The largest deficit category in the manufacturing sector was motor vehicles, with an imbalance of $111 billion.

Providing an Overall Context

In the mid-1800s, about 68% of U.S. employment was in the agricultural sector. Manufacturing accounted for only 17% of employment. Since then, the employment absorbed by these sectors has shifted dramatically. By 2001, agriculture, for example, accounted only for 1.5% of employment. But 66% of the work-eligible population does not consist of unemployed farmers. Rather, there have been dramatic increases of employment in the services sector, where employment has risen from 22% to almost 80% of the overall economy. The manufacturing sector, in turn, grew to an employment proportion of almost 30% in 1960. In the last 20 years, however, employment levels have decreased at a rising rate. At the turn of the new millennium, U.S. manufacturing

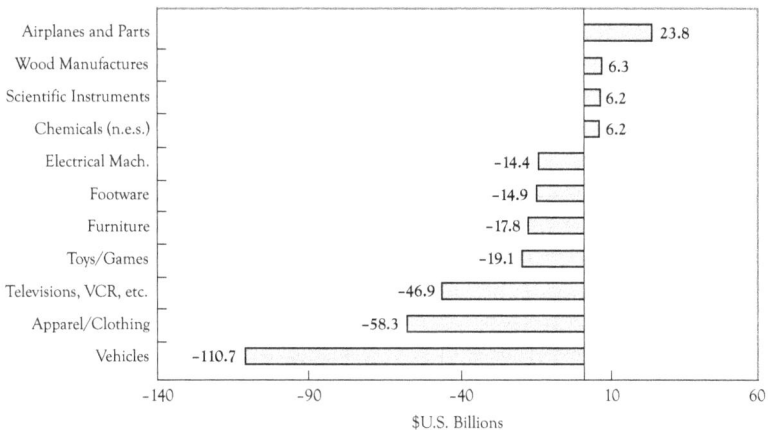

Exhibit 5.7. Key U.S. Manufactures Trade Imbalances by Commodity Group, 2002

Source: Census, 2003.

employment, at 14.8%, had decreased below the levels of when it was first officially measured.

For a global context, Exhibit 5.8 compares employment developments in manufacturing in the United States, Germany, and Japan. During the past 31 years, German manufacturing employment dropped as a proportion of gross domestic product (GDP) from 36% to 23%. The steepest decline came in the 1990s when, within one decade, employment dropped by almost seven percentage points. In Japan, the 6.5% drop in manufacturing employment from 1970 to 2001 was much milder, though as a percentage of GDP, the shift was from 33.5 to 21 percent. This is in sharp contrast with U.S. employment changes. U.S. and Japanese manufacturing employment proportions were almost the same in 1970. Since then, U.S. proportionate employment has been cut almost in half—and is now more than five percentage points lower than the Japanese manufacturing employment and almost 10 percentage points below German levels. U.S. manufacturers and their workers have, therefore, undergone the most drastic changes among the three countries when it comes to employment. While other countries have taken

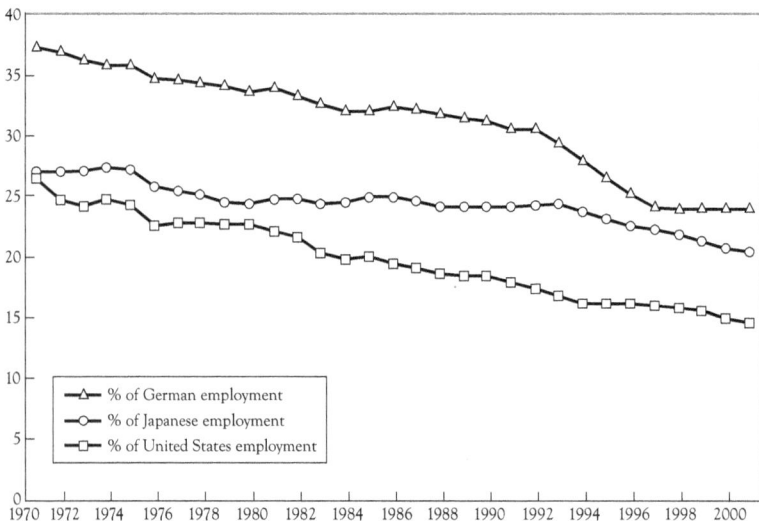

Exhibit 5.8. Manufacturing in Germany, Japan, and the United States, 1970–2000

Source: Census, 2003.

protective measures to soften the blow against their manufacturers, U.S. firms have experienced the full power of market forces.

All these shifts in employment reflected a transfer of manufacturing away from the industrialized nations toward the emerging economies. Exhibit 5.9 shows how the proportion of manufacturing has rapidly grown in nations such as Malaysia, South Korea, Thailand, and Indonesia.

Some Key Causes

Such a shift is greatly hastened when manufacturers under export. When entering international markets, firms are faced with new risks, new cultures, new processes, and new conditions such as changing exchange rates and divergent government regulations.

There are difficulties in obtaining financing for export ventures, and the regulatory rules for exporters can be complex. For many U.S. firms, the size of their home market seems to provide ample opportunity, obviating the need to learn about international prospects. As a result, U.S. firms do not take sufficient advantage of international market opportunities and underexport relative to other nations. U.S. merchandise exports comprise only 11% of GDP, compared to almost 34% for the

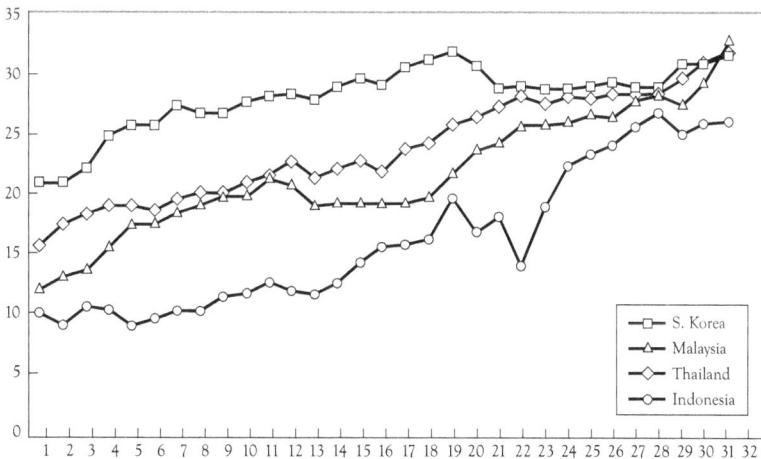

Exhibit 5.9. Manufacturing as a Percentage of GDP, 1970–2000

Source: Census, 2003.

European Union (excluding intra-EU trade) and 26% for China. On a per capita basis, in 2002 the European Union exported $7,434 for every man, woman, and child, while for the United States it was only $3,794 (Czinkota & Roukaineu, 2003).

U.S. manufacturers also contribute to the migration of plants. In order to maintain their price competitiveness many of them have established subsidiaries abroad to take advantage of lower labor costs. They specify the products to be produced, decide on the quantities to be turned out, and determine the volume of shipments back to the United States. In 2000, the latest year for which data are available, such import shipments from foreign affiliates of U.S. companies amounted to 14% of U.S. imports. In addition, many firms have developed long term supplier relationships with firms abroad, which lead to another large set of "captive" imports.

Subsidiaries of foreign firms in the United States also import from affiliated plants of their home countries. The share of U.S. imports accounted for by these foreign parents of U.S. affiliates was 20% in 2000 (Lowe, 2003). Therefore, at least one half of U.S. imports are initiated and encouraged by U.S. corporate entities who consider it good business strategy to source from abroad rather than producing in the United States.

Practical Implications

While it is comforting to point toward the gradual adjustment of employment sectors over time, individuals currently experiencing the economic shifts through their personal unemployment will see this explanation as providing little solace. The economy appears to be working quite efficiently from a long-term perspective. But the need to adjust lifestyles, obtain a new set of skills, and change location may be overwhelming to many. Similarly, such shifts have an impact on the firm's stakeholders. Companies are one piece of a mosaic that affects the appearance and stability of the other pieces. For example, the disappearance of a firm will affect the local community and government, shape the fate of local suppliers, educational opportunities, health care, and may even determine whether a community can survive.

There is also a holistic perspective, which looks beyond the immediate surroundings. When important shifts occur in the economy, one needs to consider the repercussions down the road. Otherwise it would be the rare exception to see investments for the long term common good. There would be few trees planted, lighthouses built, or basic research projects conducted.

Finally, while important, the economic dimension cannot be the only criterion driving a nation. Issues such as national security, public safety, and the overall standard of living must be considered when analyzing the importance of specific changes.

Repercussions and Concerns

The shift in U.S. manufactures trade and the continued, growing trade deficits gives rise to concerns on a macro and microeconomic level. Nations need to have a sound footing in order to be strong in their offense against terrorism, capable in their maintenance of a standard of living, and kind in their support of the poor and the ill.

On the macroeconomic level, trade deficits of the current magnitude are unsustainable in the long run. At about five percent of GDP, these trade deficits add to the U.S. international debt burden, which must be serviced through interest payments and eventually perhaps even repaid. Therefore, an improved global performance by U.S. manufacturing firms that results in an increase in their exports and an improved competitiveness with imports will be crucial for the nation.

There will be concern by the international trade community about any U.S. desire to gain more market share for its exports and to stem the rapid increase of imports. However, the United States has the right to argue for a special case. As the trade figures have shown, over the decades the U.S. market has remained wide open to imports. Even today, when faced with many international machinations, the United States continues to offer its own market and consumptive power as an economic locomotive to the world. Many nations would have fallen into the abyss of economic disaster had their exports not had virtually unfettered U.S. market access. U.S. manufacturing has already paid the price by suffering the most drastic declines among all the industrialized nations. When it comes to future trade concessions in manufacturing, it's fair for U.S. negotiators to say, "We already gave at the office."

One should also consider U.S. manufacturing capability in the context of lifestyle and national needs. When a manufacturing sector disappears domestically, it leaves behind a void that goes beyond lost jobs. Replacement parts suddenly become unavailable or much more expensive. Product reorders, now filled abroad, take weeks rather than days. Some crucial input components to other manufacturing processes may be lost or delayed, slowing down the production of related products. Particularly for industries critical to the national welfare and national security, such effects can be devastating in case of an emergency. Even if there are good relationships with the governments of the countries to which sensitive manufacturing industries migrate, one has to consider the long term. For example, how many of us would wish, in today's fog of war, to rely on old friends abroad for the rapid resupply of crucial manufactures? The much praised interdependence of globalization of manufacturing has also increased national dependence.

Then there are the effects of manufacturing migration on innovation and market responsiveness. Together, with Masaaki Kotabe of Temple University, I have analyzed the use of emerging technologies in existing products. We found that the closer companies are to their market, the more they can use such technologies in new products. Japanese companies systematically incorporate new technologies in existing products. This enables them to gain experience, debug technological glitches, reduce costs, boost performance, and adapt designs for worldwide customer benefit. As a result, they have been able to increase the speed of new product introductions, meet the competitive demands of a rapidly changing marketplace, and capture market share. The continual introduction of newer and better designed products brings a greater likelihood of market success. However, when production is removed from its primary market, such rapid response to market demands may well be dulled, which can lead to a decline in manufacturing competitiveness (Czinkota & Kotabe, 1990).

Sourcing from abroad through independent suppliers may also have long-term consequences on the processes, competence, and capabilities of firms. In a comparison between the outsourcing networks of Japanese and U.S. companies, Kotabe finds that U.S. companies gradually severed their value chain and, in search of cost efficiency, have willingly increased their dependence on foreign suppliers for components and finished products that have become technologically more sophisticated. The creation of new technology is a gradual and painstaking learning process of continual adjustment and refinement, as new productive methods are tested and adapted in the light of a company's accumulated experience. Thus, overreliance on acquisitions and new technologies from other firms may not result in the same sustainable competitive advantage available through internal development. The manufacturing shift abroad may, therefore, eradicate current technology, design, and process advantages possessed by U.S. firms, placing them and the country at further, future disadvantage.

There are also effects of manufacturing migration on cluster formation. Over the past decades many industries have gradually emerged in a cluster formation—where a diverse set of firms eventually shapes regions or centers of excellence. Such centers are characterized by strong competition from a wide variety of firms, demanding customers, and a multitude of creative and innovative suppliers. They tend to be attractive to job seekers in that particular industry, generate specific expertise, and bring in even more firms wanting to be in close proximity to industrial capability either for production or buying purposes. Silicon Valley in California or the Diamond District in New York can serve as examples.

Typically only a few firms were the originators of such a cluster of excellence. It is therefore reasonable to expect that similar developments are true in reverse. For example, the migration of a few key firms can result in the decomposition of such clusters and their relocation to other regions. Such a phenomenon may occur particularly in industries where changes in technology make skill levels less important. As the shoe and optical equipment industries have demonstrated, a decline in the skills required can lead to movement of an entire industry. Such a lumpy migration of manufacturing can then result in a greatly magnified effect on individuals and communities. Therefore, the shift of any one manufacturing firm must be seen in the context of the overall stability of existing clusters.

Some Possible Policy Remedies

The concerns raised can be addressed by various actions. One major temptation may be to press legislation against those countries and foreign industries which account for substantial imbalances in manufactures trade. Doing so, however, runs the grave risk of substituting government judgment for market direction, a replacement which has not distinguished itself by past success. Prices might rise disproportionately, consumers might be deprived of desirable goods, and firms might find their ability to export undermined.

More positive change might be achieved by encouraging existing market activities through better processes, more support, and more information. For example, export promotion can persuade U.S. manufacturers to take more advantage of international opportunities. This will require coordinated and streamlined services by government. They must include more information, a greater availability and ease of export financing, more streamlining of the logistics of international shipments, better tools for risk analysis, and better targeting for the delivery of this support. For example, there need to be more systematic efforts to introduce customer relations management (CRM) activities and benchmarks into government export promotion work. When a firm seeks governmental help with financing, communication, or its shipments, such assistance ought to be provided through one "personal export officer," regardless of which agency handles the details.

There also needs to be more emphasis on and opportunities for the bundling of products, services, financing, and the creation of global networks when it comes to the international effort. It is through such bundling that U.S. manufacturers can gain specific advantages not available to their competitors abroad. Consider one example from the automotive industry: Airbags, the global positioning system, and a telephone in a car are no longer anything special. Yet, by bundling all these components together, car manufacturers have been able to develop an entire new set of passenger assistance services which can even independently notify emergency services in case of an accident. Such combinations of available products, technology, and networks can lead to an entirely new plateau of customer satisfaction.

On the regulatory side, a stable and safe international environment is, in itself, an important support for firms. But regulations also need to incorporate an international dimension by considering the global implications and effects of regulatory actions. U.S. export control rules need to be revisited in order to ensure that they are precise and targeted, while not needlessly inhibiting to firms. The foreign availability of products needs to be taken into consideration before denying a firm the opportunity to export. If similar products are available from abroad (even though perhaps at different prices and in different quantities), the regulatory community must face a particularly high hurdle of proof of effectiveness before denying a license application. Likewise, if a U.S. firm receives an export order that requires the production inspection of the foreign buyers, visa regulations should be able to quickly accommodate the need for a brief visit by foreign customers. By delaying such visits for months, current and future manufacturing export contracts may well be in jeopardy.

There should be a systematic effort to alert customers and consumers to the long term consequences of their purchasing decisions. Their knowledge level should be addressed before the final consequences of their decisions are reached. Perhaps we can learn from the motto of a national clothing chain: "An informed consumer is our best customer." More available domestic information on manufacturing and its future may well affect some decision processes. The White House Office of Global Communication has been created to let the world know more about the United States and its intentions abroad. Perhaps a similar outreach effort should communicate the condition of manufacturing to a domestic audience.

As a caveat, it is worth noting that services are, at 79% of the workforce, the largest employing economic sector in the United States. Increasingly U.S. services industries are becoming footloose and are beginning to go global. We have all heard the stories about the back office operations in Ireland and India. These services are growing progressively sophisticated. For example, many x-ray and CT scan frames are read by radiology experts abroad. One should therefore also consider how to ensure that U.S. services firms and their employees retain international competitiveness.

There is always the question of who pays for such efforts. For the past half century, various U.S. administrations have been instrumental in opening up world markets. Congress has ratified the resulting agreements with the expectation of beneficial economic effects. However, the positive effects caused by free trade are not self-evident; they must be explained, defined, and provided by industry in a highly visible fashion on a regular basis, particularly when it comes to jobs. The public understanding of free trade and its resulting reverberation is often insufficiently addressed. In listening to some of the arguments brought forth by activists against free trade, one might gain the impression that there are no benefits at all. It is up to the beneficiaries to step up to the plate and provide positive evidence both to legislators and the public at large.

For too long, there has been little, if any, linkage between the governmental efforts that open markets and the industry response to the benefits obtained from such openings. For example, even though most trade negotiations result in both winners and losers, there are no current incentives for winners to let others share in their bounty. Similarly, there are few if any requirements placed on the beneficiaries of protective measures to convincingly demonstrate how they have used their enhanced revenues to help the transition of workers and communities. Perhaps the time is here for industries that reap the benefits of government actions to deal with the negative reverberations.

We need a program where winners chip in to pay for the cost of such adjustment. In an era of renewed budget restraint, such a program can become an essential engine for further trade liberalization. If there are trade enhancing measures for which there is insufficient public sector funding, the private sector can pay for further trade policy aims. After all, free trade carries a price.

References

Czinkota, M. R., & Kotabe, M. (1990, November/December). Product development the Japanese way. *Journal of Business Strategy, 11*, 31–36.

Czinkota, M. R., & Ronkainen, I. A. (2003). *International marketing* (7th ed.). Cincinnati: Thomson.

Kotabe, M. (1999). Efficiency vs. effectiveness orientation of global sourcing strategy: A comparison of U.S. and Japanese multinational companies. *Academy of Management Executive, 12*(4), 107–119.

Lowe, J. H. (2003, January). An ownership-based framework of the U.S. current account, 1989–2001. *Survey of Current Business*, pp. 17–19.

PART II

Competition From (Re)emerging Markets

CHAPTER 6

Have Lunch or Be Lunch

Smaller Firms Thrive in Vulnerable Markets

Michael R. Czinkota and Ilkka A. Ronkainen

The United States is in a vulnerable position when it comes to international trade. Since 1975, it has been importing more goods than it has been exporting, therefore running a continuous merchandise trade deficit. Even though overall U.S. exports surpassed $1 trillion in 2001, the deficit in the trade of goods was more than $426 billion. Ongoing annual trade deficits of this magnitude are unsustainable in the long run. Such deficits add to the U.S. international debt, which must be serviced through interest payments and eventually perhaps even repaid. Therefore, an export performance by U.S. firms that matches or even exceeds our imports will become crucial

Furthermore, exports are also an important contributor to national employment. We estimate that $1 billion of exports supports the creation, on average, of about 11,500 jobs. In its latest benchmark study, the U.S. Department of Commerce reports there were more than 8 million U.S. jobs sustained by the export of manufactured goods, which ties one out of every five U.S. manufacturing jobs directly or indirectly to exports. For example, in the state of Illinois alone, more than 360,000 jobs were linked to manufactured exports. An increase in exports can therefore be a key factor in maintaining domestic job growth.

Many see the global market as the exclusive realm of large, multinational corporations. Overlooked are the hundreds of thousands of smaller firms that have been fueling a U.S. export boom, which has supported the economy in times of limited domestic growth. The latest information from the trade data project at the Department of Commerce indicates that, between 1987 and 1999, the number of U.S. firms that export at least occasionally has more than tripled to more than 231,000. Almost 97% of these exporters were small or midsized companies.

The reason for the export success of smaller firms lies in the new determinants of competitiveness, as framed by the wishes and needs of the foreign buyers. Other than price, buyers today also expect an excellent product fit, high levels of corporate responsiveness, a substantial service orientation, and high corporate commitment. Small and midsized firms stack up well on all these dimensions compared to their larger brethren and may even have a competitive advantage.

Corporate Vulnerabilities

In spite of many advantages, smaller firms face major obstacles to international market prosperity.

Financial Issues

All firms worry about getting paid when they ship their merchandise abroad, but small and midsized exporters are particularly at risk. They need financing to cover the time lag between shipping and payment receipts as well as to offer credit to buyers. Longer distances, slower transportation, and more accommodating payment terms abroad make international transactions more expensive. These transactions also require more capital and represent a larger portion of the firm's resources than do domestic transactions. In addition, due to their size, international shipments often represent a larger degree of risk than smaller firms are willing or able to tolerate.

Exchange rate changes present a major source of vulnerability. Time passes between the initiation of an international transaction and its consummation. During that time, the firm is exposed to the effects of currency shifts. Major changes of currency value can transform a good business transaction into one that loses money.

One particular issue U.S. exporters must cope with is the competition from the Euro zone and its currency volatility. The Euro is the new international trade currency the European Union implemented widely on in 2002. Even though originally introduced at a value slightly higher than the dollar, the Euro was valued at only 0.88 during most of 2002. Consequently, U.S. imports from Europe became cheaper, but U.S. exporters found it more difficult to compete. During the latter part of last year, the Euro rose in value and now exceeds the dollar. However, this has mainly been a function of different interest rate policies, which have been guided by a flexible U.S. Fed and a very unyielding European Central Bank. Changes in bank leadership, which appear quite likely, may presage new policies and a return to a rapidly rising dollar.

Smaller firms also lack the unfettered access to global capital markets that large firms have. They still rely very heavily on mainly domestic or even local sources of money. As a result, they don't benefit from the low-cost opportunities of global capital and are not diversified enough in their sources of funds to cope with local interest rate inefficiencies. Given the increasing commoditization of goods, price shifts resulting from interest or exchange rate changes may critically affect the firm's competitiveness and profits.

Supply Chain Management

Key concerns here are the development of contacts, relationships, and networks with suppliers and the forging of a systems linkage with intermediaries and customers. In addition, there are the logistics of arranging transportation, determining transport rates, handling documentation, obtaining financial information, coordinating distribution, packaging, and obtaining insurance. The logistics are often handled by intermediaries, such as freight forwarders. This area also includes the overseas servicing of exports, where the firm needs to accommodate returns and provide parts, repair service, and technical advice. Often the solution is to open a servicing or distribution office abroad.

Timely communication among the different members of the supply chain is crucial if a firm is to perform competitively. Here again, small and midsized firms are particularly vulnerable since they may need to invest heavily in information technology—a major capital outlay. They don't have the clout of large firms that can require their international supply chain members to adapt to a standardized information system. Smaller firms have to adapt to multiple systems and find ways to make them internationally compatible—incurring additional expenses and technical difficulties.

Firms that developed elaborate just-in-time delivery systems for their international shipments were also severely affected by the border and port closures during the days following the terrorist attacks on the United States. Together with their service providers, they continue to be affected by the increased security measures. Firms now need to focus on internal security and must demonstrate to third parties how much more security-oriented they've become. In many instances, government authorities require evidence of threat-reduction efforts to speed things along. Insurance companies have increased their premiums substantially in response to new definitions of risk. Unless policy holders take major steps to reduce such risk (or assume some of it themselves), they are likely to suffer from continued premium increases.

Regulatory Issues

Another key vulnerability consists of legal procedures and typically covers government red tape, product liability, licensing, and customs/duty issues. Here, small and midsized firms are particularly exposed to changing government policies. The September 11 terrorist attacks have profoundly affected the administration of U.S. export controls and customs procedures. While larger firms have the benefit of a fully staffed department that deals with regulatory affairs, smaller exporters often face new and unfamiliar territory. For them, export control regulations are more burdensome. In addition, customs classifications and rules may require the hiring of specialists who ensure that shipments go out and come in properly reported and on time.

On the regulatory side, U.S. firms also are exposed to the vicissitudes of trade policy. Market access and market performance issues should be taken up in the Doha Round, the new conference of trade liberalization negotiations due to conclude by 2005. However, in existing trade disputes, our firms are also threatened by the retaliatory measures taken by trade adversaries overseas. Even though a conflict may be totally unrelated to their industry, U.S. manufacturers are vulnerable to foreign trade policy actions specifically designed to elicit the largest amount of pain from their victims. For example, when European countries or China react to U.S. import duties on foreign steel products, they do so by placing new (or higher) tariffs on a wide range of U.S. products. This makes many U.S. firms, including smaller producers, noncompetitive in these markets. They, in effect, pay the price for the U.S. protection of the domestic steel industry.

Market Contact

Small to midsized firms need to cope with advertising, sales effort, and obtaining marketing information. They also need to develop foreign market intelligence on the location of markets, trade restrictions, and competitive conditions overseas. For large firms, such activities are often part of market expansion, where additional activities are carried out in already familiar territory. Small and midsized firms, however, are often still at the level of international market entry, where each step requires the dedication of new resources to unfamiliar tasks. It bears remembering that any new entrant into the international market must not only match, but must exceed by far, the capabilities of the local competition overseas. After all, apart from needing to find the spare capacity among its management resources, which permits a corporate focus on and commitment to exports, the newcomer must also carry all the transaction costs associated with the internationalization process. These start with the cost of shipping and special packaging and include duties and other special international burdens.

All these obstacles, both real and perceived, can prevent firms from exporting. Many managers often see only the risks involved rather than the opportunities the international market can present. As a result, the United States still underexports when compared to other nations. U.S. merchandise exports comprise only 11% of gross domestic product (GDP), compared to 28.3% for Germany and 25.4% for the United Kingdom. On a per capita basis, in 2000 the United Kingdom exported $6,226 for every man, woman, and child. The figure for Germany was $7,498, and for the United States, only $3,878.

Opportunities for Support

Currently, U.S. export performance is insufficient given its potential. Many small and medium-sized exporters are too complacent to globalize because they're either content with a vast domestic market or fear the complexity of selling abroad. Firms that do consider global opportunities appear to be unwilling to initiate major expansions of their operations abroad because of their real and perceived risk in the international market.

One core business concern is financing. On the positive side, private lenders of trade finance are becoming more active in the United States, but they often lend at relatively high rates. U.S. exporters have the benefit of many effective federal and state government programs, such as the working capital guarantee program by the Export Import Bank of the United States (Eximbank), which provides financing assistance. There are several programs specifically designed to help small business exporters. Still there needs to be a continuous emphasis on small business lending support and a responsible adaptation of credit criteria for the conditions of small and medium-sized enterprises. For example, small and midsized firms often can't afford to provide all the detailed evaluations and documentations lenders ideally want to see.

Of key relevance is a stable financial environment, both domestically and internationally. Small and midsized firms can cope with changing conditions. However, the speed of change can severely influence or even destroy the profitability of operations. Any policy measures that affect the access to and the cost of capital of smaller firms or the exchange rate of the dollar should specifically take into account the consequences and burden that such steps would impose on U.S. exporters.

Think Internationally

In time, nearly every firm will be an international marketer, by default if not by design. As globalization expands, companies will have no place to hide. New foreign competition in their own backyards will force firms to think internationally, if only defensively. Improving offerings to combat new rivals at home might well generate new demand for a firm's goods in foreign markets. As online marketplaces bring together buyers and sellers from all over the world quickly and efficiently, Internet search engines will lead prospective customers to company Web sites, even those designed for domestic buyers only.

From most perspectives, world trade conducted by savvy international marketers is the prerequisite to global growth, prosperity, and freedom for all peoples. And for companies themselves, the choice is clear: Have lunch or be lunch.

CHAPTER 7

Export Strategies and Performance of Firms From Emerging Economies

Evidence From Brazil, Chile, and Mexico

Preet S. Aulakh, Masaaki Kotabe, and Hildy Teegen

The globalization of the business environment in recent years has made it imperative for firms to look for foreign market opportunities in order to gain and sustain competitive advantage. Trade and market liberalization policies around the globe in the last two decades, especially in the erstwhile closed economies of Asia, Eastern Europe, and Latin America, provide new market, investment, and sourcing opportunities for multinational firms (Garten, 1997). Concurrently, firms from emerging economies are a growing presence in an integrated global economy. Reinforced by the success of firms from newly industrialized countries such as South Korea, Taiwan, and Singapore, emerging economies are moving away from inward-oriented import substitution policies toward outward-oriented export-led growth (Kotler, Jatusripitak, & Maesincee, 1997). Thus, public policy instruments in emerging economies are increasingly geared to providing incentives for local firms to actively internationalize and compete in foreign markets (Kotler et al., 1997).

The international expansion of private enterprises from an emerging economy is primarily accomplished by manufacturing in the home country and exporting products to foreign markets (Vernon-Wortzel & Wortzel, 1988). In fact, the pattern of foreign expansion of these firms follows the prescriptions of both the internationalization (Johanson & Vahlne, 1977) and international product life cycle (Vernon, 1966) models: firms first expand into foreign countries through exporting and, with increased market knowledge, escalate commitments in the form of more investment-oriented entry modes. Given that a majority of firms from emerging markets are still in the early stages of the internationalization process, with exporting being the dominant mode of their foreign market participation, an important research issue is what strategies these enterprises pursue as they compete in the global competitive landscape. However, there have been few systematic studies of the export strategies followed by firms from emerging economies and the performance implications of those strategies (Dominguez & Brenes, 1997). The few studies that exist have examined the internationalization process of developing country firms (e.g., Vernon-Wortzel & Wortzel, 1988), the relationship between organizational characteristics and export performance (e.g., Christensen, Rocha, & Gertner, 1987; Dominguez & Sequeira, 1993), or the links between macro policy initiatives, trade liberalization, and economic development at the country level (Otani & Villanueva, 1990). In the contemporary environment of market and trade liberalization, the importance of private enterprises in emerging economies as engines of outward-oriented growth necessitates an examination of their export strategies for building competitive advantage in foreign markets.

The purpose of this study was to provide an understanding of the export strategies of firms from emerging economies. In particular, we developed a framework by incorporating the different strategies available to exporting firms as they compete in foreign markets and linked those strategies to export performance. A set of hypotheses was generated from this overall framework and empirically tested on a sample of firms from three key Latin American countries—Brazil, Chile, and Mexico.

Latin America, comprising Mexico and countries from Central and South America, is home to about 500 million people. The region, with an average per capita gross national product (GNP) of about $3,000, represents one-third of the developing world's economy (Dominguez & Brenes, 1997). According to Kotler, Jatusripitak, and Maesincee, Latin

American countries represent a distinct strategic group with "shared histories (e.g., import substitution), common problems (e.g., inflation), and same solutions (e.g., foreign debts)" (1997, p. 95). Although most of the countries in the region have always participated in international trade, much of this trade activity was in commodity products like oil, copper, and cocoa, owing to the region's natural resource endowments. Furthermore, most of this trade was managed by state-owned enterprises, and the limited activity in the manufacturing sector was guided by import substitution policies, under the assumption that the sizes of domestic markets and endowments of natural resources were sufficient to support industrialization (Dominguez & Brenes, 1997; Kotler et al., 1997).

However, existing economic models of reliance on natural resources and state-owned enterprises in a protectionist environment grew to be no longer feasible. Consequently, a number of Latin American countries instituted drastic reforms in the 1980s and 1990s,[1] including privatization of state-owned companies, an increased role for private enterprises in fostering economic growth, the opening of domestic markets to foreign competition to bring in capital and new technologies and provide high-powered incentives for efficient enterprises, the introduction of policy initiatives to invigorate noncommodity and higher-value-added industries, and an emphasis on export-led growth.

Although an objective of these economic reforms was to emulate Asia's export-led growth policies, liberalization in Latin American is distinct on two dimensions. First, the contemporary international liberal trade regime makes it difficult to implement export-led growth through partially protecting key industries, as does Japan and South Korea. Second, given that liberalization policies have been initiated around the globe since the 1980s, the international environment is much more competitive than the one faced in the 1970s by the Asian "tigers," thus making it difficult for firms to compete in the global marketplace solely on the basis of comparative cost advantages in labor and natural resources. Thus, we see examples of increased international participation of Latin American firms in different industries through emphasis on competitive advantages built around manufactured products, strategies based on product, service, and price differentiation, and participation in value-adding activities (Dominguez & Brenes, 1997). Since Latin American firms are competing with firms from developed countries in both domestic and international markets, an understanding of their strategies and performance can provide important insights into management thought and practice in the contemporary global environment. Accordingly, we chose three major countries of Latin American as contexts within which to explore these strategy-performance links.

Export Performance

Literature Review and Conceptual Framework

Numerous researchers have examined the strategies and performance aspects of multinational corporations (MNCs), and this collective effort has enriched relevant theory, but relatively few conceptual advances have been made regarding firms whose international participation is primarily through export operations. The few studies examining the behavior and performance of exporting firms have primarily identified management characteristics and attitudes (for instance, experience in foreign markets, cultural orientation, and risk-taking propensity), firm characteristics (firm size and international experience), and product, industry, and export market variables as key factors in explaining export initiation and performance (e.g., Aaby & Slater, 1989, Rosson & Ford, 1982). Furthermore, these studies contain diverse export performance measures, including propensity to export (Rosson & Ford, 1982), attitudes toward exports, export sales level (Madsen, 1989), and export involvement (Diamantopolous & Inglis, 1988). The diversity both of conceptualizations of determinants of export performance and of performance measures has led to inconsistent and contradictory findings and lack of a coherent theoretical framework for exporting firms (Aaby & Slater 1989).

We sought to develop a framework incorporating the various strategic factors relevant to exporting firms as they compete in the international arena and linking these factors to the firms' performance in foreign markets. In developing the hypotheses, we incorporated the special challenges faced by exporting firms from emerging economies. The main logic underlying our framework is that although organizational characteristics and managerial risk perceptions have been shown to impact internationalization behavior (the decision to initiate exports), the current global competitive environment necessitates proactive application of specific export strategies to achieve success in foreign markets.[2]

We incorporated three distinct strategic factors into our framework to explain export performance: the competitive strategies of cost leadership and differentiation, marketing standardization (or adaptation) across foreign markets, and geographical diversification of exports. There is some conceptual ambiguity in the literature as to whether these are business-level or corporation wide strategies. Since we viewed these factors in the context of exports of single or a few product offerings, we examined the strategies at the level of export operations. Thus, we investigated whether strategies of cost leadership, differentiation, marketing standardization, and geographical diversification by firms in their export operations affected export performance. In this context, we did not distinguish between business and corporation-level strategies but saw their applicability as export strategies.

The strategies of cost leadership and differentiation concern how a firm develops an advantage with respect to competitors in an industry. Firms following a differentiation strategy aim at creating a product or service that customers see as unique. This is usually accomplished through such means as a superior brand image (an example is Rolls Royce automobiles), technology (Polaroid cameras), customer service (Saturn cars), or innovative products (Rubbermaid) (Miller & Friesen, 1986a). The objective of firms following a differentiation strategy is to build customer loyalty and create barriers to entry for newcomers. Because of the loyalty created for a brand, demand is price-inelastic, leading to higher profit margins for the manufacturer. A cost-leadership strategy involves giving consumers value comparable to that of other products at a lower cost (Porter, 1986). According to Porter, cost leadership requires "aggressive construction of efficient-scale facilities, vigorous pursuit of cost reductions from experience, tight cost and overhead control, . . . and cost minimization in areas like R&D, service, sales force, and advertising" (1980, p. 35). This strategy can provide above-average returns because firms following cost leadership can lower prices to match those of competitors and still earn profits (Miller & Friesen, 1986b).[3]

Marketing standardization was defined in this study as the degree to which an exporting firm used the same marketing programs in different foreign markets (Samiee & Roth, 1992). At one extreme, an exporting firm can develop marketing programs that differ in terms of products, pricing, distribution, and promotion for individual foreign markets. On the other hand, a firm can develop one marketing program, which is then implemented in all export markets. As a strategy, marketing standardization is similar to the segment differentiation strategy proposed by Chrisman, Hofer, and Boulton (1988), with a segmented-by-market approach being akin to adaptation and a homogenous-across-markets approach equivalent to standardization (Carpano, Chrisman, & Roth, 1994; Douglas & Wind, 1987; Porter, 1986). It should be noted that marketing standardization is distinct from cost leadership and differentiation. The latter relate to a firm's posture with respect to competitors, but marketing standardization concerns the consistency of marketing programs and processes between domestic and foreign markets as well as across multiple markets. Thus, it is possible for firms pursuing cost-leadership or differentiation-based competitive strategies to implement either standardized marketing programs or to adapt their programs to individual markets.[4]

The third component of strategy considered in this study was export diversification. The number of foreign markets that an exporting firm targets is a strategic choice that can have important implications for the firm's overall export performance. Although the costs and benefits of MNCs' international diversification through foreign direct investment have been well documented (e.g., Carpano et al., 1994; Geringer, Beamish, & daCosta, 1989; Hitt, Hoskisson, & Kim, 1997; Kim, Hwang, & Burgers, 1989; Tallman & Li, 1996), the performance impact of export diversification has not been examined. In the next section, we identify the costs and benefits of geographical diversification for exporting firms and examine its performance implications.

Existing research examining the links between competitive strategies and performance has suggested both direct and contingency effects. For instance, Miller and Friesen (1986b) found that firms following any of the three generic strategies outperformed those that did not follow any one strategy; Dess and Davis (1984) suggested that firms following "pure strategies" outperformed those "stuck in the middle"; and Miller (1988) discovered that the performance impact of generic strategies was contingent on environmental factors (cost leadership worked better in stable environments, but differentiation was positively related to performance in volatile environments). The marketing standardization-performance links have also been examined in prior research, and findings have been inconsistent and often contradictory. For instance, studies have found no effects of standardization on performance (Samiee & Roth, 1992), weak links (Carpano et al., 1994), negative effects (Cavusgil & Zou, 1994), and positive effects (Kotabe, 1990). Since research findings on the performance implications of standardization and adaptation are mixed, this relationship may conceivably be moderated by different environmental factors.

In light of the above discussion, we examined the export strategy-performance relationships of emerging economy firms within a contingency framework based on the foreign market environments in which these firms compete. The important environmental factors relevant here, which have found some support in the context of developed markets, are competition and environmental uncertainty, with its underlying dimensions of dynamism and instability. Given that the firms in our sample were competing in numerous countries, each with different levels of competition and uncertainty, and that our focus was the impact of export strategies on overall export performance rather than the strategies' impact in individual markets, we used a surrogate measure for environment. Accordingly, we incorporated a *foreign market focus* variable into our framework, dichotomized into developed countries and developing countries. The rationale here was that, compared to developing country markets, developed country markets are more competitive, with large numbers of resource-endowed competitors and demanding consumers, and are more dynamic, with frequent changes in consumer tastes and introductions of innovative products and services. Differences between the competitive conditions in developed and developing markets, combined with the internal resource constraints of exporting firms from emerging economies, will lead to differing effects of cost leadership, differentiation, and marketing standardization strategies on performance for firms that compete primarily in developed countries and those focusing on developing countries.

Hypotheses

Cost Leadership, Differentiation, and Export Performance

As firms from emerging economies begin to compete in export markets in the value-added manufacturing and service sectors, their export success depends upon their ability to develop and implement unique competitive strategies. When developing strategies of cost leadership and/or differentiation, these firms have to match their internal and location-specific competitive and comparative advantages with the requirements of the external environment in which they compete. In particular, given their relatively weak technology bases, these firms concentrate primarily on mature products (Gomez, 1997; Vernon-Wortzel & Wortzel, 1988), thus precluding any competitive advantage derived from developing innovative products and/or process technologies. However, firms from emerging economies possess certain comparative advantages in terms of low labor and production costs. The fundamental issues in developing competitive export strategies for emerging economy firms then become the following: (1) Given their natural cost advantages, should they use cost leadership as their primary competitive strategy in foreign markets? (2) Since they do not have innovative products, can these firms differentiate their products along other dimensions in foreign markets and thus make differentiation their competitive weapon? (3) Is it viable for these firms to use an integrated strategy whereby they simultaneously achieve cost leadership and differentiation? We examine the viability of emerging economy firms' use of individual and integrated competitive strategies and their performance implications in the following paragraphs.

Our argument is that emerging economy firms encounter different competitive and customer environments for their products in developed and developing markets that require them to adapt their competitive strategies to the specific needs of the two types of markets. In particular, a cost-based strategy is more likely to achieve superior performance in developed country markets, and differentiation is more likely to do so in developing countries.

Developed country markets are characterized by competition (due to a history of free market economic philosophies and to the presence of both large numbers of resource-endowed firms competing in particular product markets and demanding customers) and by dynamism (due to the continuous introduction of innovative products and the frequent changes in customer tastes and preferences). Emerging economy firms exporting to these markets are at a disadvantage with respect to local firms because the latter have more financial, managerial, and technological resources; established brands; and innovative products. Furthermore, a number of studies (e.g., Cordell, 1993) have shown that consumers in developed markets perceive products and brands from developing countries negatively and generally equate them with low price and quality. Taken together, the poor quality image, focus on mature products, and resource-rich competitors make it very difficult for emerging economy firms to build advantage by differentiating their products and services. Emerging economy firms, however, do have cost advantages over competitors from developed countries. Although liberalization of trade and investment around the world in the last two decades has led to a partial expropriation of these cost advantages, since MNCs with established brands can locate their production facilities in emerging markets, domestic emerging economy firms still enjoy overall cost advantages relative to developed country firms. These advantages stem from emerging economy firms' lower R&D, product development, and marketing costs, in turn resulting from a concentration on mature products and the absence of elaborate expenditures in brand development and other areas. Thus, emerging economy firms are more likely to achieve success in developed countries by pursuing a cost-based strategy that allows them to leverage comparative cost advantages. Further, a low cost-low price strategy is compatible with consumer perceptions and expectations of products made in emerging economies.

The characteristics of markets in developing countries are different from those in developed countries. Developing countries have traditionally had protected economies. Protectionist environments, coupled with control by state-owned enterprises of much of these economies, led to situations in which consumers either faced shortages of various products or had limited choice sets to buy from. Because of these factors, the competition within product markets was low, and pent-up demand for various types of products was substantial (Arnold & Quelch, 1998; Gillespie & Alden, 1989). Thus, developing countries provided tremendous opportunities for foreign products once their markets were liberalized. In the context of this study, the question then is, What competitive strategy will lead to superior performance on the part of emerging economy firms in other developing countries? Firms from emerging economies do not have any particular cost advantage vis-à-vis other developing economy firms, since marginal differences in costs would probably be negated by transportation costs and the remaining tariff and nontariff barriers. Therefore, a cost-based strategy may not be very effective in developing countries. On the other hand, emerging economy firms can differentiate their products and services from local competitors' to build advantage. Research suggests that consumers in developing countries perceive foreign-made products (from both industrialized and developing countries) to be of superior quality and are willing to pay a price premium over domestically made products (Hulland, Todino, & Lecraw, 1996). This observation suggests that emerging economy exporters can leverage positive consumer perceptions by differentiating their products on the country-of-origin dimension and can, over time, build enduring brand reputations. Furthermore, the cost of implementing a differentiation strategy will be lower in developing countries than in developed countries since the former are less competitive markets with fewer entrenched local competitors having established brands or other reputations.

In view of the above arguments, we suggest contingency relationships between competitive strategies and export performance—specifically, that the effectiveness of cost leadership and differentiation strategies will depend on the types of foreign markets in which they are implemented. Accordingly, we tested the following contingency hypotheses:

Hypothesis 1. The use of a cost leadership strategy is more likely to enhance export performance for firms that have a developed country focus than it is for those that have a developing country focus.

Hypothesis 2. The use of a differentiation strategy is more likely to enhance export performance for firms that have a developing country focus than it is for those that have a developed country focus.

Porter (1980, 1986) argued that although firms could pursue both strategies successfully under certain conditions, such an approach could not be sustained, given each strategy's requirements (high R&D and advertising expenditures for differentiation versus scale and scope economies and low overhead for cost leadership). Thus, Porter suggested that "a firm must make a choice between [the two generic strategies] . . . as achieving cost leadership and differentiation are usually inconsistent, because differentiation is usually costly" (1985, pp. 17–18).

However, a few studies, using U.S. samples, have identified successful firms pursuing both cost leadership and differentiation (e.g., White, 1986). Hill also addressed the issue: "Porter's model is flawed in two important respects. First, differentiation can be a means for firms to achieve an overall low-cost position. Hence, . . . cost leadership and differentiation are not necessarily inconsistent. Second, there are many situations in which establishing a sustained competitive advantage requires the firm to simultaneously pursue both low-cost and differentiation strategies" (1988, p. 401). Similarly, Karnani (1984) identified numerous contextual factors that affect the ability of firms to successfully implement both strategies. Thus, both empirical evidence, mainly in the context of U.S. firms, and theoretical advances suggest that firms can, and may, need to implement an integrated strategy whereby they simultaneously differentiate and lead on cost (Hitt, Ireland, & Hoskisson, 1997).

We examine the viability of emerging economy firms' pursuing both cost leadership and differentiation. The argument put forth here is that a combination of factors related to the nature of the products exported by firms from emerging economies as well as to weak resource bases will make implementing an integrated strategy very costly and thus negatively impact export performance. In order to support our rationale, we briefly review the work of Hill (1988) and Karnani (1984).

Hill (1988) suggested that pursuing both cost leadership and differentiation can lead to superior performance when a firm can push the demand curve outward (by increasing expenditures on differentiation) but can at the same time ensure that the shift in the cost curve is smaller than the demand curve movement. He identified certain factors that will help firms accomplish this dual task: ability to differentiate, a competitive product market, switching costs for consumers, economies derived from learning, and economies of scale and scope. Similarly, Karnani (1984) pointed out that firms can achieve lower costs, independent of scale, that can allow for simultaneous achievement of both cost leadership and differentiation.

Although space does not permit us to provide a point-by-point discussion of the arguments put forth by Hill and Karnani, we would argue that some of the important conditions for successful implementation of these strategies that they identified do not hold for emerging economy firms. In particular, economies of scope and learning effects are not relevant, as most firms from emerging countries have narrow product lines, thus precluding the possibility of reducing costs by sharing resources across multiple products. Second, these firms concentrate on products that are in the growth and maturity stages and thus do not allow them to leverage steep learning curves to reduce costs faster than competitors. Third, their relative lack of experience in foreign markets and poor resource bases, relative to those of competitors from developed countries, put them at a competitive disadvantage, making it very costly for them to pursue both cost leadership and differentiation. Thus, a combination of these product-, experience-, and resource-related factors prevent emerging economy firms from effectively employing an integrated strategy in foreign markets. We tested these arguments through the following hypothesis:

Hypothesis 3. The simultaneous use of both cost leadership and differentiation strategies by firms from emerging economies is negatively related to their export performance.

Marketing Standardization and Export Performance

Yip (1992) and Samiee and Roth (1992), among others, have identified a number of benefits of using a standardized approach across foreign markets. First, substantial cost savings are realized by developing one or a few marketing programs and implementing these in multiple markets. Second, marketing program effectiveness is increased as firms can concentrate more resources behind standardized programs. Third, consistency of a marketing program (in terms, for instance, of products and advertising) across markets avoids confusion in the minds of consumers and builds brand awareness among consumer segments. Fourth, a standardized approach allows firms to quickly enter new markets and reduces the costs of simultaneously entering multiple markets. But although firms can build competitive advantage by standardizing marketing programs across markets, this approach also has limitations that explain the inconsistent and somewhat contradictory findings regarding the performance impact of standardization (Samiee & Roth, 1992). Probably the biggest drawback is related to implementation. In the case of multinationals, there is evidence that subsidiary managers responsible for marketing can be reluctant to give full support to standardized programs dictated by headquarters (Kotabe, 1992), since they perceive encroachment on their autonomy. This issue becomes even more critical for exporting firms, where marketing programs are implemented by independent distributors who tend to favor their own distinct strategies grounded in local conditions. Furthermore, exporting firms have lower bargaining power with local distributors than established MNCs. Besides the implementation difficulties, cultural, political, and economic constraints in individual markets may make it difficult for a firm to develop a standardized strategy acceptable to various country segments (Douglas & Wind, 1987). In addition, research suggests that the success of a standardized approach is contingent on the nature of the industry within which a firm competes, with global industries being more amenable to standardization than multidomestic ones (Porter, 1986).

To achieve the benefits of a standardization strategy, firms can follow two possible approaches. First, they can extend marketing programs developed for domestic markets into foreign countries. This approach is viable for firms with established brand names that are appealing to similar segments in different countries. Second, firms can proactively develop global products and programs by incorporating the diverse preferences of consumers and other external factors from various countries (the World Car approach of Ford Motor Company is an example). This action usually involves high R&D and marketing costs, high involvement of individual subsidiaries in different markets, global coordination of marketing and production, and long lead times (Kotabe & Helsen, 1998). In essence, both approaches require a combination of facilitating conditions (established global brands, intermarket segments, resources with which to develop global programs, and so forth) to be present for firms to achieve the benefits of standardization. The relevant issue in the context of this study was whether emerging economy firms have these needed facilitating conditions.

As mentioned earlier, most emerging economy firms have relatively low resource bases, lack branded (or at least, globally branded), mature products, and lack experience in foreign markets. Furthermore, since most of these firms are in the early stages of internationalization, they are not likely to have subsidiaries in foreign markets. These characteristics make it difficult for emerging economy firms to implement a standardized marketing strategy either by extending their domestic marketing programs to foreign countries or by proactive development of globally standardized products and programs. In addition, research on exporting (the primary mode of emerging economy firms' international participation) suggests that exporters are more likely to achieve superior performance in foreign countries by adapting elements of their marketing to the needs of individual markets (Cavusgil & Zou, 1994), since the market-oriented approach (adaptation) outweighs the cost savings of a standardization strategy. We hypothesize that, although exporters from emerging economies can realize some inherent benefits of standardization (lower marketing costs, speed-to-market advantages, etc.), given their lack of experience in foreign markets (which makes it difficult for them to proactively incorporate heterogeneous consumer preferences into standardized offerings) and their low bargaining power with respect to local distributors (undermining implementation), they are more likely to achieve success by adapting their marketing strategies in individual markets, especially during the early stages of international expansion. Thus, we propose the following:

Hypothesis 4. The degree of marketing standardization across foreign markets by firms from emerging economies is negatively related to their export performance.

Although we expected a negative impact of standardization on export performance, it appeared likely that this association would be stronger in developed countries. First, the market conditions in developed countries are very different from those faced by emerging economy firms in their domestic markets. Owing to the cultural distance (Kogut & Singh, 1988) between developing and developed countries and the competitive environments of the latter, exporting firms from emerging economies have to modify their marketing mixes to be successful in developed country markets. On the other hand, emerging country firms face economic and infrastructure conditions similar to those at home in other developing countries. The low cultural distance and pent-up consumer demand in developing countries puts less pressure on exporters to adapt their marketing programs and allows them more leverage in terms of extending their domestic programs into other developing country markets. Thus,

> *Hypothesis 5.* The negative relationship between marketing standardization and export performance is stronger for firms with a developed country focus than for those with a developing country focus.

Export Diversification and Export Performance

Strategic management and international business researchers have examined the impact of international diversification strategy on firm performance (e.g., Geringer et al., 1989; Hitt, Hoskisson, & Kim, 1997; Kim et al., 1989; Tallman & Li, 1996). These researchers argue that diversification into a foreign market from a firm's home base or across multiple markets allows the firm to build and sustain competitive advantage by attaining economies of scale and scope, achieving synergies across geographically dispersed locations, arbitraging across individual country markets, and leveraging ownership, internalization, and location advantages, among others (Dunning, 1988; Hitt, Hoskisson, & Kim, 1997). Empirical studies have supported the performance implications of international diversification. For instance, Kim, Hwang, and Burgers (1989) found a linear effect of international diversification on performance, and Hitt, Hoskisson, and Kim (1997) found an inverted U-shaped relationship, whereby very low levels of international diversification were insufficient to allow for any synergy gains, moderate levels of international diversification enhanced performance, and very high levels of diversification were detrimental, as costs started outweighing potential benefits.

Both of these studies, as well as Tallman and Li (1996), showed inter-active effects between international and product diversification on firm performance. Although these studies used different diversification and performance measures, the theoretical rationales and empirical findings of all three point toward international diversification as an important strategic variable for building and sustaining competitive advantage.

However, most of the literature on international diversification has focused on large MNCs and examined diversification in terms of dis-persion of value-chain operations across multiple markets accomplished through foreign direct investment. In fact, the main theoretical argu-ments made for the advantages of geographical diversification stem from internalization theory (Buckley & Casson, 1976), Dunning's eclectic paradigm (1988), and the organizational learning perspective (Kogut & Zander, 1993), all of which imply that foreign direct investment allows firms to exploit firm-specific ownership and internalization and country-specific location advantages to develop knowledge about foreign markets. Thus, existing studies do not provide insights into whether diversifi-cation advantages will accrue to firms that are not involved in foreign direct investment. This is a crucial issue for a large number of emerg-ing economy firms whose primary mode of foreign market participation is exporting. Furthermore, internationalization models (Johanson & Vahlne, 1977) suggest that firms follow a sequential path of international involvement, first expanding abroad through low-risk entry modes such as exporting. Since firms from emerging economies are still in the early stages of internationalization (Dominguez & Sequeira, 1993; Vernon-Wortzel & Wortzel, 1988), they are likely to export products from their home bases rather than engage in foreign direct investment. The primary issue for these firms is to determine the number of countries they will export their products and services to (their level of export diversification) and the impact diversification will have on export performance.

For exporting firms, the main benefits of export diversification arise from four sources. First, exporters face much higher exchange rate expo-sure than MNCs since their costs are in one currency and revenues from product sales come from the foreign market currency. This leads to high transaction risk, given that exchange rates (especially in emerging econo-mies) are volatile and futures foreign exchange markets do not exist for certain currencies. Thus, a major benefit of export diversification is minimization of transaction risks by trading in multiple currencies (Dominguez & Sequeira, 1993). Second, firms can increase market coverage for their products and services by targeting similar customer segments across countries. This advantage of export diversification is particularly strong for firms whose products are targeted to very narrow market segments. For such a product, the potential market in any one country is saturated very quickly, and the only way to expand the size of the market is to target like segments in different countries. Third, and related to the above, are the scale advantages of export diversification. Government export promotion programs in a number of emerging economies are targeted to increase export sales and, thus, firms develop products especially for export markets. Here, the only way to achieve scale advantages is to increase foreign sales, which is accomplished by simultaneously targeting a number of foreign markets. Fourth, according to the organizational learning perspective expounded by Kogut and Zander (1993) and internationalization theory (Johanson & Vahlne, 1977), exporting firms can leverage their accumulated knowledge of one country to target other economically and culturally similar foreign markets. The above discussion suggests that exporting firms can achieve and leverage their competitive advantages by targeting multiple foreign markets for their products and services.

Exporting firms also face challenges of diversification similar to those faced by MNCs (Hitt, Hoskisson, & Kim, 1997). First, increased geographical diversification increases the coordination costs of managing export operations. Cavusgil and Zou (1994) and Madsen (1989) suggested that important determinants of export performance are the amount of support provided to foreign distributors and the commitment shown to individual export markets. Thus, increased geographical diversification can spread managerial resources thinly across markets, reducing ability to support the marketing programs of foreign distributors. Second, as Hitt, Hoskisson, and Kim (1997) noted, geographical diversification increases both managerial information-processing needs, because managers must deal with culturally diverse markets, and transaction costs, which arise from the different tariff and nontariff barriers faced in different countries.

The above discussion suggests that an exporting firm has to determine its optimal level of export diversification, the point where the benefits exceed the costs. The optimal point will be a function of the resource base of an individual firm and, to a certain extent, of the product type (Madsen, 1989), but in general we expected a nonlinear relationship between export diversification and export performance. Thus, our prediction, which is in line with Hitt, Hoskisson, and Kim's (1997) findings about the international diversification of MNCs, is that increased export diversification will lead to higher performance until a certain point, after which the costs of diversification outweigh the benefits, thus reducing export performance. Thus,

> *Hypothesis 6.* The relationship between the export diversification of firms from emerging economies and their export performance has an inverted U shape; the slope is positive for moderate levels of export diversification but negative for high levels of export diversification.

Methods

Setting and Instrument Design

Data for this study were simultaneously collected from firms in Brazil, Chile, and Mexico during the period October 1996 through May 1997. A survey methodology was considered appropriate as relevant published data were either not available in these emerging markets or did not capture the specific variables of interest. An instrument was first designed in English that included questions related to the characteristics of the responding firms, different types of strategies followed in foreign markets, and aspects of export performance. After finalizing the English version, we translated the questionnaire into Spanish and Portuguese. The back-translation technique was used to accomplish item equivalence in different languages. Subsequently, similar procedures were used to translate both the Spanish and English versions into Portuguese. The Spanish and Portuguese versions were content-analyzed by academics in Brazil, Chile, and Mexico to ensure the suitability of the items in the respective business settings. Subsequently, three versions of the questionnaire were finalized, one each for Brazilian, Chilean, and Mexican firms.

Data Collection

The target sample in each country was local firms—that is, firms that were not subsidiaries of foreign multinationals—that were involved in international operations. Since the primary objective of this study was to examine the determinants of export performance, the survey included questions related to export activities.[5] The actual data collection procedure varied by venue, given particular limitations and opportunities within each country. As no single master directory of internationally oriented firms existed for any of the venues, various sources were used in each country, including chambers of commerce, published directories, and business school contacts.

Brazil

Initially, 357 firms were selected as the target sample. These firms were first contacted via phone calls (a total of 1,200 calls were made) during which the caller explained the nature of the study and asked for the name or names of those in charge of the company's export operations. Of the 357 firms, 294 were effectively contacted. In the second stage, 294 questionnaires were mailed out to these firms. However, soon after the mailing, there was a nationwide postal strike and sabotage, and numerous firms did not receive the questionnaire. Hence, some surveys had to be hand delivered or faxed to potential respondents. A total of 93 surveys were returned, out of which 80 were complete, for an effective response rate of 27.2%.

Chile

The target sample consisted of 180 manufacturing firms that traded on the Bolsa de Comercio de Santiago. Given concerns of local researchers about the feasibility of mail surveys, only 40 questionnaires were initially sent through the mail. After two reminders and extensive telephone follow-ups, only three questionnaires had been returned. Subsequently, master's of business administration (M.B.A.) students at a prominent local university were asked to contact the firms in person and get questionnaires filled out. These students hand delivered the surveys and collected them after they had been answered. A total of 92 surveys were returned, out of which 80 were usable, for a response rate of 44.4%.

Mexico

The data were collected by executive M.B.A. students of a major business school in Mexico with campuses at over 20 locations. As part of a class project, each student was given the responsibility of identifying a Mexican firm and a senior manager responsible for the firm's export operations. One of the authors then verified (1) that each student had identified a different firm and (2) that the firms were actively involved in exporting. After this verification, the students hand delivered the survey instrument to the key informants. Given this data collection approach, a 100% response rate was achieved.

Validity of Responses

Although survey research has been useful in studying organizational behavior and, in certain contexts, may be the only feasible way to get desired information (Dess & Robinson, 1984; Huber & Power, 1985), there are several concerns related to the validity of this data collection methodology. In particular, three issues have been raised: (1) selection of key informants and informant response bias, (2) nonresponse bias, which leads to a systematic exclusion of firms from a population, and (3) common method variance (Huber & Power, 1985; Podsakoff & Organ, 1986).

First, in designing the survey, we had the measures of dependent variables related to performance precede the independent variables. Second, to further minimize consistency artifacts, we interspersed open-ended questions throughout the instrument and used both Likert and semantic differential scales. Regarding key informants, we targeted managers who were explicitly responsible for their firms' export operations. All the respondents held upper-management positions and had an average 10 years of experience with their firms and an average 6.3 years managing export operations. Nonresponse bias could not be statistically examined because comprehensive secondary information was not available, and early and late respondents could not be compared, as most of the questionnaires were collected in person; however, sample characteristics point to the appropriateness of the represented firms for testing the model, in that the firms on the average had $150 million in total sales, foreign sales constituted 28.3% of total sales, and the sample firms belonged to different industries.

Finally, we examined the common method variance issue through two post hoc statistical tests. First, we used Harman's one-factor test. The logic behind this test is that if common method variance is a serious issue in a data set, a single factor will emerge, or one general factor will account for most of the covariance in the independent and dependent variables (Aulakh & Kotabe, 1997; Podsakoff & Organ, 1986). We performed a factor analysis on items related to the cost and differentiation strategies, marketing standardization, international diversification, and performance measures, extracting five factors with eigenvalues greater than one. Furthermore, no general factor was apparent in the unrotated factor structure, with factor 1 accounting for only 28% of the variance. Second, we examined the correlation between the total sales reported by the respondents and sales figures available from secondary sources. The correlation coefficient for 45 firms for which secondary data were available was .90 ($p < .0001$).[6]

Measures

Export performance was measured through a four-item scale assessing the overall role of exports in the firms' sales growth, market shares, and competitive positions, as well as the profitability of export sales. The overall coefficient alpha for the scale was .84 (Brazil, .78; Chile, .87; Mexico, .81). Table 7.2 (see Results section below) gives the items in this scale and in others used in this research.

A strategy of *cost leadership* emphasizes having efficient-scale facilities and lower costs than major competitors (Porter, 1980). Accordingly, we used a two-item Likert scale to assess this strategy ($\alpha = .68$, overall; Brazil, .60; Chile, .72; Mexico, .72). A firm following a *differentiation* strategy wishes to create a unique image for its products and services (Porter, 1980). We thus adapted a three-item scale from Aulakh and Kotabe (1997) that captured the dimensions of quality standards, image, and general differentiation with respect to competitors (α = .82, overall; Brazil, .77; Chile, .80; Mexico, .86).

A six-item scale was developed to measure the extent of *marketing standardization* in foreign countries. Accordingly, respondents were asked to indicate, on a five-point scale, the extent of their firms' standardization of product design, brand name, advertising messages, product positioning, pricing, and promotional techniques in foreign markets (α = .82, overall; Brazil, .86; Chile, .73; Mexico, .84).

Export diversification was an adaptation of the entropy measure developed by Hitt, Hoskisson, and Kim (1997). Since the primary focus of this study was to examine diversification of exports in foreign markets (geographical diversification), respondents were asked to indicate the extent of their export sales to six regions: South America, Central America and Mexico, Africa/Middle East, United States/Canada, Western Europe, and Asia/Australia. The entropy measure of export diversification of exports is defined as *Export diversification* = $\Sigma_i[P_i \times \ln(1/P_i)]$, where P_i is the sales attributed to each of the six regions and $\ln(1/P_i)$ is the weight given to each region.

To measure *foreign market focus*, respondents were asked to indicate the percentages of their foreign sales in each of the following regions: South America, Central America and Mexico, Africa/Middle East, United States/Canada, Western Europe, and Asia/Australia. The first three regions were classified as developing countries. United States/Canada and Western Europe were classified as developed countries. The Asia/Australia region consists of both developing and developed countries. We dropped this region from analyses because the percentages of sales in the two types of markets could not be distinguished, and not all of the responding firms had significant (>5%) sales in the region. For a firm to be categorized as having either a developed country or a developing country focus, 75% or more of its sales had to be in one of the groups. On the basis of this criterion, 94 firms from the sample had a developed country focus, and 102 firms had a developing country focus. The subsequent empirical analyses is based on the 196 firms that had clear developed or developing country foreign market focuses.

To control for possible confounds, we included several *control variables*. Two dummy variables, one for Mexico and one for Brazil, were used to capture any systematic differences across the three countries in the sample. We included three dummy variables to control for industry effects. Given that standard industry classifications were not available through secondary sources and that classification systems vary across countries, we asked the respondents to list the primary industries of their export products. These were then classified independently by two people and coded into different industry groups. The set of export products fell under four broad industry groups: manufactured durables, manufactured nondurables, services, and food and agricultural products. *Firm size*, measured by the natural logarithm of total sales, was used to control for economies and diseconomies of scale (Hitt, Hoskisson, & Kim, 1997). Finally, firms' *international experience*, measured as the number of years of exporting to foreign countries, was used to control for experience effects on export performance.

Psychometric Properties and Pooling Considerations

Besides the issue of translation equivalence in a cross-national sample, other factors that need to be taken into consideration were construct and measurement equivalence. To ensure that construct meanings were consistent, we took care during the questionnaire design stage, performing further empirical tests after collecting the data. A reasonably good convergence of reliability estimates across the three samples confirmed construct equivalence. We then performed three factor analyses to examine whether the factor structures were similar for the three country samples. The scale items for the three strategy variables and for the diversification and export performance measures were used in computing factor solutions. In all cases, five factors with eigenvalues greater than one emerged, and factor loadings were similar for the three samples.

After construct and measurement equivalence had been confirmed, the next step was to examine sampling equivalence. We thus compared the responding firms' means on key characteristics. There were no significant differences among the three national samples on firm size (total employment and total sales) and international experience (the number of countries in which a firm had exporting operations and the length of experience in foreign countries). Thus, the data were pooled, and subsequently reported analyses were based on the pooled data.[7] To further confirm the convergent and discriminant validity of the constructs, we performed another factor analysis with the pooled data. The five-factor solution accounted for about 69% of the variance and represented all the derived factors with eigenvalues greater than one. The pattern of observed loadings indicated that the scales represented distinct measures of the underlying constructs. Accordingly, a composite score was calculated for each multi-item scale as an unweighted linear sum of the respective item scores. Sample characteristics and factor analysis results are provided in Tables 7.1 and 7.2, respectively.

Results

The hypotheses were tested through ordinary least squares (OLS) regression analysis. We performed collinearity diagnostics by examining the bivariate correlations (reported in Table 7.3) and variance inflation factors (VIFs; reported in Tables 7.4 and 7.5). Furthermore, assumptions of equality of variance, independence of error, and normality of the distribution of errors were met for all regression equations.

Table 7.4 presents the results of a hierarchical regression analysis in which we first regressed export performance on the different strategy aspects and control variables for country, industry, size, and international experience (model 1). In the second stage, we entered the foreign market

Table 7.1. Sample Characteristics[a]

Characteristic	Brazil	Chile	Mexico
Total employment	3,347	2,567	5,735
Total sales	$250 million	$373 million	$163 million
Number of countries the firm exported to	14	13	8
Number of years of international experience	13	13	10
Percentage of exports to developed countries	23	27	68
Percentage of exports to developing countries	66	56	20
Industry			
Manufactured durables	20.5	5.6	20.5
Manufactured nondurables	65.8	44.4	32.4
Services	5.5	24.1	25.0
Food/agricultural products	8.2	25.9	22.1

[a]Except for industry, the reported values are means. Values for industry are percentages.

Table 7.2. Factor Analysis Results for Independent and Dependent Variable Scales[a]

Scale and item	1	2	3	4	5
Differentiation					
Maintaining higher quality standards for our products	−.06	.13	.06	.79	.24
Maintaining unique image for our products	.04	.10	.11	.88	.01
Differentiating products and services from competitors	−.04	.26	.26	.67	.12
Cost leadership					
Having lower costs than our major competitors	.03	.03	.04	.36	.80
Achieving economies of scale in our international operations	−.02	.13	.36	.02	.80
Marketing standardization					
Product design	.36	.52	−.08	.23	.22
Brand name	.14	.72	.07	.21	−.06
Advertising messages	−.14	.85	.06	.08	.06
Product positioning	.06	.75	.12	.20	−.07
Pricing strategy	.20	.51	.30	.02	.23
Promotional techniques	−.14	.83	−.02	−.05	.16
Export diversification	−.02	.08	−.11	−.01	.82
Export performance					
Exporting has contributed to the sales growth of our firm	09	−.03	.90	.05	.08
Exporting has improved our firm's market share	.12	.03	.87	.12	.09
Our export activity has made our firm more competitive	−.09	.06	.83	.19	.12
Profitability of our export sales	−.30	.04	.59	.06	.11
Eigenvalue	4.55	2.62	1.59	1.16	1.05
Percentage of variance explained	28.42	16.39	9.96	7.25	6.55
Cumulative percentage of variance explained	28.42	44.81	54.77	62.02	68.57

[a]Varimax rotation was performed. Factor loadings greater than measure 0.40 are shown in bold. Export diversification is a single-item entropy

focus dummy variable as well as its interactions with cost leadership, differentiation, and marketing standardization to examine the moderating effects (model 2).

The overall regression equation in model 1 is statistically significant ($F = 10.64$, $p < .001$), and the set of independent and control variables explain 50% of the variance in export performance. We had hypothesized

Table 7.3. Means, Standard Deviations, and Correlations[a]

Variable	Mean	s.d.	1	2	3	4	5	6	7	8
1. Sales	3.62	2.24								
2. International experience	2.14	1.00	.39***							
3. Cost leadership	3.94	0.97	.01	.06						
4. Differentiation	3.98	0.93	-.30***	.03	.34***					
5. Cost leadership × differentiation[b]	0.34	1.29	.04	-.14[t]	-.05	-.24**				
6. Marketing standardization	2.70	1.36	-.21**	-.05	.13[t]	.28***	-.13[t]			
7. Export diversification	-378.55	97.12	.12	.04	.01	.06	.29***	.01		
8. Export diversification squared[b]	0.99	2.78	-.10	-.26***	-.13[t]	-.13[t]	.39***	.06	.79***	
9. Export performance	3.42	1.11	-.15	.21**	.37***	.28***	-.05	.04	.03	-.24**

[a]$N = 196$.
[b]The interaction and squared terms were calculated by first standardizing the constituent parts and then multiplying the standardized variables.
[t]$p < .10$
*$p < .05$
**$p < .01$
***$p < .001$

that a firm's attempt to simultaneously achieve both cost leadership and differentiation would have a negative impact on its export performance (Hypothesis 3). This prediction was not supported, as the coefficient for the interaction term (cost leadership × differentiation) is not statistically significant ($\beta = -.07$, $p > .10$).

Hypothesis 4 states that high marketing standardization in foreign markets on the part of firms from emerging economies will lead to lower export performance. This hypothesis was supported, as the coefficient is negative and statistically significant ($\beta = -.14$, $p < .05$). To examine the curvilinear relationship between export diversification and export performance (Hypothesis 6), we included export diversification and its squared term in the regression equation. The coefficient for export diversification is positive and significant ($\beta = .40$, $p < .001$), and for the squared term, it is negative and significant ($\beta = -.56$, $p < .001$). Taken together, these findings support Hypothesis 6, showing an inverted U-shaped relationship implying that diversifying into a few foreign markets improves export performance but that going beyond a certain number of markets is detrimental to performance.

Although no specific hypotheses were proposed on the direct effects of cost leadership and differentiation on export performance, we found positive and significant beta coefficients ($\beta = .23$, $p < .001$, cost leadership; $\beta = .13$, $p < .10$, differentiation). These relationships will be discussed in more detail below. Secondly, the results also suggest that our Mexican firms had higher export performance than both the Chilean and Brazilian firms ($\beta = .29$, $p < .001$), with the Brazilian firms having the lowest export performance ($\beta = -.18$, $p < .01$). What explains these results? One factor that appears to be meaningful is economic liberalization and integration in Mexico. Its signing of the North American Free Trade Agreement (NAFTA) provided Mexico with clear, cheap, and easy exporting access to two big industrialized markets: Canada and the United States (Kotabe & Arruda, 1998). This factor only explains Mexico's export success in these industrialized markets. However, other countries, such as Columbia, have signed bilateral trade agreements with Mexico in order to use Mexico as a gateway into the NAFTA markets. These trade agreements, then, provide Mexican firms easy access to both developed and developing countries and thus have positive effects on the

Table 7.4. Results of Hierarchical Regression Analysis for Export Performance[a]

Independent variable[b]	Model 1			Model 2		
	β	t	VIF	β	t	VIF
Cost leadership	.23	3.33***	1.31	.21	2.36**	2.20
Differentiation	.13	1.84[t]	1.47	.17	1.72[t]	2.73
Cost leadership × differentiation	−.07	−1.02	1.18	−.09	−1.30	1.25
Marketing standardization	−.14	−2.12*	1.19	−.06	−0.78	2.24
Export diversification	.40	3.85***	3.00	.33	3.06**	3.29
Export diversification squared	−.56	−5.14***	3.22	−.54	−5.00***	3.28
Mexico	.29	3.31***	2.15	.24	2.54**	2.50
Brazil	−.18	−2.27*	1.75	−.14	−1.80[t]	1.82
Manufactured durables	.02	0.25	1.87	.04	0.48	1.96
Manufactured nondurables	−.11	−1.27	2.18	−.10	−1.09	2.27
Services	−.11	−1.39	1.79	−.10	−1.20	1.95
Sales	−.06	−0.61	2.28	−.06	−0.67	2.30
International experience	.14	1.85[t]	1.45	.11	1.56	1.47
Foreign market focus				.48	1.34	36.46
Foreign market focus × cost leadership				.17	0.57	25.13
Foreign market focus × differentiation				.34	−0.96	36.47
Foreign market focus × marketing standardization				−.16	−1.01	7.00

[a]All significance levels are based on two-tailed tests.

[b]Two dummy variables were created for the three countries, with Chile omitted. Three dummy variables were created for the four industry classifications, with food and agricultural products omitted.

[t]p < .10

*p < .05

**p < .01

***p < .001

Table 7.5. Results of Subgroup Analyses Examining Moderating Effects of Foreign Market Focus on Export Performance[a]

Independent variable[b]	Group 1: Developed country focus			Group 2: Developing country focus		
	β	t	VIF	β	t	VIF
Cost leadership	.40	3.24**	1.47	.21	2.00*	1.23
Differentiation	.02	0.15	1.69	.31	2.68*	1.43
Cost leadership × differentiation	−.19	−1.59	1.38	−.15	−1.47	1.09
Marketing standardization	−.24	−2.03*	1.31	−.04	−0.33	1.28
Mexico	.15	0.96	2.47	.38	2.82**	1.94
Brazil	−.10	−0.76	1.84	−.13	−1.05	1.56
Manufactured durables	.01	0.09	1.58	.00	−0.01	2.92
Manufactured nondurables	−.08	−0.62	2.18	−.22	−1.20	3.73
Services	−.10	−0.80	1.60	−.16	−0.96	2.93
Sales	−.18	−1.19	2.32	.22	1.55	2.26
International experience	.38	3.15**	1.43	.03	0.26	1.36
R^2	.35			.42		
Adjusted R^2	.24			.32		
F	3.09**			4.11***		

[a]For group 1, n = 94. For group 2, n = 102.

[b]Two dummy variables were created for the three countries, with Chile omitted. Three dummy variables were created for the four industry classifications, with food and agricultural products omitted.

[t]$p < .10$

*$p < .05$

**$p < .01$

***$p < .001$

All significance levels are based on two-tailed tests.

country's export performance. Brazil is a member of another trading bloc, Mercado Común del Sur (MERCOSUR), but the latter has met with less success in effectively opening trade among member nations (Kotabe & Arruda, 1998), making Brazil's negotiating leverage with other countries less than Mexico's. Chile's situation seems to fall in between the other two countries'. It has a long history of liberalization and, through reciprocal trade deals, has been able to build a sizable number of informal trading relationships with various countries. Also, Chile has been widely reported to be the next entrant to NAFTA, making it an attractive trading partner.

The results in Table 7.4 (model 2) also point toward the moderating effect of foreign market focus. The overall model is significant (F = 9.05, p < .001), and the change in the squared multiple correlation coefficient (R^2) of .04 when the moderating variable and the interaction terms are entered into the equation is also statistically significant (ΔF = 2.44, p < .05). Although the moderating effect demonstrated in Table 7.4 is significant overall, we do no not interpret the individual coefficients, since multiple interaction terms lead to high multicollinearity. This is apparent from the extremely high VIFs for foreign market focus and the interaction terms. To test for the moderation predicted in Hypotheses 1, 2, and 5, we used subgroup analyses. Two regression equations were estimated. In the first equation, export performance was regressed on the set of independent and control variables for the subsample of firms whose primary foreign market focus was developed countries, and the second equation was estimated for firms whose foreign market focus was developing countries.[8] The results are presented in Table 7.5.

Both the equations are significant (F = 3.09, p < .01, and F = 4.11, p < .01), with the set of independent variables respectively explaining 35 and 42% of the variance in export performance for the two groups. Hypothesis 1 states that the effect of cost leadership on export performance will be stronger for firms with a developed country focus than for those with a developing country focus. Although the beta coefficients for cost leadership for both subgroups are statistically significant (β = .40, p < .01, developed country focus; β = .21, p < .05, developing country focus), results of a Z-test (Cohen & Cohen (1983) comparing the two coefficients (Z = 1.42, p < .10) support the hypothesis that a cost leadership strategy has a stronger effect on export performance in developed country markets than it does in developing markets. Hypothesis 2 states that the effect of a differentiation strategy on export performance is stronger for firms with a developing country focus than for those with a developed country focus. This hypothesis was also supported; the coefficient for a developed country focus is not significant (β = .02, p > .10), that for a developing country focus is positive and significant (β = .31, p < .01), and the Z (1.65, p < .05) shows significant differences in the sizes of the beta coefficients. Finally, we expected that the negative relationship between marketing standardization and export performance would be stronger for firms with a developed country focus than for those with a developing country focus. The beta coefficient for the former group is negative and significant ($\beta = -.24$, $p < .05$), and that for the latter is negative but not significant ($\beta = -.04$, $p > .10$). A significant Z (1.55, $p < .05$) confirms differences in the coefficients, thus supporting Hypothesis 5.

These empirical results support five of the six hypotheses tested and collectively provide evidence for the export performance model for emerging economy firms proposed in this study. Before discussing the implications of these findings, we further examine the impact on export performance of an integrated strategy, as captured by the interaction of our cost leadership and differentiation variables. We argued, in developing Hypothesis 3, that two sets of factors (the first related to the nature of products and the second to financial and experiential resources) would prevent emerging economy firms from successfully developing and implementing an integrated strategy in export markets. Accordingly, we expected a negative relationship between an integrated strategy and export performance. However, the results do not support this hypothesis; none of the beta coefficients, for either the full sample (Table 7.4) or the subsamples (Table 7.5), are statistically significant. What explains this nonsignificance? Is it possible that some firms in our sample were able to successfully implement an integrated strategy, while others were not, so that combining results produced a neutral effect? To answer these questions, we conducted a post hoc analysis in which we examined the role of firm resources (measured in terms of size and international experience) on the integrated strategy-performance relationship. Since firm resources are likely related to the implementation of a particular strategy, we first divided the sample into two groups, large and small, on the basis of total sales. Then we examined the correlations between integrated strategy and export performance for the two groups. Neither the correlation for large firms ($r = -.05$, $p = .67$) nor that for small firms ($r = -.01$, $p = .95$) was statistically significant. Next, we did the same test for more versus less internationally experienced firms. Although the correlation between integrated strategy and export performance for more internationally experienced firms ($r = .12$, $p = .32$) is positive, and that of less internationally experienced firms ($r = -.11$, $p = .30$) is negative, neither is significant. In summary, our post hoc analyses did not provide additional insights into the relationship between export performance and use of a strategy integrating cost leadership and differentiation for firms from emerging economies.

Discussion

Understanding firms' competitive strategies has been a major focus of researchers in both management and marketing disciplines, and these efforts have provided important insights into strategic types, their impact on performance, and the contextual, organizational, and environmental factors that affect the choices and consequences of different types of strategy. Most of these models were developed to explain the competitive behavior of firms from developed countries (mainly from the "triad regions" of North America, Europe, and Japan), competing primarily within their own national markets, and of MNCs competing through foreign direct investment. Two questions about the external validity of these strategy models become relevant: First, are these models applicable to enterprises that participate in international markets mainly through export operations from their domestic bases? Second, are they applicable to enterprises from countries outside the triad, and in particular, to those from emerging markets, which operate under unique institutional pressures and have different managerial processes and resource capabilities than enterprises from developed countries? We made two contributions in this study. First, we proposed a framework that incorporates various strategic factors explaining the performance of exporting firms. In particular, we examined the effects on performance of three strategy components (Chrisman et al., 1988): competitive weapons (differentiation, cost leadership), segmentation differentiation (marketing standardization versus adaptation in targeting markets), and scope (geographic diversification). Second, we developed and empirically tested hypotheses in the context of emerging economy firms from Brazil, Chile, and Mexico. The results point to the validity of the proposed framework. We found that, with firm and industry characteristics controlled, the different strategies pursued by firms from emerging markets explain their export performance.

Managerial and Theoretical Implications

Our findings have important implications for both practice and theory. The first finding relates to the performance implications of two competitive strategies, cost leadership and differentiation. This study adds a geographical market dimension to earlier evidence that the relationship between these two strategies and performance is contingent on the environment within which they are implemented (e.g., Lim & Kim, 1988; Miller, 1988). We found that, although a cost leadership strategy tends to enhance export performance for emerging economy firms in both developed and developing markets, the impact of this strategy is more pronounced when the target market focus is on developed countries. On the other hand, a differentiation strategy leads to improved performance if the market focus is on developing countries. These findings are plausible for several reasons detailed below.

Since competition in developed country markets is intense, owing to the sophistication of consumers, the large number of competitors, and dynamism related to technology, it would be rather difficult, if not impossible, for emerging economy firms offering mature products to differentiate their products on the basis of quality and unique features and build their brand recognition in those developed country markets. Also, a number of studies (e.g., Cordell, 1993) have found that consumers in developed countries perceive products and brands from developing countries negatively and generally equate them with low price and quality. These negative perceptions will not allow firms from emerging countries to successfully create a unique image and demand premium prices for their products and services, as would be necessary to implement a differentiation strategy. Marketing products on a low-cost basis tends to be a more suitable strategy for developed country markets, as was amply demonstrated by Japanese firms in the 1960s and 1970s and by firms from the Asian tigers in the 1970s and 1980s. Since firms from emerging economies concentrate on mature products, they have cost advantages vis-à-vis developed country firms and can thus better compete through a cost leadership strategy. Thus, we found a stronger relationship between degree of cost leadership and performance in developed markets. In the case of firms whose foreign market focus was primarily other developing markets, we found stronger effects of a differentiation strategy on performance. This finding could be due to the fact that firms in our sample may not have had any particular cost advantage vis-à-vis domestic firms in the other emerging country markets, thus making a differentiation strategy a more appropriate way to gain competitive advantage. As a result, a differentiation strategy seems to be more effective for emerging economy firms within a group of countries that are at similar stages of economic development.

Our second major finding, regarding the association between degree of marketing standardization in foreign markets and performance, is twofold. First, like Cavusgil and Zou (1994), we found that standardized marketing programs tend to result in lower performance. Second, we found another contingency effect: firms using a standardized approach in developed countries have lower performance than those adapting their marketing programs, but in developing countries, the effect is not significant. Some studies have suggested that standardization might be appropriate when a firm is marketing to countries that are similar to its home market (Douglas & Wind, 1987; Samiee & Roth, 1992). This standardized marketing approach fails to work in developed countries because the cultural distance between the exporter and the market is high, with customers unwilling to sacrifice idiosyncratic preferences for lower costs.

Finally, we found that some extent of export market diversification is beneficial for reducing currency risks and attaining synergy and economies of scale. However, a high level of diversification can spread limited managerial and financial resources too thin. Such a stretch, along with high transaction and coordination costs, is detrimental to export performance, as the costs of targeting multiple markets outweigh the benefits. This finding is consistent with those of Hitt, Hoskisson, and Kim (1997), who found a similar inverted U-shaped relationship between international diversification and firm performance. However, our study provides further insights for the diversification literature, as it identifies specific advantages and disadvantages relevant to exporting firms that are different from the location and internalization benefits accruing to firms that enter foreign markets through foreign direct investment.

Further Research

According to the resource-based view of the firm (Barney, 1997), firms need to build, acquire, or identify valuable, inimitable, rare, and nonsubstitutable resources in order to gain competitive advantage. Enterprises from emerging economies traditionally had comparative cost advantages in factors of production, especially for commodity and nondifferentiated manufactured products. However, these advantages may not be sufficient in the contemporary global environment, as competition is increasingly based on differentiated products and services, and the present liberal trade regime allows firms from different countries to access location-specific factors related to factors of production.

In the preceding discussion, we suggest the possibility that the reasons behind the inability of emerging economy firms to successfully implement certain strategies include their lack of experience in foreign markets; deficiencies in managerial, financial, and technological skills vis-à-vis established multinationals from developed countries; negative brand and country-of-origin effects; and narrow product lines that preclude their taking advantage of economies of scale and scope. A fruitful area for future research would be to examine the processes through which firms can acquire these deficient resources.

One possible way could be through strategic alliances with firms from developed countries. Such alliances can potentially overcome the resource constraints of emerging economy firms as well as alleviate negative country-of-origin effects, especially if products are marketed under the developed country partners' programs. Second, there is evidence (Dominguez & Brenes, 1997) that firms from developing countries have acquired established foreign brands. These processes can potentially compensate for lack of resources and negative consumer perceptions. Furthermore, as Khanna and Palepu (1997) suggested, firms in emerging economies become part of diversified business groups in order to create entry barriers for foreign entrants and manage the political process collectively. It is conceivable that such pooling of resources within diversified groups can enhance their competitive advantages in foreign markets as well and allow them to reap both scale and scope economies.

Another related avenue for research is to further investigate the nature of participation by emerging economy firms in foreign markets. According to Craig and Douglas, a firm "must broaden its participation in the transnational value chain and gain a controlling role, if it is to develop a strong competitive position in world markets" (1997, p. 73). Finally, our study did not examine the role of organizational structures and administrative mechanisms in the implementation of successful strategies (Govindarajan, 1988; Miller, 1988). Future research can provide important insights by incorporating structural aspects in the strategy-performance models and examining if emerging economy firms use organizational forms that are similar to those used by multinationals from developed countries.

Limitations

This study has a number of limitations. The first shortcoming is that, given its exploratory nature, our measures of strategy and performance constructs were parsimonious and did not incorporate various subdimensions identified in previous research. For instance, Miller (1988) and Kim and Lim (1988) identified innovation and marketing differentiation as two subdimensions of a differentiation strategy. Second, our environmental variable, foreign market focus, was simplistic and all encompassing, and thus did not capture heterogeneity within developed and developing markets. Finally, all of our measures were perceptual and, despite our best efforts to control for informant bias and associated common method variance problems, the results of this study should be interpreted in light of the inherent limitations of a survey methodology.

Notes

1. Chile was an exception as it initiated liberalization in 1973.

2. Firm characteristics (size and experience) were used as control variables in our analyses. However, management characteristics were not included in this study either as determinants of export performance or as control variables.

3. Porter (1980) identified a third generic strategy, focus, that involves serving a specialized segment more effectively or efficiently than competitors who are competing more broadly. We incorporated only the individual and interactive effects of the cost leadership and differentiation strategies because a focus strategy involves achieving low cost or differentiation, or both (Govindarajan, 1988; Karnani, 1984).

4. For example, an exporting firm following a differentiation strategy in foreign markets can use different or similar tools to convey this differentiation in different countries. In one country, it can differentiate its products on prestige aspects, through higher pricing and distribution in luxury boutiques, for instance. In another, it can differentiate on service aspects, through distribution via an in-home sales force. In this case, although the exporter is using a differentiation strategy in both markets, it is adapting its marketing program specifically for each market. A second issue regarding marketing standardization versus adaptation concerns links to the global versus multidomestic approaches identified in the strategy literature. Global strategy deals with management of globally dispersed value chains; a multidomestic strategy refers to complete value chain management on a country-by-country basis. Product/marketing standardization has some bearing on, but is not synonymous with, the global/multidomestic strategy dichotomy. For example, Ford and Honda both use global platform strategies. Ford brings major components from several key plants around the world to produce standardized cars with identical product positioning. Honda designs its globally standardized Accord with inputs coming from Japan, the United States, and Germany, but its market positioning is adapted to individual markets.

5. The assumption made in this study is that since firms from emerging markets are relative novices in foreign markets (especially for noncommodity manufactured products), they are more likely to participate in foreign markets through exports than to use other investment modes. To verify the validity of this assumption, we asked how many foreign countries the responding firms had manufacturing operations in. Of the 228 firms that responded to this question, 212 (or 93%) reported that they manufactured in just their home countries.

6. Secondary data on export performance were not available because it is not reported in annual reports or other published sources. Given that our objective was to ensure the validity of retrospective reports, the high correlation (r = .90, p < .001) between reported and published total sales for the 45 firms suggested that the respondents were providing accurate information.

7. Pooling data from the three countries was considered necessary as the number of observations in each sample was relatively small. Furthermore, we did not expect country-specific differences in the strategy-performance relationships. However, we included two dummy variables in the regression equations to control for any country-specific effects.

8. International diversification was not included in the subgroup analysis because this variable and foreign mar- ket focus are related. Although the degree of export di- versification within developed and developing countries may have provided additional insights on its perfor- mance effects, our data did not allow this analysis since we did not have exports sales data for individual foreign markets within each group.

References

Aaby, N.-E., & Slater, S. F. (1989). Management influences on export performance: A review of the empirical literature 1978–88. *International Marketing Review, 6*(4), 7–26.

Arnold, D. J., & Quelch, J. A. (1998). New strategies in emerging markets. *Sloan Management Review, 40*(1), 7–20.

Aulakh, P. S., & Kotabe, M. (1997). Antecedents and performance implications of channel integration in foreign markets. *Journal of International Business Studies,* 28: 145–175.

Barney, J. B. (1997). *Gaining and sustaining competitive advantage.* Boston: Addison-Wesley.

Buckley, P. J., & Casson, M. C. (1976). *The future of the multinational enterprise.* London: Macmillan.

Carpano, C., Chrisman, J. J., & Roth, K. (1994). International strategy and environment: An assessment of the performance relationship. *Journal of International Business Studies, 25,* 639–656.

Cavusgil, S. T., & Zou, S. (1994). Marketing strategy-performance relationship: An investigation of the empirical link in export market ventures. *Journal of Marketing, 58*(1), 1–21.

Chrisman, J. J., Hofer, C. W., & Boulton, W. R. (1988). Toward a system for classifying business strategies. *Academy of Management Review, 13,* 413–428.

Christensen, C. H., Rocha, A., & Gertner, R. K. (1987). An empirical investigation of the factors influencing exporting success of Brazilian firms. *Journal of International Business Studies, 28,* 61–77.

Cohen, J., & Cohen, P. (1983). *Applied multiple regression/correlation analysis for the behavioral sciences.* Hillsdale, NJ: Erlbaum.

Cordell, V. (1993). Interaction effects of country of origin with branding, price, and perceived performance risk. *Journal of International Consumer Marketing, 5*(2), 5–20.

Craig, C. S., & Douglas, S. P. (1997). Managing the transnational value chain: Strategies for firms from emerging markets. *Journal of International Marketing, 5*(3), 71–84.

Dess, G., & Davis, P. S. (1984). Porter's (1980) generic strategies as determinants of strategic group membership and organizational performance. *Academy of Management Journal, 27,* 467–488.

Dess, G. G., & Robinson, R. B. (1984). Measuring organizational performance in the absence of objective measures: The case of the privately-held firm and conglomerate business unit. *Strategic Management Journal, 5,* 265–273.

Diamantopoulos, A., & Inglis, K. (1988). Identifying differences between high- and low-involvement exporters. *International Marketing Review, 5*(2), 52–60.

Dominguez, L. V., & Brenes, E. (1997). The internationalization of Latin American enterprises and market liberalization in the Americas: A vital linkage. *Journal of Business Research, 38*, 3–16.

Dominguez, L. V., & Sequeira, C. G. (1993). Determinants of LDC exporters' performance: A cross-national study. *Journal of International Business Studies, 24*, 19–40.

Douglas, S. P., & Wind, Y. (1987). The myth of globalization. *Columbia Journal of World Business, 22*(4), 19–29.

Dunning, J. H. (1988). The eclectic paradigm of international production: A restatement and some possible extensions. *Journal of International Business Studies, 19*, 1–32.

Garten, J. E. (1997). *The big ten: The big emerging markets and how they will change our lives.* New York: Basic Books.

Geringer, J. M., Beamish, P. W., & daCosta, R. C. (1989). Diversification strategy and internationalization: Implications for MNE performance. *Strategic Management Journal, 10*, 109–119.

Gillespie, K., & Alden, D. (1989). Consumer product export opportunities to liberalizing LDCs: A life cycle approach. *Journal of International Business Studies, 20*, 93–113.

Gomez, H. (1997). The globalization of business in Latin America. *International Executive, 39*(2), 225–254.

Govindarajan, V. (1988). A contingency approach to strategy implementation at the business-unit level: Integrating administrative mechanisms with strategy. *Academy of Management Journal, 31*, 828–853.

Hill, C. W. L. (1988). Differentiation versus low cost or differentiation and low cost: A contingency framework. *Academy of Management Review, 13*, 401–412.

Hitt, M. A., Hoskisson, R. E., & Kim, H. (1997). International diversification: Effects on innovation and firm performance in product-diversified firms. *Academy of Management Journal, 40*, 767–798.

Hitt, M. A., Ireland, R. D., & Hoskisson, R. E. (1997). *Strategic management: Competitiveness and globalization.* St. Paul: West.

Huber, G. P., & Power, D. J. (1985). Retrospective reports of strategic-level managers: Guidelines for increasing their accuracy. *Strategic Management Journal, 6*, 171–180.

Hulland, J., Todino, H. S., & Lecraw, D. J. (1996). Country-of-origin effects on sellers' price premiums in competitive Philippine markets. *Journal of International Marketing, 4*(1), 57–79.

Johanson, J., & Vahlne, J. E. (1977). The internationalization process of the firm: Managerial behavior, agency costs, and ownership structure. *Journal of International Business Studies, 8*(1), 23–32.

Karnani, A. (1984). Generic competitive strategies—An analytical approach. *Strategic Management Journal, 5*, 367–380.

Khanna, T., & Palepu, K. (1997). *Corporate scope and institutional context: An empirical analysis of diversified business groups.* Unpublished manuscript, Harvard University Graduate School of Business Administration, Boston.

Kim, L., & Lim, Y. (1988). Environment, generic strategies, and performance in a rapidly developing country: A taxonomic approach. *Academy of Management Journal, 31*, 802–827.

Kim, W. C., Hwang, P., & Burgers, W. P. (1989). Global diversification strategy and corporate profit performance. *Strategic Management Journal, 10*, 45–57.

Kogut, B., & Singh, H. (1998). The effect of national culture or the choice of entry mode. *Journal of International Business Studies, 19*, 411–432.

Kogut, B., & Zander, U. (1993). Knowledge of the firm and the evolutionary theory of the multinational corporation. *Journal of International Business Studies, 24*, 625–645.

Kotabe, M. (1990). Corporate product policy and innovative behavior of European and Japanese multinationals: An empirical investigation. *Journal of Marketing, 54*(2), 19–33.

Kotabe, M. (1992). *Global sourcing strategy.* New York: Quorum Books.

Kotabe, M., & Arruda, M. C. (1998, Spring). South America's free trade gambit. *Marketing Management, 7*, 38–46.

Kotabe, M., & Helsen, K. (1998). *Global marketing management.* New York: Wiley.

Kotler, P., Jatusripitak, S., & Maesincee, S. (1997). *The marketing of nations: A strategic approach to building national wealth.* New York: Free Press.

Madsen, T. K. (1989). Successful export marketing management. Some empirical evidence. *International Marketing Review, 6*(4), 41–57.

Miller, D. (1988). Relating Porter's business strategies to environment and structure: Analysis and performance implications. *Academy of Management Journal, 31*, 280–308.

Miller, D., & Friesen P. H. (1986a). Porter's (1980) generic strategies and performance: An empirical examination with American data. Part I: Testing Porter. *Organization Studies, 7*, 37–55.

Miller, D., & Friesen P. H. (1986b). Porter's (1980) generic strategies and performance: An empirical examination with American data. Part II: Performance implications. *Organization Studies, 7*, 255–261.

Otani, I., & Villanueva, D. (1990). Long-term growth in developing countries and its determinants: An empirical analysis. *World Development, 18*, 769–783.

Podsakoff, P. M., & Organ, D. W. (1986). Self-reports in organizational research: Problems and prospects. *Journal of Management, 12*, 531–544.

Porter, M. E. (1980). *Competitive strategy: Techniques for analyzing industries and competitors.* New York: Free Press.

Porter, M. E. (1986). *Competition in global industries.* Boston: Harvard Business School Press.

Porter, M. E. (1990). *The competitive advantage of nations.* New York: Free Press.

Rosson, P. J., & Ford, L. D. (1982, Fall). Manufacturer-overseas distributor relations and export performance. *Journal of International Business Studies, 13,* 57–72.

Samiee, S., & Roth, K. (1992). The influence of global marketing standardization on performance. *Journal of Marketing, 56*(2), 1–17.

Tallman, S., & Li, J. (1996). Effects of international diversity and product diversity on the performance of multinational firms. *Academy of Management Journal, 39,* 179–196.

Vernon, R. (1966). International investment and international trade in the product cycle. *Quarterly Journal of Economics, 81,* 190–207.

Vernon-Wortzel, H., & Wortzel, L. H. (1988, Spring). Globalizing strategies for multinationals from developing countries. *Columbia Journal of World Business, 23,* 27–35.

White, R. E. (1986). Generic business strategies, organizational context and performance: An empirical investigation. *Strategic Management Journal, 7,* 217–231.

Yip, G. S. (1992). *Total global strategy: Managing for worldwide competitive advantage.* Englewood Cliffs, NJ: Prentice-Hall.

CHAPTER 8

Strategic Alliances in Emerging Latin America

A View from Brazilian, Chilean, and Mexican Companies

Masaaki Kotabe, Preet S. Aulakh, Roberto J. Santillán-Salgado, Hildy Teegen, Maria Cecilia Coutinho de Arruda, and Walter Greene

Most U.S. business executives did not pay much attention to Latin America for its market opportunities until after the ratification in 1994 of the North American Free Trade Agreement (NAFTA) among Canada, the United States, and Mexico. The NAFTA awakened them to look initially to the immediate south of the U.S. border. Then exactly 1 year later, on January 1, 1995, another major free trade agreement, known commonly as the Southern Common Market or MERCOSUR (*Mercado Común del Sur*), went into effect among four countries in the Southern Cone region of South America—Argentina, Brazil, Paraguay, and Uruguay. Subsequently, in June 1996, Chile and Bolivia agreed to join MERCOSUR, extending the frontiers of the South American trading bloc. Chile joined MERCOSUR as an associate member on October 1, 1996, and Bolivia's formal association with MERCOSUR is expected to begin in 2004. Indeed, MERCOSUR'S goal is to incorporate all South American countries by 2006 before linking up with NAFTA.

Although the total gross domestic product (GDP) (on purchasing power parity basis)[1] in 1998 for the MERCOSUR region exceeds

US$1.9 trillion, comprising approximately 70% of South America's GDP and over half of Latin America's GDP, the South American market movement has failed to register in the minds of many business executives in the United States in the way NAFTA did. Brazil is by far the largest economy in Latin America, with its GDP of US$1.04 trillion in 1998, followed by Mexico and Argentina with a GDP of US$815 billion and US$374 billion, respectively. Chile, albeit with a relatively small GDP of US$185 billion, is considered a country with the most progressive privatization programs in place in Latin America.

Despite a recession under its current austerity program and its currency depreciation that rocked the MERCOSUR region in 1999, Brazil's movement toward a more liberalized market environment seems irreversible. At the "Summit of the Americas" in April 1998, both Chile and Mexico were lauded for their continued successful economic reform. Consequently, Latin American countries—led by Brazil. Chile, and Mexico—have attracted an increasing amount of foreign direct investment for lucrative business opportunities.

A promising regional economy in Latin America could offer sizable business opportunities and attract foreign investment in the region. However, the United States and other foreign companies remain wary about the region's traditional economic and political volatility despite its broad economic reforms and democratic changes. Although these concerns have been further exacerbated by the recent financial turmoil in several Southeast Asian countries, executives of those U.S. and other foreign companies also know that they would have to take risks cautiously and exploit business opportunities for first-mover advantage (Kotabe & de Arruda, 1998).

Trends in Latin American Commercial Collaboration

An increasing number of firms in Latin American countries are partnering with foreign firms to enhance their own competitive positions. Our study seeks to explore the following issues in alliances: Latin American firms' motivations to form alliances, structures of these alliances, and their performance evaluations. Although existing studies have historically examined the dyad of strategic alliances from a perspective of developed countries (e.g., the United States), our study explores the issue from a perspective of companies in emerging Latin American economies.

First, the motivations of these Latin American firms for seeking commercial collaboration need to be understood. In particular, we examine what Latin American companies want from their partnership with companies from developed countries (DC companies), what DC companies offer to Latin American companies, and their concordance or discordance in their respective objectives. Knowing what they are seeking through allying will benefit firms interested in collaborating in the region.

Second, the structure of these alliances will be examined. To achieve the alliance motivations and objectives, how do Latin American companies structure their alliances with DC companies? We examine their equity structures and types of alliances to gain some insight into the structural issues.

Third, we address the behavioral aspects of their collaboration to identify how the management of these collaborative relationships is perceived by Latin American partners. Then we present the criteria that these Latin American firms use to evaluate the success of their cross-border partnerships, as well as the actual performance of their alliances based upon these criteria. The results of this discussion of their relationships and success criteria/performance will be followed by normative suggestions for firms currently collaborating with or wishing to collaborate with firms from Latin American Newly Industrialized Countries (NICs).

The Importance of Collaboration in Latin America

Current discussion surrounding the potential for a western hemispheric free trade area ("Free Trade Area of the Americas") highlights the vast benefits to firms engaged in trade in the region (Mackay, 1997). Brazil's current and Chile's associate membership in MERCOSUR and Mexico's membership in NAFTA give these nations an important leadership role in further integration within the Americas. Given this region's historical "third world" status, however, little attention has been given to business phenomena in Latin America. This lack of attention presents an acute limitation for U.S. firms in particular, given what many believe to be the inevitable broadening and deepening of commercial linkages within the Americas.

Little empirical work exists to guide managers interested in engaging in business in Latin America or with Latin American counterparts (Gillespie & Teegen, 1995).

MERCOSUR, NAFTA, and the European Union

Historically, MERCOSUR countries had animosity toward the U.S. extraterritorial influence on South American politics and economy whereas they maintained amicable postcolonial cultural ties with Western Europe. As a result, MERCOSUR has enjoyed closer economic relationships with European countries than with the United States. Indeed, a free trade agreement is expected to be signed by the European Union (EU) and MERCOSUR during the first Latin American-European Union Summit in 1999, the first region-to-region free trade accord across the ocean.

MERCOSUR member countries collectively exported US$77 billion and imported US$83 billion in 1996. Although the intraregional trade among MERCOSUR member countries constituted nearly half of their international trade, some 23% (or US$18 billion) of MERCOSUR'S total exports went to the EU, 15% (or US$12 billion) to NAFTA, and 9% (or US$7 billion) to Asia (China, Japan, South Korea, and ASEAN). The total MERCOSUR imports were distributed as follows: 26% (or US$21 billion) from the EU, 22% (or US$18 billion) from the United States, 7% (or US$6 billion) from Asia, and 45% from the rest of the world.

Although the share of MERCOSUR's trade volume with the EU fell from 32% to 24% between 1990 and 1996, this relative decline was attributed to European companies' increased direct investment in MERCOSUR for increased local operations. MERCOSUR countries have absorbed 70% of EU investment in the American region in recent years. Most of EU investments are directed increasingly to telecommunication, air transportation, automobile, tourism, and financial services industries. Consequently, the economic relationships between EU and MERCOSUR are becoming ever closer, as are business collaborations between European and South American companies.

Concerning NAFTA, there have been negotiations for establishing the "Four plus Three" agreement between MERCOSUR and the NAFTA member countries for the creation of the American Free Trade Area (AFTA). Presently, formal relationships exist only between MERCOSUR and the United States, in fulfillment of the 1991 "Tour plus One" agreement, but this agreement has been far from active. Initially, the United States had some doubt about the Southern Cone integration process. At the same time, the MERCOSUR countries raised vexing issues related to NAFTA, including the rules of origin for NAFTA imports.

Furthermore, the Clinton administration's failure to secure fast-track trade negotiating authority in the Congress is increasingly viewed by MERCOSUR countries as emblematic of the lack of U.S. commitment to hemispheric cooperation. Unfortunately, the negotiations between the United States and MERCOSUR are further strained by the recent ill-timed Asian financial crisis, which had a ripple effect on South American countries, particularly on Brazil. Consequently, many U.S. companies have become late comers in entering South American markets and are in search of local partners as well.

Commercial Collaboration

Of particular interest to managers is the notion of commercial collaboration. By commercial collaboration, we refer to the various alliances and partnerships that have proliferated among firms across the globe. These arrangements vary from license agreements to franchising to technology transfers to coproduction accords. The key elements of commercial collaboration are the maintenance of legal independence of the partners (as opposed to the merger or acquisition cases), and the longer term nature of the relationships that goes beyond a single market transaction (as in the case of a single-shot purchase/sale between two independent firms). We allow here for the formation of equity joint ventures between the partners—a third, legally separate entity from the parent firms—in our definition of commercial collaboration in this analysis. Although historically foreign firms seeking entry into Latin American markets were legally obliged to form equity joint ventures with local partners, these arrangements are rarely required today in the region. A clear result of these eased equity participation restrictions is the growth in nonequity forms of collaboration in Latin America.

The global trend toward collaborative organizational forms/strategic alliances is consistent with the Latin American regional experience. In fact, Latin America has a long tradition of economic integration initiatives between nations. As has been argued elsewhere (Teeyen, 1998), economic integration is often discussed in terms of collaboration at the national level, yet actual integration is a firm-level phenomenon. Without *firms* collaborating, *economies* are not integrated. Given the importance of the region in terms of current economic integration as well as its clear potential for expanded economic integration, and given the prerequisite role of firm-level collaboration for economic integration to take place, a further understanding of interfirm collaboration is a critical need for learning about business in Latin America.

Latin America's economic liberalization has brought with it increased competitive pressure on domestic firms from newly entering competitors from abroad. Many of these formerly protected firms have been unable to face this challenge; others have engaged in strategic alliances to better position themselves in the newly opened economies.

Concomitant with economic liberalization in the region has been impressive economic growth and gains in related areas such as inflation control and balance of payments position. In Brazil, Chile, and Mexico, a middle class started to emerge with significant purchasing power and sophistication. Access to information from abroad regarding consumption options and standards has inspired local consumers within these markets to demand higher quality goods and services (Kotabe & de Arruda). Many firms seek alliances to better respond to consumer demand within these markets.

Alliances for market entry have often been examined—largely from the perspective of firms from the triad. Yet, if firms are to produce better relationships in collaboration with Latin American partners, *their* perspectives must be assessed. Any normative implications for foreign firms seeking entry into these markets via partnerships with local firms will therefore need to address why Latin American firms are motivated to collaborate. In addition, knowing how they view the relational aspects of these collaborations will help guide managers on how to build relationships and interact with these partners. Lastly, gauging how these firms measure alliance success and understanding their assessments of alliance success are critical to ensuring satisfied partners. At a minimum, a healthy international alliance with a Latin American partner requires that they find the alliance successful. This research examines the perceptions of Latin American firm managers who are engaged in alliances with foreign firm partners in addressing these important collaboration issues.

Data

The data for this study consisted of local manufacturing companies that had a significant presence in their respective markets in Brazil, Chile, and Mexico. In all cases, data were collected from them via a common survey instrument. The sample consisted of 80 Brazilian, 80 Chilean, and 82 Mexican firms. The data collection procedure is summarized in the Appendix.

Partner firms represented in this sample are from Latin America, North America, Europe, and Asia. Although some differences exist in a number of demographic characteristics among Brazilian, Chilean, and Mexican firms, our preliminary analysis[2] shows that their response patterns on various variables on collaborations were deemed comparable. Therefore, the following analysis was conducted on the aggregate sample.

Thirty-six percent of the sample consisted of consumer goods companies, and 34%, industrial goods companies. On the average, companies in the sample, employing 3,830 people, had an annual sales volume of US$150 million; the average number of foreign partners was 7.3 per firm; and the average length of the relationships was 7.4 years. Latin American firms in the sample, on the average, generated 28.3% of their total revenue from foreign sales. Those firms that had U.S. partners tended to be somewhat larger in size than those that had non-U.S. partners. The sample makeup is presented in Table 8.1.

Latin American Perspectives on Collaboration

To better understand collaboration patterns, we queried Latin American allying firm managers on what we believe to be comprehensive dimensions of alliances: why they ally with a foreign partner (motivations), how they structure their alliance relationships, what criteria they utilize in gauging alliance success, and finally how they rate their alliances based upon their

Table 8.1. Firm Characteristics

Variable	Total sample	Brazil	Mexico	Chile	Firms with U.S. partners	Firms with non-U.S. partners
Consumer goods (%)	36.0	29.3	40.9	37.5	39.1	33.4
Total sales ($ million)	150.0	231.3	505.0	376.0	330.0	256.0
Total employees	3,830	3,347	5,735	2,567	4,687	3,005
Number of partners	7.3	8.0	8.2	5.8	6.9	7.0
Relationship length (years)	7.4	9.3	6.0	6.9	6.6	8.1
Foreign sales (%)	28.3	13.2	43.3	28.3	32.8	24.0

selected criteria for success. Thus, our examination conceptually covers the alliances from inception through management and to evaluation.

Motivations for Strategic Alliances

There exists a rich literature in why firms might seek collaboration in their competitive efforts (Hagedoorn, 1993; Hamcl, 1991; Ohmae, 1989). Firms seek partners when the resources available to them within the firm are insufficient to meet the competitive challenges they face in their markets. Additionally, where firms are resource capable, they make strategic choices regarding the deployment of these scarce resources, recognizing the opportunity costs of their utilization. By partnering, firms can leverage the resources of their allies whereby each firm can specialize in the deployment of resources and operational areas for which they are relatively advantaged. As in the case of gains from trade between nations based upon comparative advantages, firms can gain through alliances with others who have complementary resources and who are comparatively advantaged in distinct areas.

Additionally, the literature has pointed to competition-motivated alliance behavior. By allying with a potential competitor, this firm may be co-opted, thus reducing the net competitive intensity a firm faces. Furthermore, by joining forces, allying firms can effectively raise barriers of entry to other parties wishing to enter a competitive arena (geographic or product-based).

Table 8.2. Six Major Motivations for Latin American Firms to Ally

Access to foreign partner's technical expertise	Access to foreign partner's marketing expertise	Access to financial resources	Direct access to foreign markets	Risk and cost reduction	Competitive move
Access to partner's expertise in: • Technology • Product market knowledge • Material • Suppliers • Products/services • Important customers	Access to partner's expertise in: • Geographic markets • Product markets • Geographic market knowledge • Marketing infrastructure • Recognized brands	Access a partner's • Capital • Long-term credit	• Overcome trade barrier/restriction • Obtain regulatory permission • Access labor	• Reduce risk • Reduce costs	• Block competitors • Co-opt competitor and make ally

Note: These six factors were generated from a factor analysis of the original list of 21 strategic alliance motivations discussed in the literature.

Lastly, by sharing resources, collaborators can reduce the costs and risks associated with participating in a given venture. In this way, an individual firm's probability of success overall is enhanced; resources are freed up to engage in other avenues.

The alliance managers in this study report a wide range of motivations for allying with these foreign firms.[3] As shown in Table 8.2, our analysis shows six major categories of motivations for Latin American companies to ally with partners from developed countries.

Access to a Foreign Partner's Technical Expertise

The most important motivation relates to access to a foreign partner's expertise, as discussed above, with resources including supplier connections and materials as well as technology and product market knowledge. This motivation is tied closely with a strategic concern for firms in many liberalizing countries. Decades of protected markets constrained Latin American companies' access to technological expertise and efficient suppliers. Local suppliers in that era were not subject to the competitive pressures that prioritize responsiveness to customer needs in areas such as consistently high quality products and timely delivery. In postliberalization Latin America, firms eagerly seek supply relationships with foreign partner firms that have high quality and performance standards. Linkages of this sort are required for these Latin American firms that themselves now face competitive pressures that can be addressed through effective supply chain management and assurances of high quality inputs domestically as well as from abroad.

Access to a Foreign Partner's Marketing Expertise

Access to a foreign partner's marketing expertise is the second most important motivation for these Latin American firms. This factor includes marketing infrastructure and relationships with important customers. Economic liberalization, coupled with advances in communications, has created strong pressures for Latin American firms to better respond to consumer needs both domestically and internationally. Foreign partners, with greater experience in competitive market places can provide their allies with knowledge that can be transferred to the domestic markets in Latin America. Among the largest Latin American economies, domestic markets in Brazil, Chile, and Mexico are of insufficient scale in many industries for production and marketing efficiencies. By accessing a foreign partner's marketing infrastructure and client bases abroad, these firms can more readily tap into scale advantages as well as new areas for sales growth. This access is particularly useful in nations, such as the United States, that allow dutyfree entry for certain products from Latin America.

Access to a Foreign Partner's Financial Resources

Accessing a foreign partner's financial resources (capital and credit line) further motivates many of these Latin American firms to collaborate. This result is not surprising given the prevalence of capital constraints on many Latin American firms. Domestic credit is scarce, and that which is available tends to be prohibitively costly for these firms. Nascent stock markets in the countries have eased capital access pressures for only the largest Latin American firms, but the Mexican economic crisis and most recently, the Brazilian government's austerity program show how these events affect portfolio investment stability. Direct investment in firms tends to be more stable, but implies a loss of control that many firms are not willing to cede. By joining forces with capital-rich partners, Latin American allies can access funds whereby maintaining their legal independence.

Direct Access to Foreign Markets

Direct access to foreign markets is sought by many Latin American companies via their alliances with foreign companies by receiving regulatory permission to enter through the alliance and by utilizing the geographic market knowledge of the partner. The concern about regulatory permission is most notable for alliances with firms from countries that are not economically integrated with the home country of the Latin American ally. To access those markets. Latin American companies must identify a foreign firm that incorporates their components and in-process goods into its finished products or jointly develops products to gain access to the foreign partner's market. In many cases, this takes the form of a joint venture formation. Even where a Latin American firm can freely enter the foreign partner's market in regulatory terms, lack of knowledge about the market itself poses a significant barrier to successful entry. Many of these Latin American companies are new to the global business milieu, and thus lack the experience to know where, when, how, and if to adapt their product offerings, promotion, pricing, and distribution when entering a given market, such as the United States. This need to access geographic market knowledge is likely to be most pressing in those markets representing large cultural distances from the Latin American allies' home markets.

Risk and Cost Reduction

Risk and cost reduction also motivates Latin American firms to ally. By partnering with another firm, costs are often shared, reducing the financial investments necessary for any individual firm to undertake a given business venture. Clearly reducing financial investments in the business reduces the downside risk of their loss in the event of business failure. Another important way in which alliances allow firms to reduce risk is through diversification. By partnering with a firm in a different geographic market and/or different product market, losses in one market may be offset by gains in others, reducing the risk of the partner firm's overall portfolio of investments. Where firms in an alliance specialize, they reduce costs and risk for the overall venture: each partner has already invested in progress along a given learning curve and the alliance then captures the benefits of this learning from both partners. Finally, by allowing for greater market access, and by avoiding duplication of efforts through rationalization, allying firms can further reduce costs of participating in their joint business.

Competitive Move

Lastly, competitive moves also motivated Latin American companies to collaborate with firms outside their borders. This motivation relates to partnering with the intention of bettering the firm's potential in competitive field by blocking or co-opting potential competitors. By partnering with other firms, strong entry barriers are created that serve to limit the effective competition in a given product or geographic market. By partnering with a potential competitor, that firm is converted into an ally (at least concerning the scope of the alliance) instead of a firm against which to compete.

Structure of Strategic Alliances

Now that we have examined the issue of partnering motivations, we explore in this section how they structure these alliances. Alliances by their very nature require the partnering firms to structure how to interact with each other. In particular, we examine three aspects of the alliances: types of alliances, equity structure, and business dependency. These interactions have been shown to produce both positive and negative outcomes for collaborating firms. By interacting with a partner, information is exchanged that might provide occasions for partners to behave opportunistically. Without a hierarchical control structure in place, independent allying firms could become strong competitors through pursuing self-interest at the expense of their partner who shared information. Partners, then, could take advantage of the firm in ways that might jeopardize the success of the alliance or the future viability of the firm itself.

The types of alliances, equity structure, and business dependency are presented in Table 8.3.

The types of alliances along the value chain correspond, without doubt, to the very reasons why Latin American companies want to ally with foreign partners. When Latin American host companies and foreign partners develop alliances on a cross-equity participation basis, the host companies tend to have a lower equity position in their foreign partners irrespective of type of alliances formed. In our sample, Latin American host companies, on the average, had an 8.1% equity stake in their foreign partner companies, whereas the foreign partner companies had a 14.3% equity stake in the Latin American partners. This significant difference in mutual ownership may well be due to the fact that foreign companies are generally larger than Latin American companies. However, when they have a joint venture—a separate legal entity—as a form of their alliance, both parties to the alliance tend to have a fairly

Table 8.3. Types of Alliances, Equity Structure, and Business Relationship

Type of alliance	Technical assistance	Legal protocol	Marketing arrangement	Management	Assistance	Production arrangement
Specific arrangement	Technical training	License/patent	Procedural accord	Management contract	Production	
Start-up assistance	Brand/Trademark licensing	Marketing agreement	Service agreement	Assembly		
Process initiation		Distribution accord				
Research and development						
In the case of equity participation in partner company						
Host company's[a] equity position (%)	7.0	5.3	6.0	11.3	8.6	
Foreign partner's equity position (%)	12.9	14.2	11.1	13.6	12.4	
In the case of equity participation in a separate joint venture[b]						
Host company's equity position (%)	20.7	15.2	18.3	22.7	22.2	
Foreign partner's equity position (%)	21.3	18.8	21.5	26.4	24.7	
Percentage of business coming from the company's relationship with its partner						
Host company's dependency on foreign partner	28.6	30.4	29.9	31.6	33.4	
Foreign partner's dependency on host company (%)	13.0	12.4	17.8	16.5	21.9	

[a]Host company—Latin American company.

[b]The sum of equity ownership positions for a joint venture does not add up to 100% due to multiple-partner arrangements in most cases.

similar equity participation, with Latin American companies owning 19.0% of the joint venture stake and foreign partners owning 21.7%. This small difference is not statistically significant. This similar level of equity stake between them generally seems to apply to all types of alliances. Overall, whether alliances are by way of mutual equity participation or by formation of joint ventures, equity participation seems to be a form of "mutual hostage" arrangement to firm up each partner's legal stake in the other.

Interestingly, when it comes to the volume of their business attributable to the alliances, Latin American partners seem to have relatively much more to gain from the relationship than foreign partners do. This is true whether or not the joint venture form of alliances is used. On average, Latin American partners draw 26.9% of their business from their affiliations with their foreign partners through increased regional sales as well as increased exports, whereas foreign partners have some 17% of their business coming from these alliances. Particularly, when they have legal protocol transfer arrangements including transfer of technology licenses and brand/trademark franchises, Latin American companies seem to have a much higher relative stake on the alliances than foreign partners. Given the technological gap that usually exists between developed country partners and Latin American companies, a wider gap in their respective stake is understandable.

A firm can trust its partner if it is deemed to behave reliably and competently. Because partnering provides opportunities for specialization of activities among alliance partners, firms explicitly and/or implicitly delegate responsibilities to their allies. This delegation requires trust on the part of these partnering firms that the counterpart will behave as expected in a given situation. According to our sample, most Latin American alliance managers expressed a high level of trust in their foreign alliance partners, and indicated that their partners tended not to behave opportunistically.

As organizational forms, alliances allow firms to engage in business activities and transactions in a manner that allows for eased adaptation to market conditions. Binding rules of incorporation (as in the case of a merger, acquisition, or subsidiary relationship) can thus be avoided and the alliance can take advantage of opportunities quickly. However, such responses require the alliance organization to be flexible in interfacing with the market. This need for flexibility extends also to the relationship between the partners. In international alliances such as these, distinct national cultures and often distinct organizational cultures become intertwined in the alliance. This cultural blending requires flexibility on the part of the partnering firms; without flexibility in adapting, the alliance would perish under the pressures of constant internal turmoil. The Latin American alliance managers found their relationships with foreign firms to be characterized by high levels of flexibility.

Knowing that these relationships are well managed by the partnering firms and Latin American partners are benefiting from the alliances, we now address the issue of performance assessment in these alliance relationships.

Performance Criteria

Of paramount importance for understanding alliances with Latin American firms is understanding how the managers of these alliances evaluate the collaboration's performance. Although the literature on commercial relationships and marketing orientation points to the need to assess and address the evaluation criteria of relationship partners, U.S. managers are generally ignorant of how Latin American firms managers view success in partnerships. The Latin American managers in our sample were asked to identify the three criteria that they deem most important in their alliance success evaluations. To categorize these responses, three independent judges were used in classifying the criteria. Upon initial classification, the judges discussed categorization until complete concordance was achieved.[4] Fourteen categories of performance/success criteria were determined, and are presented in Table 8.4.

The most frequently cited performance criterion (38%) concerns *technology and innovation*. Firms in these Latin American NICs are increasingly cognizant of their need to enhance their competitiveness via innovation, and thus evaluate their alliances accordingly. Economic liberalization in these markets exacerbates this concern with technological advancement.

Sales growth and market share are cited by nearly a third of the firms in the sample as critical performance criteria. With limited domestic markets in terms of size and purchasing power, this concern is particularly relevant to these Latin American alliance managers. The alliances that

Table 8.4. Performance Success Criteria for Strategic Alliances

Success criterion	Level of importance (% firms)[a]	Performance rating[b]
Technology/innovation	38	3.5
Sales growth/market share	29	3.0
Market access/knowledge	24	3.7
Profits	19	2.9
Relationship/trust	18	3.2
Capital, credit, and foreign exchange	13	3.9
Image, brand, and reputation	12	3.7
Supplies and suppliers	9	3.1
Product access	9	3.2
Costs	7	3.7
Customer service/satisfaction	4	3.9
Production/economies of scale	4	4.4
Training/support	4	4.3
Market power/competitive position	2	3.8

[a]The percentage of Latin American companies that indicated a given criterion within the three most important criteria for alliance success.

[b]Based on a 5-point scale rating; 1 = Not at all successful . . . 5 = Extremely successful.

allow for such expansion are those that these firms will tend to seek and will evaluate highly.

Market access is also important to these firms; given their relatively small domestic markets, this is not surprising. Also given movements toward economic integration, alliances that allow for quick entry into newly "opened" partner countries are given premium status.

The traditional performance measure of *profitability* is cited by one-fifth of the respondents. Although not as important as the previously mentioned performance criteria, clearly these firms are also concerned with profits gained through their foreign partnerships. For many of these managers, although profitability is an obvious eventual criterion for success in the alliance, other strategic objectives in the short and medium term may be seen as more important outcomes of the alliance.

Many firms in this sample (18%) also deem *relationship and trust* criteria as important in evaluating the alliance's performance. Eased decision making and a reduced need to protect against a partner's opportunism that can result from high levels of trust in alliances likely motivates this evaluation. This finding is consistent with the high emphasis placed on relationships in Latin American culture.

All remaining success criteria have been mentioned by less than one-fifth of the respondents and are thus deemed to be not as universal in characterizing these Latin American firms' evaluation criteria.

Performance Evaluation

Based upon the performance criteria discussed above, the respondent firms were asked to evaluate their alliance's performance on the criteria they cited. These evaluations were on a scale from 1 (not at all successful) to 5 (extremely successful). The results of this analysis are also presented in Table 8.4.

On average, these managers rate the success of these alliances as fairly good according to their own criteria. Semantically, these managers would rate their alliances' success somewhat better than midway between extremely successful and not at all successful.[5] Thus, this analysis would indicate that these alliances generally perform well.

However, by mapping the performance evaluation to each corresponding success criterion, a troubling fact emerges. Those success criteria that were most frequently mentioned as being *important* in gauging alliances are precisely those criteria on which these Latin American firm managers give relatively *poor* performance evaluations: technology and innovation, sales growth/market share, and market access and knowledge. This is so despite the significant business stake that those Latin American companies already attribute to those aspects of the alliances.

This result indicates clearly that work must be done by foreign partners collaborating with Latin American firms—especially in terms of those frequently mentioned success criteria on which foreign partners are not doing as well as perceived by the Latin American managers. The issues they deem important in these alliances are not, by and large, being met satisfactorily by their partners.

As managers of firms from NICs, it is clear why these criteria would be so frequently mentioned in deeming an alliance successful. Firms collaborate to compete. For firms emerging from markets that traditionally have been strapped with low productivity and low quality products (due to protected markets that dampened the need to be efficient, effective, and competitive), innovation and technology are highly valued outcomes sought through collaboration with partners rich in those resources.

Similarly, economic liberalization in all three of these Latin American NICs has been accompanied by intense competitive pressure within their domestic markets. This pressure, coupled with gains possible through economies of scale (and thus larger production quantities), has urged these firms to seek new markets for their products. Economic liberalization in other nations offers further incentive for these firms to want foreign market access. Yet histories of import substitution throughout Latin American deprived companies in these nations of the ability to learn about business in other markets; their production and energies were focused on supplying the domestic market exclusively. Without knowledge of foreign markets, these firms seek foreign partners with knowledge about and competitive infrastructures already created within those foreign markets. Thus, the criteria of sales growth/market share and market access are clear areas that these firms would want to have addressed in their alliances.

The poor performance of these firms' foreign partners with regard to the criteria the Latin American managers deem important (technology and market access/sales growth) highlights the inherent tension built into collaboration and international collaboration in particular. Both technology and market knowledge (which is necessary for effective access and subsequent sales growth) can be core competencies of firms—competencies that allow the foreign firm to successfully compete in a product/technology/geographic area.

By collaborating with a Latin American firm wherein these sensitive resources are passed through, the foreign firm may be effectively creating a strong competitor. This risk of competitor creation is particularly acute in this context given the justifiable concerns over intellectual property protection in Latin America.[6] Historically protected markets that used to deny reciprocal access still strain foreign firms' desire to perform along this dimension in their collaboration with Latin American firms.[7]

Conclusions

This survey of Latin American managers regarding their commercial collaboration has yielded important results for firms allying with them currently or with plans to do so in the future. It also offers valuable insights for local managers in understanding the relevant dimensions they must emphasize when building a strategic alliance with a foreign partner. These firms are motivated to enter into alliance relationships for a variety of motivations; this is consistent with the experience of firms from many nations as cited in the literature. Resource acquisition, competitive posturing and risk/cost reduction are variously sought by these firms through alliances with foreign partners.

In general, the management of these alliances is running smoothly. Mutual ownership stakes in the alliances seem to provide a sense of security to both parties, although Latin American partners tend to have a higher business stake in the relationships. These Latin American companies have indicated that their relationships with their foreign counterparts are largely acceptable; they view them as flexible. Foreign partners have largely abstained from opportunistic behavior, and the relationships tend to be stable. These favorable ratings by Latin American managers of their alliances speak well of their foreign partners. Presumably, this trusting of partners does not extend in the other direction; if it did, it is assumed that foreign firms would be less reluctant to perform in terms of providing access to technology to their Latin American partners.

It can be surmised that many of these foreign firms' concerns in regards to providing the Latin American firms access to their markets (allowing them to grow sales) and providing them with innovative capabilities would be mitigated through significant and sincere efforts on the part of these Latin American firms' governments to enhance foreign firms' access into their markets (reciprocity) and to ensure effective protection of intellectual property rights.

Firms that wish to ally with Latin American firms can make significant strides in enhancing their Latin American partner's perception of success along the innovation and market access criteria that they most seek even where government-sponsored safeguards and opportunities are lacking.

In terms of innovation and technology access, alliances can be structured in ways that limit the repercussions of information leakage to the partner through passing on second generation technology. This practice, however, may not appease the Latin American managers who undoubtedly seek state-of-the-art technology from their partners. By sharing this sort of technology on a limited basis, the foreign partners can test the trustworthiness of their Latin American partner before granting carte blanche access to the whole range of technology the firm has in place. Finally, by structuring alliances in such a way that the Latin American firm makes investments in the relationship that would enhance the competitive position of the foreign partner in exchange for access to the technology, that foreign partner will gain sufficiently to potentially offset the loss of competitive posture from technology leakage. An example of the sort of investment that a Latin American firm partner could make to offset the risk would be in promotion of the foreign firm as an ally to local consumers. In this way the Latin American firm would allow its brand equity to "carry over" to the partner firm, creating brand identification for the foreign firm in the Latin American market.

Market access concerns can be best addressed by focusing on alliances that are more vertical, or complementary, than horizontal in nature. Where the partnering firms produce products or services that are largely substitutes, reciprocal market access is nearly impossible. By granting a substitute product access to the firm's domestic market, it is effectively creating competition there. However, where the firm's product/service is up/down stream or complementary to the partner's product/service, competitive benefits such as better customer service can result. In this way, by carefully selecting partners based upon their business niches, granting market access to an ally can enhance a firm's competitive position.

By knowing empirically what motivates these Latin American firms to seek foreign partners, and perhaps most importantly how their success is evaluated and currently is rated, managers wishing to partner with firms from this region are better prepared to enter into meaningful and successful alliances there. Recommendations obviously include sustaining the successful track record of alliance management. Given the strong relationship orientation of Latin America culturally, the importance of these factors cannot be overstated.[8]

Furthermore, foreign firms must recognize that their Latin American counterparts will typically be seeking market access and technology access. If these firms are unprepared to facilitate their Latin American counterparts in these efforts, they must recognize the likelihood that their partners will remain unsatisfied, despite the foreign firms' best efforts in the relationship area. Until foreign firms feel as though assisting their Latin American counterparts with market access and technology access would not pose a risk to their competitiveness and/or allow for some sort of important reciprocation, these firms would unlikely placate their Latin American firm allies.

Appendix: Methodology

Survey Instrument

The survey instrument was originally developed in English and was translated into Portuguese and Spanish (Brazil, and Chile/Mexico, respectively) by native speakers who are professors of business. Back translation was performed on each local language instrument until conceptual and functional equivalence had been achieved. In each venue, business professionals and academics were consulted regarding issues of interpretation, ease of understanding, and face validity. These checks ultimately yielded instruments that were deemed to be reliable and valid, and equivalent in English, Spanish, and Portuguese.

Data Collection

The actual data collection procedure varied by venue, given particular limitations and opportunities within each country. Unfortunately, in none of these venues does a "master directory of international collaborations" exist. Thus, a most challenging aspect of the data collection concerned the identification of firms with international collaboration experience. This was accomplished through different means in each venue.

Brazil

Before data collection, many corporate directories and Chambers of Commerce were consulted.[9] In addition, one of the authors consulted contacts through a prominent business school in São Paulo in identifying firms. Firms were initially contacted by telephone to ensure that they bad experience collaborating with a foreign firm. The survey instrument was sent by mail, and most were undelivered due to an unexpected lengthy postal strike and sabotage. The instruments were either personally delivered or faxed to the target firms. A total of 335 survey instruments were successfully delivered to target firms, with 103 returned. Formal refusal to participate came from 84 firms. A total of 80 questionnaires were returned completed, and represented Brazilian firm collaborations with firms from North America, Western Europe, and Asia.

Chile

Potential firms for inclusion in the study were identified through listing on the Santiago Stock Exchange, local chambers of commerce, and contacts from a prominent local university. Additional firms were identified by referrals from other firms contacted. The survey instrument was initially mailed to the identified firms, with a very low response rate of only 2%, despite reminder letters and follow-up telephone calls. The data collection effort was then modified and personal interviews with key informants were conducted in which the respondents replied to the survey questions. This process was conducted by one of the authors, his research assistant, and a group of MBA students as part of an International Business class at a prominent local university in Santiago. As a result of this process, 180 firms were contacted initially, and 92 firms completed questionnaires. Of these 92 questionnaires, 80 were retained as the other 12 contained excessive missing data.

Mexico

One of the authors was giving a course on international strategy to MBA students via satellite to 20 campuses within Mexico. As a class project, the students at each campus were responsible for identifying a local firm with international collaboration experience. The students then personally delivered the questionnaire to the key informant in the firm, and collected the completed questionnaire from that individual a week later. A total of 103 surveys were distributed in this manner. An independent graduate assistant in Mexico then contacted each firm in the sample to verify the response to three items, as a way of ensuring valid data collection: that the key informant had personally replied to the items of interest. In 21 of the cases, the key informant's failure to respond consistently with answers recorded on the survey instrument and/or excessive missing data deemed the response unreliable, and these surveys were discarded from further analysis, resulting in a final sample size from Mexico of 82 responses. Most partner firms in this sample are from the United States, although partners from other countries are also represented.

Notes

1. As the exchange rates fluctuate irregularly and do not necessarily reflect the purchasing power of the foreign currencies vis-a-vis the U.S. dollar, the GDP is expressed in real purchasing power in dollar terms.

2. Principal components factor analysis was used to determine factor structure. All constructs used in this study were found to be universal irrespective of nationality of firms.

3. A list of 21 motivations for collaborating with a foreign partner were identified from the literature and through a pilot study with 18 firms in Mexico who had allied with a foreign firm. For each of these motivations, the respondents in the current study were asked to indicated the importance of the particular motivation in forming the alliance under review on a live point scale anchored by "not at all important" and "extremely important" (Contractor & Lorange, 1988).

4. Upon initial classification, at least two judges were in agreement in 82.7% of the cases categorized (559/676 criteria provided by respondents). Upon later consultation, complete agreement was achieved for all 676 cases. These classifications were used for subsequent analyses.

5. This semantic evaluation corresponds to an average success rating across success criteria of 3.59. Recall that this rating is on a 5-point scale in which 5 represents "extremely successful."

6. Note that in Brazil, Mexico, and Chile, strong intellectual property protection has been officially legislated. Effective enforcement of existing laws and policies, however, is not consistent.

7. Despite significant progress made through the WTO in terms of multilateral free trade, protection of markets still exists in many forms throughout the world. This limited reciprocity is, of course, country-dependent; for U.S. firms allying with Mexican partners, this argument against providing their Mexican partner access to the U.S. market does not hold. Similarly, for an Argentine

firm partnering with a Brazilian ally, MERCOSUR legislation provides for "free" reciprocal market access. For other country pairings, however, this type of reciprocal access does not hold.

8. All three of these countries have been found to be culturally collectivistic, although Mexico and Chile more so than Brazil (Hofstede, 1991).

9. The directories consulted were as follows: *Gazeta Mercantil-Balanço Anual* (1995), *Exame-Maiores e Melhores* (1995), *American Chamber of Commerce Yearbook* (1995), and EPIL Industries Yearbook (1990/1991). The Chambers of Commerce (in Brazil) that were consulted are as follows: Argentina, Belgium-Luxembourg, Canada, Chile, France, Germany, Great Britain, MERCOSUR, Holland, Italy, Japan, Portugal, Spain, Sweden, Switzerland, Venezuela, and the Manufacturing Industry Federation of the São Paulo State.

References

Contractor, F. J., & Lorange, P. (1988). Why should firms cooperate? The strategy and economics basis for cooperative ventures. In F. J. Contractor & P. Lorange (Eds.), *Cooperative strategies in international business* (pp. 3–28). Lexington: Lexington Books.

Gillespie, K., & Teegen, H. (1995, Winter). Market liberalization and international alliance formation: The Mexican paradigm. *Columbia Journal of World Business, 30*, 58–69.

Hagedoorn, J. (1993). Understanding the rationale of strategic technology partnering: Interorganizational modes of cooperation and sectoral differences. *Strategic Management Journal, 14*(5), 371–386.

Hamcl, G. (1991, Summer). Competition for competence and inter-partner learning within international strategic alliances. *Strategic Management Journal, 12*, 83–104.

Hofstede, G. (1991) *Cultures and organizations: Software of the mind.*

Kotabe, M., & de Arruda, M. C. C. (1998, Spring). South America's free trade gambit. *Marketing Management, 7*, 38–46.

Mackay, D. (1997, September). FTAA: Prospects and challenges. *OAS Working Paper.*

Ohmae, K. (1989, March–April). The global logic of strategic alliances. *Harvard Business Review, 67*, 143–154

Teeyen, H. (1998). New actors: Business and their strategic alliances. In R. Fernandez de Castro, S. Weintraub, & M. Verea de Campos (Eds.), *The new agenda for the bilateral relationship: The United States and Mexico*. Mexico City: Fondo de Cultura Press.

CHAPTER 9

Marketing's Contribution to the Transformation of Central and Eastern Europe

Reiner Springer and Michael R. Czinkota

Introduction

The transformation from planned to market economy is a worldwide phenomenon. The majority of countries in transition are former socialist nations in Europe and the successor states of the Soviet Union. Transformation means a change of systems, a paradigm change in politics and economics. The transformation process starts with a planned economy and is aimed at a market economy, but it may pass through various interim stages which vary from country to country according to historical background, concept, speed, and acceptance of transformation. All the countries started into the transformation process without an accepted and comprehensive theory of system change (Wagner, 1991, p. 17). To understand the magnitude of the scope, the tasks, and the problems of system transformation in Central and Eastern Europe, Table 9.1 contrasts key business dimensions of planned and market economies (Jens, 1993; Schüller, 1991).

History has proven that planned economies are less efficient than market economies. The reasons for the disintegration and collapse of the socialist system are manifold, but lack of efficiency and motivation are key. Problems of motivation were mainly caused by the principle of socialist equality where everyone was to live according to his needs,

Table 9.1. Contrast of Planned and Market Economies

Criteria	Planned economy	Market economy
Decision making	Highly centralized, party government; planning bureaucracy is taking economic decisions related to the macro and microeconomic level; political administrative-dominated management of economy and companies; price regulation by the state	Autonomy of companies; limited or no interference of the state
Information gathering	Top-down planning process, especially quantitative balancing of output and input on the macro and micro level	Price-market mechanism
Ownership of the means of production	State-owned companies; sometimes cooperative property	Private property
Motivation	Moral and material incentives directed at the fulfillment of national economic plans	Maximizing of profits; development of individual personality

not according to his own effort and contribution. The lack of efficiency resulted from the primacy of politics and dominance of national plans, which prevented the development of markets as a place of exchange, eliminated the signaling function of the price mechanism, and inhibited the market orientation of companies. Marketing as a corporate strategy was undesirable since its full implementation would have strengthened the position of companies and managers and reduced the power of the party and the state bureaucracy. In terms of priorities, state control vastly outranked corporate efficiency and customer satisfaction. This choice of priorities was maintained with relative ease, since, due to a lack of democracy, customers and managers were very limited in their ability to complain effectively.

A successful transformation of planned to market economies requires the development of a market orientation in the transition countries. This affords a unique opportunity but also an obligation for marketing to help restructure society and business processes in order to improve the standard of living. Yet, there has been little established knowledge about how marketing can be used to facilitate economic transitions (Olivier, 1991). This article will assess what marketing knowledge and practice has done in the past, what marketing has accomplished during the ongoing transformation, and what it can do in future to improve the functioning of economies in transition.

The Past

Marketing as management concept was not used in the planned economies of the former socialist countries for two main reasons: First, political and ideological beliefs prohibited the acceptance and use of marketing, since national economic plans rather than the market regulated and managed the economy and the economic behavior of companies, suppliers, buyers, and consumers. Some countries even prohibited the use of the term *marketing*, since it was labeled as capitalistic and therefore negative, and believed to manipulate consumers against their own will. In East Germany the term *Murktarbeit* (market work) was used. In Poland, Hungary, or Czechoslovakia the national languages did not provide an equivalent term. Secondly, markets in which demand consistently outstripped supply offered neither a basis nor an incentive to use marketing. Virtually anything produced was sold based on a guarantee by the national economic plan and state-controlled distribution systems (Mayer, 1976; Naor, 1986, 1990; Samli, 1986).

Although the socialist economies did not permit the implementation of marketing as a management concept, companies operating in planned economies used various tools of marketing in an unsystematic way. In evaluating the role of marketing in planned economies, one can distinguish three segments of the economy: internal activities of domestic businesses, external activities of domestic firms due to international business efforts, and the internal repercussions from the export activities of foreign companies.

In their internal domestic business, firms did not aim to create customer value but rather focused on meeting quantitative targets set by the plan. In general, supply was smaller than demand, prices were set by the state, and distribution channels were fixed. Companies were production oriented and used marketing instruments only selectively. In preparing plans, market research determined the quantitative development of demand; occasionally, point of sales advertising was used to get rid of surplus stocks; fairs and exhibitions were attended to introduce new products; the transportation and distribution of products were optimized by using network planning techniques; and individual and organizational buyers learned how to develop incentives in order to source inputs in short supply. Since demand was larger than supply, consumer behavior developed buying criteria atypical for market economies. As consumers did not have a choice between a variety of offers, price and quality did not play a major role in the buying decisions. Simply to obtain a product was a major source of satisfaction.

The external efforts of domestic companies were mainly export oriented. In doing business with other centrally planned economies the need for marketing was low, since trade and product exchanges were regulated by long-term trade agreements and agreed upon pricing rules. Trade with the West required a more comprehensive use of marketing instruments. Foreign trade organizations (FTOs) were authorized by the state to handle all export and import operations. As a consequence, these FTOs, rather than manufacturers, used marketing approaches and, over time, acquired solid experience in doing business in Western markets. The marketing strengths of these FTOs were market research, channel management, use of fairs and exhibitions for introducing and selling products, adapting products to specific customer needs, competitive pricing, use of counter-trade, negotiation skills, and exploiting loopholes in the import and export regulations of their target markets.

The international business activities of Western companies in planned economies were heavily influenced by the foreign trade monopoly in the East and the export control policies in the West (Czinkota & Dichtl, 1996). The inward trade monopoly limited business activities to the import of goods and simple licensing agreements. Western companies did not have access to end users and had to deal with FTOs only. Market research focused on analyzing general economic developments and economic plans to identify specific business opportunities. The participation in fairs and exhibitions played a key role in establishing business contacts with decision makers in government and party circles. Distribution was not important since the FTOs were completely in charge of domestic allocation.

In sum, there was no marketing culture and marketing based behavior of suppliers and buyers in the socialist planned economies. Due to political, economic, and systemic constraints, managerial readiness and capability to use marketing as a management concept did not exist. Manufacturers held a monopolistic position and were told by the planning bureaucracy what to produce. Therefore, they did not need marketing to determine and satisfy the needs and wants of customers. Consumers did not have buying options, and chased products rather than select them. Without functioning markets in planned economies, marketing as a management concept could not work.

Changes During Transition

Transition Shapes and Requires a Marketing Environment

Replacing the political and economic system of socialism with a new democratic and market-driven system is the objective of transition. However, the precise expectations of the new economic system vary from country to country. Most countries in transition prefer the German or Swedish type of social market economy, where markets are heavily influenced by government, to the United States or British type of a less restrained market economy. This attitude may well be the result of a distrust in the invisible hand and a continued belief in government intervention by the population and is of major relevance for political and economic reforms in Central and Eastern Europe. During the introduction of a market orientation, the people of Central and Eastern Europe have both hopes and fears. On the one hand, people expect an immediate improvement in their personal economic situation. On the other hand, they fear to be without shelter, to be steamrolled by an unknown and antagonistic system. Therefore, any policy of transition has to make sure that the population accepts reforms and can endure the transformation from the old to the new system. Since the rules as well as the advantages and the disadvantages of the new system are unknown to the population, the aims, content, and mechanism of any reforms must be explained constantly to generate broad support for and acceptance of change. Differences in the explanatory success by governments may be a reason why the transition to a market economy is progressing at differing speeds and with different success from country to country. Fear and the need for popular support may also explain why the majority of countries is preferring a step-by-step transformation process. In other words, in the long run a gradual transition seems to be more successful than shock therapy.

The transition process will be a success only if the new political and economic system is accepted by the vast majority of the population, generates internal and external political and economic stability, and improves the social well-being and standard of living of the population. In the end, transition has to increase the political, economic, technological, and social proximity between the countries in transition and the countries in the industrialized West. If there is no real hope for substantial improvement in the future, then the transformation to the new system has failed.

The transition process has disbanded the bloc of socialist countries. The formerly Eastern bloc is not a bloc anymore but a group of countries with the same political past but a varying political, economic, and social future. The ongoing transition will deepen the differences between countries. Based on the speed and success in transition, countries can be clustered in progressive reformers (Czech Republic, Hungary, Poland, Estonia, Lithuania, Latvia, and Slovenia), reformers on the brake (like Slovakia, Russia, Bulgaria, and Romania), and late, reluctant reformers (member states of CIS except Russia).

The success of economic reforms depends heavily on comprehensive and speedy political and legal reforms. The institutional, organizational, and legal changes have been accomplished relatively fast in most of the countries in transition. But political behavior, practiced democracy, implementation of enacted laws, and legal certainty are lagging behind. A perspective of the status of system reforms by countries in transition can be gained from Exhibit 9.1.

The success of transition depends heavily on the acceptance of the new political and economic system by the elite and, even more importantly, by the whole population. According to polls taken, the acceptance of a market economy as the right way into the future differs widely between the countries in transition. Whereas in Poland and Croatia 60% of the people accept a market orientation, only 42% of the Czechs, 37% of the Hungarians, and 24% of the Russians and Ukrainians agree with this direction of transition (Business Central Europe, 1997, p. 67). These figures raise the question why, after almost 10 years of transition only a relatively low percentage of people (and voters) have accepted a market

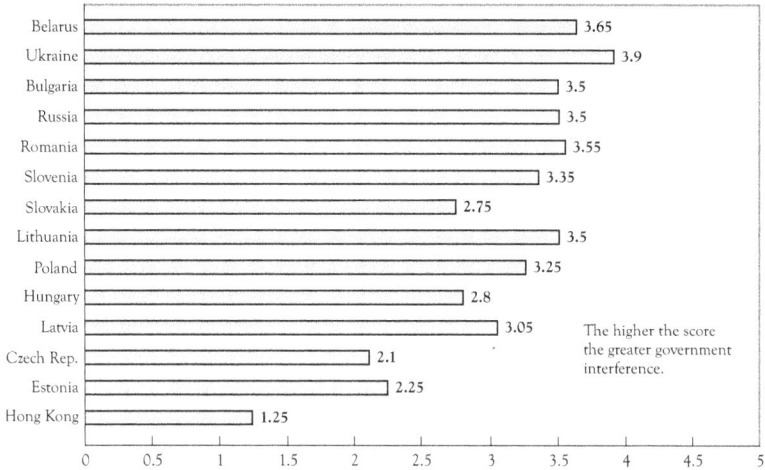

Exhibit 9.1. Index of Economic Freedom Ranking

Source: Transition, 1997.

orientation as the best way of system change. The reasons may be manifold but are basically rooted in unfulfilled expectations. People hoped for quick improvements in their standard of living, politicians promised more than they could deliver, political freedom was taken for granted and valued as an extraordinary achievement only at the beginning of the transformation process. Combined with a low readiness for hardships, the results of transition have led to disappointment and disenchantment. Many people now only remember the bright side of life under socialism and forget the dark side and the missed opportunities.

Although the transition to a new political and economic order seems to be irreversible, the establishment of a market system may take longer than expected. The process will be accompanied by developments that are not in line with market-oriented behavior and cause instability and irritation especially for outsiders. The transition from a planned to a market economy is changing the marketing environment in Central and Eastern Europe gradually although substantially. These changes bring about a new political, economic, financial, and legal framework for consumer behavior and doing business in the region (Czinkota, Gaisbauer, & Springer, 1997; Healey, 1994; Huszagh, Huszagh, & Hanks, 1992; Hooley, 1993; Mueller, Wenthe, & Baron, 1993). Since there is a strong interdependence between the marketing environment and the way marketing can be implemented by the players in the market, the impact of transition on consumers/customers and suppliers/companies shall be discussed next. In this context it is important to notice that the shift in marketing and managerial behavior of suppliers, customers, decision makers, and politicians is lagging behind the changes in the marketing environment. This gap between framework changes and behavioral changes may lead to conflicts, backward-oriented decisions by local politicians and managers, and an eventual slow-down in the process of transition.

Consumers and Customers Adapt to Marketing

A major feature of the marketing environment in Central and Eastern Europe is the slow and sometimes contradictory shift in the market constellation from a seller's market to a buyer's market. This shift is accompanied by long-lasting transition crises and output losses in all countries of transition. In 1997 only Poland and Slovenia surpassed or reached the gross domestic product (GDP) level of 1989, all the other countries are still below this level. Russia has reached 59% and the Ukraine 37% of the 1989 GDP (data compiled from EBRD, 1997a, 1997b). These output losses mean that there are fewer products and services available, and that both consumption and investments are decreasing. In addition some of the domestic products are in short supply or are being replaced by foreign products. With net monthly wages in manufacturing between $55 in the Ukraine and $329 in Poland (EBRD, 1996), the buying power among countries differs widely and is growing mainly in the progressive transition economies.

The transition crisis has fueled the shadow economy, which may compensate at least partially for the output losses registered in the official economic sector. In 1995, the size of the shadow economy was estimated to be 19% of GDP in Central and Eastern Europe, 44.8% in the European part of the CIS, and 20.4% in Central Asia (EBRD, 1997a, p. 76).

Because of these economic conditions, the majority of households in Central and Eastern Europe have not yet improved their economic situation. Only 17% of questioned households confirm that their current economic situation is now better than under the planned economy, 46% of the households hope that the situation will improve in the future (Rose & Haerpfer, 1996). As a result, many people question the wisdom of transition and protest against the transition course in elections.

The general picture hides the fact that social gaps are growing and that the number of both poor and rich people is increasing. The so-called newly rich in Russia and in other countries constitute an interesting segment of customers for high-priced Western products.

The trend toward a market economy has affected the buying behavior of consumers. Limited purchasing power and the possibility of choice have led to more Western-style yet still rational buying behavior. Price and quality have become dominant buying criteria (Shama, 1992; Feick, Coulter, & Price, 1995). Consumers prepare the buying decision for long-lasting products very carefully in order to make sure that limited funds are spent wisely. Consumers demand information from suppliers to make the buying decision. Improvements in purchasing power will, perhaps, lead to more emotional buying behavior.

Country-of-origin issues have an impact on the buying behavior of consumers in Central and Eastern Europe (Gajewski, 1992; Good & Huddleston, 1995; Ettenson, 1993; Papadopoulos, Heslop, & Beracs, 1990). Immediately after the opening toward the West, consumers saw domestic products to be of inferior quality and rushed to buy foreign products to try out the unknown. In consequence, imports of Western products surged, international brands captured market share, and domestic manufacturers fired workers or even closed down. But now consumers return to local products, especially foodstuffs and low-tech products. Consumers have recognized that the quality of foreign products is not much better and that local products are much cheaper. Buying national also saves jobs. This ethnocentric buying behavior may also be partially explained by the still prevailing collectivism and national pride.

Advertising as a marketing tool is relatively new for customers in Central and Eastern Europe (Church, 1992; Heyder, Musiol, & Peters, 1992). In 1995 advertising expenditures per capita in Central and Eastern Europe were on average one-tenth of the expenditures in Austria: for instance, Poland, $24; Slovakia, $27; Hungary, $50; Czech Republic, $55; and Slovenia, $64 (Brenner, 1997, p. 47). Advertising has to reduce the information deficit of consumers with regard to goods, services, and conditions offered. It should reflect the differences in buying behavior and culture. Therefore, the style of advertising messages implemented in the East and in the West needs to differ. Eastern consumers prefer rational-based advertising, which explains the features of products and provides valuable information for preparing and making the buying decision. Advertising must help the consumer navigate in an ever-broadening array of products, and develop the kind of sovereignty needed to hold his ground in an economic system that demands personal decisions. Marketing, and especially advertising, run the risk of being rejected if customers are misled. For example, life style advertising used in the West rarely works in the East, because the lifestyles portrayed are far removed from reality. Therefore, marketing should present reliable and checkable facts to consumers in order to overcome the mistrust still emanating from their experience with ideological propaganda.

In this context branding plays a very important role. Since markets are flooded with new and very often unknown products, brands must serve as a guide through this increased offer. Customers in Central and Eastern Europe no longer consider international brands as superior per se. Sometimes they even develop brand loyalty toward local brands to protect themselves against everything foreign and to keep alive elements of the past they can personally relate to. Therefore, local brands can be as valuable as international brands; they just have to be positioned differently. In consequence, foreign companies should offer a mix of local and international brands. This will permit a much more precise targeting of various customer segments, taking into account the widespread differences in income levels and ethnocentric consumer behavior.

During the transition process, marketing has contributed by educating the consumers and by helping them to develop and practice patterns of thinking and behavior based on the rules of the market economy and to cope with the challenges arising from the new economic order. Especially, the buying behavior has been changed: Consumers compare and evaluate offers; demand explanations from the sellers; buy if they have a need, not if products are on the shelf; buy less frequently; and visit modern shopping facilities. Overall, consumers recognize that they are moving into a stronger position vis-à-vis the seller, and make use of a developing consumer sovereignty. By doing so, consumers gain some independence and freedom in making their own decisions.

Companies and Suppliers Learn to Operate in a Competitive Setting

The privatization of state-owned companies in Central and Eastern Europe and the opening of the countries in transition toward the world economy have substantially changed the economic setting for corporations. The privatization of state-owned companies is a central area of economic reform in Central and Eastern Europe. In mid-1997, the share of the private sector in GDP ranged between 75% for the Czech Republic and 20% for Belarus (EBRD, 1997a, p. 14). These figures provide, at best, an indication of the change of the legal status of formerly state-owned companies. They give no indication regarding the restructuring of socialist companies into market-oriented companies. The key question in this context is whether privatization will lead to a turnaround of formerly state-owned, hardly competitive, and plan-based companies into market-oriented and competitive companies. The majority of Eastern companies are far from competitive. Labor productivity in manufacturing is around 50% or even lower compared to Western companies. In 1994, half of the companies were profitable (Czech Republic, 81%; Hungary, 68%; Bulgaria, 34%) 15% of all companies or fewer (Poland, 14%; Bulgaria, 9%) had a positive cash flow (EBRD, 1996). Many companies lost their markets either to foreign competitors penetrating Eastern markets with Western products or because of the breakdown of trade relations with other formerly socialist countries.

What went wrong? Why have the new ownership and the prospects for profits not accomplished the necessary turnaround to a larger extent? Here are some of the reasons: Privatization did not provide enough fresh capital for needed investments, which delays technological restructuring. The implemented privatization schemes did not force out the old management. Many companies were privatized by changing the legal status from a state-owned company to a share-holding company with the state, state-controlled banks, or investment funds as owners so that the ownership did not really change. In some instances wild and uncontrolled privatization caused a drain on material and financial resources of Eastern companies undercutting their chances for survival. This all means that the turnaround of Eastern companies from plan-managed companies into market-oriented companies is far from complete. The transition on the company level has just started and will take years. Especially, changes in management styles and managerial behavior will progress only if a constant transfer of management know-how from the West to the East takes place.

All these developments contribute to a lack in competitiveness of the majority of domestic Eastern companies. Most of them still base their competitiveness on cost advantages, employ short-term survival tactics, and have not developed a long-term customer-oriented strategy. Such an approach works as long as competition is still underdeveloped and Eastern companies maintain a reasonable market share in a more or less protected domestic market. With progress in transition, competition will intensify and domestic Eastern companies will have to adopt a market orientation if they want to stay in the market. From a competitive perspective, there are currently two segments in the transition markets: domestic companies compete in one segment and foreign firms in the other. This is possible since the segments represent different clusters of customers being targeted by a different positioning of products and services mainly in regard to price and quality. Over time, foreign companies will be able to penetrate the segments of the Eastern companies because foreign companies have started production in Central and Eastern Europe and can therefore, due to low production costs, compete on price as well. It will be much more difficult for Eastern firms to penetrate the Western segments based on quality.

An example for the two segments within the markets of Central and Eastern Europe is the retail system. Western retail chains like Auchan, Leclerc, Metro, Tesco, Carrefour, Kaisers, Tengelmann, Billa, Meinl, and others are moving into Central and Eastern Europe on a large scale. They implement a greenfield strategy and do not cooperate with local retail systems. Western retail chains are hence competing against local retail outlets, which offer a much narrower assortment, hardly carry foreign products, and provide poor facilities (e.g., no parking). Compared to Western Europe, small shops still dominate the retail system in Central and Eastern Europe, but emerging supermarkets will accelerate the concentration process in the retail system. Eastern consumers have started to accept the foreign retail outlets and no longer visit the shop around the corner several times a week. The entry of international retail chains leads to a substitution of local products by international brands. Based on buy national attitudes many customers complain to be forced to buy foreign products even though the Hungarian milk or apple is as good as the foreign product. Therefore, those international retailers that offer local products may have a competitive advantage over retailers who focus mainly on international products. In the long run, local retailers will survive only if they form joint ventures among themselves, open modern sales outlets, and implement a customer orientation. But already marketing has changed the retail system in Central and Eastern Europe to the benefit of the customer.

The Eastern companies competitive in Western markets are mainly those in a progressive privatization stage or joint venture companies with foreign participation (the car manufacturer Skoda/VW for instance is contributing 8% of all Czech exports). Eastern companies base their competition in Western markets mainly on cost advantages. They offer low-priced products at a relatively low technological level, so that a major quality gap continues to exist. A comparison of the average quality levels of products imported by Western buyers from various countries can be seen in Exhibit 9.2.

On the whole, the penetration of the markets in Central and Eastern Europe by foreign companies as exporters and investors has fueled competition and is forcing domestic companies to adapt. Even though there has been a large inflow of foreign direct investment (FDI) since 1989, these cumulative FDI inflows from 1989 to 1997 are just $153 per capita (EBRD, 1998, p. 12). A comparison with the investment flows into the former East Germany lends perspective. By the end of the decade, Western Germany will have transferred $1 trillion to Eastern Germany (Czinkota, 1998). In spite of the transfer of almost $65,000 per capita, major discontent and inequity between the two German regions are likely to persist.

There are some indications that even the limited foreign investment inflows may not continue at the same speed due to political and legal uncertainties and cultural conflicts. Based on their experience, foreign companies operate more cautiously and place heavy emphasis on risk control and risk avoidance. In recent times, an increasing number of foreign companies prefers build strategies to buy strategies when entering Central and Eastern Europe since the turnaround of old companies is time consuming, very costly, and much more difficult than expected.

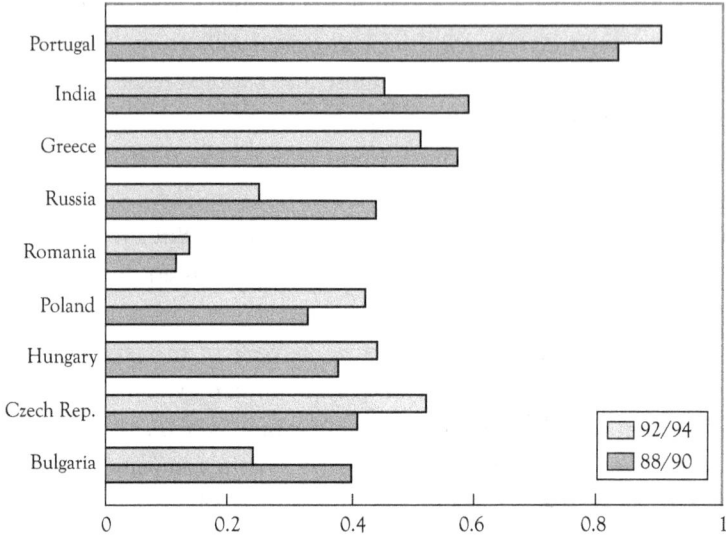

Exhibit 9.2. Quality Gap Between Machinery Produced Imported from Central and Eastern Europe and European Union (EU) Average

EU average = 1.

Source: EBRD, 1997a.

Some companies even disengage from foreign investments, especially in countries that lag behind in political and economic reforms. They find that the benefits of cheap labor and other low cost production factors are being more than absorbed by higher costs in logistics and other operating costs (Hauch-Fleck, 1997, p. 31).

This may explain why contract manufacturing is a market entry mode of increasing importance since capital commitment is low, market exit is possible in a very short time, but the benefits of low cost production factors can still be exploited. More than 50% of all foreign contract manufacturing by German companies takes place within Central and Eastern Europe; more than 15% of all German imports from Central and Eastern Europe are deliveries from contract manufacturing operations (Handelsblatt, 1995, p. 16). There is a shift of contract manufacturing from Asia to Central and Eastern Europe.

In joint ventures cultural conflicts often turn out to be a reason for failure. Western companies tend to overlook that patience and thoroughness, knowledge of the country, good personal contacts, local presence of a decider from the Western partner, stable and reliable supply networks, effective and accepted organizational structures, and effective control mechanism are key success factors of joint ventures in Central and Eastern Europe (Trommsdorff, Binsack, Drüner, & Koppelt, 1995; Trommsdorff & Schuchardt, 1998).

The marketing environment in Central and Eastern Europe is still different compared to the marketing environment in the industrialized West. This is illustrated by the fact that low purchasing power, import restrictions, low price stability, and uncertain legal conditions are major barriers for market entry into Central and Eastern Europe (Handelsblatt, 1997, p. B 5).

Marketing Management Will Be Learned

Management styles and managerial behavior are determined by the political and economic system and cultural values of a society. As this foundation is changing, management will change as well. Management tools can be learned in school, but managerial behavior will be learned mainly by doing. This means that as the transition progresses, the behavior of managers in the East is adjusting to the needs of a market economy (Pribova & Savitt, 1995; Tesar & Nieminen, 1994). This process takes time and the adoption of new management skills is lagging behind.

It seems to be especially difficult to give up the managerial behavior learned under the conditions of a planned economy. On the whole, managerial behavior in Central and Eastern Europe is influenced by typical cultural standards, which have their roots in the socialist economic system. Using the five cultural dimensions of Hofstede (1991), one can argue that Central and Eastern Europe is characterized by high power distance, low individualism, masculinity, high uncertainty avoidance, and short-term orientation. In the planned economies managers implemented orders handed down by the national economic plan, the party, or the state planning bureaucracy. The decision process and the areas of responsibility were structured very clearly as a top-down model, so that an interaction across hierarchical borders was almost impossible. Managers and their staff were not accustomed to take risks and postponed necessary decisions while waiting for orders from above. With the ongoing transition, companies gain autonomy and independence, which requires managers to take responsibility and to prepare and implement decisions on their own. Middle management, especially, still waits for orders from above and demonstrates insecurity when confronted with the need for fast decision making. On the other hand, within working groups or teams, low individualism prevailed so that a "we" attitude and collective pride developed in connection with solidarity among group members which contributes to a friendly working climate and efficiency. Transition also caused a shift from a long-term orientation under the planned economy to a short-term orientation, which is directed at survival.

The obvious deficit in marketing behavior in Central and Eastern Europe is the lack of customer orientation and the weak striving for customer satisfaction. With competition still underdeveloped and customers less demanding, companies only now start to care about customer needs. The necessary change toward a marketing orientation of the Eastern companies is not so much an issue of modern marketing skills, methods, and instruments but mainly a behavioral problem. Its success will require management to grasp the meaning and the philosophy of marketing as a conceptual tool and managerial system that are instrumental to generating profits for the company and to improving the well-being of consumers and society at the same time.

The gap between existing management skills and needed management skills can be narrowed by the transfer of management know-how from West to East. For such a transfer to be successful, however, it needs to achieve a linkage between knowledge, learning, and actual change. Well-entrenched societal structures, at least in the short run, may not be overcome by learning alone. For example, in many Central European firms, a move up on the career ladder still depends on seniority, with little attention paid to capability or expertise. In order to encourage market-oriented thinking, the system needs to show that knowledge causes advancement.

But knowledge alone is not sufficient. It must be translated into changed behavioral patterns on part of all employees—the ones interacting directly with customers as well as the senior executives. Many indigenous firms face a dilemma here. In some of them, senior management has a vision of a marketing orientation, but is unable to have this vision understood or implemented by employees. In others, some employees are trying to apply new ways of thinking, but they are ignored or dismissed by their managers who are not yet ready for employees who participate or speak up. Only those firms that manage to synchronize management and labor in their thinking about a market orientation are able to achieve lasting shifts in behavior and performance. They are the ones that focus systematically on improving behavioral skills such as communication, decision making, customer orientation, and team building (Czinkota & Springer, 1997).

Future Contributions of Marketing

Marketing will evolve with the ongoing transformation. The shifts elated to transition are only the beginning of a process. But the announcement of reforms and the intention to establish a market economy do not autmatically result in change itself. For example, the abolition of a centrally planned economy does not create a market economy. Laws permitting the emergence of private-sector entrepreneurs do not create entrepreneurship. The reduction of price control does not immediately make goods available or affordable. The abolition of monopolies will not lead to competition overnight. Highly prized fundamentals of the market economy such as the reliance on competition, the support of the profit motive, and the willingness to live with risk on a corporate and personal level are not yet fully accepted (Czinkota & Ronkainen, 1998, p. 776).

Transition is a learning process that needs time and requires a readiness for change on the individual, company, and societal level. Some claim that transition will be a success only when the levels of technological and economic development, income, and consumption are similar to the standards of the industrialized West. This is at least the target and promise set out by politicians in East and West. If the GDP per capita is a valid benchmark then it will take decades, or even generations, before the East catches up. As Exhibit 9.3 indicates, leading reformers like Slovenia or the Czech Republic will reach between 80 and 90% of the EU-average GDP per capita in the year 2010. Other countries are even further behind. Measured this way, it will take a long time to determine the degree of transition success and provide ample room for disagreements, discontent, and reversals of policies.

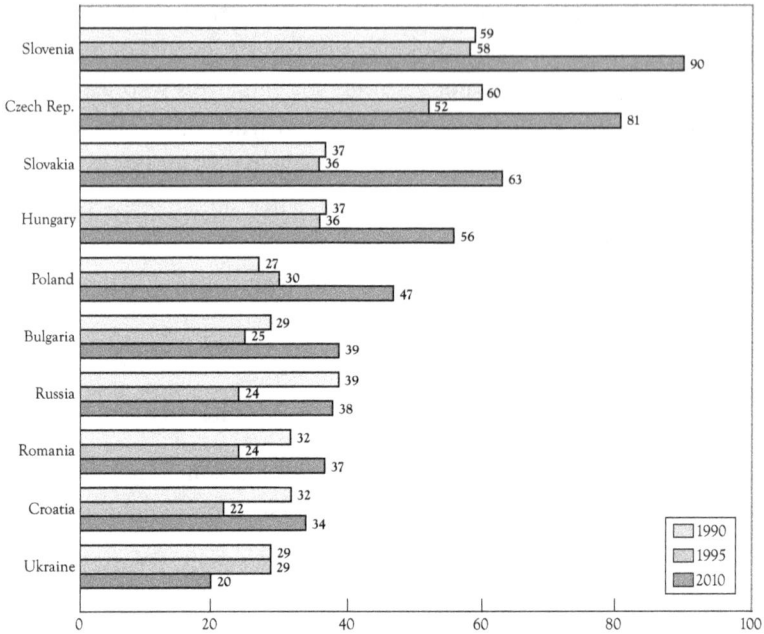

Exhibit 9.3. *GDP per Capita in Central and Eastern Europe Compared to EU Average*

Source: EBRD, 1996, 1997a, 1997b.

But perhaps the forecasts that use short-term situations and conditions to produce long-term projections are limited in their value. We believe that the success of transition needs to be measured not by any particular arbitrary outcome, but by the direction taken by an economy—a direction which attributes value to individual well-being, choice, and empowerment, but also does not neglect the importance of overall societal welfare. Marketing may not succeed in placing the primacy of consumption on the same pedestal that it has in the West. Market forces, however, are instrumental in signaling demand and in helping to determine the allocation of resources.

Nonetheless, existing social structures and expectations may result in the emergence of new marketing concepts or new marketing applications that blend the old with the new. For example, the prized marketing dimension of individual ownership of products may give way to the concept of "product use" and thus permit a more rapid increase in overall welfare levels than would otherwise be possible. A transformation of the spirit of collectivism may give unexpected rise to new concepts of voluntary individual social responsibility, or lead to consumption priorities, which are more oriented toward intangibles. In such instances the implementation of marketing would shift markedly, requiring a major redesign of payment flows, product life cycles, product positioning, and distribution strategies.

The disintegration of the Iron Curtain has introduced marketing thought into Central and Eastern Europe. The entry and presence of Western companies will continue the nurturing of a marketing system. The emergence of an economic area covering the whole of Europe and the enlargement of the European Union toward the East will promote the harmonization of Western and Eastern marketing systems and lead to some convergence of marketing strategies and management styles. But the speed and the outcome of the transformation will vary by country, based on each nation's popular aspirations, leadership, and endowments and on its relationships with the global market. Export-influenced growth will be important. Many Western countries and firms will be surprised by, and will need to adjust to, newly arising competition emanating from the East. However, most of the causes for growth will be rooted in the domestic economy and its institutions and processes. Marketing can contribute to the transition process by informing the population, guiding the leadership, inspiring competition, encouraging supportive global economic relations, and offering choice. But economic interests are only one dimension in an interconnected world, which also looks toward issues such as security, peace, and personal fulfillment. As a discipline, marketing has an opportunity to assume a major role by shaping society and the future of history. However, in this process marketing will not be the focus, but rather the means to an end, the support that helps to achieve a better society. Marketing must also be ready to adapt to local conditions, to reflect newly emerging national priorities, and to offer itself to develop new economic relational approaches, which will lead to growing individual and societal contentment.

References

Brenner, E. (1997). *Werben oder Sterben, Gewinn, 16*(3), 46–48.

Business Central Europe. (1997, May).

Church, N. (1992). Advertising in the Eastern Bloc: Current practices and anticipated avenues of development. *Journal of Global Marketing, 5*(3), 109–129.

Czinkota, M. R. (1998). Hungary in the global economy: Strategies for improved competitiveness. *European Business Journal, 10*(1), 39–45.

Czinkota, M. R., & Dichtl, E. (1996). Export controls and global changes. *Der Markt, 35*(138), 148–155.

Czinkota, M. R., Gaisbauer, H., & Springer, R. (1997). A perspective on marketing in Central and Eastern Europe. *The International Executive, 39*(6), 831–848.

Czinkota, M. R., & Ronkainen, I. A. (1998). *International marketing* (5th ed.). Fort Worth: Dryden Press.

Czinkota, M. R., & Springer, R. (1997) Managementausbildung in Rußland unter den Bedingungen der Transformation zur Marktwirtschaft. *Der Markt, 36*(141), 51–62.

EBRD Transition Report Annually. (1996). *Transition report 1996.*

EBRD Transition Report Annually. (1997a). *Transition report 1997a.*

EBRD Transition Report Annually. (1997b). *Transition report update 1997b.*

EBRD Transition Report Annually. (1998). *Transition report update 1998.*

Ettenson, R. (1993). Brand name and country of origin effects in the emerging market economies of Russia, Poland and Hungary. *International Marketing Review, 10*(5), 14–36.

Feick, L., Coulter, R. H., & Price, L. (1995). Consumers in the transition to a market economy: Hungary, 1989–1992. *International Marketing Review, 12*(5), 18–34.

Gajewski, S. (1992). Consumer behavior in economics of shortage. *Journal of Business Research, 24*(1), 5–10.

Good, L. K., & Huddleston, P. (1995). Ethnocentrism of Polish and Russian consumers: Are feelings and intentions related? *International Marketing Review, 12*(5), 35–48.

Handelsblatt. (1995). No. 206.

Handelsblatt. (1997). No. 77.

Hauch-Fleck, M. L. (1997). Blauäugig kalkuliert. *Die Zeit, 44*(24), 10.

Healey, N. M. (1994, Spring). The transition economies of Central and Eastern Europe: A political, economic, social and technological analysis. *Columbia Journal of World Business*, pp. 62–70.

Heyder, H., Musiol, K., & Peters, K. (1992, March). Advertising in Europe: Attitudes toward advertising in certain key East and West European countries. *Marketing and Research Today*, pp. 58–68.

Hofstede, G. H. (1991, November/December). *Cultures and organizations: Software of the mind.* New York: McGraw Hill.

Hooley, G. (1993). Raising the Iron Curtain: Marketing in a period of transition. *European Journal of Marketing, 11/12*, 6–20.

Huszagh, S. M., Huszagh, F. W., & Hanks, G. F. (1992). Macroeconomic conditions and international marketing management. *International Marketing Review, 9*(1), 6–18.

Jens, U. (1993). Schocktherapie oder Gradualismus? Zur Transformation einer Zentralverwaltungswirtschaft. *Wirtschaftsdienst, 3,* 158–164.

Mayer, C. (1976). Marketing in Eastern European socialist countries. *University of Michigan Business Review, 28*(1), 16–21.

Mueller, R. D., Wenthe, J., & Baron, P. (1993). The evolution of distribution systems: A framework for analysing market changes in Eastern Europe: The case of Hungary. *International Marketing Review, 10*(4), 36–52.

Naor, J. (1986). Toward a socialist marketing concept: The case of Romania. *Journal of Marketing, 50,* 28–39.

Naor, J. (1990). Research on Eastern Europe and Soviet marketing: Constraints, challenges and opportunities. *International Marketing Review, 7*(1), 7–14.

Olivier, M. (1991, Spring). Eastern Europe: The path to success. *Columbia Journal of World Business,* pp. 10–14.

Papadopoulos, N., Heslop, L., & Beracs, J. (1990). National stereotypes and product evaluations in a socialist country. *International Marketing Review, 7*(1), 32–47.

Pribova, M., & Savitt, R. (1995). Attitudes of Czech managers toward markets and marketing. *International Marketing Review, 12*(5), 60–71.

Rose, R., & Hearpfer, C. (1996). Fears and hopes: New democracies barometer survey. *Transition, The World Bank, 7*(5–6), 14.

Samli, C. (1986, Winter). Changing marketing systems in Eastern Europe: What Western marketers should know. *International Marketing Review,* pp. 7–16.

Schüller, A. (1991). Probleme des Übergangs von der Staatswirtschaft zur Marktwirtschaft. In *Zur Transformation von Wirtschaftssystemen: Von der sozialistischen Planwirtschaft zur sozialen Marktwirtschaft.* Marburg: Arbeitsberichte zum Systemvergleich.

Shama, A. (1992). Transforming the consumer in Russia and Eastern Europe. *International Marketing Review, 9*(5), 43–59.

Tesar, G., & Nieminen, J. (1994). Management conflict in joint ventures: A bilateral perspective. In P. Chadraba & R. Springer (Eds.), *Proceedings on the conference on marketing strategies for Central and Eastern Europe.* Vienna.

Trommsdorff, Binsack, Drüner, & Koppelt. (1995). *Erfolgreich kooperieren in Osteuropa.* Köln.

Trommsdorff, V., & Schuchardt, C. (1998). *Transformation osteuropäischer Unternehmen.* Wiesbaden.

Wagner, H. (1991). Einige Theorien des Systemwandels im Vergleich: Und ihre Anwendbarkeit für die Erklärung des gegenwärtigen Reformprozesses in Osteuropa. In K. Backhaus (Ed.), *Systemwandel und reformen in östlichen wirtschaften.* Marburg.

CHAPTER 10

Three Dimensional

The Markets of Japan, Korea, and China Are Far From Homogeneous

Masaaki Kotabe and Crystal Jiang

Asia is one of the world's most dynamic regions, and offers multiple opportunities for businesses and investors. In terms of its nominal gross domestic product (GDP) in 2005, Japan had the largest economy ($4.80 trillion), followed by China ($1.84 trillion) and Korea ($.72 trillion). China's real purchasing power exceeds $7 trillion, Japan's is estimated at $4 trillion, and Korea's is estimated at $1 trillion. These giants' combined purchasing power is comparable to the $12 trillion U.S. economy.

One of the challenges faced by American and other Western multinational companies is a tendency to lump together these markets and assume that Asian consumers have similar tastes and preferences, moderated by different income levels. This is not only a very shortsighted view, but also a risky assumption when entering these markets.

Asian countries have distinct cultural, social, and economic characteristics that affect consumer behavior, with consumers in Japan, Korea, and China differing in brand orientations, attitudes toward domestic and foreign products, quality and price perceptions, and technology feature preferences. A comparative analysis of consumer behaviors can help companies identify effective marketing strategies, and enable them to successfully tackle these Asian markets (see Table 10.1).

Executive Briefing

Globalizing markets might not mean that markets have become similar. Although multinational companies tend to believe that all Asian markets are the same, a comparative analysis proves that consumers in Japan, Korea, and China differ in their brand orientations, attitudes toward domestic and foreign products, quality and price perceptions, and product feature preferences. To ensure success, companies must set aside narrow and risky assumptions, and tailor country-specific strategies to target these consumers.

Brand Orientation

Japan

Of all the developed countries, this is the most brand conscious and status conscious. It is also intensely style conscious: Consumers love high-end luxury goods (especially from France and Italy), purchasing items such as designer handbags, shoes, and jewelry. Since 2001, Hermes, Louis Vuitton (commonly referred to as LVMH), and Coach have opened glitzy flagship stores in Tokyo and enjoyed double-digit sales growth. And the country represents 20% of Gucci's worldwide revenue, 15% of LVMH's, and 12% of Chanel's. It seems that a slumping economy has not inhibited its consumers.

Eager to "know who they are," they prefer brands that contribute to their senses of identity and self-expression. These highly group-oriented consumers are apt to select prestigious merchandise based on social class standards, and prefer products that enhance their status. Accordingly, they attach more importance to the reputation of the merchandise than to their personal social classes.

Noticeably, the country's consumer markets have expanded to China and Korea. In Shanghai or Seoul, you can see the influence of Japan's fashion trends and products. There's even a Chinese word for this phenomenon: *ha-ri*, which means the adoration of Japanese style.

Table 10.1. Market Characteristics of the Three Largest Asian Economies

	Japan	Korea	China
Population (2005)	127 million	48 million	1,306 million
Nominal GDP (2005) ($)	4.80 trillion	.72 trillion	1.84 trillion
GDP purchasing power parity (2004) ($)	3.7 trillion	.92 trillion	7.3 trillion
GDP per capita purchasing power parity (2004) ($)	29,400	19,200	5,600
GDP real growth rate of country (2004) (%)	2.9	4.6	9.1
Degree of luxury brand consciousness	Very strong	Strong	Varied
Preference for foreign products	Strong (particularly for European products)	Weak	Very strong
Price/quality perception	Extremely quality demanding	Polarization of consumption	Very price conscious
Importance of high-tech features on new products	Very high	Very high	Varied

Sources: Central Intelligence Agency, World Factbook, and Index Mundi.

Korea

Consumers have very sophisticated tastes, show immense passion for new experiences, and favor premium and expensive imported products. In 2004, the Korean Retail Index showed continuous growth of premium brands in certain product categories, such as whiskey, shampoo, and cosmetics. Consumers also demonstrate great interest in generational fads (expressions of their generations and cultures, not just of their economics or regions), thereby selecting products that follow their generations' judgments and preferences.

China

Roughly 10–13 million Chinese consumers prefer luxury goods. The majority of them are entrepreneurs or young professionals working for foreign multinational firms. Recent studies found that 24% of the population, mostly in their 20s and 30s, prefers new products and considers technology an important part of life. (Those in their 40s and 50s are price conscious, brand loyal, and less sensitive to technology.) With higher education and purchasing power, this generation is brand and status conscious. It considers luxury goods to be personal achievements, bringing higher social status.

Purchasing behavior tends to vary regionally. Consumers in metropolitan areas follow fashions/trends/styles, prefer novelty items, and are aware of brand image and product quality. These consumers live on the eastern coast—in major cities such as Shanghai, Beijing, Shenzhen, and Dalian. There, luxury brands such as Armani, Prada, and LVMH are considered prominent logos for high-income clientele.

According to LVMH, this country is its fourth-largest market in terms of worldwide sales. It's no wonder that many high-end firms label these consumers "the new Japanese": a group of increasingly wealthy people hungry for brands and fanatical about spending.

Domestic Versus Foreign

Japan

Although consumers are extremely demanding and have different perceptions of products made in other countries, they are generally accepting of quality foreign products. However, Japan is mostly dominated by well-established companies such as Canon, Sony, and Toyota. Many globally successful firms experience great difficulty gaining footholds.

In this market, Häagen-Dazs Japan Inc. succeeded the exit of competitor Ben & Jerry's, dominating the premium ice cream market with a 90% market share. It successfully delivered the message of a "lifestyle-enhancement product" with word-of-mouth advertising, garnering a flood of free publicity. The company flourished by promoting high quality with local appeal.

Korea

These consumers hold negative attitudes toward foreign businesses; the majority believes that these businesses transfer local wealth to other countries, and crowd out small establishments. Consumers are very proud, and demonstrate a complicated love-hate relationship with foreign brands.

Very few consumers understand or speak English, let alone the languages of their closest trading partners: Japan and China. Often, Korean campaigns require significant rebranding—use of localized brands—to influence local perceptions. According to an official at Carrefour (the world's second-largest retailer), the company has difficulty expanding its investments into other provinces because of excessive regulations, and hasn't done enough research to keep up with Korean consumers' needs.

Nevertheless, the country is increasingly comfortable with the presence of foreign companies in previously closed industries. (In fact, the society is much too uncritical and passive in the acceptance of foreign—especially American—products.) And consumers are far less brand conscious than before, and will embrace new products from unknown companies.

China

Attitudes toward foreign products differ, depending on consumers' age groups. Companies can no longer view this country's youth through the lens of traditional cultural values; this generation considers international taste a key factor in making decisions. Conversely, the mature generation (55 years and older) expresses a definite preference for locally made products. In general, consumers believe imported products under foreign brand names are more dependable.

Many foreign companies (e.g., Nike, Nokia, Sony, and McDonald's) have replaced unknown local brands. The country retains more than 300 licensed Starbucks outlets, and chairman Howard Schultz says of this market, "In addition to the 200 million middle-to-upper-class segments of the population that are typically customers for upscale brands, there is a growing affinity from the younger, affluent consumer for Western brands."

However, some foreign companies—with an increased focus on local appeal—have lost their prominent brands' images to domestic rivals, ultimately forfeiting their market share. After all, when this country's consumers are inspired by design and function, they prefer domestic brands because of their good value for the money.

Quality and Price

Japan

These consumers are the world's strictest when it comes to demand for product quality, and they clearly articulate their needs/desires about a product or packaging operation. They view information other than price (e.g., brand, packaging, and advertising) as important variables in assessing quality and making decisions. Compared with Chinese and Korean consumers, they have much higher expectations for products—and are willing to pay premium prices for them. In agricultural produce, for example, they are less tolerant of skin blemishes, small size, and uniformity.

Foreign companies that don't fully understand and meet consumers' needs/expectations struggle with their investments. Although Wal-Mart dwarfs the competition (with $285 billion in 2004 global sales) and owns 42% of all Japanese supermarket chains, it faces losses there. Its "everyday low prices" philosophy doesn't seem to attract Japanese consumers, because they often associate low price with low quality: *yasu-karou, waru-karou*— cheap price, cheap product.

To cater to these consumers, manufacturers have adopted a total quality approach. To survive fierce local competition, Procter & Gamble sought the best available materials for product formulations and packaging. In the process, it learned some invaluable lessons on how to improve operations, and obtained new product ideas from consumers. (Interestingly, the company took this education on the Japanese way of interacting with consumers and applied it globally.) Today, the country serves as Procter & Gamble's major technical center in Asia, where it develops certain global technologies.

McDonald's opened its first store in Tokyo's Ginza district, which is identified with luxury brand-name goods. It purchased expensive land— not justified by the limited profits of a hamburger establishment—to boost the quality image of its product. Today, McDonald's Japan has grown to become the country's largest fast-food chain.

In terms of cost, the younger generation prefers low-priced products— everything priced at 100 yen (similar to U.S. dollar stores). The "two extreme price markets" segmentation model explains how consumers value lower prices for their practical use while paying premium prices for self-satisfaction, social status, and the quality of products—especially those from Europe. As a result, anything that falls in the middle of the price range—such as the country's designer brands—generates petty profits.

Korea

Consumption has been sluggish since the Asian financial crisis of 1997–1999. However, the younger generation is at the forefront of a new and emerging pattern; it holds opposing expectations of/preferences for low-priced and high-priced goods. When purchasing high-tech or fashion-related items, these consumers prefer well-known brands, and tend to purchase expensive goods to attain psychological satisfaction. Yet they are willing to purchase unbranded goods with low prices, as long as the basic features are guaranteed. It has taken several decades for discount stores to surpass the retail market.

China

Most consumers are price sensitive, and try to safeguard part of their income for investment. In 2005, many global automakers readjusted their strategies in this country, based on demand predictions that most consumers would purchase cars priced less than $12,000. One popular Chinese automaker, Chery, priced its QQ model between $5,500 and $7,500; another aggressive domestic automaker, Xiali, priced its cars at similarly affordable prices.

Although this market is lucrative with growing demand, foreign brands (e.g., Honda, General Motors, and Volkswagen Group) cannot compete with Chinese automakers' competitive prices. And when the younger generation worships Western and luxury brands—in eagerness to establish its social identity—it might prefer pirated versions to domestic ones, making anticounterfeiting control a major issue for companies.

Technology Features

Japan

Because of the country's harmonic convergence of the domestic market and the industrial sector, consumers have always preferred high-tech gadgets. According to an estimate by the World Bank Group, the country possesses 410,000 of the world's 720,000 working robots (which perform useful chores and provide companionship). Its electronics companies create gizmos by borrowing new concepts from the computer industry, such as personal video recorders, interactive pagers, and Internet radios.

Instead of looking for cost or value, consumers are willing to pay for better and cooler features and technological sophistication. Largely because of Japan's small living quarters, manufacturers have become experts at miniaturizing and creating multifunction devices. For instance, Sony's PlayStation Portable compacts the power of the original PlayStation into a palm-sized package. According to the company, it can deliver music and MPEG-4 video, can display photos, and even offers a Wi-Fi connection for wireless gaming and messaging. It's also no wonder that the country welcomed Baroke, the first company to successfully produce quality sparkling and still wine in a can.

Korea

The most wired country in the world is a leader in Internet usage and high-tech industries such as mobile phones, liquid crystal displays (LCDs), and semiconductors. It also has widespread broadband, and high volumes of personal computer ownership. While mobile phone sales have cooled in Japan, these consumers continue to trade in phones for newer models about every six months.

According to a Samsung Research Institute survey, consumers prefer to express themselves without following social conventions. The Cyworld virtual community Web site, for instance, provides a subscriber with a private room, a circle of friends, and an endless range of "home" decoration possibilities and cool music. Ever-widening cyberspace reaches more than one-fourth of the population. The younger generation in particular enjoys virtual shopping malls and e-commerce.

China

It is imperative for companies to understand the major differences in consumer behavior between generations. Young Chinese consumers (typically affluent segments in the prosperous cities) are passionate about the latest developments. Recent studies found that 24% of the population—most with ages in the early 20s or 30s—prefer new products and consider technology an important part of life. Those in their 40s–50s, on the other hand, are price conscious, brand loyal, and less sensitive to technology.

Advice and Recommendations

Marketers need to tailor country-specific strategies to target consumers in Japan, Korea, and China. The existence of strategically equivalent segments (e.g., the younger generation, with its propensity to purchase high-quality, innovative, and foreign products) suggests a geocentric approach to global markets. These similarities allow for standardized strategies across national boundaries. By aggregating such segments, companies not only preserve consumer orientation, but also reduce the number of marketing mixes they have to offer—without losing market share, marketing, advertising, research and development, and production throughout Asia.

Moreover, because product design, function, and quality determine consumers' experiences, companies must simultaneously incorporate all areas—such as product development and marketing—to establish commanding positions in mature markets. Once they create positive images in these countries, success will be forthcoming.

Japan

- This is the most profitable market for luxury goods companies. The key to success is promotion of high quality, local appeal, and a sense of extravagance.
- As one of the most volatile markets, it requires a steady flow of new stimuli with an improved rhythm of innovations. To survive, companies must continuously develop new products

and establish prestigious brand value. If they can succeed there, then they can do so anywhere.

- Picky Japanese consumers clearly articulate their requirements about products or packaging operations. As a result, companies can use the country as their technical center—to gain firsthand experience in satisfying consumers in the region.
- These consumers are willing to pay for better and cooler features and technological sophistication. Companies can win their hearts by introducing gizmos.
- Because significant differences exist among generations, and those differences will translate into diverse consumer behaviors, segmentation marketing (identifying variations based on age, region, and gender) is best. Companies must be aware of these differences, and understand what kinds of products/services can meet the market segment's needs. For example, Coca-Cola has introduced more products here than anywhere else, including coffee and green tea beverages that appeal to Japanese tastes. As a result, its net operating revenue represents more than 60% of the total Asian segment (20% of its worldwide revenue).

Korea

- A consumer-oriented approach is crucial for identifying tastes and blending in, rather than being viewed as foreign. Careful market, brand, and advertising testing is imperative.
- It can be difficult to enter this market alone; strategic alliances with domestic companies are a practical way to understand local preferences when introducing a global brand.
- If foreign companies make greater efforts to intensify their involvements with—and long-term commitments to—the country's economic development, then consumers' perceptions of an "invasion" will dissipate over time.
- Product design directly affects a company's competitiveness. This and brand power can overcome product quality, and even product functions. To present the best product design to its consumers, Samsung Electronics hired an influential British

industrial designer. According to the company's Economic Research Institute, a good design "provides a good experience for consumers"; it looks different, feels good, is easy to use, and has an identity.

China

- Foreign companies can no longer wait; the market for consumer goods is growing rapidly, stimulated by a strong economy.
- Its diversity and the vastness of its consumer base make it critical for companies to segment consumers based on demographic, geographic, and psychographic/lifestyle variations.
- Because of the younger generation's brand orientation, promoting symbolic value is imperative for conspicuous and inconspicuous foreign products.
- Multinational companies can't assume that their first-mover advantages will be rewarded for brand recognition and established distribution channels.
- Cost-conscious consumers are quite unpredictable, so companies should avoid a too-high premium price strategy. Instead, they should research quantitatively acceptable price/value trade-offs by category.
- Because local brands are on the rise, foreign companies must work harder to localize research and development and the contents of their products. They must also better evaluate the market and the potential for long-term growth. Without competitive pricing and world-class product design/quality, companies will have a tough time surviving.

Company executives must remember that not all countries are created equally. By understanding and learning to appreciate the differences and similarities between these three Asian purchasing giants, companies from other countries can immerse their organizations seamlessly.

PART III

Global Sourcing and Supply Chain

CHAPTER 11

Global Sourcing Strategy and Sustainable Competitive Advantage

Masaaki Kotabe and Janet Y. Murray

Introduction

Global competition suggests a drastically shortened life cycle for most products and no longer permits companies a polycentric, country-by-country approach to international business. If companies that have developed a new product do follow a country-by-country approach to foreign market entry over time, a globally oriented competitor will likely overcome their initial competitive advantages by blanketing the world markets with similar products in a shorter period of time. Indeed, it is imperative for companies to continuously create and acquire capabilities that would help generate a sustainable competitive advantage over their rivals. Increasingly, how to source globally has become a critical strategic decision that is influenced by the capabilities needed to compete.

Barney (1991, p. 102) has stressed that a firm possesses sustained competitive advantage when it adopts a strategy that is "not simultaneously being implemented by any current or potential competitors and when these other firms are unable to duplicate the benefits of this strategy." Unfortunately, product innovation alone cannot guarantee that a firm would enjoy sustainable competitive advantage. Instead, it is of utmost importance for a firm to complement its product innovation with strong manufacturing and marketing capabilities. This is primarily because, in today's highly competitive market, legal means of protecting proprietary technology have become ineffective as new product innovations are easily reverse engineered, improved upon, and invented around by competitors without violating patents and other proprietary protections (Baumol, Nelson, & Wolff, 1994; Levin, Klevorick, Nelson, & Winter, 1987). Production sharing facilitates technology diffusion through official and unofficial channels among competitors. Obviously, the value of owning technology has lessened drastically in recent years as the inventing company's temporary monopoly over its technology has become transitory.

History has shown repeatedly that in a highly competitive environment many manufacturers begin to either produce in lower-cost locations or outsource components and finished products from lower-cost producers on a contractual original equipment manufacture (OEM) basis. However, companies increasingly outsource to gain access to suppliers' capabilities (Barney, 1999). Global sourcing strategy generally refers to management of (a) logistics identifying which production units will serve which particular markets and how components will be supplied for production and (b) the interfaces among R&D, manufacturing, and marketing on a global basis. The ultimate objective of global sourcing strategy is for the company to exploit both its own and its suppliers' competitive advantages and the comparative locational advantages of various countries in global competition.

First, we explain the nature of global sourcing strategy as practiced by multinational companies in the last 20 years and explore its long-term strategic implications. The world economy in the last two decades of the 20th century was generally characterized by relatively consistent economic growth and predictable currency fluctuations. While the nature of global competition remains the same, the global market environment has drastically changed in the last several years starting with the Asian financial crisis that took place in 1997. Therefore, second, we explore some sourcing strategy implications under current turbulent times.

Global Sourcing as a Business Practice

Without established sourcing plans, distribution, and service networks, it is extremely difficult to exploit both emerging technology and potential markets around the world simultaneously. As a result, the increased pace of new product introduction and reduction in innovational lead time calls for more proactive management of locational and corporate resources on a global basis. We emphasize logistical management of the interfaces of R&D, manufacturing, and marketing activities on a global basis—which we call global sourcing strategy—and also the importance of retaining the company's capability and gaining access to suppliers' capabilities to design and develop major components and finished products. These capabilities allow the company to better understand the cost and quality implications of its sourcing relationship with its suppliers.

Global sourcing strategy requires a close coordination among R&D, manufacturing, and marketing activities across national boundaries (Kotabe & Helsen, 2004, ch. 10). There always exist conflicts in the tug-of-war of differing objectives among R&D, manufacturing, and marketing. Excessive product modification and proliferation for the sake of satisfying the ever-changing customer needs will forsake manufacturing efficiency and have negative cost consequences, barring a perfectly flexible computer-aided design (CAD) and computer-aided manufacturing (CAM) facility. CAD/CAM technology has improved tremendously in recent years, but the full benefit of flexible manufacturing is still many years away. Contrarily, excessive product standardization for the sake of lowering manufacturing costs will also be likely to result in unsatisfied or under-satisfied customers. Similarly, innovative product designs and features as desired by customers may indeed be a technological feat but might not be conducive to manufacturing. Therefore, topics such as product design for manufacturability and components/product standardization have become increasingly important strategic issues. It has become imperative for many companies to develop a sound sourcing strategy in order to exploit most efficiently R&D, manufacturing, and marketing on a global basis.

Executives should understand and appreciate the important roles that product designers, engineers, production managers, and purchasing managers—among others—play in corporate strategy development. Let us look at Toyota's global sourcing strategy as an example.

Toyota is equipping its operations in the United States, Europe, and Southeast Asia with integrated capabilities for creating and marketing automobiles. The company gives the managers at those operations ample authority to accommodate local circumstances and values without diluting the benefit of integrated global operations. Thus, in the United States, Calty Design Research, a Toyota subsidiary in California, designs the bodies and interiors of new Toyota models, including Lexus and Solara. Toyota has technical centers in the United States and in Brussels to adapt engine and vehicle specifications to local needs. Toyota operations that make automobiles in Southeast Asia supply each other with key components to foster increased economies of scale and standardization in those components—gasoline engines in Indonesia, steering components in Malaysia, transmissions in the Philippines, and diesel engines in Thailand. Toyota also started developing vehicles in Australia and Thailand in 2003. These new bases develop passenger cars and trucks for production and sale only in the Asia-Pacific region. The Australian base is engaged mainly in designing cars, while the Thailand facility is responsible for testing them (*Nikkei Net Interactive*, 2002).

In addition to capitalizing on the comparative advantages of different sourcing locations and its own unique capabilities by designing and manufacturing certain components in-house, Toyota also reaps the advantages of outsourcing. To outsource components and parts, Toyota adopts both the arm's-length and partner models in managing their external suppliers. It would purchase necessary, but nonstrategic inputs from independent suppliers on an arm's-length basis to obtain a lower cost for these inputs. Examples would be belts, tires, and batteries that are not customized and do not differentiate its products from its competitors. Strategic inputs that are of high value and provide differentiation (e.g., transmission, engine parts) are sourced from suppliers based on strategic partnerships to gain access to suppliers' capabilities (Dyer, Cho, & Chu, 1998). As a result, Toyota is able to combine its own and its suppliers' unique capabilities to obtain a sustainable competitive advantage over its rivals.

Trends in Global Sourcing Strategy

Over the last 20 years or so, gradual yet significant changes have taken place in global sourcing strategy. The cost-saving justification for international procurement in the 1970s and 1980s was gradually supplanted by quality and reliability concerns in the 1990s. However, most of the changes have been in the way business executives think of the scope of global sourcing for their companies and exploit various opportunities available from it as a source of competitive advantage. Peter Drucker, a famed management guru and business historian, once said that sourcing and logistics would remain the darkest continent of business—the least exploited area of business for competitive advantage. Naturally, many companies, regardless of their nationality, that have a limited scope of global sourcing are at a disadvantage over those that exploit it to the fullest extent in a globally competitive marketplace.

Manufacturers were under pressure to compete on the basis of improved cost and quality as just-in-time (JIT) production was adopted by a growing number of companies. JIT production requires close working relationships with component suppliers and places an enormous amount of responsibility on purchasing managers. Furthermore, sourcing directly from foreign suppliers requires greater purchasing know-how and is riskier than other alternatives that use locally based wholesalers and representatives. Locally based representatives are subject to local laws and assume some of the currency risk associated with importing. However, now that purchasing managers are increasingly making long-term commitments to foreign suppliers, direct dealings with suppliers are justified.

As a global company adds another international plant to its network of existing plants, it creates the need for sourcing of components and other semiprocessed goods to and from the new plant to existing plants. Global manufacturing adds enormously to global sourcing activities either within the same company across national boundaries or between independent suppliers and new plants. Mature companies are increasingly assigning independent design and other R&D responsibilities to satellite foreign units so as to design a regional or world product. As a result, foreign affiliates have also developed more independent R&D activities to manufacture products for the U.S. markets in addition to expanding local sales (Kotabe & Swan, 1994).

Logistics of Sourcing Strategy

Sourcing strategy includes several basic choices companies make in deciding how to serve foreign markets. One choice relates to the use of imports, assembly, or production within the country to serve a foreign market. Another decision involves the use of internal or external supplies of components or finished goods. Therefore, the term "sourcing" is used to describe management by multinational companies of the flow of components and finished products in serving foreign and domestic markets.

Sourcing decision making is multifaceted and entails both contractual and locational implications. From a contractual point of view, the sourcing of major components and products by multinational companies takes place in two ways: (1) from the parents or their foreign subsidiaries on an "intrafirm" basis and (2) from independent suppliers on a "contractual" basis. The first type of sourcing is known as intrafirm sourcing. The second type of sourcing is commonly referred to as outsourcing. Outsourcing can further be broken down into two types: on an arm's length or strategic partnership basis. Similarly, from a locational point of view, multinational companies can procure components and products either (1) domestically (i.e., domestic sourcing) or (2) from abroad (i.e., offshore sourcing).

In developing viable sourcing strategies on a global scale, companies must consider not only manufacturing costs, the costs of various resources, and exchange rate fluctuations, but also availability of infrastructure (including transportation, communications, and energy), industrial and cultural environments, the ease of working with foreign host governments, and so on. Furthermore, the complex nature of sourcing strategy on a global scale spawns many barriers to its successful execution. In particular, logistics, inventory management, distance, nationalism, and lack of working knowledge about foreign business practices, among others, are major operational problems identified by multinational companies engaging in international sourcing.

Some studies have shown, however, that despite, or maybe, as a result of, those operational problems, *where* to source major components seems much less important than *how* to source them (Kotabe & Swan, 1994; Murray, Kotabe, & Wildt, 1995). Thus, when examining the relationship between sourcing and competitiveness of multinational companies, it is crucial to distinguish between sourcing on an "intrafirm" basis and sourcing on a "contractual" basis, for these two types of sourcing will have a different impact on their long-run competitiveness.

Intrafirm Sourcing

Multinational companies can procure their components inhouse within their corporate system around the world. They produce major components at their respective home base and/or at their affiliates overseas to be incorporated in their products marketed in various parts of the world. Thus, trade does take place between a parent company and its subsidiaries abroad and also between foreign subsidiaries across national boundaries. This is often referred to as intrafirm sourcing. If such in-house component procurement takes place at home, it is essentially domestic in-house sourcing. If it takes place at a company's foreign subsidiary, it is called offshore subsidiary sourcing. Intrafirm sourcing makes trade statistics more complex to interpret, since part of the international flow of products and components is taking place between affiliated companies within the same multinational corporate system, which transcends national boundaries. The most recent United Nations official report shows that in 1999, about 34% of world trade is managed by multinational companies on an intrafirm basis (Hamdani, 1999).

Outsourcing

As discussed earlier, Dyer et al. (1998) have observed that Japanese companies make a distinction of outsourcing as to whether it is based on an arm's length or a strategic partnership basis. In the 1970s, foreign competitors gradually caught up in a productivity race with U.S. companies. This coincided with U.S. corporate strategic emphasis shifting from manufacturing to finance and marketing. This strategic shift was based chiefly on a cost–benefit analysis that manufacturing functions could, and should, be transferred to independent operators and subcontractors, depending on the cost differential between in-house and contracted-out production. A company's reliance on domestic suppliers for major components is basically a domestic purchase arrangement. Furthermore, in order to lower production costs under competitive pressure, U.S. companies turned increasingly to outsourcing of components and finished products from abroad, particularly from such countries as China, Singapore, South Korea, Taiwan, Hong Kong, and Mexico. Initially, subsidiaries were set up for production purposes (i.e., offshore subsidiary sourcing), but gradually, independent foreign suppliers took over component production for U.S. companies. This latter phenomenon is usually called offshore outsourcing (or offshore sourcing, for short).

Outsourcing helps reduce fixed investment in in-house manufacturing facilities and thus lower the breakeven point, which subsequently helps boost an outsourcing company's return on equity (ROE). Thus, if corporate executives' performance is evaluated on the basis of their contribution to the company's ROE, they tend to have a strong incentive to increase outsourcing.

Unlike their U.S. counterparts who historically managed all suppliers in an arm's-length fashion, Japanese companies managed their outsourcing activities based on the types of inputs sourced. Although many studies of supplier–assembler relationships in Japan implied that all suppliers are part of the *keiretsu*, this perception is inaccurate (Dyer et al., 1998). Japanese companies differentiate strategic suppliers (*kankei kaisha*) that fall into the *keiretsu* category from independent suppliers (*dokuritsu kaisha*) that do not. In utilizing both types of outsourcing, Japanese companies are able to achieve economies of scale using arm's length transactions. At the same time, they also gain access to their suppliers' capabilities for strategic inputs by using strategic partnerships. In general, "these inputs are not subject to industry standards and may benefit from customization due to multiple interaction effects with other components in the final product" (Dyer et al., 1998, p. 71). It is this unique combination of the firm's and its suppliers' capabilities in producing differentiated components in a product that would provide the firm with sustainable competitive advantage.

Potential Pitfalls in Global Sourcing

As stated earlier, global sourcing strategy requires close coordination of R&D, manufacturing, and marketing activities, among others, on a global basis. While national boundaries have begun losing their significance both as a psychological and as a physical barrier to international business, the diversity of local environments still plays an important role not as a facilitator, but rather as an inhibitor, of optimal global strategy development. Now the question is how successful multinational companies can circumvent the impact of local environmental diversity.

These counteracting forces have since been revisited in such terms as "standardization versus adaptation" (1960s), "globalization versus localization" (1970s), "global integration versus local responsiveness" (1980s), and, most recently, "scale versus sensitivity" (1990s). Terms have changed, but the quintessence of the strategic supply-side and demand-side dilemma that multinational companies face today has not changed and will probably remain unchanged for many years to come.

One thing that has changed, however, is the ability and willingness of these companies to coordinate various activities in an attempt either to circumvent or to nullify the impact of differences in local markets to the extent possible. It may be more correct to say that these companies have been increasingly compelled to take a global view of their businesses, due primarily to increased competition, particularly among the triad regions of the world, namely, North America, Western Europe, and Japan. This contemporary view of competitive urgency is shared by an increasing number of executives of multinational companies, irrespective of nationality.

While U.S. multinational companies have subsidiaries all over the world, they have been somewhat reluctant to develop an integrated and well-coordinated global strategy that European and Japanese multinational companies have managed to establish. In addition, U.S. multinational companies have historically managed their outsourcing activities on an arm's-length basis only to achieve efficiency. Indeed, European and Japanese multinational companies have heavily invested in, and improved upon, their strengths in manufacturing that many U.S. multinational companies have tended to ignore. Furthermore, foreign multinationals, with Japanese companies in particular, have capitalized on differentiated outsourcing to achieve both efficiency and effectiveness. In contrast, U.S. companies tend to rely more on a sequence of new product introductions as a way to maintain their competitive advantage than on well coordinated manufacturing strategy. The lack of emphasis on manufacturing activities has been traced to U.S. management's strategic emphasis having drifted away from manufacturing to marketing and to finance over the years.

As a result, manufacturing management gradually lost its influence in the business organization. Production managers' decision-making authority was reduced such that R&D complied and marketing imposed its own delivery, inventory, and quality conditions, but not productivity considerations. In a sense, production managers gradually took on the role of outside suppliers within their own companies. Production managers' reduced influence in the organization led to a belief that manufacturing functions could be transferred easily to independent operators and subcontractors, depending on the cost differential between in-house and contracted-out production. Thus, in order to lower production costs (i.e., to improve ROE) under competitive pressure, U.S. multinational companies turned increasingly to outsourcing components and finished products from such countries as China, South Korea, Taiwan, Singapore, Hong Kong, and Mexico, among others. Akio Morita, a cofounder of Sony, a highly innovative Japanese electronics company, once chided such U.S. multinational companies as "hollow corporations" that were increasingly adopting a "designer role" in global competition—offering innovations in product design without investing in manufacturing process technology and simply putting their brand names on foreign-made products (Special report: The hollow corporation, 1986).

However, we should not rush to a hasty conclusion that outsourcing certain components and/or finished products from foreign countries will diminish a company's competitiveness. Many multinational companies with plants in various parts of the world are exploiting not only their own and their suppliers' competitive advantages (e.g., R&D, manufacturing, and marketing skills) but also the locational advantages (e.g., inexpensive labor cost, certain skills, mineral resources, government subsidy, and tax advantages) of various countries. Thus, it is also plausible to argue that these multinational companies are in a more advantageous competitive position than are domestic-bound companies.

Then, is the "hollowing-out" phenomenon not indicative of a superior management of both corporate and locational resources on a global basis? What is wrong, if any, with IBM procuring most of its components for its personal computers from independent domestic and foreign suppliers? How about Honeywell marketing in the United States the products manufactured in its European plants? Answers to these questions hinge on a company's ability and willingness to integrate and coordinate various activities and also strategically capitalizing on outsourcing activities based on the types of advantages desired.

Long-Term Consequences

There are two opposing views of the long-term implications of offshore sourcing especially for strategic inputs, dependent on whether the company would differentiate outsourcing activities based on an arm's-length or strategic partnership basis. Many successful companies have established strategic partnerships with their suppliers by developing a dynamic virtual organizational network through increased use of joint ventures, subcontracting, and licensing activities across international borders. However, if suppliers for strategic inputs are managed based on an arm's length basis, there could be negative long-term consequences resulting from a company's dependence on independent suppliers and subsequently the inherent difficulty for the company to keep abreast of constantly evolving design and engineering technologies without engaging in those developmental activities. In this case, companies fail to coordinate and integrate their suppliers' design and production as part of their own activities, as would be the case using strategic partnerships. These two opposing arguments will be elaborated below.

Benefits of Virtual Network

A network of loosely coupled strategic alliances allows each participant to pursue its particular competence. Therefore, each network participant can be seen as complementing rather than competing with the other participants for the common goals. Strategic alliances may even be formed by competing companies in the same industry in pursuit of complementary abilities (new technologies or skills) from each other.

The advantage of forming a virtual network is claimed to be its structural flexibility. Such a network of loosely coupled partnerships can accommodate a vast amount of complexity while maximizing the specialized competence of each member and provide much more effective use of human resources that would otherwise have to be accumulated, allocated, and maintained by a single organization. In other words, a company can concentrate on performing the task at which it is most efficient. This approach is increasingly applied on a global basis with countries participating in a dynamic network as multinational companies configure and coordinate product development, manufacturing, and sourcing activities around the world.

First, due to the need for fast internationalization and related diversification, such alliances provide a relatively easy option to access the world markets, thus allowing the firms in the network to create and maintain a sustainable competitive advantage by combining capabilities and technologies in a unique way. Second, reduced investment requirement for each participating company helps improve its ROE. Thus, for example, AT&T needed Olivetti's established European network to enter the European market for telephone switchboard equipment. Similarly, Toyota established a joint venture with General Motors so that the Japanese carmaker could learn to work with United Auto Workers (UAW) union members while General Motors could learn JIT inventory management from Toyota.

Dependence

In contrast with outsourcing based on strategic partnerships, companies that rely on independent external sources of supply of major components tend to forsake part of the most important value-creating activities to, and also become dependent on, independent operators for assurance of component quality. Furthermore, those multinational companies tend to promote competition among independent suppliers, ensure continuing availability of materials in the future, and exploit full benefits of changing market conditions. In addition, in an arm's length arrangement, competing firms (e.g., in the United States) tend to share a common set of suppliers (Dyer et al., 1998), thus diluting the degree of differentiation of these major components to the buying firms. By attempting to maintain various sources of supply and a high degree of relative bargaining power, companies (e.g., in the United States) may have also restricted the size and scale of their suppliers. Furthermore, individual suppliers are forced to operate in an uncertain business environment that inherently necessitates a shorter planning horizon. The uncertainty about the potential loss of orders to competitors often forces individual suppliers to make operating decisions that will likely increase their own long-term production and materials costs. In the process, this uncertain business environment tends to adversely affect the multinational companies sourcing components and/or finished products from independent suppliers. The rapid decline of IBM offers a vivid classic example of the problems caused by its dependence on independent suppliers for crucial components in the personal computer market.

Gradual Loss of Design and Manufacturing Abilities

Those multinational companies that depend heavily on independent suppliers on an arm's-length basis (i.e., without integrating their suppliers into their activities) also tend in the long run to lose sight of emerging technologies and expertise, which could be incorporated into the development of new manufacturing processes as well as new products. Thus, continual sourcing from independent suppliers, as opposed to sourcing based on strategic partnerships, is likely to forebode companies' long-term loss of the ability to manufacture at competitive cost and, as a result, loss of their global competitiveness. However, if technology and expertise developed by a multinational company are exploited within its multinational corporate system (i.e., by its foreign affiliates and by the parent company itself), the company can retain its technological base to itself without unduly disseminating them to competitors. The benefit of such internalization is likely to be great, particularly when technology is highly idiosyncratic or specific with limited alternative uses, or when it is novel in the marketplace. For such a technology, the market price mechanism is known to break down as a seller and potential buyers of the technology tend to see its value very differently. Potential buyers, who do not have perfect knowledge of how useful the technology will be, tend to undervalue its true market value. As a result, the seller of the technology is not likely to get a full economic benefit of the technology by selling it in the open market.

In addition, by getting involved in design and production on its own or through strategic partnerships, the multinational company can keep abreast of emerging technologies and innovations originating anywhere in the world for potential use in the future. Furthermore, management of the quality of major components is required to retain the goodwill and confidence of consumers in the products, which may be impossible using arm's-length outsourcing. Maintaining the ability to develop major components and finished products in-house or via strategic partnerships allows the company to better understand the cost and quality implications of its sourcing relationship even with its suppliers.

Global Sourcing Strategy in an Unstable World Economy

Since the Asian financial crisis took place in 1997, the world economy has continued to stagnate with many uncertainties that have ensued. The financial crisis in Asia was followed by the terrorist attack on America in 2001 and Argentina's financial crisis worsened in 2002. These crises have finally sent the world economy into a global slowdown. Furthermore, the aftermath of the U.S.-led war against Iraq and the mysterious illness, known as severe acute respiratory syndrome (SARS) spreading from China in 2003 continue to curb the weak world economy from recovering.

As a result, Asia's once booming economies are still fragile, liquidity problems are hurting regional trade, and losses from Asian investments are eroding profits for many multinational companies. Many U.S. companies that have large investments in Asia have reported less than expected earnings. For example, the unsettling ups and downs of the Dow Jones Industrial Average reflect the precarious nature of U.S. investments in Asia. These economic, political, and natural crises and their ramifications could not only have far-reaching economic consequences but also force many companies to adopt new business views and practices for competing around the world at the dawn of the new century.

The global strategy models popularized by Bartlett and Ghoshal (1989) and Porter (1986), among others, are predicated on a complex configuration of assets and capabilities that are specialized but also dispersed. Let us focus on Asia, as it is a major region in which many multinational companies have established procurement bases. Many foreign companies operating in Asian countries tend to procure certain crucial components and equipment from their parent companies or from strategic suppliers overseas. Now that Asian currencies depreciated precipitously during the region's financial crisis, those foreign companies are faced with those imported components and equipment whose prices have gone up enormously in local currencies. In other words, the more dispersed the company's and its suppliers' assets and capabilities are, the more difficult it is for them to manage wild currency fluctuations. Financial hedging has failed to help much.

Companies that have localized procurement do not have to be affected easily by fluctuating exchange rates. As a result, many companies are also scurrying to speed steps toward making their operations in Asian countries more local. Suffering from the recession in their domestic market as well as being most seriously affected by the Asian financial crisis, Japanese companies seem to stay one step ahead of U.S. and European competitors in this localization strategy. Since the yen's sharp appreciation in the mid-1980s, Japanese manufacturers have moved to build an international production system less vulnerable to currency fluctuations by investing in local procurement and more recently have begun to transfer R&D activities to local markets (*Nikkei Weekly*, 1998, 2001). In addition, these Japanese companies have demanded that their strategic suppliers also locate their supply base in these local markets. A case in point: After Honda set up its production in Marysville, Ohio, many of Honda's Japanese suppliers have also invested in Ohio or elsewhere in the United States for producing components and parts to be close to Honda's assembly plant.

When financial hedging could not cope with the extensive currency fluctuations, companies are known to resort to operational hedging. Operational hedging is to shift production and procurement abroad to match revenues in foreign currency. For example, by producing abroad all of the products a company sells in foreign markets, this company could create an operational hedge by shielding itself from fluctuating exchange rates (Bodnar & Marston, 2002).

This localized production and marketing strategy is fundamentally different from local responsiveness, as originally envisioned by Bartlett and Ghoshal (1989). Current localization movement is to address the wild, and sometimes unexpected, currency fluctuations rather than local market needs per se. On the other hand, due to constant cost pressures from many competitors, the need for global integration still remains strong for the sake of cost efficiency.

However, a number of new questions have begun to emerge. In an era of technological obsolescence, no one company possesses the capabilities needed to maintain a sustainable competitive advantage for long. Would outsourcing based on strategic partnerships take on a more important role than in-house sourcing? How could the benefits of global integration be achieved in a localization strategy? Could the results of homegrown R&D activities be easily transferred to local subsidiaries or affiliates for local product development? How could a transnational company manage increasingly localized production and marketing without relinquishing too much autonomy to local subsidiaries and affiliates? These questions beg for answers.

Summary and Future Directions

The scope of global sourcing has expanded over time. Whether or not to procure components or products from abroad was once determined strictly on price and thus strongly influenced by the fluctuating exchange rate. Thus, the appreciation of the dollar prompted companies to increase offshore sourcing, while the depreciation of the dollar encouraged domestic sourcing. Today, many companies consider not simply price but also quality, reliability, and technology of components and products to be procured. These companies design their sourcing decision on the basis of the interplay between their competitive advantages and the comparative advantages of various sourcing locations for long-term gains.

Global sourcing strategy requires close coordination of R&D, manufacturing, and marketing activities on a global basis. Managing geographically separated R&D, manufacturing, and marketing activities, those companies face difficult coordination problems of integrating their and their suppliers' operations and adapting them to different legal, political, and cultural environments in different countries. Furthermore, separation of manufacturing activities involves an inherent risk that manufacturing in the value chain will gradually become neglected. Such neglect can be costly, as continued involvement in manufacturing tends to lead to pioneering product design and innovation over time. An effective global sourcing strategy calls for continual efforts to streamline manufacturing without sacrificing marketing flexibility.

The global strategy model of the 1980s–1990s drove home why it is imperative for globally operating companies to develop an organizational mechanism by which to benefit from both global integration and local responsiveness. Depending on dispersed assets, specialized operations, and interdependent relationships among units of a company, Bartlett and Ghoshal (1989), for example, described the plausible parent-subsidiary relationships for "peacetime" transnational solutions. However, they fell short of offering specific solutions as to how to cope with the world market not so peaceful, characterized by wild and unpredictable currency fluctuations as well as other unfortunate regional events. They developed a very useful conceptual framework to address the climate of the time of the 1980s–1990s. The climate has changed since the Asian financial crisis that wreaked havoc over what could otherwise have been a stable and growing world economy.

Although it is beyond the scope of this article, one broad solution may be found in modular production, or the application of modular design capabilities in product development (Bettis & Hitt, 1995; Sanchez, 1999; Schilling, 2000). Again, this view is consistent with global marketers' four alternative specifications on global product policy. Modular production generally refers to the process of assembling final products from a number of predetermined and interchangeable modules. The fundamental difference, however, is that modular production could reduce the inherent difficulty in technology transfer, in particular, that of tacit knowledge, between units of a company, thereby making decentralized/localized production feasible without losing the benefits of global integration. Another solution is attaining strategic flexibility in sourcing. Companies should design their structure to include a combination of a quasi-hierarchical and a pure hierarchical governance structure for different activities or operations in order to "integrate, build, and configure internal and external competences to address rapidly changing environments" (Teece, Pisano, & Shuen, 1997, p. 516). A combination of a quasi-hierarchical (e.g., strategic partnerships with suppliers) and a pure hierarchical governance structure allows a firm not only to exploit its own capabilities, but also to explore new capabilities or technologies through learning from its partners, sharing risks, and gaining synergy.

Clearly, more research is needed. One thing is clear: Globally operating companies need to be in constant search of methods to "kill two birds with one stone," or meeting supply-side and demand-side counteracting forces head-on for their sustainable competitive advantage.

References

Barney, J. B. (1991). Firm resources and sustained competitive advantage. *Journal of Management, 17*(1), 99–120.

Barney, J. B. (1999). How a firm's capabilities affect boundary decisions. *Sloan Management Review, 40*(3), 137–145.

Bartlett, C. A., & Ghoshal, S. (1989). *Managing across borders.* Boston: Harvard Business School Press.

Baumol, W. J., Nelson, R. R., & Wolff, E. N. (1994). *Convergence of productivity: Cross-national studies and historical evidence.* New York: Oxford University Press.

Bettis, R. A., & Hitt, M. A. (1995). The new competitive landscape. *Strategic Management Journal, 16*(Special Issue), 7–19.

Bodnar, G. M., & Marston, R. C. (2002). *A simple model of foreign exchange exposure* (Working Paper). Philadelphia: University of Pennsylvania.

Dyer, J. H., Cho, D. S., & Chu, W. (1998). Strategic supplier segmentation: The next "best practice" in supply chain management. *California Management Review, 40*(2), 57–77.

Hamdani, K. (1999, September 26–28). The role of foreign direct investment in export strategy. Paper presented at the 1999 Executive Forum on National Export Strategies, International Trade Centre, the United Nations.

Kotabe, M., & Helsen, K. (2004). *Global marketing strategy* (3rd ed.). Hoboken, NJ: Wiley.

Kotabe, M., & Swan, K. S. (1994). Offshore sourcing: Reaction, maturation, and consolidation of U.S. multinationals. *Journal of International Business Studies, 25*(First Quarter), 115–140.

Levin, R. C., Klevorick, A. K., Nelson, R. R., & Winter, S. G. (1987). Appropriating the returns from industrial research and development. *Brookings Papers on Economic Activity, Issue 3,* 783–831.

Murray, J. Y., Kotabe, M., & Wildt, A. R. (1995). Strategic and financial performance implications of global sourcing strategy: A contingency analysis. *Journal of International Business Studies, 26*(First Quarter), 181–202.

Nikkei Net Interactive. (2002, December 4). Toyota, Nissan, Mitsubishi to expand overseas development bases. Retrieved December 4, 2002, from http://www.nni.nikkei. co.jp

Nikkei Weekly. (1998, January 12). Manufacturers reshape Asian strategies. 1 and 5.

Nikkei Weekly. (2001, June 18). Japanese R&D trickling overseas: Skilled, cheap work forces in other Asian nations attracting Japanese firms. Retrieved June 18, 2001, from http://www.nni.nikkei.co.jp

Porter, M. E. (Ed.) (1986). *Competition in global industries.* Cambridge, MA: Harvard Business School Press.

Sanchez, R. (1999). Modular architecture in the marketing process. *Journal of Marketing, 63*(Special Issue), 92–111.

Schilling, M. A. (2000). Towards a general modular systems theory and its application to inter-firm product modularity. *Academy of Management Review, 25,* 312–334.

Special report: The hollow corporation. (1986, March 3). *Business Week,* pp. 56–59.

Teece, D. J., Pisano, G., & Shuen, A. (1997). Dynamic capabilities and strategic management. *Strategic Management Journal, 18*(7), 509–533.

CHAPTER 12

Outsourcing, Performance, and the Role of E-Commerce

A Dynamic Perspective

Masaaki Kotabe, Michael J. Mol, and Janet Y. Murray

Introduction

History has repeatedly shown that in a highly competitive global environment, many manufacturers begin to either set up manufacturing facilities in lower-cost locations or outsource components and finished products from lower-cost producers on a contractual original equipment manufacture (OEM) basis. Without established sourcing plans, distribution, and service networks, it is extremely difficult to exploit both emerging technology and potential markets around the world simultaneously. As a result, the increased pace of new product introduction and reduction in innovational lead time calls for more proactive management of locational and corporate resources on a global basis. Following this trend, increased outsourcing of manufacturing activities has become a prominent part of the restructuring of firms' supply chains since the 1990s. Many academics and consultancy firms seem to support the view of outsourcing as one of the key drivers of superior performance.

Outsourcing strategy is part and parcel of the value chain of corporate activities. Outsourcing strategy not only affects but also is affected by the other aspects of the firm's supply chain. Levy (2005) has asserted that the core driver of the latest form of global outsourcing is the increasing organizational and technological capacity of firms in decoupling and coordinating a network of remotely located external suppliers performing an intricate set of activities. Thus, executives should understand and appreciate the important roles that product designers, engineers, production managers, and purchasing managers, among others, play in global sourcing strategy development. Let us look at Toyota's global sourcing strategy as an example.

Toyota is equipping its operations in the United States, Europe, and Southeast Asia with integrated capabilities for creating and marketing automobiles. The company gives the managers at those operations ample authority to accommodate local circumstances and values without diluting the benefit of integrated global operations. Thus, in the United States, Calty Design Research, a Toyota subsidiary in California, designs the bodies and interiors of new Toyota models, including Lexus and Solara. Toyota has technical centers in the United States and in Brussels to adapt engine and vehicle specifications to local needs. Toyota operations that make automobiles in Southeast Asia supply each other with key components to foster increased economies of scale and standardization in those components—gasoline engines in Indonesia, steering components in Malaysia, transmissions in the Philippines, and diesel engines in Thailand. Toyota also started developing vehicles in Australia and Thailand in 2003. These new bases develop passenger cars and trucks for production and sale only in the Asia-Pacific region. The Australian base is engaged mainly in designing cars, while the Thai facility is responsible for testing them.

In addition to capitalizing on the comparative advantages of different sourcing locations and its own unique capabilities by designing and manufacturing certain components in-house (i.e., insourcing), Toyota also reaps the advantages of outsourcing. To outsource manufacturing activities, Toyota adopts both the arm's length and partner models in managing its external suppliers. It would purchase necessary, but nonstrategic inputs from independent suppliers on an arm's length basis to obtain a lower cost for these inputs. Examples would be belts, tires, and batteries that are not customized and do not differentiate its products from its competitors. Strategic inputs that are of high value and provide differentiation (e.g., transmission or engine parts) are sourced from suppliers based on strategic partnerships to gain access to suppliers' capabilities, and yet other activities are still performed inside Toyota (Kotabe & Murray, 2004). In 2000 Toyota was approached by General Motors and Ford to jointly develop an online business-to-business (B2B) automotive components clearinghouse. Although Toyota declined to join because it was not convinced of the wisdom of standardizing parts with other automakers, General Motors and Ford, along with Daimler-Chrysler, proceeded to create Covisint to jointly address escalating costs and inefficiencies in their supply-chain management.[1]

In this chapter, we seek to bring together various empirical trends and to provide a coherent explanation for these. As the Toyota example shows, the first trend is that we see increased, but not unlimited, outsourcing. The second trend, which we discuss relatively sparingly (for more details see, for example, Van der Valk & Wynstra, 2005), is in an increase in partnership-type supplier relations. And the third trend is the adoption of electronic commerce (e-commerce) in these supplier relations. In Section 2 we conceptualize global sourcing strategy. In Section 3 we raise the question of how outsourcing affects firm-level performance by arguing that there is an inverted-U shape relationship between them. Section 4 takes up the theme of e-commerce, and describes how the introduction of e-commerce in supplier relations affects this inverted-U shape relationship. We conclude by sketching some managerial and research implications of our work.

Global Sourcing Strategy

Global sourcing strategy refers to identifying which production units will serve which particular markets and how components will be supplied for production, and thus includes a number of basic choices companies make in deciding how to serve various markets. One choice relates to the use of imports, assembly, or production within the country to serve a foreign market. Another decision involves the use of internal or external supplies of components or finished goods. Therefore, the term "sourcing" is used to describe how multinational companies manage the flow of components and finished products in serving foreign and domestic markets.

Sourcing decision making is multifaceted and entails both contractual and locational implications. From a contractual point of view, the sourcing of major components and products by multinational companies takes place in two ways: (a) from the parents or their foreign subsidiaries on an "intrafirm" basis and (b) from independent suppliers on a "contractual" basis. The first type of sourcing is known as insourcing. The second type of sourcing is commonly referred to as outsourcing. Outsourcing can further be broken down into two types: on an arm's length or strategic partnership basis. Similarly, from a locational point of view, multinational companies can procure components and products either (a) domestically (i.e., onshoring) or (b) from abroad (i.e., offshoring).

In developing viable sourcing strategies on a global scale, companies must consider not only manufacturing costs, the costs of various resources, and exchange rate fluctuations, but also availability of infrastructure (including transportation, communications, and energy), industrial and cultural environments, the ease of working with foreign host governments, and so on. Furthermore, the complex nature of sourcing strategy on a global scale spawns many barriers to its successful execution. In particular, logistics, inventory management, distance, nationalism, and a lack of working knowledge about foreign business practices, among others, are major operational problems identified by multinational companies engaging in global sourcing.

Some studies have shown, however, that despite—or maybe as a result of—those operational problems, *where* to source major components seems much less important than *how* to source them (Kotabe & Swan, 1994; Mol, van Tulder, & Beije, 2005; Murray, Kotabe, & Wildt, 1995). Thus, when examining the relationship between sourcing and competitiveness of multinational companies, it is crucial to distinguish between insourcing and outsourcing, for these two types of sourcing will have a different impact on their long-term competitiveness.

Insourcing

Multinational companies can procure their components inhouse within their corporate system around the world. They produce major components at their respective home base and/or at their affiliates overseas to be incorporated in their products marketed in various parts of the world. Thus, trade takes place between a parent company and its subsidiaries abroad, and also between foreign subsidiaries across national boundaries. This is often referred to as insourcing. If such in-house component procurement takes place at home, it is essentially onshore insourcing. If it takes place at a company's foreign subsidiary, it is called offshore insourcing. Insourcing makes trade statistics more complex to interpret, since part of the international flow of products and components is taking place between affiliated companies within the same multinational corporate system, which transcends national boundaries. One-third of multinational companies' trade is accounted for by insourcing activities between the multinational parent company and its affiliates or among those affiliates (UNCTAD, 2002).

Outsourcing

Dyer, Cho, and Chu (1998) have observed that Japanese companies make a distinction of outsourcing as to whether it is based on an arm's length or a strategic partnership basis. In the 1970s, foreign competitors gradually caught up in a productivity race with U.S. companies. This coincided with U.S. corporate strategic emphasis shifting from manufacturing to finance and marketing. This strategic shift was based chiefly on a cost–benefit analysis that manufacturing functions could, and should, be transferred to independent operators and subcontractors, depending upon the cost differential between in-house and contracted-out production. A company's reliance on domestic suppliers for major components is basically a domestic purchase arrangement (i.e., onshore outsourcing). Furthermore, in order to lower production costs under competitive pressure, U.S. companies turned increasingly to outsourcing of components and finished products from abroad (i.e., offshore outsourcing), particularly from such countries as China, India, South Korea, Taiwan, Hong Kong, and Mexico. Initially, subsidiaries were set up for production purposes (i.e., offshore insourcing), but gradually, independent foreign suppliers took over component production for U.S. companies. This latter phenomenon is usually called offshore outsourcing (or offshore sourcing, for short). Although there are exceptions such as Philips and Sanofi-Aventis, many European firms have been relatively slow in adopting offshore outsourcing strategy.

Outsourcing helps reduce fixed investment in in-house manufacturing facilities and thus lower the breakeven point, which subsequently helps boost an outsourcing company's return on equity (ROE). Thus, if corporate executives' performance is evaluated on the basis of their contribution to the company's ROE, they tend to have a strong incentive to increase outsourcing. This financial logic appealed in particular to U.S. corporate executives who tend to be evaluated on relatively short-term results.

Unlike their U.S. counterparts who historically managed all suppliers in an arm's length fashion, Japanese companies managed their outsourcing activities based on the types of inputs sourced. Although many studies of supplier–assembler relationships in Japan implied that all suppliers are part of the *keiretsu*, this perception is inaccurate (Dyer et al., 1998). Japanese companies differentiate strategic suppliers (*kankei kaisha*) that fall into the *keiretsu* category from independent suppliers (*dokuritsu kaisha*) that do not. In utilizing both types of outsourcing, Japanese companies are able to achieve economies of scale using arm's length transactions. At the same time, they also gain access to their suppliers' capabilities for strategic inputs by using strategic partnerships for improved long-term performance (Dyer et al., 1998). Therefore, the performance implications of outsourcing strategy are multifaceted and require careful examination.

Outsourcing and Firm Performance

Outsourcing has become one of the buzzwords in managerial practice today. Similarly, it has received an increasing amount of academic attention (Domberger, 1998; Leiblein, Reuer, & Dalsace, 2002; Porter, 1997; Quinn, 1999). Yet, conflicting predictions have arisen over its performance implications with varying attention for its benefits and drawbacks. Practitioners are now beginning to doubt whether universally prescribing outsourcing is the right way to go (Doig, Ritter, Speckhals, & Woolson, 2001). Indeed, Gottfredson, Puryear, and Phillips (2005) found that about 50% of firms in their sample reported that their outsourcing programs fell short of expectations. Only 10% were highly satisfied with the cost savings, and 6% were highly satisfied with their offshore outsourcing overall. Similarly, Booz Allen Hamilton recently found that the success rate of outsourcing deals from the customer's perspective was only 12% (*The global outsourcing*, April 3, 2006). Likewise, some researchers have even suggested that outsourcing may not be directly related to performance (Leiblein et al., 2002).

Thus, our thinking on outsourcing strategy and firm performance may have to be redefined. Watson, Zinkhan, and Pitt (2004) offer a useful theoretical framework for examining the performance implications of outsourcing strategy. When independent firms operate in a network, they face two kinds of costs (coordination costs and suboptimality costs) depending upon the level of their autonomy in the network. While their autonomous operations may lower coordination costs within a network (albeit maintaining their own respective capabilities), such autonomous operations may result in less than optimal performance for the network as a whole. On the other hand, while more coordinated operations by network firms may improve network performance, such coordinated operations may result in increased coordination costs.

The outsourcing strategy literature offers arguments both for and against outsourcing strategy. In essence, those who argue in favor of outsourcing strategy base their argument on the benefit of reduced coordination costs as a result of increased autonomous operations by firms in a network. This argument is based primarily on short-term benefits. On the other hand, those who argue against outsourcing strategy derive their view primarily from increased coordination costs as a result of the network firms' increased attempt to accomplish an optimal network performance. Their argument is based more on long-term benefits.

Short-term vs. long-term views on outsourcing seem consistent with institutional perspectives on managerial innovations (Westphal, Gulati, & Shortell, 1997). Early adopters of outsourcing strategy indeed experienced efficiency gains as they were able to reduce fixed investment in in-house manufacturing facilities and boost their ROE. Later adopters may have jumped on the outsourcing bandwagon to gain institutional legitimacy or because of competitive pressures in the industry, despite some inherent uncertainties about the long-term costs and benefits of outsourcing strategy (Abrahamson & Rosenkopf, 1993). Naturally, some deviation from an optimal level of outsourcing is bound to occur and bandwagoning can provide one important explanation for it.

We posit that the outsourcing-performance relationship inherently takes on an inverted-U shape, implying that there is an optimal degree of outsourcing for every individual firm and that as a firm deviates further from its optimum, either by insourcing or outsourcing too much, its performance will suffer disproportionately. Based on this perspective, we first address these arguments and then combine them to develop a dynamic perspective of the performance implications of outsourcing strategy for firm performance. Note that our focus is not on any single outsourcing decision or transaction, but rather on the overall extent of outsourcing of a business unit, across all of the activities performed to meet customer demand.

The Case for Outsourcing

Various arguments have been supplied to make the case for outsourcing. We briefly outline these arguments to explain why firms would want to outsource.

Strategic Focus/Reduction of Assets

Through outsourcing activities, a firm can reduce its level of asset investment in manufacturing and related areas. Therefore, stock markets usually react favorably to outsourcing since more or less similar absolute profit levels can be obtained with lower fixed investments (Domberger, 1998). Furthermore, outsourcing can help the management of a firm redirect its attention to its core competencies, instead of having to possess and keep updated a wide range of competencies.

Complementary Capabilities/Lower Production Costs

External suppliers are often highly specialized in the production of components or products, allowing them to produce at lower costs than the outsourcing firm could due to scale economies. Therefore, a firm can improve production cost levels by outsourcing noncore activities (Hendry, 1995; Quinn, 1999). Firms are increasingly relying on third-party specialists to help with administrative matters, thus avoiding the high cost of new technology, and allowing their own human resources professionals to focus on transforming their human capital into a real strategic advantage (Corbett, 2006). Indeed, Everest Research Institute's recent study found that human resources outsourcing arrangements increased by more than 40% in 2005 alone (Corbett, 2006).

Strategic Flexibility

Global outsourcing may increase the firm's strategic flexibility. By using outside sources, it is much easier to switch from one supplier to another (Harris, Giunipero, & Hult, 1998). If an external shock occurs, firms are better able to deal with it by simply increasing or decreasing the volumes obtained from an external supplier. If the same item were produced in-house (i.e., insourcing), there would not only be high restructuring costs, but also a much longer response time to external events.

Avoiding Bureaucratic Costs

Rising production costs are associated with internal production (D'Aveni & Ravenscraft, 1994). More generally, there is a lack of a price mechanism and economic incentives inside a firm (Domberger, 1998). To the extent that such incentives are missing, firm efficiency will suffer as a consequence.

Relational Rent

In recent years, many researchers have argued that certain relationships with external suppliers can deliver competitive advantage (e.g., Dyer & Singh, 1998). By outsourcing items and then building idiosyncratic and valuable relationships with suppliers, firms may be able to innovate, learn, and reduce transaction costs.

The Case Against Outsourcing

Extant literature on outsourcing strategy has also highlighted the disadvantages of outsourcing strategy.

Interfaces/Economies of Scope

Firms may benefit from internalizing production through scope economies (D'Aveni & Ravenscraft, 1994). Kotabe (1998) has suggested that
manufacturing firms, in their outsourcing decisions, ought to reflect on
the interfaces among R&D, manufacturing, and marketing. If there are
important interfaces between activities, decoupling them into separate
activities performed by separate suppliers will generate less than optimal
results and potential integration problems.

Hollowing Out

Firms that excessively outsource activities are hollowing out their competitive base (Kotabe, 1998). Once activities have been outsourced, it
tends to become difficult to differentiate a firm's products on the basis of
these activities. Furthermore, a firm could lose bargaining power vis-à-vis
its suppliers because the capabilities of the suppliers increase relative to
those of the firm.

Opportunistic Behavior

External suppliers may behave opportunistically (Williamson, 1985) as
their incentive structure varies widely from that of the outsourcing firms.
Opportunistic behavior allows a supplier to extract more rents from the
relationship than it would normally do, for example by supplying a lower
than agreed-on product quality or withholding information on changes
in production costs.

Rising Transaction and Coordination Costs

Hendry (1995) has emphasized the issue of the high coordination costs
incurred due to excessive outsourcing. Firms are limited in their capacity
to work with external suppliers as partners, and therefore have to prioritize external partners. If they simultaneously invest time in and pay attention to all external suppliers, this would induce very high coordination
costs indeed. Rottman and Lacity (2006) recently concluded that U.S.
customers micromanage their offshore suppliers to a much greater degree

than they manage their domestic suppliers. They found that transaction costs for offshore projects neared 50% of contract value, compared to 5 to 10% for domestically outsourced projects.

Limited Learning and Innovation

A form of learning that is deemed especially important for attaining tacit knowledge is learning-by-doing. External suppliers will acquire tacit knowledge by performing the activity, but in this case the outsourcing firm cannot appropriate all benefits. Appropriation of innovations and rents is always a problem in buyer–supplier relationships (Nooteboom, 1999) because both parties will try to obtain as many private benefits as possible. Furthermore, it may become more difficult to innovate, given differing incentives and the subsequent lack of interfaces between firms.

Higher Procurement Costs Due to Fluctuating Currency Exchange Rates

During the Asian financial crisis, many foreign firms operating in Asian countries learned an invaluable lesson on the negative impact of fluctuating currency exchange rates on their procurement costs and profitability. Multinational companies (MNCs) operating in Asian countries tend to procure certain crucial components and equipment from the parent companies and other suppliers using global outsourcing. When Asian currencies depreciated precipitously, these MNCs' subsidiaries were faced with imported components and equipment whose prices had increased enormously in local (i.e., Asian) currencies. In other words, the more dispersed these MNCs' assets, capabilities, and activities are due to global outsourcing, the more difficult it is for them to manage wild currency exchange rate fluctuations, and the higher the probability that they will suffer from increased procurement costs and lower profits (Kotabe, 2002).

A Dynamic Perspective

Given the conflicting predictions on the performance impact of outsourcing, with some arguments in favor of outsourcing yet others against it, there is a need to synthesize the arguments. We approach this by evaluating the proposed consequences of each. Proponents of outsourcing argue that firms which procure almost all of their activities internally will be so far removed from the market that their efficiency tends to suffer. In other words, if almost no outsourcing is undertaken, there will be no benchmark available that would permit a firm to judge how efficient its own activities are relative to the market. If outsourcing is undertaken, such a beacon exists. The less outsourcing, the more inefficient firms tend to be.

However, others have argued that insourcing has its merits. Put differently, outsourcing also seems to have negative effects on a range of performance indicators. Thus, there are reasons to argue for a negative relationship between outsourcing and performance. Opponents of outsourcing particularly warn of the long-term detrimental effects of excessive outsourcing. Firms that become hollow or virtual lack a solid basis for competing, and can neither innovate enough nor learn much. The disadvantages of outsourcing are at their worst when firms outsource (almost) everything.

In general, one could argue that there is a feasible range of outsourcing strategies where firms can uphold reasonable performance. If, however, they implement either very high insourcing or very high outsourcing, their competitive position and performance will suffer deeply. Simply stated, too little outsourcing tends to result in internal bureaucratic and other nonmarket inefficiency, while too much outsourcing tends to result in external relational inefficiency and technological dependence. Moving toward a high level of insourcing (i.e., vertical integration) implies that firms could lose touch with the efficient production propagated by markets. They could face staggering production costs as some U.S. and British conglomerates discovered in the 1980s and 1990s before being dissolved. The reverse can be equally true. As has been argued by Chesbrough and Teece (1996), *virtual* is not always virtuous. This is a lesson many dot-com firms have learned over the past several years. Their extreme degree of outsourcing, coupled with a lack of internal capabilities has led to very high transaction costs, for example, in terms of having to obtain those capabilities externally through acquisitions in the stock market, or even losing touch with reality (Doig et al., 2001; Krugman, 2001).

Combining these two perspectives, we expect an inverted-U shape relationship, since the extremes produce the worst possible outcomes, while there is some optimum in the middle (see Exhibit 12.1). In other words, a firm has some overall optimal level of outsourcing that lies in between complete integration (i.e., insourcing) and complete outsourcing. This explains why firms never integrate all of their activities nor outsource them all. Also, one should note that we do not argue there is a universal single optimum. Rather, each firm will have its own optimal level, depending on factors at the country, industry, firm, and transaction levels.

Another justification for this proposed relationship is to consider a firm as a bundle of activities needed to satisfy customer demand. To the left of the optimum we find activities that should be best outsourced because the costs of insourcing do not outweigh the benefits. This includes, at very low levels of outsourcing (i.e., near the left-hand extreme of Exhibit 12.1), activities that are simply procured in an arm's length manner. For these activities it is very costly to make the wrong decision— to insource when outsourcing is much more appropriate. As we move towards the optimum, we find activities where it becomes progressively less clear that outsourcing is the best solution. These activities should still be outsourced, but will be outsourced through partnerships with external suppliers. This involves reciprocal sharing of knowledge with the supplier undertaking production of the activity

As we move beyond the optimum, on the right-hand side of Exhibit 12.1, we will first find activities for which integration is the better choice, but not by a large margin. These will be produced by the firm itself but with inputs from suppliers and others (open innovation R&D activities could be an example). As we move closer to the right-hand extreme of Exhibit 12.1, we find activities for which insourcing should be an

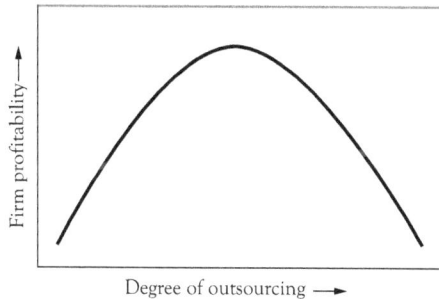

Exhibit 12.1. The relationship between the degree of outsourcing and firm profitability.

increasingly obvious choice, and for which making the wrong choice (i.e., outsourcing instead of insourcing) is an increasingly costly mistake. Outsourcing of top management of a firm comes to mind as an example of this category.

Some Empirical Illustrations

In a separate paper (Kotabe & Mol, 2005), we tested this hypothesized relationship empirically and found compelling evidence in favor of it. The test involves around 1,100 manufacturing businesses operating in the Netherlands. We regressed their overall performance on their overall outsourcing level and a range of control variables, in line with the level of analysis proposed in this chapter, and take into account a time lag to counter problems of reverse causality. The tests also showed that the steepness of this curve is moderated by the level of uncertainty the business faces, which confirms the importance of the dimensions suggested by transaction cost economics.

Other empirical research confirms that there is indeed a spread of activities similar to that suggested by the curve presented in Exhibit 12.1. There are those activities that are almost always outsourced, and for which it matters more how outsourcing is organized. Poppo and Zenger (1998), for instance, investigate different types of supplier relations in IT outsourcing. There are activities which are closer to the optimal level and which can either be outsourced or integrated. The popular press regularly publishes stories on failed outsourcing attempts and management consultants have started to suggest there should be some balance in a firm's outsourcing levels, arguing that "farming out in-house operations has become a religion. Now it must be tempered by reason" (Doig et al., 2001, p. 25). Abrahamson (2004) discusses how Cisco outsourced, integrated, and again outsourced a particular project over a 2-year time span. Parmigiani (2007) discusses why firms would simultaneously make and buy the same goods, reminiscent of earlier discussions of taper integration in the literature. And there is still a class of activities (a class that is probably shrinking, as we will discuss in Section 4) that is never outsourced and therefore not researched in any detail either. A prominent example would be the making of outsourcing decisions and the subsequent management of outsourcing. Firms keep these activities in-house.

The Impact of E-Commerce

This hypothesized relationship can be further extended to bring in the other empirical trends mentioned in the introduction—partnership relationships with suppliers and the rise of ecommerce. We use the term e-commerce broadly to refer to exchanges culminating in transactions between buyers and suppliers based on computer and information technology. Examples might include electronic (Web-based) auctions, Electronic Data Interchange (EDI), file-sharing protocols for product design, and perhaps even video conferencing.

Technological change can alter the effectiveness of the make and/or buy options because it affects transaction and production costs and firm capabilities.[2] New technology can, for instance, enable instant contact with a supplier or electronic information sharing between buyers and suppliers (Eng, 2004). These types of information sharing can facilitate coordination between various players in a supply chain and thus lower transaction costs. As Hamel (2000, p. 99) succinctly put it, "The fact remains that vertical integration, which was in the past a response to high transactions costs (which could be lowered by bringing key functions inside the corporate boundary), is becoming less critical in a world where real-time information allows for transparency and trust between business partners." Hence e-commerce helps facilitate partnership relations with outside suppliers.

There is a long-standing debate around the possible effects of IT and e-commerce on outsourcing levels. First, it is argued that that IT reduces the transaction costs associated with operating in the market (e.g., Malone, Yates, & Benjamin, 1987). Furthermore, reduced communication costs as a result of IT even permit smaller suppliers to extend their geographical market boundaries (e.g., Downes & Mui, 1998). Because of these lower transaction costs, it is argued that markets become relatively more beneficial when compared to hierarchies. Hence, the increasing use of IT should lead to more outsourcing, and developments in IT indeed are a prime, if not the prime, driver of outsourcing. On the other hand, other authors countered this notion. Clemons, Reddi, and Rowe (1993) spoke of the move towards the middle, by which they implied the formation of networks and partnership relations rather than either markets or hierarchies. Because information becomes so much easier to spread to many actors simultaneously through electronic means—for example, by copying multiple recipients into an e-mail—IT supports electronic networks. Holland and Lockett (1997) described the formation of such networks in more details by explaining how the introduction of EDI solidified existing cooperative relations rather than leading to more market-like conditions. These authors therefore believed that the introduction of information systems further promotes the formation of interfirm networks of perhaps changing composition in which cooperative ties are formed between buyers and suppliers. The option of creating networks of suppliers, facilitated by e-commerce, makes outsourcing an even more interesting option.

Regardless of the specific form that buyer-supplier relations takes on, whether it be arm's length market-like relationships or cooperative network relations, there therefore appears to be broad agreement that the introduction of new information technology supports more outsourcing, or put more negatively, makes vertical integration a less attractive alternative, although IT can also lower the internal costs of communication substantially. This impact may differ according to the stages of the sourcing process. E-commerce is particularly effective in reducing the costs and increasing the effectiveness of search. Internet technology, for instance, can now be used to search for providers of offshore outsourcing services all over the globe. But the costs of evaluating these suppliers and their product and service offerings are harder to change through the use of e-commerce alone. Evaluation normally involves getting to know the other party in details, finding out about the other party's history of relations with other buyers through personal connections and establishing effective communications. E-commerce now lends itself somewhat for these purposes, but virtual networks are, and will remain at best, an imperfect substitute for real networks. This is especially true in B2B transactions, where orders are normally specified.

All things considered, e-commerce has a positive impact on the degree of global outsourcing as well as the sophistication with which such outsourcing takes place. This implies that the introduction of e-commerce has two parallel consequences. First, it raises the optimal level of outsourcing. The curve we portrayed in Exhibit 12.1 shifts towards the right-hand side as e-commerce is introduced into a supply chain. This confirms what so many observers have suggested: firms not only are outsourcing much more than in the past, say 20 years ago, but they can actually profitably do so. At the same time, e-commerce does not fundamentally alter the relationship between outsourcing and performance. That is, there are still very real limits to how much a firm should outsource and deviations from the optimum continue to be costly. Even in a world full of e-commerce, firms need to keep performing some activities in-house to maintain effective and differentiated in the eyes of their customers.

Second, as e-commerce gets introduced, and outsourcing levels go up, firms will increasingly engage in partnership relationships with suppliers. E-commerce enables the transfer of relatively more complex and made-to-order components and services to remote external suppliers. As firms outsource more activities, they also enter that range of more complex and made-to-order components and services, after having already outsourced their simple and off-the-shelf components and services at some point in the past. This is an indirect effect of outsourcing, and it implies that e-commerce creates more challenges in terms of managing supplier relations and supplier networks. In other words, there is a clear link between the introduction of e-commerce, increases in outsourcing, and more partnership relations and supplier networks. There is also a link to subsequent increases and decreases in firm performance, based on how well firms adapt to these changed circumstances.

Conclusions and Managerial Implications

We have presented a novel perspective on outsourcing and firm performance, arguing there is an inverted-U shape. Although this is based on the age-old notion that "too much of a good thing may be a bad thing," or what is known as diminishing returns in economics, it provides newness in applying that principle to the study of outsourcing, and in detailing the advantages and disadvantages of outsourcing that help produce such a curve. It also helps us understand in a more systematic way how it is that e-commerce produces higher optimal, and actual, levels of outsourcing.

Based on our discussion, managers should rethink and redesign their global outsourcing activities. Many managers have a strong general sense for what constitutes a sound outsourcing policy. They realize that outsourcing every activity may lead to disasters, just as much as they recognize that not all activities should be insourced. However, we suggest the above can improve managerial decision making in various respects.

There is currently a tendency in practice to describe (performance) problems related to outsourcing as "implementation issues." Managers often assume that outsourcing is the proper design choice, so they attribute the unsatisfactory performance to implementation problems in that suppliers are not well equipped—insufficient guarantees are built into contracts or market circumstances change rapidly. We suggest that there are much more fundamental objections against outsourcing that have nothing to do with implementation problems. Rather, there are limits to outsourcing and many inputs of a firm should not be outsourced. Our work confirms managerial intuitions that there is an optimal level. Thus, we help lower the uncertainty surrounding managerial decision making on outsourcing and also improve its quality.

Managers are often not conscious of the fact that there is an optimal degree of outsourcing for their entire portfolio. Instead of using this portfolio level, they tend to see the good or the evil of outsourcing or insourcing particular items or activities in that "outsourcing is more than a bidding process. Companies don't do enough analysis before they jump into it" (*The global outsourcing*, April 3, 2006, p. S4). This helps explain why in practice outsourcing often looks like a bandwagoning process. Likewise, many academic approaches have centered on analyzing single make or buy decisions. To some extent this is appropriate, since outsourcing decisions are made on an irregular basis. However, the performance advantages of outsourcing will only materialize when a firm has the organizational capacity to integrate outsourced items/activities into its operations. Furthermore, many companies make outsourcing decisions by evaluating only a few options on the basis of their previous experience and by what their competitors are doing (Farrell, 2006). For example, in June 2006, Apple Computer pulled the plug on a call center in India due to the high cost of operating there (Kripalani & Burrows, 2006), although many managers still perceive India as a low-cost location for call centers.

Managers are in need of guidelines as to where the optimal point lies for their particular business at a particular time. Based on the extant literature and our current research, we can suggest several indicators to help answer that question including asset specificity, uncertainty, firm competencies, industry trends, and firm nationality and location. These factors will help determine what is optimal for a particular firm at a particular time. Timing is crucial, as the optimal point will change due to changes inside and outside the firm. In this chapter, we examined one particular type of change, the introduction of e-commerce. E-commerce increases optimal outsourcing levels, and managers ought to be cognizant of this. As new e-commerce opportunities arise in their environment, the pressure to outsource more activities will mount.

What would really be useful from a managerial perspective is a model that helps determine what the optimal degree of outsourcing is for a firm. Upon determining that, managers could prioritize their set of activities and outsource until they more or less reach optimality. Such a model provides the next challenge for the academic community. As outsourcing strategy is a dynamic process, competing firms may not accurately grasp the full benefit (and cost) of outsourcing activities due to causal ambiguity. Simply bandwagoning on the first-mover's current outsourcing strategy offers no guarantee for improved performance. We suggest that tackling that challenge involves a broader behavioral understanding of how outsourcing trajectories of firms change over time and within industries.

Notes

1. Although its success is debatable, Covisint today supports over 250,000 users, representing more than 30,000 organizations in over 96 countries in the global automotive industry (Applegate & Collins, 2005).

2. We readily acknowledge that there are many other factors influencing optimal and actual outsourcing levels. These would include all kinds of other technologies than e-commerce, like transportation technology or managerial technology, as well as institutional factors. Institutional factors may include items like contract law, international trade regimes, intellectual property rights regimes, and economic

liberalization. A full discussion of what causes changes in outsourcing levels over time clearly extends beyond the boundaries of this paper. So while we acknowledge these other factors, our focus will be on e-commerce alone.

References

Abrahamson, E. (2004). *Change without pain: How managers can overcome initiative overload, organizational chaos, and employee burnout*. Boston: Harvard Business School Press.

Abrahamson, E., & Rosenkopf, L. (1993). Institutional and competitive bandwagons: Using mathematical modeling as a tool to explore innovation diffusion. *Academy of Management Review, 18*(3), 487–517.

Applegate, L. M., & Collins, E. L. (2005, June). Covisint (A): The evolution of a B2B marketplace. *Harvard Business School Case, 1*, 1–29.

Chesbrough, H. W., & Teece, D. J. (1996). When is virtual virtuous? Organizing for innovation. *Harvard Business Review, 74*(1), 65–72.

Clemons, E., Reddi, S. P., & Rowe, M. C. (1993). The impact of information technology on the organisation of economic activities: The "move to the middle" hypothesis. *Journal of Management Information Systems, 10*(2), 9–33.

Corbett, M. (2006, August). Solving the puzzle: Third-party specialists are helping globetrotting companies put the right people in the right places. *Fortune, 7*, 58.

D'Aveni, R. A., & Ravenscraft, D. J. (1994). Economies of integration versus bureaucracy costs: Does vertical integration improve performance? *Academy of Management Journal, 37*(5), 1167–1206.

Doig, S. J., Ritter, R. C., Speckhals, K., & Woolson, D. (2001). Has outsourcing gone too far? *McKinsey Quarterly, 26*(4), 26–37.

Domberger, S. (1998). *The contracting organization: A strategic guide to outsourcing*. Oxford: Oxford University Press.

Downes, L., & Mui, C. (1998). *Unleashing the killer app: Digital strategies for market dominance*. Boston: Harvard Business School Press.

Dyer, J. H., Cho, D. S., & Chu, W. (1998). Strategic supplier segmentation: The next "best practice" in supply chain management. *California Management Review, 40*(2), 57–77.

Dyer, J. H., & Singh, H. (1998). The relational view: Cooperative strategy and sources of interorganizational competitive advantage. *Academy of Management Review, 23*(4), 660–679.

Eng, T. Y. (2004, February). The role of e-marketplaces in supply chain management. *Industrial Marketing Management, 33*, 97–105.

Farrell, D. (2006, June). Smarter offshoring. *Harvard Business Review*, pp. 85–92.

The global outsourcing. (2006, April 3). *Fortune, 100*, S2–S17.

Gottfredson, M., Puryear, R., & Phillips, S. (2005, February). Strategic sourcing—From periphery to the core. *Harvard Business Review*, pp. 132–139.

Hamel, G. (2000). *Leading the revolution*. Boston: Harvard Business School Press.

Harris, A., Giunipero, L. C., & Hult, G. T. M. (1998, September). Impact of organizational and contract flexibility on outsourcing contracts. *Industrial Marketing Management, 7*, 373–384.

Hendry, J. (1995). Culture, community and networks: The hidden cost of outsourcing. *European Management Journal, 13*(2), 218–229.

Holland, C. P., & Lockett, A. G. (1997). Mixed mode network structures: The strategic use of electronic communication by organizations. *Organization Science, 8*(5), 475–488.

Kotabe, M. (1998). Efficiency vs. effectiveness orientation of global sourcing strategy: A comparison of U.S. and Japanese multinational companies. *Academy of Management Executive, 12*(4), 107–119.

Kotabe, M. (2002). To kill two birds with one stone: Revisiting the integration / responsiveness framework. In M. Hitt & J. Cheng (Eds.), *Managing transnational firms* (pp. 59–69). New York: Elsevier.

Kotabe, M., & Mol, M. J. (2005). *Outsourcing and firm profitability: A negative curvilinear effect*. Working Paper. London: London Business School.

Kotabe, M., & Murray, J. Y. (2004). Global sourcing strategy and sustainable competitive advantage. *Industrial Marketing Management, 33*(1), 7–14.

Kotabe, M., & Swan, K. S. (1994). Offshore sourcing: Reaction, maturation, and consolidation of U.S. multinationals. *Journal of International Business Studies, 25*(1), 115–140.

Kripalani, M., & Burrows, P. (2006, June). India: Why Apple walked away. *Business Week, 19*, 48.

Krugman, P. (2001, April). Reckonings: Chip of fools. *New York Times*.

Leiblein, M. J., Reuer, J. J., & Dalsace, F. (2002). Do make or buy decisions matter? The influence of organizational governance on technological performance. *Strategic Management Journal, 23*(9), 817–833.

Levy, D. L. (2005). Offshoring in the new global political economy. *Journal of Management Studies, 42*(3), 687–693.

Malone, T. W., Yates, J., & Benjamin, R. I. (1987). Electronic markets and electronic hierarchies. *Communications of the ACM, 30*(6), 484–497.

Mol, M. J., van Tulder, R. J. M., & Beije, P. R. (2005). Antecedents and performance consequences of international outsourcing. *International Business Review, 14*(5), 599–617.

Murray, J. Y., Kotabe, M., & Wildt, A. R. (1995). Strategic and financial performance implications of global sourcing strategy: A contingency analysis. *Journal of International Business Studies, 26*(1), 181–202.

Nooteboom, B. (1999). *Inter-firm alliances: Analysis and design*. London: Routledge.

Parmigiani, A. (2007). Why do firms both make and buy? An investigation of concurrent sourcing. *Strategic Management Journal, 28*(3), 285–311.

Poppo, L., & Zenger, T. (1998). Testing alternative theories of the firm: Transaction cost, knowledge-based, and measurement explanations for make-or-buy decisions in information services. *Strategic Management Journal, 19*(9), 853–877.

Porter, M. E. (1997). *On competition* Boston, MA: Harvard Business School Press.

Quinn, J. B. (1999). Strategic outsourcing: Leveraging knowledge capabilities. *Sloan Management Review, 40*(3), 9–21.

Rottman, J. W., & Lacity, M. C. (2006). Proven practices for effectively offshoring IT work. *Sloan Management Review, 47*(3), 56–63.

Van der Valk, W., & Wynstra, F. (2005). Supplier involvement in new product development in the food industry. *Industrial Marketing Management, 34*(7), 681–694.

Watson, R. T., Zinkhan, G. M., & Pitt, L. F. (Summer 2004). Object-orientation: A tool for enterprise design. *California Management Review, 46*, 89–110.

Westphal, J. D., Gulati, R., & Shortell, S. M. (1997, June). Customization or conformity? An institutional and network perspective on the content and consequences of TQM adoption. *Administrative Science Quarterly, 42*, 366–394.

Williamson, O. E. (1985). *The economic institutions of capitalism*. New York: Free Press.

United Nations Conference on Trade and Invesment. (2002). *World investment report 2002*. Geneva: United Nations.

CHAPTER 13

Outsourcing Service Activities

Gaining Access to New Ideas and Flexibility Will Allow Service-Buying Firms to Remain Competitive

Masaaki Kotabe and Janet Y. Murray

Traditionally, "make vs. buy" decisions were made by companies marketing tangible goods only. However, thanks to factors such as global competition and technological and telecommunication advances, service firms now enjoy the flexibility to outsource some of the service activities provided to their customers. In a study conducted by the Outsourcing Research Council, executives reported that approximately one-third of their firm's operating budget was spent on outside services. Likewise, executives who attended the 1999 Outsourcing World Summit reported that their outsourcing expenditures increased by 21% over the previous year.

For example, Charles Schwab now outsources development and management of its e-business services to IBM's Global Services unit. IBM's Global Services unit is a leader in technology services, which accounts for 29% of the company's sales and 17% of profits. The ability to provide e-business services to major customers, such as Charles Schwab, has helped contribute to IBM's overall financial health, despite flat hardware and modest software sales growth.

As this example suggests, outsourcing of service activities provides advantages not only for the service-buying firm, but also for its suppliers and customers. Through outsourcing of service activities, the service-buying firm can focus on its core competencies (i.e., using insourcing for the core service activities that it can do best) and be flexible enough to meet the ever-changing demand in the marketplace by designing the service package and outsourcing remaining noncore service activities from the best-in-class providers. Consequently, the service firm's suppliers have access to a wider customer base through providing service activities to the service-buying firm. The service-buying firm's customers in turn receive service activities performed by a multitude of more efficient specialized service providers, thus enjoying convenience and extra value.

Although service-buying firms enjoy greater leverage, they should also be aware of the potential problems related to outsourcing of service activities. First, by outsourcing service activities, a service-buying firm takes on the role of a channel member (i.e., a middleman of services). Regardless of whether the services provided to its customers are insourced or outsourced, the customers often do not know who the actual service provider is. Consequently, if customers complain about the outsourced service quality, the service-buying firm's brand image would be tarnished. Second, if the outsourced service activity is inseparable from the core services the firm provides to customers and if it happens to be the only time

Executive Briefing

Service firms seem to have begun outsourcing part of their service activities in much the same way as manufacturing firms have sourced components and finished goods in the past 30 years. However, little is empirically known about the nature of service-sourcing strategy. What types of service activities are conducive to outsourcing? Which factors are considered important in selecting suppliers for outsourcing service activities? How would service-outsourcing strategy affect firm performance? We have found that, similar to components and finished-goods procurement, supplementary service activities are increasingly outsourced. Furthermore, outsourcing of supplementary services seems to affect the service firm's market performance.

when they are exposed to the human element, the service-buying firm would lose its only chance to have direct contact with those customers. Therefore, the service-buying firm may not have the opportunity to build relationships with its customers.

Developing effective sourcing strategies has become critical to improving service firms' market performance. To remain competitive, service firms need to be aware of the opportunities available to them through strategic outsourcing activities.

Strategic Outsourcing

Firms must first address the following question: Which service activities should be outsourced?

Similar to goods-manufacturing firms, services provided by service firms essentially consist of a set of interrelated activities (i.e., the value chain). The value chain of service activities includes the design, manufacturing, marketing, and supporting activities. In examining outsourcing decisions for service activities, it is imperative that service firms differentiate the two types of service activities involved—core service activities and supplementary service activities. Core service activities are the essential set of service activities the firm (e.g., a supermarket) must provide in order to participate in its market (i.e., retailing services). In other words, if a service firm does not do a good job in providing the core service activities, it will eventually go out of business. Supplementary services are either indispensable for the execution of the core service activities or are available only to improve the overall quality of the core service bundle (e.g., delivery services).

Before developing a competitive strategy, firms should first classify their service activities into core and supplementary service categories. Since providing core service activities is the reason that service firms exist, we would expect most, if not all, service firms to provide core services by themselves. However, supplementary services are those services that are mainly used for differentiation purposes (which often do not fall into the core competency domain to the service firm), and they are prime candidates for outsourcing.

Since the opportunities for strategic outsourcing lie in the area of supplementary service activities, we looked at the following questions:

What are the characteristics of supplementary service activities? What is the level of outsourcing for supplementary service activities? Which factors are considered important in selecting suppliers for supplementary service activities? How would outsourcing of supplementary service activities affect firm performance? We used a survey of Fortune 500 U.S. service firms and their major subsidiaries operating in the United States. Among the 100 executives responding, 35% worked for firms in financial business (banks, securities, and insurance), 19% in utility, 13% in transportation, 8% in construction, 8% in publishing/communication, 5% in retailing/wholesaling, 4% in health care, and 8% in other service sectors. This study is based on one of the very few primary databases available in examining service sourcing opportunities.

Supplementary Services

Respondents reported that, on average, core service activities constituted 78% of the value of services offered to their customers, while the remaining 22% were supplementary service activities, Respondents were then asked to evaluate the 20 characteristics of supplementary service activities. As we looked for the main characteristics, we searched for consistency, depth, and consensus in their responses. Our analysis indicated that 11 of the 20 characteristics consistently converged into four discrete categories that represented the nature of the supplementary service characteristics. They are (a) highly specialized investments needed to provide supplementary service activities, (b) high innovativeness of the supplementary services, (c) demand uncertainty, and (d) low availability of the supplementary service activities. Summary findings are reported in Table 13.1.

Respondents reported the two most important characteristics of their supplementary service activities are the high levels of specialized investment required for both capital and human resources (a mean value of 3.71 on a 5-point scale) and the high level of innovations (a mean value of 3.46 on a 5-point scale) involved in the supplementary service activities. Increasingly, service firms are capitalizing on technological innovations in serving their customers better and also in changing the way supporting activities are performed. Service firms that regularly research and introduce service innovations continue to gain a series of temporary advantages over their

Table 13.1. Characteristics of Supplementary Services

Characteristics	Level of characteristics (Very low = 1 . . . 5 = Very high)
Specialized investments • Major investments and training needed • Professional skills required • Specialized know-how required	**3.71**
Innovativeness • Service innovation • Process innovation • Applications to service innovation • Applications of process innovation	**3.46**
Demand uncertainty	3.07
Availability • Number of external suppliers available • Possible to import services • Possible to have different suppliers to perform different aspects of services	**2.69**

Note: The numbers in bold indicate that responses are significantly different from a neutral response of 3.

competitors. These service innovations help maintain service quality, replace workers by machines for repetitive tasks, and involve customers in service delivery through self-service. Because the use of continuous innovations is a source of competitive advantage for firms, specialized know-how is often involved, and intensive training must be provided to the service providers to improve their skills in performing the supplementary services.

In addition, respondents reported that the level of the demand uncertainty of supplementary services was only moderate (a mean value of 3.07 on a 5-point scale). As supplementary service activities are often used to augment the overall quality of the core service bundle, production and consumption don't need to take place in the same location and at the same time.

Consequently, it is much easier for service firms to manage the seasonality of demand for supplementary service activities. However, respondents also stated the availability of suppliers to perform the supplementary service activities is low (a mean value of 2.69 on a 5-point scale). This seems to pose a constraint on finding qualified suppliers to perform the service activities.

Since many service firms are not able to provide all the service activities in house, it is important for them to concentrate their investment and managerial resources on areas that yield a competitive advantage over their rivals. Therefore, the next crucial issue is to decide whether to insource or outsource the needed supplementary service activities. Respondents reported that 19% of the value of the supplementary service activities was outsourced (i.e., provided by independent suppliers).

What Are the Deciding Factors?

Because of the significant advantages that service-buying firms realize through outsourcing supplementary service activities, potential suppliers of the outsourced service activities should know what factors potential customers (i.e., service-buying firms) think are important in supplier selection. This will give supplying firms insight into how to tailor their strategies to gain customers. Initially, respondents were asked to rate the importance of 22 items in influencing supplier selection. Our analysis showed that 13 of those 22 items consistently converged into five discrete categories of supplier selection factors. In order of importance (as rated by executives), they are (a) supplier's competency (a mean value of 4.72 on a 5-point scale), (b) service quality control (a mean value of 4.44), (c) transaction-cost drivers (a mean value of 3.43), (d) supplier's brand image (a mean value of 3.37), and (e) supplier's country characteristics (a mean value of 2.46). Summary findings are reported in Table 13.2.

Supplier's competency and the ability of the service-buying firm to control service quality are rated as the two most important factors in supplier selection of supplementary service activities. Since the service-buying firm acts as a middleman between its supplier and its customers when outsourcing supplementary service activities, customers seldom know that the services delivered to them are in reality performed by the firm's suppliers. Therefore, the service-buying firm has to be extra cautious about the service quality of the outsourced supplementary service activities. For outsourced physical goods, a buying firm can evaluate the quality of the goods involved before the purchase is made. However, with services, the same supplier may provide services of varying quality. Thus, it is important for the service-buying firm to ensure that the outsourced service quality of the suppliers is consistent. Consequently, the overall competency of the supplying firm, measured by its reliability and performance, is considered the foremost important factor in supplier selection. In other words, the service-buying firm needs to find out whether there are highly competent suppliers from which to outsource. If competent external suppliers are available, the service-buying firm should consider outsourcing. Otherwise, the service-buying firm may consider performing these services by itself. In addition, although highly competent suppliers are available, the supplying firm needs to devise a scheme the service-buying firm can rely on in order to check the quality of the services delivered by its suppliers.

Transaction-cost drivers are considered the third most important factor in supplier selection. Some of the supplementary services contain proprietary know-how, require major investment, and are provided to customers frequently. For service activities that have these characteristics, the service-buying firm should consider performing the service activity by itself. This is because the service firm can keep its proprietary know-how to itself without unduly disseminating it to an outside party when outsourcing is used. Moreover, it is easier to control the quality of these service activities if they are performed in house. Equally important is that for service activities that require major investment in training, performing these services in house would eliminate the risk of the service-buying firm being held hostage by the service-supplying firm, since alternate suppliers may not be readily available in the marketplace.

Supplier's brand image is considered somewhat important in selecting suppliers. In addition to relying on the reliability and performance of potential suppliers, the intangible quality indicator of supplier's brand image also serves as a cue to the quality of the service activity to be performed.

Supplier's country factors are not considered as an important factor in supplier selection. Since supplementary services are additional services provided by the service-buying firm to augment the core service package, these services often are not consumed and produced simultaneously. Thus, the supplier's country characteristics for outsourcing supplementary services do not seem to pose a great risk.

Table 13.2. Factors Influencing Outsourcing of Supplementary Services

Factors	Importance (Very unimportant = 1 ... 5 = Very important)
Supplier's competency • Reliability • Performance	**4.72**
Control • Firm's ability to control service quality	**4.44**
Transaction-cost drivers • Proprietary know-how • Major investments and training • Transaction frequency	**3.43**
Supplier's brand image • Experience • Overall reputation • Nationality	**3.37**
Supplier's country factors • Currency exchange rate • Similarity in culture • Country risks	**2.46**

Note: The numbers in bold indicate that responses are significantly different from a neutral response of 3.

The Perceived Importance

Respondents were asked about the perceived importance of outsourcing of supplementary services (all items of perceived importance of different sourcing strategies were measured using a 5-point scale: 1 = very unimportant; 5 = very important). Since many firms still believe they must deliver all services to their customers by themselves, regardless of whether these services are core or supplementary service activities, we also asked respondents to rate the perceived importance of insourcing supplementary services. On average, respondents reported that insourcing and outsourcing supplementary service activities are both important strategies in achieving the desired level of market performance. However, on average, respondents placed a higher importance on insourcing (a mean value of 4.01 on a 5-point scale) over outsourcing (a mean value of 3.51). Because respondents rated supplier's country characteristics as an unimportant factor in supplier selection, we were interested to know how respondents viewed the importance of sourcing from U.S. vs. foreign-based suppliers.

The results showed that U.S. sourcing (a mean value of 3.78 on a 5-point scale) is perceived as much more important than foreign sourcing (a mean value of 2.40).

The Effects

In addition to examining the perceived importance of different sourcing strategies (i.e., insourcing or outsourcing, and sourcing from U.S. or foreign-based suppliers) on market performance, we also investigated the actual relationship between these sourcing strategies with different aspects of performance (i.e., strategic performance and financial performance) relative to the service firm's three largest competitors. Strategic performance is a two-item measure that includes market share and sales growth rate, while financial performance is a three-item measure that includes return on sales, return on investment, and return on equity. The analyses showed that insourcing and foreign sourcing of supplementary services was negatively related to both strategic and market performance. Conversely, outsourcing and domestic sourcing (i.e., using U.S. based sourcing) of supplementary service activities was positively related to both strategic and financial market performance. Interestingly, the findings of the sourcing strategies-actual performance relationships are inconsistent with the sourcing strategies-perceived performance relationships.

Implications

Recently, service firms have begun to realize that outsourcing of service activities is no longer a tactical approach to reducing costs. Rather, strategic sourcing involves focusing on a firm's core competency and outsourcing the remaining noncore activities in order to reap the benefits of its suppliers' economies of scale and scope. In addition, the evaluation of whether a service activity should be outsourced by a service firm or not affects both the service firm's suppliers and its customers. Hence, the examination of strategic sourcing involves how sourcing influences the entire value chain, creating competitive advantage to the service firm through a combination of internal core competencies and outside suppliers' strengths.

There are important implications for service firms. As supplementary service activities play such a crucial role in strategic outsourcing, service firms need to know the unique characteristics of supplementary service activities. Our analysis showed that the delivery of supplementary service activities generally requires highly specialized investments (i.e., major capital investments and training, professional skills, and specialized know-how needed), and this type of service activity is generally highly innovative (i.e., in terms of service and process innovations and the number of potential applications of the innovation). This concurs with the Outsourcing Institute's (a trade group) observation that continuous, creative, and quick innovations are an impetus to business success. Firms simply cannot survive without having goods and services breakthroughs on a regular and predictable basis. Outsourcing is a way to respond to this highly volatile, innovate-or-die Darwinian world. As pointed out by Frank Casale, president of the Outsourcing Institute, firms increasingly leverage outsourcing to assist innovation through providing information, procedures, business methodologies, new product development, and ongoing services. Through outsourcing, firms continuously gain access to new ideas, fresh perspectives, and flexibility to remain competitive.

Because supplementary service activities generally require highly specialized investments and are innovative in nature, respondents also reported that this type of service in general has low availability. Although the number of suppliers available to provide the supplementary service activities is limited, firms should not jump to the conclusion that these supplementary service activities should be performed in house. One effective alternative is to find strategic partnering firms to become suppliers who have the competency to deliver innovative supplementary service activities and the ability to make the necessary investments. Through the use of competent partnering firms, the service-buying firm would have a tighter control on the service quality of the outsourced supplementary service activities, which in turn fulfills the two most important requirements of supplier selection—supplier's competency and service quality control.

The next important finding is that the perceived higher importance of insourcing over outsourcing of supplementary service activities, as rated by respondents, did not match the actual effects of insourcing and outsourcing of supplementary service activities on market performance. Many service providers still have the mindset that all services should be performed in house, without realizing that this is an outdated mode of thinking in the Internet era. The new business model requires a service firm to continuously design an innovative service package to remain distinctive in the marketplace. However, the delivery of the part of the service package that does not fall within the core competencies of the firm should be outsourced, preferably through strategic partnerships. In other words, the challenge for the service firm is to design a package (including other supplementary services in addition to the core service) that is desired by its target market, while the actual delivery of some (if not all) of these supplementary services may be performed by outside "best-in-class" suppliers. Therefore, the ability of a service firm to find a strategic partner to provide the needed supplementary services and maintain the relationship is a source of competitive advantage. The firm can strategically outsource some of its supplementary services and focus on its core competencies. In doing so, the firm is able to maximize returns on internal resources by concentrating investments and energies on what it does best. In addition, as James Brian Quinn and Frederick G. Hilmer have stressed, the firm is able to leverage "the full utilization of external suppliers' investments, innovations, and specialized professional capabilities that would be prohibitively expensive or even impossible to duplicate internally."

Suppliers of supplementary services should take note of the many opportunities available in servicing those firms that are in different industries. Through strategic partnerships with these firms, the supplying firms can have access to a much wider customer base and achieve further economies of scale. In conclusion, strategic sourcing of supplementary service activities represents a win-win situation for both service-buying and supplying firms.

Additional Reading

Casale, F. (1999). *The rise of the chief resource officer.* New York: The Outsourcing Institute.

Murray, J. Y., & Kotabe, M. (1999, September). Sourcing strategies of U.S. service companies; A modified transaction-cost analysis. *Strategic Management Journal, 20,* 791–809.

Quinn, J. B., & Hilmer, F. G. (1994, Summer). Strategic outsourcing. *Sloan Management Review, 35,* 43–55.

CHAPTER 14

An Evolutionary-Stage Model of Outsourcing and Competence Destruction

A Triad Comparison of the Consumer Electronics Industry

Masaaki Kotabe, Michael J. Mol, and Sonia Ketkar

Introduction

Offshoring and outsourcing remain high on managerial agendas, although the type of sourcing that grabs most headlines and managerial attention tends to change fairly rapidly. In the late 1980s and early 1990s global sourcing of components and products was seen as a key trend among manufacturing firms. The mid-1990s saw corporations farm out information technology activities on a large scale. Currently major trends are business process outsourcing to countries like India and South Africa and the continuing shift of manufacturing activities to China. The latter types of offshoring and outsourcing are not only highly contentious politically but also pose managerial dilemmas.[1]

Until quite recently it was generally accepted that outsourcing, and especially outsourcing across borders, was primarily implemented to cut costs in order to maintain competitiveness. An argument commonly used by decision makers and academic writers alike is that outsourcing, the reliance on external suppliers for the delivery of components and entire products, leads to an increased focus on remaining activities (Quinn, 1999). By keeping in-house a more limited number of activities, managers can devote more attention to maintaining a world-class level in those activities. Because (foreign) suppliers likewise target their efforts, it is possible to obtain specialized help from outside suppliers with much lower production costs, so the argument goes. Of course, these lower production costs are at least partly offset by higher transaction costs, because of the difficulties associated with sourcing across borders (Mol, van Tulder, & Beije, 2005). This comparative cost approach is relatively well understood and has been widely implemented by practitioners, although firms often fail to take into account the true total costs of ownership in make-or-buy and offshoring decisions, as we demonstrate in this chapter. The disadvantage of this approach is that it is relatively static.

In recent years a second argument has therefore been added to sway managers toward outsourcing. Outsourcing can be a means of accessing supplier competences that would otherwise remain inaccessible, or it can even serve as the gateway to the creation of competences that reside in the relationship between the firm and its supplier (Dyer & Singh, 1998). Toyota, for instance, has been able to distill a competitive edge from long-term and intimate relations with suppliers like Nippondenso. Thus one might argue that the effects of outsourcing on the acquisition of competences have now come to the fore in managerial practice and academic literature. Outsourcing can be a source of both cost savings and competence acquisition.

Like in the popular press, much of the outsourcing literature is focused on its immediate impact in the form of potential cost savings. For the simplest forms of outsourcing (e.g., those involving procurement of commodity goods and services), this makes sense, as an outsourcing decision will have no implications beyond the current bookkeeping period. Where more complicated forms of outsourcing are concerned, this is normally not the case. For instance, it took the UK government and Network Rail 10 years and several deadly incidents to reconsider the outsourcing of maintenance that accompanied the privatization of the railroads (Economist, 2005). At the heart of these problems was the gradual erosion of knowledge on the technical state of the railways and a lack of technological investments that could have helped detect impending failures.

But any understanding of the long-run consequences of outsourcing should also include how it could affect a firm's ability to maintain appropriate skill levels and upgrade its competitive position, not just cut costs in the short run. This is much less well understood and a less popular route of scholarly investigation. It has been noted that the long-run consequences of outsourcing are sometimes not particularly comforting (Bettis, Bradley, & Hamel, 1992; Kotabe, 1998; Doig, Ritter, Speckhals, & Woolson, 2001). However, no general explanation has so far been provided for how outsourcing could lead to deterioration in a firm's competence base. Therefore we ask the question, How does outsourcing affect competences? By doing so we reverse the questions that various authors (e.g., Barney, 1999; Quinn, 1999) have addressed.

Researchers often focus on comparing the current governance costs of in-house production with those of external offerings. Transaction cost economics argues that outsourcing levels ought to be the results of levels of asset specificity, business uncertainty, and the frequency of transactions (Leiblein, Reuer, & Dalsace, 2002; Williamson, 1985). This approach has obvious merits for its simplicity and its ability to correctly predict the governance structure of many transactions. It has also been argued, however, that there is a range of transactions for which it is not particularly apt (Barney, 1999). Barney (1999) argues that transaction cost arguments are too static to cope with more dynamic industries, especially those with blurred industry boundaries. Transaction cost economics focuses on current transaction characteristics, but if important future learning and change can occur, current governance costs may not be a proper predictor for future governance costs and optimal outsourcing choices.

Such shifts can occur in technologically uncertain and intensive industries, such as the electronics industry. In fact, we would argue that this is exactly what has been happening in the electronics industry over the past few decades. Firms have had to face major technological shifts, such as that from analog to digital technology. They also faced stiff global competition and business cycles, for instance, in consumer electronics (CE) and semiconductors. For this type of industry additional analytical tools may be required that incorporate long-term change into viability assessments on outsourcing. So far empirical investigations on the effects of outsourcing over longer time periods are scarce (with some exceptions, like the semilongitudinal study of D'Aveni and Ravenscraft, 1994). Also relatively sparse are discussions of forms of international outsourcing, as much published work seems to be focused on single countries and treats outsourcing as either a strictly domestic issue or is agnostic as to outsourcing locations. We seek to address both issues, broadly asking the question how changes in outsourcing levels and locations change competence development inside the firm.

We longitudinally analyze and compare the cases of three major electronics manufacturers, Emerson Radio from the United States, Japan's Sony, and Philips from the Netherlands, focusing particularly on how these firms changed their sourcing strategies over time. Using these cases we then construct a stage model that relates offshoring and outsourcing to competence development inside the firm and shows that a vicious cycle may emerge. We describe the specific conditions under which such a cycle comes into existence, especially the loss of competitiveness in manufacturing in firms' home bases. The stage model helps managers to understand for which activities and under which conditions outsourcing is not a viable option.

Methodology: Content Analysis

Because this research question includes a longitudinal element, it cannot be adequately captured by survey or cross-sectional research. Therefore, we used content analysis of news articles, company documents, industry trends, books and other published reports, as well as personal interviews pertaining to the CE industry in general and our three firms in particular. We focused on our three firms mainly because our initial review of the data documents revealed that the stages cycle emerged most conspicuously in these firms. Also, in order to keep our cases clear and discrete, we restricted our analysis only to these firms. The fact that all three firms hail from different parts of the triad, allows us to capture different development paths in their home country electronics industries.

The time period ranged from 1954 to 2007 and we reviewed the content from around 50 different sources. Where possible, we were able to compare different reports of the same firm information or event as recounted by various reporters. We also compared what was reported against interviews on outsourcing we held with electronic firms (not reported here) and against what other authors have written about outsourcing and subcontracting in the electronics industry (Kenney & Florida, 1995). An in-depth analysis of our sources suggested that there was a similar pattern in the histories and behavior of all three firms over time even though the timing (actual years) did not correspond for the firms. Emerson Radio (United States) for example, went through its outsourcing experiences much earlier than Philips and especially Sony.

Global Consumer Electronics Industry

No explanation of CE firms is complete without a brief introduction to the dynamics underlying the industry in the years when the specter of global competition first appeared. The worldwide CE industry has seen much international competition since the 1950s. The Western world dominated the field of CE until this time and the 1950s witnessed the advent of the Japanese competition, which began with the export of transistors. Soon, Japanese CE firms such as Sony, Matsushita, and others became a force to reckon with. In particular, rivalry in television technology was the most intense in the 1970s. It is difficult to pinpoint exactly when global competition became so fierce among firms in the triad region. But, in 1951, when MITI (Ministry of International Trade and Industry, Japan) permitted Japanese companies to enter into licensing agreements for television technology with foreign firms, several Japanese companies signed pacts with U.S. companies, such as RCA. At the time, MITI expected to receive only a few applications for approval but it ended up authorizing around 37 applications (Partner, 1999). As electrical goods rapidly permeated Japanese society, local companies grew larger and developed a competitive edge based on a quick learning process and low labor costs.

U.S. companies, such as Emerson Radio, RCA, Zenith, and Magnavox also realized that they could gain cost-based competitive advantage by subcontracting assembly and later on manufacturing operations to their Asian partners at lower costs. Hence, around the 1960s and 1970s, outsourcing became popular with many U.S. firms. In subsequent years, Japanese CE firms acquired technology from U.S. companies, gained technological competency, and launched new technologically advanced products derived from their own R&D. Competition between U.S. firms and their Japanese counterparts heated up when Japanese firms entered the U.S. domestic market and began selling their products at lower prices. This led U.S. firms to charge dumping allegations against the Japanese firms. The developments in the industry that followed show that U.S. companies rapidly increased outsourcing and in turn their dependence on their Japanese partners first for radios and later on for television sets. By the end of the 1960s, there were no U.S. radio manufacturers left in the United States (Partner, 1999).

A discussion of the European CE industry is mostly an account of Philips and its activities. There was probably only one other company, Thomson of France, that was as active in the industry, more so than firms such as Siemens and Telefunken. Like some U.S. firms (National Union Electric and Zenith), European firms felt threatened by Japanese competition in the CE industry. Prompted by a turbulent environment after the 1970s and lobbying for protection from non-European rivals by influential firms like Philips, Europe implemented new policies. European CE firms were also granted subsidies. Especially in the 1980s, the European Union (EU) stepped in to defend its CE firms from Japanese penetration of its markets. Nevertheless, the European CE industry went through a series of restructurings into the 1990s like the major turnaround operation "Centurion" at Philips.

To illustrate the intensity of rivalry and firms' attempts to outdo each other through innovation and imitation, let us take this example. As the story goes, in 1963, Philips gave the world the audiocassette, which was a noise reduction innovation because Philips eliminated the background tape sound. Based on this product, in 1964, a Sony employee proposed the idea of a videocassette. Finally, by 1976, Sony introduced its Betamax VCR in the United States. In late 1977 RCA launched its VHS SelectaVision VCR format that was made by Matsushita. This product was an improvement on Sony's Betamax, which could record for only an hour. Thus, an innovation/product introduction by one firm was very quickly followed by the creation of another entrant that sought to gain market share. We historically examine the corporate strategies, trials, and tribulations of three companies, Emerson Radio (United States), Royal Philips Electronics (The Netherlands-Europe), and Sony Corp. (Japan) in the field of CE. We focus on firm decisions related to entertainment products groups, namely audio, video, and television products in these companies. Every product introduction has been built on and upgraded from previous technology. The three companies in our sample have slightly, and sometimes even drastically, changed their corporate strategies innumerable times in the last 30–40 years. We focus on those strategies that are relevant to outsourcing.

All three firms, Emerson Radio, Philips, and Sony were technological pioneers at some point in the early days of CE. While Emerson Radio discovered a way to retain its market share by supplying CE products at low prices, Philips "became Europe's core consumer electronics learning base," and Sony revolutionized the industry with its miniaturization of CE products (Chandler, 2001, p. 221). So, how did these firms acquire technological competences? And how did these firms start losing their technical prowess?

Overview of Three Companies

Emerson Radio (United States)

From pioneer and maker of CE products to distributor recites the Emerson Radio saga in a sentence. The company's history is complex because it changed ownership a few times. Emerson Radio & Phonograph, as the company was originally called by its founder Max Abrams in 1922, mass-produced radios around the time of World War II. Its radios were known to be very modern for their time and decorative in appearance. It also manufactured phonographs and TVs. In 1965, it was taken over by National Union Corp. (NUC)[2] and in 1975 Major Corp. (a phonograph manufacturer founded in 1956) bought its brand name for CE from NUC and changed its own name to Emerson Radio.

Emerson Radio obtained technology mainly through its own efforts and through acquisitions. Soon after entering the radio business, the company introduced the first radio-phonograph combination sold in the United States. In 1932, it launched its popular miniature radio, which was around 8 1/2 inches by 6 1/4 inches wide, and Emerson Radio was the leader in the manufacture and sale of miniature radios. By 1938, it had sold over 1 million of these radios. In 1954, years before Japan's Sony became famous for miniaturization of CE products, Emerson Radio introduced the tiniest radio to date, which measured 3 1/2 × 3 × 3/4 inches. This achievement made Emerson Radio the largest producer of tiny radios in the world. It was so technologically advanced in the 1950s that it planned to "build a radio, using transistors instead of tubes, so small that it can be worn like a wrist watch" (Forbes, 1954, p. 22). After World War II, it introduced one of the first television sets in the United States; this caused earnings to more than double by the mid-1950s. Emerson Radio also had R&D labs in the United States. By this time, Emerson Radio had a solid brand name and superior technological capabilities and attempted to capture nearby markets, mainly in Canada and Latin America. However, as more players entered the emerging television industry, competition at home grew and Emerson started cutting the price of its television sets in order to survive in the market. It is around this time when the company realized that it needed to take drastic measures to subsist in the industry and it did (explained in the following section). In 1953, Emerson Radio launched the first compatible color TV receiver and, in 1958, it acquired further technological capabilities when it bought CE inventor DuMont's television sets, phonograph, and high-fidelity stereo equipment operations. By the early 1960s Emerson Radio had developed production capabilities complemented by a strong brand name in CE. But even then, in the battle for market share and the onslaught of foreign CE firms, U.S. producers like Emerson Radio were fast losing market share. In the latter half of the 1960s, although American companies such as RCA, Westinghouse Electric, Admiral, and General Electric were struggling to make profits and hang on to their businesses, Emerson managed to continue making a profit (*New York Times*, 1981). Emerson built a large customer base and acquired a significant portion of the market by eventually setting up cost-efficient manufacturing operations in East Asia to deliver electronic products at reasonable prices to middle-class American citizens. It was indeed one of the very first U.S. companies to popularize such manufacturing strategies. In the short run profitability grew, but in the long run it faced several problems due to excessive outsourcing.

Philips Electronics (The Netherlands)

Philips was established in the Netherlands in 1912 and grew to be the largest European CE company and one of the largest in the world. Its main activity was electrical lighting, but it acquired a leading position in CE before the mid-1970s when Japanese companies entered Europe. From the time it was set up, Philips was based on R&D and developed its own technologies and mostly kept R&D in-house in various labs across Europe. This enabled it to increase its own product portfolio from the 1920s. However, during World War II, several of its European operations were destroyed. Postwar Philips enhanced its technical capabilities by relying on color TV technology licensed from RCA, like most of the Japanese CE firms in the 1970s. At the same time, Philips's research efforts proved to be beneficial for Japan's Matsushita because Philips owned 35% of Matsushita, which depended on Philips's R&D. Philips entered into collaborations and joint ventures for innovation and new product development in the 1980s. Its most successful collaboration was with Sony to launch the compact disc (CD) system. However, by the late 1990s, Philips had lost its once superior technological capabilities.

Sony Corporation (Japan)

Although Sony did not invent the transistor, it was the first company to launch the transistor radio and this innovative feat played a major role in Sony's emergence as a technological leader (Partner, 1999). Founded in 1953, Tokyo Tsushin, as the company was originally called before its name was changed to Sony, quickly built a reputation for itself in Japan and soon in the rest of the world. In 1953, Sony signed a pact with U.S.-based Western Electric to learn its transistor technology and then conducted its own research on radios. In 1955, Sony introduced its first transistor radio, TR-55, into the market. Just like Sony, other U.S. and Japanese manufacturers had developed their versions of the transistor radio around the same time and sold those in the U.S. market. But, in the international arena, Sony had to compete not only with other Japanese contenders but also with the U.S. and European ones, which already had brand equity and established distribution networks. In 1982, Sony introduced the TV Walkman, a technological breakthrough in those days.

Throughout this era, Sony, like most other Japanese companies relied on in-house R&D, continually increasing R&D spending over the years, for instance, by 9.6% in 1983 to $90.6 million. Sony, like most other Japanese CE firms, initially followed a conservative policy by keeping R&D in-house, but eventually gave in to financial concerns (brought about by an inability to meet high demand and fierce rivalry) and resorted to outsourcing. Hence, the 1990s saw "a shift from a technology-based company to a product-based company," in the words of Kutaragi, president of Sony Computer Entertainment Corp. (*Nikkei Weekly*, 2003). In the next section we examine the dynamic shifts, in four different stages, in the sourcing strategies employed by Emerson, Philips, and Sony. Table 14.1 contains a summary.

Stages Over Time

Stage 1: Offshore Sourcing (Setting Up a Foreign Subsidiary in Low-Cost Locations)

Before plunging headlong into the establishment of foreign manufacturing subsidiaries, CE firms dabbled in foreign transactions. After Emerson faced trouble selling its television sets amid tough competition and after trying out the price-cut strategy, the company found another way to increase profits—by lowering costs. In 1956 sales fell from over $87 million to $74 million while earnings were a meager $84,850. Then the company moved further to set up cost-efficient manufacturing operations in East Asia in the 1960s.

Philips, on the other hand, had been collaborating with foreign companies, starting in 1916 with General Electric, to exchange technical know-how and experience. Although the company had been engaged in foreign trade activities, foreign investment were not established until in the 1920s. Philips moved many of its production plants out of the Netherlands to avoid high tariffs leaving behind unemployed people. This was the first time it set up offshore production. In the following years, Philips closed down some more plants in the Netherlands. It followed an aggressive expansionist policy in the next decade and set up several subsidiaries in different parts of the world. By the late 1960s, Philips had manufacturing operations in several parts of the world, including

Table 14.1. Evolution of Outsourcing Strategy

Firm	Characteristics	Trigger	Stage 1	Stage 2	Stage 3	Stage 4
Emerson (1922)	• Manufacturing—decentralized • R&D—centralized	Increased cost competition	Outsourcing deals with U.S.'s Admiral and East Asian manufacturers	Falling out with Admiral and relying completely on foreign original equipment manufacturers (OEMs). Emerson in charge of design but not manufacture.	Realization of the loss of technology to East Asian OEMs	Complete reliance on outsourcing; unrelated diversification
Philips (1912)	• Manufacturing—decentralized • R&D—decentralized	Increased cost competition	Setting up manufacturing subsidiaries in Taiwan, etc. (1980s)	Selling its foreign factories and increasing outsourcing from Taiwan and Korea (1980s)	Loss of DVD technology to Japanese (1990s)	Increased R&D in-house and stepped up outsourcing as well (1990s)
Sony (1953)	• Manufacturing—centralized • R&D—centralized	Foreign market access	Setting up manufacturing subsidiaries in the United States, Brazil, Taiwan, etc. (1970s)	Selling some of its manufacturing plants to Solectron and outsourcing more to independent manufacturers (1990s)	Realization of the loss of innovative capabilities (2003)	Reduced outsourcing for high-tech components and increased in-house production of high-demand products (2000s)

Singapore, Indonesia, South Africa, Kenya, and also Algeria in the early 1970s. Almost all of these places were low cost locations. In 1968, the company's profits rose by 10%. Philips set up operations in low cost Taiwan (1970), where it began production of monochrome picture tubes (by 1989, this facility had become the world's largest tube manufacturer and Philips had a total of five plants in Taiwan). In 1974, the company discontinued its noncolor picture tube production in the United Kingdom and moved production to low cost locations. Around this time CE companies the world over were involved in similar moves to low cost regions for manufacturing. By 1974, Philips already had TV and audio plants in Singapore, a black-and-white TV plant in Taiwan, a stereo plant in Brazil, and an electronics production plant in South Korea.

Philips suffered a setback in profits in the fourth quarter of 1975. This was also a turning point for Philips as it faced tough competition from the Japanese companies. Philips's video technology, V2000, was in direct competition with Beta and VHS—that is, the Japanese VCR systems. By the end of the 1970s, the Japanese companies had entered Europe and formed partnerships and collaborations and this helped them gain a foothold and market share in Europe. Although the V2000 format developed by Philips was technologically superior to the Japanese VCR systems, the V2000 system failed partly due to Philips's inability to find partners (Dai, 1996). This was the beginning of the collaborative era for Philips, during which it went on an alliance spree and partnered with several foreign firms. Philips increased its presence in Japan by buying a stake in Japan's Marantz in 1980 from U.S.-based Superscope that owned a majority stake in the company. Marantz, then owned by Philips, soon became its base in Japan for the production of goods at low costs. Hence, as time went by, Philips, like other CE firms had spread itself over several low cost regions, which enabled it to compete more efficiently in the industry.

Sony set up its first foreign production plant, Champagne Plant, in 1959 in Hong Kong. It was a transistor radio assembly plant through a local firm that provided all the capital and managed the business. It was only a contractual agreement for production. Goods at this plant (mainly assembled transistor radios) were then sent to Europe, Australia, Canada, and other areas. However, Sony already shut down the plant in 1961 due to some undisclosed "disagreement" with the local firm, making for an unsuccessful first move abroad. Compared to most U.S. firms, Sony moved operations abroad much later. Competition in the industry compelled it to set up several foreign plants in the 1970s. In 1973, Sony formed Sony do Brazil. In the same year, Sony also denied reports that it would second source products from National Semicon. By 1973, Sony was manufacturing radios, black and white TVs, and tape recorders in its Sony Korea subsidiary. It also formed a joint venture with a Korean partner, Hwasin Industries, for production of color TVs. Following a drop in overall sales, Sony reorganized its distribution network. Other foreign subsidiaries set up in the 1970s and 1980s include audio manufacturing subsidiary, Sony da Amazonia, in Brazil; a VCR factory in Taiwan and in Malaysia; an audio tape manufacturing subsidiary, Magneticos de Mexico, a joint venture with Motoradio; Sony Videobras for video tape manufacturing; and several others worldwide. It also established Sony Precision Engineering Center in Singapore to manufacture optical pick-ups for CD players and joint production of CE products with a Chinese trading firm. Most of these offshore plants were in low cost locations and involved joint production with local partners.

Until the late 1980s, Sony kept R&D in Japan. By 1988, Sony had considerably increased offshore production. The company claimed that the appreciation of the yen prompted it to expand overseas production because this made it less profitable to manufacture goods in Japan. In the 1980s around 20% of Sony's production was undertaken by its foreign plants, and it felt the need to further increase manufacturing overseas. Sony aimed to develop its Asian plants as supply centers for high-technology products. The company hoped that it would achieve at least 35% of manufacturing outside of Japan in the 1990s. Thus, it moved toward increasing offshore production in the 1980s. But, in 1985, Sony announced that it would start shifting focus from CE to business customers in response to a fall in profits. It also started setting up regional R&D and engineering centers in 1989 such as Advanced Video Technology Center (AVTC), the development base for high-definition TV (HDTV) in San Jose in the United States. By the first half of the 1990s, Sony had over 20 R&D centers outside Japan.

All three firms perceived the need to lower manufacturing costs, and Philips and Sony responded to this need by setting up plants in low-cost locations, as did their industry rivals. Emerson seemed to opt directly for sourcing components and then final products from overseas manufacturers, which were low-cost producers. CE firms often followed each other to low cost destinations in Asia, thereby overturning each other's temporary gains and then reentering the race to reduce costs even further. Nevertheless, this opening move to low cost regions seemed to be successful as profits rose initially in all three cases. The relentless pursuit of advanced technologies, however, soon prompted CE firms to reduce costs even further, which characterizes stage 2 of our model.

Stage 2: Phasing Out (Transferring Production to Independent Operators)

U.S.-based Emerson Radio moved through the stages of the model we will conceptualize later much faster than the other two firms. After the takeover by NUC, Emerson Radio continued to produce television sets and other CE products. However, sales were low and profits remained elusive. Emerson Radio began operating in the red under NUC, with the problem being apparently too little volume to cover fixed costs. Between 1967 and 1971 the division lost about $27 million. In order to reduce fixed costs, NUC outsourced manufacturing of Emerson Radio's CE products to U.S.-based Admiral Corp. Under the pact, Emerson Radio was in charge of designing, engineering, and marketing. At the same time, Emerson also imported home entertainment products and some other CE goods from East Asian manufacturers. However in 1973, Admiral terminated its contract with Emerson Radio, which was thereafter dependent almost entirely on Asian OEMers (original equipment manufacturers) for its products.

Philips went through its own share of problems, and after profits took a beating in 1975, it was encouraged to further lower its fixed cost levels by increasing its reliance on offshore manufacturers. The company continued to phase out production in higher-cost locations, such as its color TV manufacturing plant in Canada, and moved further production offshore. In 1981, it set up its seventh factory in Singapore for the production of radios, increased its investment in product development and automation in Singapore, and also set up an audio equipment plant in China in 1985.

In 1980, Philips restructured its organization. The V2000 debacle had hit Philips hard. Until then, it was a prosperous organization but after the V2000 case, profitability fell. At the time, it introduced its make-or-buy policy. Under this new policy, the company withdrew itself from certain industries such as military and defense. The company that was managed thus far as locally responsive in its various markets started moving toward globalizing its businesses, divesting itself of noncore operations, and entering joint ventures for production. In the later 1980s, Philips's chairman-CEO at the time clarified the new direction of the company by stating, "On a world scale, you must be selective and stick to what you can do best" (*TV Digest*, 1988, p. 10). It also sold its white goods unit to Whirlpool and its minicomputers unit to Digital Equipment. Under its agreement with Whirlpool, Whirlpool was to own 53% of the joint venture with Philips, but soon Whirlpool bought out Philips's stake in the company. Philips continued to sell white goods until the 1990s when it disengaged itself from the business entirely. In 1981, Philips spun off its electronics parts subsidiary and in a series of sales a few years later and sold two more electronics component units to Cambridge Electronics Industries. In 1981 Sanyo acquired Philips's UK color TV production plant to sell its own color TV sets. In 1983, after the failure of its V2000, Philips bought VHS models from Matsushita in Japan and sold them in Australia and New Zealand. NAP (North American Philips, Philips's U.S. subsidiary), on the other hand, purchased TV sets from Matsushita for sale under the Magnavox, Philco, and Sylvania brands in the United States. Japan's Pioneer was also supplying compact disc players to NAP. Matsushita also supplied VCRs to be sold under the Magnavox brand name in the United States. Thus NAP was entirely dependent on products supplied by Japanese companies.

What is notable about Philips's strategies is its proclivity to form joint ventures. After the 1980s, the company ended up with many pacts with foreign CE companies for joint production or R&D in Asia. Significant examples of these are joint production of VHS recorders in South Korea with local Dong Won Electronics and the venture for compact disc players with Shenzhen Shen Fei Laser of China. These enabled the partner in the venture to learn from the more technologically advanced Philips. Philips gradually increased reliance on these partners, and in many cases the partners finally took over operations from Philips. Philips had a videodisc laser optics factory in Shenzhen, China, and it also formed a partnership with China's Shenzhen Advanced Science and Technology Development Company to produce cassettes for Philips in the 1980s. The output was to be used for the Chinese market as well as different world markets. By the end of 1989, Philips had increased its dependence on this plant and begun manufacturing CD boom boxes, laserdisc players, and optical discs. This 50–50 joint venture with Shenzhen used Philips's equipment worth $40 million and also employees and technicians trained by Philips. In 2001, Philips reduced its share in the joint venture. But by this time, the Chinese partner had ample opportunity to acquire knowledge about Philips's technology. Philips also had a 20% stake in a VCR, and other components, production plant in Czechoslovakia. Philips was providing this plant with production facilities, know-how, information systems, and employee training—all forms of tacit knowledge.

Other divestments include the sale of Philips's 35% stake in Matsushita[3] to Matsushita's parent company, which had by then learned most of Philips's technologies and product development capabilities in CE products, the sale of its manufacturing division in South Korea to South Korean investors, and the sale of plants that were manufacturing television and audio equipment in Singapore and Brazil in 1998. As recently as September 2002, Philips sold its contract-manufacturing unit for CE goods (PCMS, set up by Philips in 1999) to the U.S.-based EMS (electronics manufacturing services) company, Jabil Circuit, Inc. Under the pact, Philips guaranteed sales worth $4 billion to Jabil over a period of 4 years even after the unit was sold. Jabil also acquired nine of Philips's plants (mostly in low cost locations worldwide) and 5,000 employees, which include 150 design engineers.

The year 1997 was significant for Philips in that, followed by a loss of $349 million in 1996, the company went through a series of measures to boost profits, and these included a host of outsourcing deals. Executive VP-CFO Eustace said, "In the past, we did not 'contain our creativity', under the label of freedom, we were spending an enormous amount of money on R&D" (*TV Digest*, 1997a, p. 12). This statement indicates the direction of Philips's upcoming strategies toward outsourcing whereby it reduced its R&D expenditures. In October 1997, Philips moved from in-house production of 19–20-in. TV tubes to sourcing them from Samsung and Toshiba. In the same year, it sold its TV plant in Greeneville, Tennessee, in the United States to Taylor-White. As recently as 2001, Philips laid off employees at its own VCR factory in Austria and instead moved production of VCRs to Japan's Funai Electric. Philips gradually reduced its R&D function for CE products and ultimately lost its technological capabilities (next stages).

Like the American and European CE firms before it, Sony also eventually gave in to pressures and increased its reliance on outside operators and slowly moved toward outsourcing deals with foreign firms. But, some of Sony's first outsourcing ventures were with domestic companies that it was familiar with. For example, Sony's audio speaker manufacturing subsidiary Audio Research was launched in 1969 as a joint venture of Sony and Pioneer but Sony acquired it in 1972. In 1983, it sold Audio Research in Japan to Minebea, a Japanese producer of ball bearings. Nevertheless, Sony maintained ties with Audio Research in the form of an outsourcing relationship whereby Sony continued to be its customer and provided it with R&D support. Their relationship constituted a typical Japanese-style *keiretsu* relationship.

Sony also entered into agreements with many different firms in low cost countries to supply components. In October 2000, Sony was outsourcing 60–70% of its radio and speakers manufacturing and around 50% of its component stereos to Chinese equipment makers. The company claimed that outsourcing to Asian countries such as China and Taiwan would boost its competitiveness against Western firms.

Sony went on to increase outsourcing to other firms such as U.S.-based personal computers and telecommunications equipment manufacturer, Solectron[4] in 2000. Under the pact, Solectron acquired two of Sony's manufacturing units: one in Japan and the other in Taiwan. Solectron was to retain the employees at the factories and supply products to Sony as well as to other customers. Solectron had been expanding through mergers and had previously acquired Singapore's NatSteel Electronics for $2.4 billion in anticipation of catering to Japanese business (Wilson, 2001). By outsourcing production, Sony hoped to lower costs and increase profitability.

Thenceforth, Sony continued to divest its manufacturing operations in an attempt to reduce fixed investment. At the extreme, Sony even considered outsourcing production of its core CE production to its unit, Aiwa, of which Sony owned 50% at the time. Regarding Sony's decision to outsource production to third parties, the company's president, Ando, was reported as saying, "There will be some products on which we think it better to entrust the production also to non-Sony group companies and business partners, and we currently outsource some audio products" (*AFX News*, 2000). Sony was outsourcing some manufacturing to Celestica, Flextronics, and SCI systems. The move to increase outsourcing followed a fall in profits in 1999. By March 2003, Sony had reduced the number of its factories worldwide from 70 (in 1999) to 54. Sony hoped that by outsourcing, it could reduce the fixed costs of manufacturing by transferring it to other contractor firms and instead be involved more in the design and planning stages of products. Sony planned to increase its reliance on products from Taiwanese vendors to $938 million by 2001.

Thus, stage 2 was marked by significant divestitures by our firms, some of which were to local partners in foreign locations. This enabled the firms to reduce fixed costs but this move gradually pushed these firms into stage 3 of our model. As outsourcing appeared to produce short-term benefits, the CE firms increased their reliance on foreign firms and were soon exposed to the long-term effects of outsourcing.

Stage 3: Increasing Dependence on Foreign Suppliers

In the case of Emerson Radio, NUC sold the brand name to Major Electronics in 1973. U.S.-based Major Electronics used to produce radios, tape recorders, and other equipment. In 1968 the company began importing these products from overseas establishments and became a distributor of finished Far Eastern goods. When it took over Emerson Radio, it was buying 80% of its components and products from East Asia. In 1980 Emerson Radio dropped its last U.S.-made product—the phonograph line—because labor costs had made it unprofitable. Thus Emerson was completely dependent on foreign suppliers for all its finished products. As firm president Stephen Lane commented, "I think most of the profits we've made have been because of controlling overhead and purchasing" (*Forbes*, 1981). According to Lane, "Our philosophy is simple, that is, to have the best of two worlds. To be in sophisticated, state-of-the-art products by maintaining our own engineering and design capabilities here and keeping close tabs on quality control at all our vendors, and at the same time being able to react quickly to changes by having no hard assets, which would mean worrying about keeping factories going and people employed in a recession" (Mehler, 1984, p. 86). Other than manufacturing capabilities, Emerson Radio also lost its design and technical capabilities as it made its fortune by persuading its East Asian suppliers to imitate high-end, branded (Sony, Panasonic) CE products and then selling them to consumers at much lower prices. Based on published records, around the mid-1980s, Emerson Radio had outsourcing deals with over 15 Asian suppliers, which depended on Emerson for over 90% of their business. In November 1984, Lane claimed, "It's been 12 years since we achieved our running goal of 5 [percent] net of sales" (Mehler, 1984, p. 87). About this time, Emerson possessed design and engineering capabilities only for audio products, "But, in the video area, outside of the cabinetry, the U.S. firm has deferred to the superior design skills of its Japanese suppliers, such as Mitsubishi" (Mehler, 1984, p. 86).

Emerson struggled to hang on to its CE business. In 1985, it acquired a CE company H. H. Scott, a relatively small producer of audio equipment; in 1986, it introduced Asian-made refrigerators to the market; and in the following couple of years added several more electronics-related products to its range including computers in 1990. However, by 1991, it had withdrawn the H. H. Scott line and some other CE products. In the late 1980s, having lost its CE capabilities, it had begun diversifying into other areas. By the early 1990s, Emerson Radio was heavily in debt of over $200 million. To add to that, it was involved in lawsuits and in 1993, the company finally filed for bankruptcy. What remains of the old Emerson Radio today is its brand name. Even today the company capitalizes on the brand by licensing it to other CE firms. Philips experienced its own share of troubles due to increased outsourcing. In 1988, Philips' woes reflected those of the U.S. CE firms not too long ago. Philips's income fell again and the company claimed that competition from the Far East led to its problems. As Philips itself established plants abroad and outsourced production, it gradually increased its dependence on these foreign suppliers and unintentionally but invariably passed on tacit knowledge. The Philips-Sony liaison was a particularly interesting one.

It began in October 1979, when the two companies joined hands to use each other's patent rights for certain products (tapes, cassettes, discs, etc). This pact gave Sony access to Philips's V2000 system as well as its CD-audio system. Industry analysts concluded that due to this arrangement, Sony learned to manufacture its own optical videodisc for consumer use although the company denied these charges. Philips meanwhile had plans to launch videodiscs in Europe by 1980. Philips made consumer versions while Sony made industrial videodiscs until 1982 when Sony announced that it would sell its videodiscs in Knoxville, NAP's hometown.

Philips continued to post lower income forecasts toward the end of the 1980s and planned to cut its workforce by 10,000–20,000 globally in the following years. The company hoped that its initial measures for cost cutting would increase profitability. But, in 1988, Philips lowered its forecast for the year and announced that it would take severe measures to improve its operations through further cost cutting. In reaction to lower earnings, the company reduced its European plants from 170 to 110 in the next 5 years and also shifted more production to Mexico and Taiwan. The company already operated plants in these countries at the time and this shift increased the company's reliance on these foreign plants. It hoped to cut costs by $400 million. The company started to improve profitability for a while until profits fell again. And so the efforts went on. Toward the end of the 1990s, Philips was looking for buyers for its TV assembly plant in Juarez, Mexico (*TV Digest*, 1998).

In the late 1980s Philips was involved in R&D of LCD (liquid crystal display), a joint project of four of Philips's divisions, CE, lighting, research, and components. Although a certain part of the development efforts used to take place at headquarters in Eindhoven, the Netherlands, production was shifted to the Philips-owned plant, Marantz, in Japan. In 1986, Philips reorganized Marantz Japan into an R&D base. Prior to 1988, NAP outsourced production of TVs to Matsushita but in 1988, Marantz (Marantz Japan Inc., or MJI) began shipping VCRs to the United States for sale under Philips's brand. In 1988, Philips manufactured liquid display TVs at the Marantz plant and later increased its reliance on that manufacturing facility by producing wireless radio equipment in 1991 and new CD players in 1999. In 1997, Marantz introduced its own (Marantz-branded) low price version (with some small changes) of Philips' television models in Asia. Hence, Marantz, of which Philips owned 50.6% at the time, had learned Philips' technology, upgraded its competences and forward integrated into launching and marketing its own line of similar products. Finally, in 2001, Philips reduced its controlling ownership stake in MJI, which also acquired the "Marantz" brand and its business in Europe and the United States from Philips and established its own units in these places. The companies still maintained working relations in many areas, but MJI also developed and introduced its own products (mainly audio equipment) under its own brand name, Marantz. A year later, in 2002, Philips further reduced its stake to 14.7% in MJI when MJI merged with U.S.-based Denon Ltd.

The late 1990s was the age of DVD technology in the CE industry, and ideally Philips should have been a formidable contender. But, by his own admission, the Philips Sound & Vision chairman and CEO said, with respect to Philips' DVD program in the United States, "We've had to catch up on DVD in every sense of the word. We didn't have a DVD program 12 months ago and now we've launched a player" (*TV Digest*, 1997b, p. 15). The company launched a DVD player that was being sourced from Toshiba (Japan). By the end of the 20th century, Philips was on its way out of the CE industry having lost most of its development capabilities.

Meanwhile, Japan's Sony faced its own set of challenges with its partners. Even after selling its audio speaker manufacturing subsidiary Audio Research to Minebea in 1983 (explained in stage 2 above), Sony maintained ties with Audio Research in the form of an outsourcing relationship whereby Sony continued to be its customer and to provide it with R&D support. The following year, Minebea set up its own subsidiary for audio R&D by merging Audio Research (acquired from Sony) with another of its divisions, Minebea Denshi Co., Ltd. In this manner, Minebea learned Sony's audio research capabilities.

What started off as simple contractual agreements with foreign operators eventually led Sony to increase its reliance on its partners. Agreements also took the form of joint ventures. For example, in 1992, Viettronics Tan Binh, a Ho Chi Minh City, Vietnam-based local electric appliance maker, was in a licensing pact with Sony to produce color TVs and audio players. In 1994, Sony established a joint venture with the same company to manufacture 14-inch and 21-inch Trinitron color TVs and audio products for the Vietnamese market. Thus, with this new venture in 1994, Sony in fact increased its dependence on Viettronics (from licensing to joint venture) to jointly manufacture goods at low cost.

After the Solectron deal in 2000, Sony announced that it would farm out more production to independent manufacturers if need be. It also finalized plans to create engineering, manufacturing, and customer services units to cater to the needs of Sony and other firms that outsourced production. Taiwan being a source of low cost labor, Sony increased its reliance on Taiwanese firms to supply its products. In merely a period of 1 year, Sony bought goods worth $2 billion from Taiwan in 2001, which was an increase of seven times on the year 2000. Such was the extent of its increasing reliance on subcontractors.

In February 2003, Sony entered a contract with Oak Technology to supply decoder chips to Sony, which would replace IC (integrated circuit) chips developed by Sony's in-house facility. To start with, the decoder chips were to be used in Sony's digital TVs to be sold in Japan, but Oak Tech planned to supply chips for use in Sony's products sold in Europe and the United States later on. Previously, Oak Tech was in a similar decoder supply pact with Sony for its personal video recorders in Japan. Oak Tech also supplied chips to other CE companies like Thomson and Daewoo—another example of Sony's ever growing dependence on external suppliers and the increasing capabilities of such suppliers.

The year 2003 witnessed an awakening at Sony. Touted as the "Sony Shock," Sony incurred a net loss of $927 million in the first 3 months of 2003. Many said that Sony's state reflected that of the Japanese CE industry and also the economy as a whole. But the unpredictable global environment and the company's activities in the past few years might have exacerbated its performance. Sony had introduced only a few "new" products in the recent past, and to add to that, it was losing its once feted technological ability to innovate. The company used to "generate huge profit from its vertically integrated business model in which it developed high-performance parts . . . on a commercial basis before anyone else and released hit products based on them" (*Nikkei Weekly*, 2003). However, in the 1990s, it lost a major part of its technological glory. According to Ken Kutaragi, president of Sony Computer Entertainment and a recent addition to Sony's top management team, "top management chose not to continue investing in technology" (SinoCast China IT Watch, 2003).

Sony's technological excellence and product creativity were further tarnished by recalls in 2006 of Sony-made lithium-ion batteries used for notebook computers. The Sony batteries have been blamed for causing some Dell and Apple computers to overheat and catch fire. As if to rub salt into Sony's wounds, due to delays in production of blue laser diodes, a key component of Blu-ray Disc players, Sony was also forced to postpone the European release of the PlayStation 3 game console from November 2006 to March 2007. Sony's current crises are also attributed to its increased outsourcing by farming out a large part of production of these components to EMS (electronic manufacturing services) companies (*Nikkei News*, 2006).

Stage 4: Industry Departure
From or Reduction of Outsourcing

As time went by, Emerson Radio and Philips lost their place in the CE industry. Emerson Radio moved through the first three stages of the model so quickly that it did not get a chance to salvage itself and instead sought to diversify into other, sometimes unrelated areas. The brand name "Emerson" was associated solely with CE and having lost its technological competences, the firm is presently struggling to survive. Philips managed to shift its focus away from CE to its lighting and other businesses and managed to survive but not as a significant CE player.

Although Philips was originally founded as a lighting company, it made a very successful transition into CE and maintained its foothold in the industry for several decades. What is evident is that at several times Philips experienced declining profitability, restructured its organization and altered its strategies. Prior to the 1970s, Philips changed its strategy from one of local responsiveness to a more global strategy and reduced product lines. Then at the time of the failure of its V2000 home video system around 1980, Philips believed that it was probably due to its lack of partnership with other companies to effectively commercialize its technology (Dai, 1996). More recently, in 1996, Philips incurred a loss of $349 million on year and the company once again decided to increase outsourcing and increase its reliance on third party manufacturers. As of 2002, Philips planned to increase outsourcing of chip production from 10% to between 20 and 30%. The company also increased its reliance on products from United Microelectronics Corp. and Singapore-based Chartered Semiconductor Manufacturing. Thus, Philips never reduced outsourcing but instead increased it. In June 2001, Philips even abandoned its wireless phone manufacturing efforts, and to cut costs, it also reduced its interest in its Chinese R&D plant by transferring control over to its Chinese partner, which was to make phones and supply them to Philips for sale under Philips's name. At the dawn of the 21st century, Philips was no longer an independent producer in the CE industry. It sold off its remaining CE divisions including Polygram and "to emphasize the shift of Philips' business out of CE, the CEO, Cor Boonstra, moved Philips' headquarters from Eindhoven to Amsterdam" (Chandler, 2001, p. 221). Today, Philips markets CE products, but its main focus is on its other divisions, such as lighting and semiconductors.

The only company that is still active in the industry, Sony, is learning the hazards of excessive outsourcing and gradually reducing its reliance on outsiders for its core products. Although Sony is better known for CE than semiconductors, it uses semiconductors in many of its CE products (digital cameras, camcorders). In 1998, Sony's profits fell along with those of other Japanese companies in the semiconductors industry such as Toshiba and Fujitsu. However, the slump was attributed to lower demand for their products. Surprisingly, in 2000, Sony reduced outsourcing for semiconductors by 5% and also shifted to in-house production of some of its "most-wanted" products like personal computers, camcorders, and digital cameras. There is no hard evidence that shows why Sony reduced outsourcing for its core products, but this move followed a fall in profits in 1999. In the year 2000, Sony announced that it would set up a "supervisory company," which would be responsible for management of design, purchase, and manufacturing for several of Sony's plants. Thus, although Sony has not entirely eliminated its dependence on outsourcing to keep costs under control, it has moved toward in-house production of its popular moneymaking products. Also, the establishment of a company to monitor production indicates a very cautious components strategy. As Sony president Ando said, "Engineering and manufacturing are (some of) Sony's key strengths. That is why key products will be done by our own internal production, not OEM" (*Financial Times*, 2000, p. 36).

The fear of technology falling into the wrong hands also extends to national governments. In 2000, the Japanese government imposed an export control on Sony's PlayStation 2 (PS2) electronic game console. PS2's 128-bit central microprocessor developed by Sony and Toshiba had twice the raw number-crunching power of Intel's most advanced Pentium chip used in professional desktop computers. When coupled with a video camera, the PS2 could make an ideal missile-guidance system (*Economist*, 2000, Re, 2003). Then in 2001, Sony was to outsource the console of its PS2 product to Taiwanese firms capable of producing at low costs. There were two drivers for this outsourcing initiative. First was Sony's inability to meet demand and second was Microsoft's move to outsource the XBOX (in direct competition with PS2) to firms in Taiwan. The U.S. and Japanese governments asked Sony to keep production and assembly of the console in Japan lest the Taiwanese firms (who were low cost subcontractors) could learn the DVD application of the console's chip and use it for military purposes (Yu & Teng, 2001). In 2001, Sony also announced that it would not expand outsourcing of its personal computers production at its plant in China.

Although on the surface it appears to have evaded the grave dangers of excessive outsourcing by contracting out only "peripheral operations," it continues to face the danger of losing its core competences. In May 2002, Sony stressed the fact that it was keeping key technologies in Japan as compared with other Japanese makers who were throwing away their future due to outsourcing. In September 2002 it was reported that "three of Japan's leading electronics manufacturers will start making DVD recorders, reversing a trend for outsourcing the production of such items" (Pilling, 2002). Sony is one of those companies. Whereas on one hand, Sony reacted to its weakening situation by reducing outsourcing for its core operations, it continued to outsource peripheral technologies. Sony did not focus on increasing investment in developing technology or its reinstating control over manufacturing operations until its awakening in 2003. In 2003, the company took proactive measures to improve its position in the industry. Under the leadership of Kutaragi, it has charted out a course to bring it back to its role as a technological leader. For the purpose, it planned to invest $8.6 billion in "electrical equipment and electronics over 3 years and the introduction of in-house production and centralized management of key components" (*Nikkei Weekly*, 2003). Sony also revealed that it would reduce the number of components used to 100,000 parts (90% decrease) by the year 2005 and also indicate 20,000 standard parts to be shared by engineers, companywide. By doing so, it would be able to shorten the time taken for new product development. In late 2005, Sony announced that under the leadership of its first-ever foreign chief executive Howard Stringer, it would reduce 10,000 jobs and close 11 of its 65 plants to boost profits at its electronics unit. However, these cuts and closures were not expected to affect jobs and plants in China, its low cost manufacturing location.

A Stage Model

With these cases in hand, we can now construct a stage model around outsourcing and competences that draws upon existing theory, specifically the resource-based view and dynamic capabilities perspective (Barney, 1991; Leiblein, Reuer, & Dalsace, 2002; Teece, Pisano, & Shuen, 1997) and work on value appropriation in alliances (Nooteboom, 1999). The relationship between outsourcing and a firm's competences, the set of routines in which it has specialized, is a complex one. On the one hand, outsourcing can free up resources that can be used to speed up or redirect competence development in other areas, the argument used by some proponents of outsourcing (Quinn, 1999). In our cases, however, we observe the inverse effect as over time outsourcing seemed to lead to a loss of competences. Our stage model contains a description of the process through which such competence loss occurs. We then tackle the question under which conditions such a process presents itself and, related to that, when it does not.

The resource-based view of the firm suggests that firms can be conceived of as controlling bundles of resources—also called competences (Barney, 1991; Wernerfelt, 1984). These competences are constructed through previous experience and over time. When resources are valuable, hard to imitate, and substitute and rare, they can lead to sustainable competitive advantage (Barney, 1991). The dynamic capabilities approach (Teece, Pisano, & Shuen, 1997) adds to this a process perspective by suggesting that capabilities are constructed through evolutionary, path-dependent, processes. Outsourcing invariably involves ceding some control over resources, for instance, in the form of transferring machinery, technology, and/or people. In an arm's-length transaction, all control is ceded. In a cooperative or partnership outsourcing relationship, firms arguably maintain some control over resources, even if these physically reside at suppliers.

In such relations there are two key questions. The first question is how much value is created and the second is who gets to appropriate that value (Nooteboom, 1999). Value creation is not a central concern here, but suffice it to say that various mechanisms can be instated by the outsourcing partners to create additional rents (Dyer & Singh, 1998). In our cases, lack of value appropriation is the central concern—one that has been addressed in the literature as well (Nooteboom, 1999; Porter, 1980; Teece, 1986, 2000). One way in which insufficient value appropriation may occur is when in-house competences are leaked to the supplier, for instance, in the form of the supplier taking on board the outsourcing firm's intellectual property rights (Teece, 2000), a problem especially prevalent when no institutional guarantees are provided (Teece, 1986). The supplier may subsequently start to compete head-on with the outsourcing firm or supply to competing firms leading to a loss in bargaining power (Porter, 1980). Another possibility is the gradual erosion of the firm's internal competences because it can no longer engage in learning-by-doing leading to hollowing out (Bettis, Bradley, & Hamel, 1992; Kotabe, 1998).

Our stage model, based on the three CE cases, integrates both streams of literature. We suggest that firms need to maintain and develop their competence base in order to sustain their advantages vis-à-vis competitors, but may be unable to do so when engaging in (international) outsourcing because they cannot distill enough value from their relations with suppliers. We propose that there is a *"vicious outsourcing cycle,"* which occurs when the future need for in-house competences differs substantially from the currently perceived need and firms are unable to bridge that difference because they are too dependent on outsourcing. Specifically, a vicious outsourcing cycle can occur when firms either lose competences whose contribution is not understood well enough or close off trajectories of competence learning that prove to be important in the future. One might alternatively refer to these conditions as causal ambiguity and uncertainty. Exhibit 14.1 describes the different stages of the outsourcing cycle.

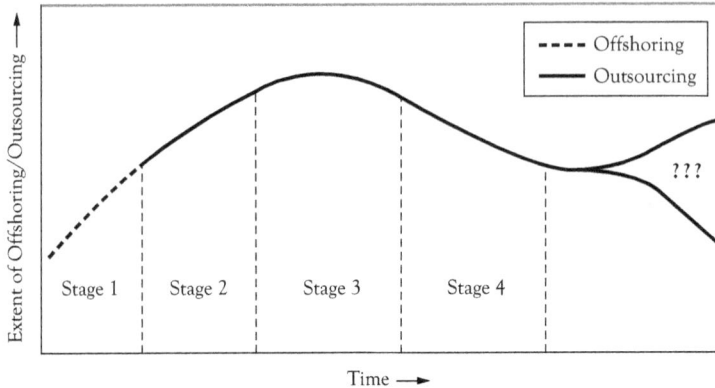

Stage 1: Offshore sourcing by setting up a foreign subsidiary
Stage 2: Phasing out of foreign subsidiary to independent operators
Stage 3: Increasing dependence on suppliers leading to less value appropriation
Stage 4: Industry departure or reduction of outsourcing

Exhibit 14.1. The Outsourcing Cycle

In stage 1, firms see an opportunity to lower their production costs by shifting in-house production to a different country. As we showed above, Philips, for instance, set up plants in a wide range of low labor cost countries in the 1960s. Vernon's (1974) IPLC model clearly illustrates this stage. Because of substantial labor cost differentials, the existing production location, which is normally the firm's home country in the early stages of internationalization, is no longer seen as competitive. Sometimes other, more qualitative factors, such as the need to access new customers or suppliers, may come into play as well as has been documented in the literature on plant locations and facility management (Ferdows, 1997). In terms of Dunning's (1988) organization, location, and internalization (OLI) model, which intends to explain when certain types of internationalization may or may not occur, activities are transferred from the home base to low-cost countries in order to benefit from L-type advantages available in these offshore locations and because a firm possesses the O-type advantages necessary to engage in international production. As a consequence of this decision, production and engineering capabilities are transferred and replicated abroad. Such a decision will bring relief in the short term as it allows the firm to maintain or improve its margins. As suggested above, Emerson increased its profits in 1959 after a cost-cutting operation.

However, because most locations are not unique, competitors can easily replicate location decisions, and perhaps even improve on them. There are many instances of an industrywide bandwagon where firms all relocate to the same country, for example, in textiles production. The classic description of such bandwagons in international business is Knickerbocker's (1973) work on "follow-the-leader" in foreign direct investment. In other words, after some time competitors will offset any temporary gains from a production shift. If cost pressures remain high and there is overcapacity in the industry, the firm finds itself in need of taking additional measures. In our cases this tended to show up in the form of some immediate financial crisis, which came upon each of the three firms at some point in time.

When responding to such a crisis, one important option is to sell off the foreign production plant to an independent operator and outsource production to this firm or simply to outsource without selling existing assets—stage 2 of the model. As we saw, Emerson for instance started to make extensive use of Asian OEMs. Referring again to the OLI model, the advantages of internalization (I) seem to have disappeared to the point where the market (outsourcing) is seen as a better solution. If these advantages decrease, outsourcing becomes a more viable option. In the case of Sony this occurred when it outsourced most of the making of stereo equipment to Chinese suppliers. Production and engineering capabilities are now transferred to, or replicated by, the supplier because the outsourcing firm will help it set up production. Thus the value appropriation issues mentioned earlier (Nooteboom, 1999; Teece, 2000) emerge.

Given that there are such issues around value appropriation, what motives do firms have for moving from stage 1 to stage 2 of our model? An outsourcing firm replaces internal fixed costs by the production costs of outside suppliers, which are variable from its perspective. This lowers the breakeven point, providing the firm with more flexibility to respond to unforeseen changes, which are quite common in the CE industry. In particular, it helps the firm to reduce the size of potential losses. Since in our cases outsourcing often appears to be a consequence of a drop in sales and profitability, this move seems sensible if further drops can be expected. Financial markets for instance may appreciate such decisions in the context of the CE industry where firms like Emerson and Philips saw themselves confronted with ever more intense competition from Asian producers. In case of a crisis the alternative to outsourcing is to restructure internally, which often does not involve terminating the production of specific components, like outsourcing may do, but of entire products. The wholesale closure of plants can be socially and politically sensitive and costly, and therefore outsourcing may be a preferred solution.

But if the firm outsources its fixed costs in this way, these costs will still have to be borne by the independent supplier instead. Unless that supplier can find a way to be more cost-efficient and to make these costs variable, such a move could amount to a mere accounting fallacy. Perhaps some managers and some investors buy into this but we have little hard evidence that is the case. Yet, as illustrated by the emergence of EMS companies, there are reasons to believe that independent suppliers can be more cost-efficient and can make better use of fixed investments. First, independent local suppliers, operating in a low cost location, do not have to bear the same overheads that producers from more expensive countries, like Emerson, Philips, and later Sony, faced. They are run locally and, being a much smaller firm, can also be more nimble. Second, and related to the first point, their expenses for research and development are much lower, at least initially, as they import more advanced technology from elsewhere. Philips and Sony, for example, have large R&D bases because they want to be first movers in new technologies, whereas the supplier in a low cost country would be content with adopting new technologies invented by others. Perhaps more importantly, the outsourcing firm needs to spread its fixed costs over a relatively fixed volume of products but the independent supplier has the option to supply other customers, thereby reusing its assets. So after outsourcing takes place, the supplier can enjoy larger economies of scale in production, resulting in further lower average costs because fixed costs are spread over a higher volume of production. For example, this logic applied to Aiwa, as Sony was contemplating to outsource more production to it.

Furthermore, outsourcing changes the incentive structure of the independent supplier in important ways. Some arguments for this may be found in Grossman and Hart's (1986) "theory of costly contracting," also known as the property rights approach. They suggest that outsourcing takes place when it is relatively easy to write complete contracts, in which specific rights can be assigned to both the outsourcing firm and its supplier. When this is the case, there is no longer an incentive for the outsourcing firm to own and vertically integrate the supplier (Grossman & Hart, 1986). For this to happen, a supplier must develop a set of distinct production capabilities for a component or product, to which property rights may then be assigned. These distinct capabilities can develop if the product architecture is well understood, allowing for easy separation of tasks. Once the supplier has gained its independence, it can then develop its capabilities further, which leads to future cost improvements. The supplier will have an incentive to develop its production capabilities because these will directly drive its cost levels, and hence its profitability, and indirectly its ability to retain the outsourcing firm as a customer in the future and to attract further customers. Because both the outsourcing firm and potential future customers will be making a comparison of their own production capabilities with those of the supplier firm, the supplier's odds of attracting future business increase with improvements in those capabilities (Jacobides & Winter, 2005). In Quinn's (1999) view, the supplier builds these advantages, to the extent that it can become best-in-world in the production of this component or product, through increasing focus.

Over time several changes can occur that alter the balance of decision making and push firms into stage 3. One change, quite common in the context of emerging countries, is learning by the supplier, which can take the forms of increased productivity and upgraded production capabilities, as discussed above. Philips experienced this in its earlier ventures with Japanese producers and Sony found this out in Taiwan. If supplier productivity is increased by learning-by-doing and this increase is shared exclusively with the outsourcing company and not with its competitors, there is no real problem. However, when suppliers manage to upgrade their own competences, there is little to prevent them from forward integration into the firm's markets. Thus the supplier can easily become a competitor. Emerson found itself competing against the Asian producers who were initially its suppliers. The buyer now has serious problems to appropriate as much value from the relationship as it would like to. When the gain of a buyer-supplier alliance is no longer shared evenly in the eyes of the buyer, it may want to reconsider its motives for having entered that alliance (Doz & Hamel, 1998).

The bargaining constellation is a second area of possible change (Porter, 1980). When the supplier starts to supply to competing firms as well, it will grow in size, become less dependent on the original buyer, and raise prices, which may pose the outsourcing firm with the need to build up alternative supply sources, if that is possible in the first place. Rather than the supplier being captive, the buyer can become captive this way. A third change can be in the outsourcing firm's in-house capacity to produce and engineer the product. Because the firm no longer produces the product, it will become more difficult to keep particularly tacit knowledge about production technology up-to-date as loss of manufacturing experience leads to a loss in development capability, particularly for existing products (Dankbaar, 2007). Emerson for instance had clearly given up on the idea of retaining any production knowledge in-house. This may also affect the ability to implement engineering changes. The supplier will need to become involved in the design of the next generation of the product. Under each of these scenarios, there is change that occurs after initial contracting and that increases the outsourcing (buyer) firm's long-term dependence on the supplier because that supplier now possesses more competences relative to the buyer.

Because our evidence on stage 4 is limited as the electronics industry is still evolving, our discussion of it is perhaps best interpreted as a form of informed theoretical speculation. When faced with a situation like stage 3, firms essentially have two options in stage 4. Firms can exit the industry altogether as Emerson and, to some extent, Philips have done. Or they can decide to take activities back in-house, as Sony has begun doing in recent years. This choice can be likened to Hirschman's (1970) exit-voice model, where decision makers also have the choice between departing from the scene and engaging and confronting a problem. Leroy's (1976) detailed empirical work on U.S. multinational firms' production location decisions along the international product life cycle (IPLC) model points to this strategic dichotomy. He traced their production location decisions over time. In reality, a majority of U.S. multinationals stopped short of reaching the last stage of the IPLC as theorized by Vernon (1974), where the subsidiaries of those U.S. multinationals based in developing countries would have become the net exporters to the United States of what had once been products innovated in the United States. His conclusion alluded to U.S. firms' reliance on product innovations and reluctance to investing in manufacturing process innovations. This finding is consistent in a way with later studies that found the sustained competitiveness of many Japanese firms resulting from their pursuit of process innovations (e.g., Cusumano, 1988; Kotabe, 1990). Exiting the industry equates to admitting the competence loss is too large to overcome.

Facing the problem, like Sony, sounds like a much easier task than it actually is. First, it will require precisely those fixed investments that the firm's business model is no longer based on. Thus the question is how to fund this reversal and make it consistent with the firm's strategy. Second, the firm will by now have lost much of its ability to produce and engineer the product and will have to seriously update its competences by training people and obtaining knowledge externally. Both may come at a high price, particularly since the competitive and technological landscapes may have changed substantially in the meantime. Hence in stage 4 there is no ideal solution to the problems around competence losses that a firm has accumulated through the first three stages.

The stage model raises several further questions. One is why the loss of competences would occur, as it appears to be inconsistent with perfectly rational managerial decision making. Several reasons come to mind. A lack of foresight perhaps produced by technological or volume uncertainty is one possibility. Differing estimations of the buyer's and the supplier's ability to develop the underlying competences in the future could be another. Another possible reason is strategic myopia that makes the short-term consequences of not outsourcing, in the form of higher fixed costs and higher production costs, look worse than the long-term consequences of outsourcing, in the form of a loss of technological prowess (Bettis, Bradley, & Hamel, 1992; Doig et al., 2001; Kotabe, 1998). For instance, the more immediate trigger for outsourcing decisions in our cases appeared to be a downturn in business cycles and short-term losses that firms were facing. Outsourcing may also be perceived as a response to adverse demand conditions because of its propensity to lower the break-even point. This could be framed as a "Faustian dilemma."[5] Because of immediate pressures to compete in the marketplace, firms need to focus and streamline their production activities. But in order to do so, they have to "sell their soul," namely their core assets and capabilities, which in the long run will catch up with them. Viewed in this way, there is no myopia but simply a lack of strategic choice. This determinism inevitably drives firms toward more outsourcing. A further implication is that causality in our model may well run in both directions, since poor results lead to more outsourcing as much as more outsourcing may lead to poorer results.

A second question is why our three case study firms experienced their outsourcing cycles and resulting competence losses at different points in time, with Emerson being first in roughly the 1950s to 1970s, Philips following in roughly the 1970s to 1990s, and Sony being last in roughly the 1980s to 2000s. Other CE producers from the same triad regions seemed to go through the same timing. We would like to suggest that it is a combination of the cost competitiveness of the home country and the mental models and financial incentives of managers in the country that are responsible for such differences in timing. Over time, and with the development of their home economies, firms found that their home country simply could not compete with offshore locations anymore because labor costs were too high. This effect may have occurred in the United States before it did in Europe, partly because European firms were more effective at limiting imports from lower cost producers. In Japan it may again have come at a later time—not until the 1980s. But managers in these countries are also different. In Japan, outsourcing is seen as a problem-solving tool, while in the United States it tends to be a problem-removal tool (Kotabe, 1998). And U.S. managers are given incentives to achieve good short-term results, encouraging them to find cost savings through outsourcing, while this is less true for European (especially Germanic) managers or Japanese managers. The latter group is rewarded for market share growth more than for financial results alone (Kotabe, 1998). Our earlier quote from the Emerson executive illustrates the point.

A third point is whether firms necessarily need to go through all stages for the competence loss to occur. Although this is ultimately an empirical question, our cases seem to show that all three firms went through the first three stages in more or less chronological fashion. In stage 4 they took different routes, however, with Sony appearing to use a voice engagement strategy and Emerson and Philips preferring an exit strategy. So there are different responses to the loss of competences through outsourcing. At the same time we think it is feasible that some firms, like small- and medium-size firms (SMEs), never set up foreign operations but immediately engage in international outsourcing. Mol, van Tulder, and Beije (2005) seemed to have evidence for this in their empirical study. Such firms will probably transfer fewer assets and less knowledge to their foreign suppliers and are therefore perhaps not as prone as larger firms to competence losses. The smaller volumes these firms produce might also make it less attractive for their suppliers to engage in forward integration. This touches upon the intriguing and more general issue how inward and outward internationalization processes are related.

Finally, we would like to raise the related issue of the conditions under which this stage model is most likely to apply. Several requirements appear to apply. First, there is causal ambiguity and uncertainty over future technological and competence trajectories as discussed above. In transaction cost economics terms, this implies that asset specificity levels cannot be estimated with much certainty, and are subject to change, and that uncertainty makes it difficult to contract with suppliers. Second, the rise of new, lower cost producers in emerging countries that puts additional competitive and cost pressures on incumbents from developed countries. Third, the presence of international trade regimes that allow for this type of outsourcing. And finally a certain size of production is needed as well. Therefore, we think the stage model may be generalized to some situations, especially larger firms competing in highly competitive and technologically intensive industries. One interesting thought experiment is whether Chinese automobile and component suppliers are going to benefit from collaborative agreements with Western producers and the purchase of technology like the acquisition of the remains of Rover in the United Kingdom.

Conclusions and Implications

Outsourcing can be more than a cost-cutting device and potentially contributes to a firm's competence base (Quinn, 1999). There are, however, circumstances under which outsourcing leads to competence destruction. Through documenting the experiences of three firms in the CE industry we illustrated how such competence destruction through outsourcing takes place and coined it the vicious outsourcing cycle. Clearly not all outsourcing processes will adhere to such a cycle. When firms outsource competences that later become important platforms for growth and innovation, the vicious outsourcing cycle can occur. This stands in contrast to the use of outsourcing to obtain new competences (Barney, 1999; Quinn, 1999), because in our cases supplier competences appear to be less complementary and more overlapping, which generates the possibility of forward integration by suppliers. In such instances it is important for firms to consider the future value of in-house production rather than merely the present costs of keeping production in-house versus outsourcing it.

For instance, it was evident in the Philips case that on the basis of its past capabilities in R&D, it should have been able to compete in the DVD market. But due to excessive outsourcing of components and products before the age of the DVD, it "did not have a DVD program" in the U.S. market as conceded by Philips Sound and Vision chairman and CEO Doug Dunn (*TV Digest*, 1997b, p. 15). Its European DVD launch also proved to be unsuccessful. One of the main reasons was that Philips' DVD technology MPEG-2 suffered due to unavailability of software. Future prospects for availability of content for these players were also bleak. This preempted the introduction of products based on Philips' DVD technology later on that were based on its own previous DVD technology. To revert back to basics proved to be harder than expected because regaining technical abilities included building plants and incurring other prohibitively high costs. Philips's case was also unique because the company's own technologies (e.g., V2000 for videos and MPEG-2 for DVDs) found no support in the market and were largely unsuccessful. Therefore, in such cases, many firms have no choice but to buy products from overseas manufacturers in order to remain in the industry.

Information contained in our sources seems to indicate that most CE firms were similarly faced with few choices: either to exit the product line(s) because sales were dropping or to go abroad like their rivals were doing and lower costs. It is unclear as to whether or not these firms and others lacked foresight. Based upon patterns in our data, it appears as though it started off as one decision, which led to an increasing dependence on suppliers, as our model proposes. These firms progressed through the stages of the model as they faced pressures to meet demand, lower prices, and so on. Thus, the increasing outsourcing relationships and their outcomes were the culmination of this gradual process. Upon the sale of Philips' Greenville TV plant (Tennessee, United States) in mid-1997, Philips Sound & Vision chairman-CEO Doug Dunn said it was "a tough decision, I don't take any joy in selling or closing down assets" (*TV Digest*, 1997b, p. 14).

Firms do not need to go through all stages of this cycle for its effects to become visible. Sometimes they do not use offshore subsidiaries but instead opt to go straight for outside suppliers from abroad. Emerson Radio at some point in time looked to nearby Canada and Latin America to set up subsidiaries but it eventually relied mainly on external Asian suppliers for its components and finished products. Emerson Radio only went through two of the stages of the cycle and much faster than the other two firms. This was probably due to the market it faced in the United States, which was severely competitive. Philips, on the other hand, appears to have gone through the first three stages and never really got back to being a technological leader in CE. It would be interesting to observe what pattern other CE firms have followed. Furthermore, one might expect firms in other industries, where international competition has emerged later than in CE, to show a similar pattern at some point in the future.

From a decision maker's viewpoint the vicious outsourcing cycle is more than just a cause for cautionary behavior. It provides managers with an important criterion for future outsourcing decisions: To what extent does the activity that we are considering to outsource embody competences that matter for our future growth and innovation potential? And are we sure that the competences contained in this activity are all easily observable? This criterion does not need to replace more traditional considerations of cost minimization or those that are based on comparisons between the firm's current resource stock and that of its potential suppliers, but it is a useful supplement to such considerations. In addition to short-term considerations, firms and their managers also need to think about long-term variables such as future growth, continued innovation, and sustainability of competitive advantage, all three of which are inextricably linked together. There is no *a priori* correct answer to the question whether outsourcing is good or bad for the development of competences inside the firm. Its consequences hinge on the circumstances under which outsourcing takes place and how these conditions then change over time.

In technologically intensive industries such as CE, continued innovation is the key to future growth and sustainability of competitive advantage. But in order to innovate, firms need to learn to identify those competences that underlie components and could possibly lead to the development of unanticipated technology or products in the future. The ability for identification is often elusive or is sometimes sacrificed by myopic managers and managers suffering from the Faustian dilemma we discussed. Managers need to tell themselves not to think in terms of "just one more component" to be outsourced. The three firms in our sample had the potential to innovate but they started giving it away bit by bit. This does not mean that firms should necessarily increase their R&D budget or keep all production activities in-house. But it calls for more judicious outsourcing strategies. Some firms have recognized this need, for example, Sony, which has shifted some of its manufacturing for semiconductors back in-house. Semiconductors, used in almost all electronic equipment today, are the basis for future innovation and being knowledgeable about the process for making semiconductors should ideally enable Sony to sustain its technological capabilities. Another important step forward seems to be the ability to move from one type of product to the next. Emerson never really made it beyond the radio and started losing out when it missed out on the DVD revolution. So firms that outsource need to think about how they can proceed to entirely new products without having productive capacity. That may require different forms of cooperation in the research and development stage, for instance with specialist manufacturing outsourcing companies such as Flextronics, which unfortunately were not around yet when Emerson and Philips made their decisions.

Notes

1. Although our model includes an "offshoring" stage, which refers to the transfer of activities across geographical borders but inside a firm, we almost exclusively discuss the "outsourcing" stage that follows it because it involves activities that are both transferred across geographical borders and performed by outside suppliers and hence is the more complex issue.

2. In 1970, NUC charged its Japanese competitors with attempting to drive U.S. TV makers out of the domestic market by dumping or selling foreign made televisions at artificially low prices. This was one of the most controversial disputes in the industry at the time and the largest antitrust case against Japanese

competitors. But in 1981, a federal court judge ruled that NUC and Zenith had been unable to provide sufficient evidence to support their charges.

3. Matsushita also acquired Philips's main U.S. subsidiary Magnavox in 1992.

4. U.S.-based Solectron is one of the world's fastest growing electronics manufacturing services (EMS) provider. Its offerings include product design and manufacturing.

5. This term is courtesy to one of our reviewers' suggestions.

References

AFX News. (Ed.). (2000, October 18). Sony may sell more production plants after solectron deal. *AFX News.*

Barney, J. B. (1999). How a firm's capabilities affect boundary decisions. *Sloan Management Review, 40*(3), 137–145.

Bettis, R., Bradley, S. & Hamel, G. (1991). Outsourcing and industrial decline. *Academy of Management Executive, 6*(1), 7–16.

Chandler, A. (2001). *Inventing the electronic century.* New York: Free Press.

Cusumano, M. A. (1988). Manufacturing innovation: Lessons from the Japanese auto industry. *Sloan Management Review, 30*(1), 29–39.

Dai, X. (1996). *Corporate strategy, public policy and new technologies: Philips and the consumer electronics industry.* London: Elsevier Science.

Dankbaar, B. (2007). Global sourcing and innovation: The consequences of losing both organizational and geographical proximity. *European Planning Studies, 15*(2), 271–288.

D'Aveni, R. A. & Ravenscraft, D. J. (1994). Economies of integration versus bureaucracy costs: Does vertical integration improve performance? *Academy of Management Journal, 37*(5), 1167–1206.

Doig, S. J., Ritter, R. C., Speckhals, K., & Woolson, D. (2001). Has outsourcing gone too far? *McKinsey Quarterly, 4*, 22–37.

Doz, Y. L., & Hamel, G. (1998). *Alliance advantage: The act of creating value through partnering.* Boston, MA: Harvard Business School Press.

Dunning, J. H. (1988). The eclectic paradigm of international production: A restatement and some possible replications. *Journal of International Business Studies, 19*(1), 1–31.

Dyer, J. H. & Singh, H. (1998). The relational view: Cooperative strategy and sources of interorganizational competitive advantage. *Academy of Management Review, 23*(4), 660–679.

The Economist (Ed.). (2000, April 22). War games. *The Economist, 60–61.*

The Economist (Ed.). (2005, April 9). Parked. *The Economist.*

Ferdows, K. (1997). Making the most of foreign factories. *Harvard Business Review, 75*(2), 73–88.

The Financial Times (Ed.). (2000, October 19). Sony sells factories in streamlining move. *The Financial Times*.

Forbes (Ed.). (1954, June 15). In tune with Emerson, *Forbes*, pp. 22–23.

Forbes (Ed.). (1981, July 20). A dangerous dream? *Forbes*, p. 52.

Grossman, S. J., & Hart, O. D. (1986). The costs and benefits of ownership: A theory of vertical and lateral integration. *Journal of Political Economy*, *94*(4), 691–719.

Hirschman, A. O. (1970). *Exit, voice, and loyalty: Responses to decline in firms, organizations, and states*. Cambridge, MA: Harvard University Press.

Jacobides, M. G., & Winter, S. G. (2005). The co-evolution of capabilities and transaction costs: Explaining the institutional structure of production. *Strategic Management Journal*, *26*(5), 395–413.

Kenney, M., & Florida, R. (1995). The transfer of Japanese management styles in two U.S. transplant industries: Autos and electronics. *Journal of Management Studies*, *32*(6), 789–802.

Knickerbocker, F. T. (1973). *Oligopolistic reaction and multinational enterprise*. Boston: Division of Research, Graduate School of Business, Harvard University.

Kotabe, M. (1990). Corporate product policy and innovative behavior of European and Japanese multinationals: An empirical investigation. *Journal of Marketing*, *54*(2), 19–33.

Kotabe, M. (1998). Efficiency vs. effectiveness orientation of global sourcing strategy: A comparison of U.S. and Japanese multinational companies. *Academy of Management Executive*, *12*(4), 107–119.

Leiblein, M. J., Reuer, J. J., & Dalsace, F. (2002). Do make or buy decisions matter? The influence of organizational governance on technological performance. *Strategic Management Journal*, *23*(9), 817–833.

Leroy, G. (1976). *Multinational product strategy: A taxonomy for analysis of worldwide product innovation and diffusion*. New York: Praeger.

Mehler, M. (1984, November 14–27). Every which way is up for Emerson. *Financial World*, pp. 86–87.

Mol, M. J., van Tulder, R. J. M., & Beije, P. R. (2005). The antecedents and performance consequences of international outsourcing. *International Business Review*, *14*(5), 599–617.

New York Times (Ed.). (1981, October 19). Emerson perseveres with heart device. *New York Times*.

Nikkei News. (Ed.). (2006, October 7). Sony's technological leadership in jeopardy. *Nikkei News*.

Nikkei Weekly. (Ed.). (2003, September 16). Maverick on board to revive sony. *Nikkei Weekly*.

Nooteboom, B. (1999). Innovation and inter-firm linkages: New implications for policy. *Research Policy*, *28*(8), 793–805.

Partner, S. (1999). *Assembled in Japan: Electrical goods and the making of the Japanese consumer.* Berkeley: University of California Press.

Pilling, D. (2002, September 9). DVDs made in Japan. *The Financial Times* (London), p. 30.

Porter, M. E. (1980). *Competitive strategy.* New York: Free Press.

Quinn, J. B. (1999). Strategic outsourcing: Leveraging knowledge capabilities. *Sloan Management Review, 40*(3), 9–21.

Re, R. (2003). PlayStation2 detonation. *Harvard International Review, 25*(3), 46–50.

SinoCast China IT Watch. (2003, October 6). Sony to reform production management model in China.

Teece, D. J. (1986). Profiting from technological innovation: Implications for integration, collaboration, licensing, and public policy. *Research Policy, 15*(6), 285–305.

Teece, D. J. (2000). *Managing intellectual capital: Organizational, strategic, and policy dimensions.* Oxford: Oxford University Press.

Teece, D. J., Pisano, G., & Shuen, A. (1997). Dynamic capabilities and strategic management. *Strategic Management Journal, 18*(7), 509–533.

TV Digest. (1997a, February 17). Grundig charges push Philips back into red, *TV Digest*, pp. 12–13.

TV Digest. (1997b, June 30). Philips plans 2 DVD players for Europe, *TV Digest*, pp. 14–15.

TV Digest. (1998, September 21). Weekly news, March–December 1988. *TV Digest.*

Vernon, R. (1974). The location of economic activity. In J. H. Dunning (Ed.), *Economic analysis and the multinational enterprise.* London: George Allen & Unwin, 89–114.

Wernerfelt, B. (1984). A resource-based view of the firm. *Strategic Management Journal, 5*(2), 272–280.

Williamson, O. E. (1985). *The economic institutions of capitalism.* New York: Free Press.

Wilson, D. Ready to turn the key: Asia's contract manufacturers are poised for Japanese hand-offs. *Electronic Business Asia.* May 20, 2001. Retrieved June 20, 2007, from http://www.eb-asia.com/EBA/issues/0105/0105c-story.htm

Yu, S., & Teng, W. July 2, 2001. Retrieved June 20, 2007, from http://www.DigiTimes.com

CHAPTER 15

The Overlooked Potential for Outsourcing in Eastern Europe

Detlev Hoch, Michal Kwiecinski, and Peter Peters

With less than 1% of the world's $30 billion market for offshore IT and business process outsourcing (BPO), Eastern Europe lags far behind more prominent locations, including India, Ireland, Malaysia, and the Philippines (see Exhibit 15.1). Our research suggests that this may soon change: demand for offshoring[1] among Western European companies rose by half from 2004 to 2006, with Eastern Europe emerging as a favorite destination.

Although Eastern Europe's governments have not wooed business as effectively as those of the more established destinations, offshoring in that region offers three primary advantages: low wages comparable to India's, a relatively low risk profile for key factors such as reliable infrastructure, and cultural and geographical proximity to Western Europe. McKinsey estimates that offshoring activity in Eastern Europe could triple, to more than 130,000 jobs, from 2005 to the end of 2008 (see Exhibit 15.2). What's more, given the relatively low pace of the region's wage inflation (see Exhibit 15.3), along with abundant output from local universities, this talent source could remain economically competitive for at least 15 years.

Eastern Europe is a particularly attractive option for Western European companies. Not only is it nearby, but companies can often find language capabilities (especially French and German) that are less readily available in India or Southeast Asia. At the same time, the new members of the European Union (EU)—particularly the Czech Republic, Hungary, Poland, and Slovakia—can offer average labor cost savings of 40 to 60% over costs in Western Europe, while cities in EU-candidate and non-EU countries can offer cost advantages of 60 to 80%.

However, choosing a suitable location isn't just a matter of picking the right country; employment costs differ widely among cities because of limited labor mobility and varying unemployment rates. Companies should look beyond the first-wave locations (such as Bratislava, Budapest, Kraków, and Prague), where wages for experienced workers are rising faster than inflation. Instead, they should begin to explore midsize cities with little or no offshoring activity but large talent pools, where the labor cost advantage is more likely to remain attractive for the next decade.

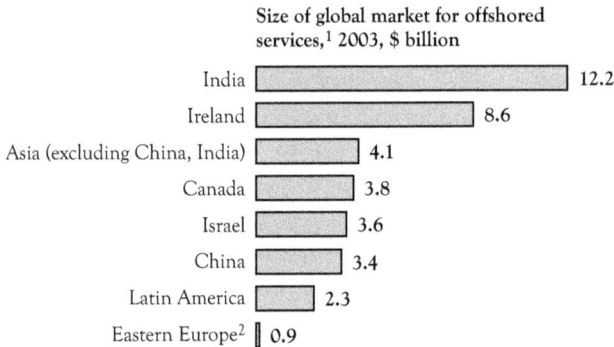

Size of global market for offshored
services,[1] 2003, $ billion

India	12.2
Ireland	8.6
Asia (excluding China, India)	4.1
Canada	3.8
Israel	3.6
China	3.4
Latin America	2.3
Eastern Europe[2]	0.9

Exhibit 15.1. A Small Share

Historically, Eastern Europe captured only a fraction of global offshoring activities.

[1]Includes business process offshoring and IT, both captive and outsourced.

[2]Only includes data for Czech Republic, Hungary, Poland, Romania, Russia, and Ukraine.

Source: Enterprise Ireland; Gartner; IDC; government Web sites and software associations for countries shown; ministry of information technology for various countries; National Association of Software and Service Companies (Nasscom); U.S. country commercial reports; McKinsey Global Institute analysis.

Demand for offshoring in Eastern Europe,
thousands of FTEs, cumulative[1]

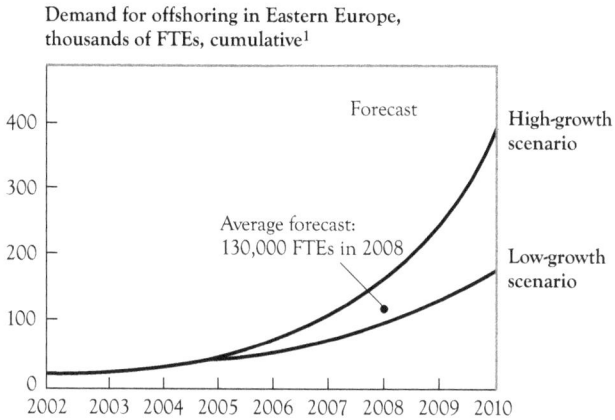

Exhibit 15.2. Forecast for Growth

Demand for Eastern European offshoring is expected to grow to 130,000 full-time equivalents (FTEs) in 2008.

[1]Offshoring = business process offshoring and IT, both captive and outsourced; Eastern Europe = Bulgaria, Czech Republic, Hungary, Poland, Romania, Russia, Slovakia; FTEs = full-time equivalents.

Source: McKinsey Global Institute analysis.

Compound annual growth rate
of wages, 2004–04,[1] %

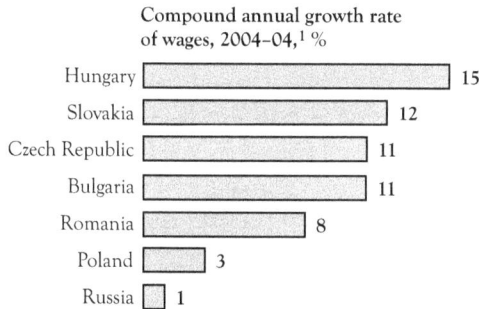

Exhibit 15.3. Modest Wage Growth

Wage levels are expected to rise only slightly.

[1]For LABORSTA category "Financial intermediation"; wages expressed as euros.

Source: LABORSTA; McKinsey analysis.

Beyond the well-known capitals, Eastern Europe has 40 to 50 provincial cities with universities large enough to supply a highly skilled labor force, along with cultural environments that lend themselves to the creation of suitable clusters of employers for university graduates (see Exhibit 15.4). This wealth of options can help companies reduce their labor costs and spread potential risks across a portfolio of locations with different risk profiles by taking into account the reliability of infrastructure, political stability, and the possibility that talent might emigrate, be enticed by competitors, or prove less capable than anticipated.

Most service centers in Eastern Europe today are so-called captives—they are owned by the companies sending them work. Independent Eastern European providers of IT and business process services have a significant opportunity. But with few exceptions—Luxoft in Russia and Ericpol Telecom in Poland, for example—these companies are not on the map compared with better known global and Indian players, some of which are setting up their own centers in Eastern Europe. So far, homegrown players have merely responded to local opportunities instead of seeking out seemingly more difficult global markets.

There are several reasons for this caution. First, Eastern European IT services providers, at their current scale, have difficulty keeping up with the 20% growth they can generate in their domestic markets. Second, regulations and inconsistencies in labor laws complicate expansion beyond

Selected Eastern European cities with universities, by tier

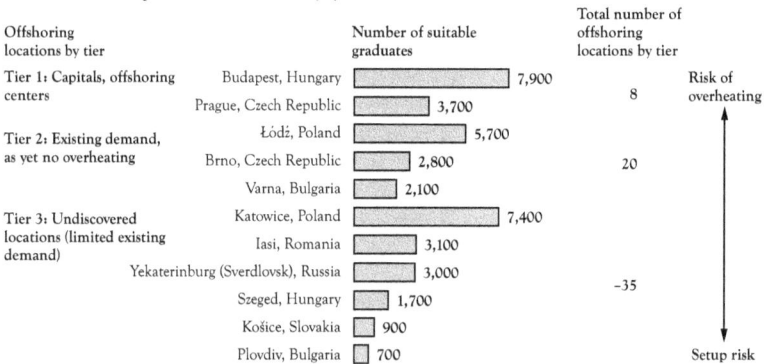

Offshoring locations by tier	Number of suitable graduates	Total number of offshoring locations by tier
Tier 1: Capitals, offshoring centers	Budapest, Hungary — 7,900	8 Risk of overheating
	Prague, Czech Republic — 3,700	
Tier 2: Existing demand, as yet no overheating	Łódź, Poland — 5,700	20
	Brno, Czech Republic — 2,800	
	Varna, Bulgaria — 2,100	
Tier 3: Undiscovered locations (limited existing demand)	Katowice, Poland — 7,400	
	Iasi, Romania — 3,100	
	Yekaterinburg (Sverdlovsk), Russia — 3,000	−35
	Szeged, Hungary — 1,700	
	Košice, Slovakia — 900	
	Plovdiv, Bulgaria — 700	Setup risk

Exhibit 15.4. The Path Less Taken

Many seemingly undiscovered locations for offshoring exist in Eastern Europe.

national borders—expansion that is a necessary precursor to gaining scale comparable to that of the global providers. Finally, continental European companies have been slower to embrace offshore outsourcing than have those in the United Kingdom and the United States, which traditionally favor the English-speaking countries in Asia. The opportunity for local service providers prepared to step up to the challenge, either alone or with the help of private equity firms, is tempting. Luxoft, for example, has grown at an annual rate of 60 to 70% for each of the past 5 years. In 2005 the company had revenues of $45 million.

Cities and nations also have a stake in this growth opportunity. Perhaps drawing on the experiences of the Indian trade association Nasscom,[2] they should work with service providers to develop a regional effort to expand the market. A full-time team that promotes a city as an offshoring destination and supports investors in their search for talent and infrastructure can make a big difference to the development of a local market. Lódz, in Poland, has undertaken one such initiative, which has been helping to make the city a developing hub for services in BPO and IT. Local governments also can work with companies to restructure regulations in ways that facilitate cross-border growth.

Notes

1. Offshoring and its close cousin nearshoring are relative terms. North American corporations refer to the transfer of work to Caribbean countries as nearshoring. Western European companies use that term for the transfer of work to Eastern Europe.

2. National Association of Software and Service Companies. The group includes the country's leading IT services providers.

CHAPTER 16

How to Be an
Outsourcing Virtuoso

Vinay Couto and Ashok Divakaran

Not so long ago, some observers were nearly ready to declare outsourcing dead. A series of well-publicized corporate outsourcing and offshoring failures—involving Dell, Lehman Brothers, J. P. Morgan Chase, J. Sainsbury, and Sears—had led to the conclusion that the future of the global business services industry was questionable. Some analysts predicted a backlash in public opinion, in which the loss of jobs in North America and Western Europe would make outsourcing politically unfeasible. Others argued that in a world of increasing political volatility and security risk, the offshoring of business services could not continue to grow.

These predictions have proven wrong.

Instead, the outsourcing industry—the international conglomeration of firms that provide services in information technology, customer care, finance, human resources, engineering, procurement, real estate and facilities management, and data analytics, among other offerings, that replace in-house selling, general, and administrative (SG&A) functions—is becoming ever more sophisticated and, for many customers, indispensable. In 2004, the International Data Corporation (IDC) valued the annual global business process outsourcing (BPO) market at $382.5 billion, a 10.8% jump over 2003. IDC estimates that by 2009 the market will hit $641.2 billion. Such growth—nearly 11% per year—is a testament to how thoroughly outsourcing is now woven into the fabric of international commerce.

This growth has also left suppliers with a variety of questions about the future of the services they provide. And for the corporate customers who contemplate introducing or expanding an outsourcing strategy, especially for those who have experimented with outsourcing unsuccessfully, a significant level of apprehension and uncertainty remains.

This dichotomy—visible but isolated failures on one side, complex but resoundingly successful outsourcing deals on the other—leads to two conclusions. First, the industry has not stabilized to the point where outsourcing any particular business activity is a guaranteed safe choice. Second, much value can be obtained from outsourcing if it's done right, and there clearly is a right way to do it.

"Most companies that are outsourcing for the first time don't know how to approach it," says Ralph Szygenda, the chief information officer of the General Motors (GM) Corporation. Over the last decade, Mr. Szygenda has taken his company through three distinct and highly complicated phases of information technology (IT) outsourcing that have led to $12 billion in savings and a complete technological overhaul. An evolving set of skills, not just at GM but at dozens of companies on both the supplier and the customer side, is coalescing into a body of best practices as the industry matures.

The pioneers of these practices are today's outsourcing virtuosos. On the supply side, they're creating instruments of unprecedented power for delivering global business performance. And on the demand side, they're learning to play those instruments with unprecedented mastery. No individual or company has all the answers, but a clear view is emerging of how the industry should continue to meet the challenges of a fast-moving marketplace with ever more demanding customers and how companies can fashion the most effective outsourcing approach for the future. We discussed these insights with five leaders in charge of successful outsourcing programs at Procter & Gamble, Innovene (a chemicals firm), Duke Energy, General Motors, and Texas electric utility TXU Energy, and with leaders of five prominent providers of outsourcing services: TCS, 24/7 Customer, Augmentum, Cognizant, and IBM.

The Industry Matures

To a casual observer, the outsourcing industry might well appear to share many characteristics with the dot-com economy. It is caught up in a classic boom business environment, with all the exuberance, hype, and dynamism that attend industries in the midst of wild expansion. The market appears to be going in two directions. On one hand, compelled by what appears to be expanding business opportunities, the BPO market is attracting many new firms from different segments of the IT services industry, such as software providers, data center outsourcers, and offshore application developers. On the other hand, the market has embarked on its first major wave of consolidation as the larger firms with deep pockets gobble up smaller competitors and expand their capabilities.

In this environment, pure-play process providers are finding it difficult to compete against established market leaders without an expanded offering and a world-class technology platform. Other firms with a limited number of BPO contracts are discovering that subscale operations cannot deliver the value necessary to grow their businesses. Several of these firms are dropping out of the BPO market or merging with larger firms that have the resources to compete. Service standards are still emerging and pricing models still evolving; legal protections are inconsistent, and the roster of providers and offerings is always shifting. Hence the woes that many client companies have experienced with outsourcing.

But amid the ferment, several trends are shaping the offerings of the most successful providers.

An Expanding Global Footprint

The marketplace for outsourcing is far more varied than it was a few years ago, with competitors of all sizes operating primarily from India, China, and the Philippines and offering their wares to customers around the world. Like their clients, they are spreading globally to make the most of international diversity, balancing the capabilities, language capacity, cultural affinities, and cost structures of a variety of regions. The more forward-looking suppliers include Western behemoths like IBM, which recently announced its intent to triple its investment in India to $6 billion over the next 3 years. They also include Indian providers such as TCS, which has offices in 34 countries on six continents, and 24/7, which is scaling up a center for global services based in the Philippines. With the leading players globalizing their operations, some distinctions between "Western" and "offshore" vendors are starting to erode, including their capabilities and even their pricing.

"The traditional regional outsourcer is going to have a very rough time competing with the global players," says Michael Cannon-Brookes, IBM vice president for business development in China and India. "You've got to have the talent, you've got to have the infrastructure, and you've got to have the processes."

As outsourcing customers develop globally standardized processes and systems, they are beginning to place more weight on vendors' abilities to provide equally standardized capabilities and processes. In the long term, for example, work delivered from a center in Bratislava, Slovakia, will have to be fundamentally the same as that delivered from Hyderabad, India. Much of this movement toward global harmonization is being driven by multinational giants such as GM, for which the benefits of standardization are immense.

"In 2003, GM truly started globalizing its business processes. Until then, we had different processes by region," observes Mr. Szygenda. "Now GM is beginning to run as one coordinated company throughout the world. We can design, develop, and distribute products from any part of the world to any other part of the world. There are no longer regional boundaries." This globally unified approach enables suppliers to build a powerful risk mitigation strategy, insulating them from catastrophe in the face of operational failures in portions of their supply chain. Says Mr. Szygenda, "We wanted [the vendors] to see that this wasn't just good for GM, it was good for them and maybe the IT industry."

Increasing Sophistication

It has taken years for outsourcing to grow up. Analysts have long predicted that outsourcing would evolve beyond the commodity services that have been its bread and butter and into areas that are more critical to the global success of customers. But through the 1990s, the outsourcing industry was fairly stable, dominated by large North American and European players—Accenture, ACS, Capgemini, EDS, IBM, and a few others—focused predominantly on information technology. The industry came to be governed by mega one-stop-shop deals under which vast portions of the IT and administrative functions were bundled and out-sourced to a single provider; a labyrinthine, rigid 10-year-plus contractual infrastructure; a measurement culture focused on cost rather than service levels; and shaky relationship management not always appropriate to the scope and demands of the engagement. This environment grew not only out of the suppliers' business model and cultural baggage, but also from the customers' own tendency to turn to outsourcing as a quick-hit pana-cea to reduce short-term costs, and a belief that contractual complexity enabled greater customer control.

Meanwhile, a quiet revolution was occurring abroad. Fueled by the Internet, plummeting telecommunication prices, government incentives, and growing awareness of the cost advantages and abundant skilled labor pool in India, offshore BPO made its first forays into Western enterprises on two fronts. First, a select group of companies, including General Elec-tric, American Express, and British Airways, set up their own offshore units for processes such as customer call centers, back-office administra-tion, and systems development. Second, a handful of Indian providers, including TCS, Infosys, Wipro, and Satyam—seeing opportunity in extending their service offering and aware of companies' growing appe-tite for cost reduction—began to expand beyond IT into the same areas of work that the privately owned captives were engaged in. Along the way, their investments in systems and scale began to pay off, and the case for BPO grew to encompass not just cost advantage but also increased quality and effectiveness. As Mr. Cannon-Brookes put it, customers saw that BPO could "take your mess for less, transform it, run it, and add real value."

Other companies soon began implementing their own comprehensive outsourcing arrangements. In 2003, Procter & Gamble contracted its IT processes to Hewlett-Packard, its human resources services to IBM, and its facilities management to Jones Lang LaSalle. Each of these engagements has yielded improvements in service and efficiency. "We thought we were doing good work by any standards, but the rigor and the quality of the measures in a commercial partnership are on a completely different scale," says Filippo Passerini, P&G's chief information officer. "Our partners brought a whole new level of methodology and discipline to the process."

The menu of BPO offerings continued to expand. Sophisticated end-to-end services are now available in human resources, finance, and procurement, along with such forward-looking offerings as analytics, advanced customer care, and innovation. Many companies use BPO as a springboard for building capabilities in knowledge process outsourcing— a subset of BPO requiring a much higher level of expertise in such areas as product development, clinical trials, research and analytics, media production, and animation.

Over the last few years, new suppliers with nothing to lose and everything to gain—and, consequently, a mind-set that is more attuned to customer needs—have entered the fray. Pushed by buyers to demonstrate business value, service providers are building robust, highly tailored offerings that deliver economic, strategic, operational, and human resources benefits. Further, they are differentiating their offerings in some cases based on industry expertise. Within industries, service providers are standardizing business processes to meet customer demands for cost savings, as buyers now refuse to pay the 10 to 20% premium for tailored processes. This standardization is setting the stage for the proliferation of one-to-many solutions.

Consolidation of Suppliers Into Two Primary Business Models

Although the mix of supply options is still in flux, two types seem likely to prevail in the end: large, full-service vendors (tier one firms) and specialist vendors (tier two firms) that serve niche markets, such as animation production houses for media companies. Because tier one firms work on a global scale, with multinational clients and immense resources, there is not room for many of them. "When we started this business 12 years ago, there were 700 or 800 firms in India that had the same idea," says Francisco D'Souza, COO of Cognizant, a leading U.S. provider. "Today, there are four tier one firms. That's just an artifact of a maturing market and of the importance of scale."

As the tier one firms standardize their business processes and evolve their contractual practices, they will increasingly seek to help their customers transform their operations through outsourcing—with decisive impact on customers' processes, management approaches, and outcomes. Mr. D'Souza is convinced that this evolution offers a significant opportunity to engage more deeply with his clients: "It's not about delivering technology solutions. It's thinking about how we make our customers' businesses stronger at the end of the day. As a part of that, we've made a big effort to build within our teams experience and expertise about the industries that we serve. We want not just technologists, but technologists who understand, for instance, financial services, health care, or retail. Ultimately, everything you do needs to impact the top line or the bottom line or the cycle time of your client."

There are many barriers to this goal in the short term, including the providers' own relative lack of experience, but eventually such an approach could become the dominant method of the most successful players. Rather than task-based or time-based billing, "value-differentiated pricing is going to be very key," says Subramanian Ramadorai, CEO of TCS, one of India's oldest and largest outsourcing providers. "If I can improve the efficiency or performance of your process, we can structure a deal that benefits both of us. For example, if we automate a manual process—create a design model based on a CAD drawing into which you can simply enter your parameters—we can both share the savings." Further, Mr. Ramadorai would like to develop new services in partnership with clients. "We'll be able to charge for the intellectual property we help create, provided we can quantify the benefit to the customers," he says.

Interoperable, Commoditized Services

At the same time, the market will evolve to become significantly more accessible. Or so predicts A. R. Mullinax, executive vice president of Duke Energy Business Services. He envisions outsourcing eventually resembling a utility computing model, where services are purchased à la carte, as needed, without costly up-front investments and transition times. "Instead of having to go through the formality of sourcing contracts with long, fixed terms, we'll buy services as one-time hits. It'll be more like a competitive retail market for commodities," says Mr. Mullinax. "Five years from now, customers will be able to say, 'I just want a commodity accounts receivable billing service.' That doesn't exist today. You have to go through a big contract or you've got to get the software and your own computer." In the future, instead of committing to a 5- or 10-year agreement for accounts receivable services, customers will be able to plug into the service for short-term needs. Before this can become a reality, however, companies will need to let go of their proprietary processes and systems, and vendors will need to build capabilities and scale around a common set of standards.

Challenges and Caveats

Outsourcing is now entering a transitional period in which the most sophisticated suppliers and customers will shape the structure of the business-to-business service environment around the world. Every business, large or small, will eventually be plugged into this network of interoperable, interwoven processes. Tapping this network will be an absolute requirement for success. Not plugging in will cost a company its competitive edge.

To be sure, a number of challenges will inhibit the industry. These include credibility: Vendors will still need to convince would-be customers that they are capable and reliable, particularly for more knowledge-centric work. They will also need to reassure customers that sensitive information is safe in their hands. Says Leonard Liu, CEO of Augmentum, a supplier based in Shanghai, "It's a problem that can be managed. We have a very stringent security system. But more important than that—the really, really important thing—is the culture. We must have a culture of high integrity, ethics, and discipline, so our people will not misuse our customers' intellectual property."

There are also profound implications for workforce management as the key differentiators change from cost to quality and service effectiveness, the offerings shift from simple transactions to higher-end segments of the value chain, and the delivery model moves from local to global. The business model of the future, with vendors serving as extensions of a company's internal work force, and the need to manage a standard and interoperable business model globally, will require a clear labor sourcing strategy along with global training and knowledge management programs. It will also require a focus on such intangibles as cultural alignment across several dimensions, including the customer's business culture and goals, the customer's own customers, and the cultural norms of each country that the supplier serves. The longer-term direction toward transformational outsourcing will also drive vendors to invest far more heavily in people who oversee the customer relationship and steer the ship—project managers and account managers.

Labor sourcing, in particular, is a growing challenge. The battle for talent has become intensely competitive in China, India, and other emerging markets. Finding and retaining the right people, especially highly educated employees with the skills to take on complex assignments, is the biggest headache for most service providers, especially in the face of burgeoning demand. "We were very clear we were not going to grow too rapidly in the first 2 years," says P. V. Kannan, CEO of 24/7 Customer, a leading Indian BPO provider with relatively low churn rates. "We controlled growth until we understood how to scale without losing quality. Our biggest focus was developing a process for taking new employees who didn't know anything about call centers or claims processing and making them very competent in a specified time period." That discipline has paid off; 24/7 is now one of the most highly regarded outsourcing players, with 100% yearly growth since its founding in 2000 and exceptionally laudatory service rankings from its customers.

Mr. Kannan's concern does not stop at 24/7's walls. He also expresses interest in improving the Indian public education system. "We are talking to competitors about various education proposals. For example, can we just make all our training materials open source? Can 24/7 contribute some of what we've learned about quality for everyone to use as a basis for training?" he asks. "How do we create a talent engine?"

Masterful Customers

For most users of outsourcing services, successful design and execution of an outsourcing plan is extraordinarily difficult to pull off, especially when the processes make use of several companies with separate global supply chains and footprints. But it's possible to do it right, especially given the fundamental power shift in the outsourcing market. The customer is the new king. As global buyers have progressed along the learning curve, they have gained the knowledge and buying power to demand service excellence and significant cost savings from providers. Insights from the leaders we consulted, along with our own experience, suggest that there are five

requirements for any company embarking on an outsourcing strategy—
approaches that are indispensable to successful execution.

Commit From the Top and Move Quickly

Like any transformational initiative, outsourcing requires explicit resolve
from senior management. Outsourcing efforts tend to involve multiple
functions—many that are decentralized and owned by autonomous divisions—and carry significant implications for spending and for individual
staffers. They are thus vulnerable to internal resistance, and senior management's unequivocal support is essential. Top-down determination can
help sweep away much internal resistance. At TXU, C. John Wilder set
the tone and paved the way for success. "Our chairman and CEO said,
'We're going to move from concept to reality without delay,'" recalls Kris
Hillstrand, chief information officer. "This wasn't an exercise in 'I wonder
if we should do this.' It was an exercise in 'We're going to get this done.'"

For companies that have decided to move forward with an ambi-
tious outsourcing arrangement, the most successful programs are enacted
quickly. P&G completed its deal with Hewlett-Packard in only 5 months.
"We had the critical junctures of the deal process scheduled down to the
day, down to the hour," says Mr. Passerini, P&G's CIO. "I learned a lot
of things in that process. For example, large meetings with a lot of people
are inefficient because they dilute accountability. For the HP deal, which
was very complex, we held well-organized, all-day meetings in which
all the key players—70, 80, or 90 people—would call in or come by at
appointed times, participate, and then move on. That enabled us to make
30, 40, or 50 key decisions in a single day and not bog down the process
or the people involved."

Aside from its operational and cost virtues, executing swiftly and
deliberately sends an unmistakable message of resolve. "The biggest risk
of all is indecision," says Duke Energy's Mr. Mullinax. "Know what your
strategy is as a corporation, align with it, know that you're accountable
for delivering it, and then make some decisions and move forward."

Understand Why You're Doing It and Articulate the Reasons Clearly

It is far easier to get people to mobilize behind a potentially controversial initiative if the business reasons for doing so are clear. Some executives can spin a great story at first, but can't get others to follow through because the executives don't seem to believe it themselves, or they contradict it with halfhearted, "flip-flopping" decisions. The decision to outsource must have a compelling business rationale. Management must have an acute grasp of what the company is trying to achieve—cost reductions? optimized processes? better service levels? more for less? innovation?— and keep these priorities in mind as it evaluates options.

Equally critical, the outsourcing decision should be based on a business case that is built on hard analysis. Without a granular understanding of the underlying costs, both tangible and intangible, of each process, a precise grasp of the potential benefits is nearly impossible. No one will really know what constitutes success, and such uncertainty can lead to evaporation of senior and line management support. At TXU, "we worked hard to establish our baseline operating costs with real accuracy," says Mr. Hillstrand. "Our finance folks had to assemble, disassemble, slice, dice, understand overheads and allocations and all of the components of cost associated with a large component of the business. Then they had to articulate it crisply, in a way that could be consumed by the third-party providers. Getting that baseline straight was a very intense and important effort."

Be Partners, Not Just Customers

Many companies try to manage service providers not as partners but as virtual lackeys, negotiating them down to prices that are unsustainable over the long term, holding them to encyclopedic contracts with impractical service-level and reporting commitments, and micromanaging the process of service delivery beyond the point of usefulness. This approach is fundamentally misaligned with both the basic objectives of an outsourcing arrangement and the realities of the new, more complex outsourcing world. When relationships between the parties focus primarily on the transaction, with each side seeking the better deal, the result is often antagonism; even when the relationship remains amicable, it is not conducive to long-term success.

By contrast, executives who have gotten the greatest benefit from their broad outsourcing arrangements have built relationships of mutual trust with their vendors. "You have significantly less control than you would have with people reporting directly to you and salary management control, performance reviews, and other tools at your disposal," says Mr. Passerini of P&G. "This new model is more challenging, and more demanding to manage, but it is significantly better for our business."

Outsourcing customers place an extraordinary amount of knowledge—and faith—in the hands of service providers. They entrust vendors with critical business processes, sensitive data, proprietary business knowledge, and even basic control over implementation and ongoing quality. "If you're going to outsource a service, you must turn its delivery over to the supplier rather than use them as a body shop; you have to focus only on putting the proper processes in place to monitor how they're delivering," says Ray Mohundro, former CIO of Innovene.

Enlightened companies have figured out how to strike the right balance between rigor and flexibility, so that they don't micromanage but also don't "turn over the keys" to the outsourcer. They rely on such mechanisms as governance structures with clearly defined decision rights—agreed on in advance by both parties—from the executive level all the way down to the day-to-day users of the service. In addition, service-level agreements, performance dashboards (which deliver live data from the suppliers), formal business reviews, and rewards and penalties for meeting or falling short of service levels all help to minimize surprises. These companies rigorously manage to outcomes (the "what"), not to inputs (the "how"). That frees up the providers to bring invaluable new thinking into the process. "We didn't tell the companies where to move people and how they were required to meet our needs in various places throughout the world," says Mr. Szygenda of GM. "They had to come up with innovative ideas, and they were able to do that. Not having that requirement internal to GM let us move unbelievably fast."

An outcomes-based approach takes much of the administrative burden off the shoulders of the customer, and providers are often better equipped to deal with those burdens. "As it turns out, the market does a better job configuring itself than we would have," says Mr. Hillstrand. "When the market configures itself to your scope, the configurer owns the seams and that's desirable." For example, when Capgemini subcontracted certain facets of its TXU work, the provider did a much better job, in Mr. Hillstrand's view, of shaping the subcontracts than TXU would have.

Embrace Complexity and Learn to Manage It

Outsourcing was once a fairly simple affair: Pick from a fairly limited menu of options (IT applications and infrastructure, payroll, accounts payable or receivable, benefits administration, basic customer support), frame up some request for proposals (RFPs), send them off to a few big vendors, negotiate a 10-year deal, and get through a predictable, often painful transition period.

No longer. Complexity has crept in on every front: the number of vendors, the number of countries from which they can deliver services, delivery models (onshore, nearshore, or offshore), and the sheer scope of offerings have all expanded considerably over the last few years. So has the variety of commercial and contractual models (Will risks and gains be shared? If so, to what extent? Will it be a bundled deal with a single vendor or a best-of-breed partnership with a network of multiple vendors?). In addition, the industry thinking is evolving, calling into question many so-called best practices, such as signing long-term deals, building offshore captives, and sourcing multiple functions or processes with a single vendor to maximize leverage. These apparent complexities and increasing degrees of freedom have added to the overall confusion, and erected an intimidating barrier to entry for companies that have little experience with outsourcing.

But this complexity can work to the customer's advantage; it translates into greater choice, and thus greater customer empowerment and better results in the long term. Although the emerging best-of-breed model implied by the larger field of choices may mean more up-front work prior to the deal, and more management complexity afterward, it will almost always result in an outsourcing arrangement that is well adapted to the needs and characteristics of individual customers. And industry leaders are harnessing this complexity to their advantage.

GM, for example, announced in February that it would split its $15 billion contract for information technology services among a number of providers—EDS, HP, IBM, Capgemini, Covisint, and Wipro—to encourage competition, to decrease risk exposure, to increase competition, to take advantage of offshore pure plays for discrete activities, and to challenge providers to address the automaker's needs. GM also slashed the contract term from 10 years to 5 years to shield itself from long-term financial risk, improve management of outsourcing deals, and ensure more accountability from outsourcers.

To manage multiple sourcing contracts without spiking budgets and creating suffocating bureaucracy, companies are becoming more adept at managing the multiple delivery models, pricing structures, and business metrics contained within multiple vendor relationships. They are installing centralized vendor management functions with talented personnel who are skilled at overseeing strategic vendor relationships, monitoring vendor performance, ensuring compliance with service-level agreements, and keeping vendors abreast of evolving company strategies and priorities.

Be a Visionary

As outsourcing becomes increasingly strategic, so too must the role of the business leaders who control IT and BPO. The new generation of outsourcing leaders is always thinking beyond the boundaries of their own function and, in some cases, even beyond the boundaries of existing market capabilities. They wear two hats: that of the functional leader who is accountable for excellence in service delivery; and that of the senior enterprise leader who sees how this vibrant new market of innovative services can solve the broader business's most pressing challenges.

In many instances, visionary business leaders are helping shape the market for future growth. GM's Ralph Szygenda was instrumental in driving several vendors to globalize their capabilities to meet one of GM's key requirements—a worldwide delivery model. He says, "I talked to the CEOs of the IT companies and I said, 'Hey, I've got this problem. Not only is this an issue for GM, but you're impeding the growth of your own business. Every time you go into a new engagement, you're reinventing processes to run your business. And by the way, hardly anybody's going to use one IT company ever again, given significant off-the-shelf products, ubiquitous telecommunications, and integrated IT services. So now why don't you make it easier for customers, from an integration viewpoint?' I urged them to build the foundation, to do the fundamental process work to standardize collaboration across their businesses." Mr. Szygenda's efforts encouraged GM's outsourcing partners to retool their businesses for the long haul. He helped them understand the evolving needs of major clients, and together they created fungible processes that the partners could in turn offer to other clients.

Similarly, P&G enabled its suppliers to enhance their offerings. According to Mr. Passerini, "For all three of our suppliers, our business was not flat-out outsourcing. It was a way for each to build internal capabilities to go to market. For example, HP had declared that they wanted to move into the IT business services industry. P&G's business gave them instant credibility in the market. IBM already was strong in IT outsourcing, but wanted to move into HR, so they created their HR division, acquiring our world-class assets, people, processes, and systems. Jones Lang LaSalle already was working in facilities management, but it was not as multinational as we were. So the P&G business gave it an instant global footprint." Clearly, only the largest multinationals have enough influence to shape the vendor base. But the implicit point holds for any customer: Don't settle for the market's status quo. A proactive approach might just pay off in services that can transform your company.

Mr. Szygenda, Mr. Passerini, and the other leaders we spoke to are learning to take calculated risks that lead to significant upgrades in efficiency and quality. They all have developed what Mr. Passerini calls "a completely new set of skills" for dealing with a strategic tool that constantly shifts shape. "The world is no longer about monolithic integration of businesses. It is about agility, responsiveness, flexibility, and, more and more, working within a network. So we really had to learn how to operate in a networked business," he says.

Integral to that new set of skills are the ability and willingness to look beyond the "core functions"—traditionally the partition that separated indispensable competitive advantage from transactional services—when considering what activities to outsource. In recent years, the notion of what functions must stay in-house to maintain a company's competitive edge has become far more fluid. Industries such as financial services, pharmaceuticals, and consumer electronics have led the charge by outsourcing such "core" areas as product development, market research and analytics, advanced customer care, and clinical trials.

"You must always focus on what it is you're in business for," says Mr. Mullinax of Duke Energy. "We're a utility business. We generate and deliver power, and we collect for the services; we move natural gas. We make our money by having very reliable service and having the expertise to deal with the regulatory bodies. Everything else behind that is a service that you can source in a variety of ways."

Like Mr. Mullinax, Mr. Hillstrand of TXU rejects the standard core-versus-noncore dividing line. "I don't think we'd impose any artificial limits" on what to outsource, he says. "Every time we look at our business, we look at it with an eye to making it better. Do I think that we're married to our own steel? Or that there are certain things that we simply would never let go of? Not necessarily." He is always searching for better ways to serve TXU's constituents. "We don't hesitate to look at the tools that are out there, whether that's development of joint ventures, disposition of assets, or reconfiguration of businesses into a synthetic arrangement of ourselves and best-in-class providers to achieve a financial and operational outcome that's really desirable to us." This attitude is integral to the "distinct competency around outsourcing" that Mr. Hillstrand says TXU is developing in its leadership.

Over the past few years, academic researchers like Charles Handy and Shoshana Zuboff have written about the deliberate design of "flat" and "networked" corporations. But ironically, it's the rough-and-tumble world of Asian and emerging-nation outsourcing providers that has created actual networked businesses as a model for the future. There's a growing awareness that, despite the potential pitfalls, outsourcing has become the sine qua non of the successful global corporation. "Every day some part of our business—and this is an evolving discipline for TXU—is asking itself, 'Are we the natural owner of function X?'" says Mr. Hillstrand. That kind of continuous self-examination may ultimately turn out to be the most significant aspect of the new outsourcing—and potentially the gateway into yet another, still more sophisticated wave of virtuoso activity.

PART IV

Meeting Old and New Global Challenges

CHAPTER 17

The Brand Challenge

Are Global Brands the Right Choice for Your Company?

Johny K. Johansson and Ilkka A. Ronkainen

In the last few years, a number of companies have engaged in brand pruning efforts with the aim of reducing brand portfolios to manageable sizes. Preference has naturally been given to global brands given their prominent positions. (For example, according to Unilever executives, three-fourths of the company's business comes from 20 global brands.) Many local brands are being evaluated according to their potential as global candidates or as examples of best practice that could be applied elsewhere. The bottom line for global companies is that there aren't enough resources to go around to manage scores of local brands that are not truly different.

Global brands, like any facet of global marketing, are supposed to benefit from the scale and the scope that having a presence in multiple markets brings. As global retailers gain more power, marketers may feel more pressure to have brands that can travel with their customers. Another justification for a global presence is fueled by the increasing similarity that consumers are displaying in terms of their consumption habits and preferences. It has also been argued that global brands are perceived to be more value added for the consumer, either through better quality (as a function of worldwide acceptance) or by enhancing the consumer's self-perception as being cosmopolitan, sophisticated, and modern.

Internally, global branding can be seen as a tool to tighten organizational relationships using the transfer of best practice in brand management, as well as programs like brand stewardship through brand management teams at headquarters or designated centers of excellence. Concentrating resources and efforts on a limited number of brands should bring about improved results. For example, Unilever has singled out six brands for special attention in the personal care category, all of which showed double-digit growth in 2002.

While the level and effects of globalization can be disputed, the critical question is whether a brand's image will carry over effectively to other markets. Efforts to standardize brand names by eliminating local brand names have met with consumer hostility, and globally branded items introduced into product lines have not always received the enthusiastic support of country managers. Consumers' behavior may have converged, but some markets continue to have their own idiosyncrasies that can prove fatal to globalization efforts. The ability of a global product to penetrate individual markets is determined to some extent by the product category in question. Global brands may have more success in high-profile, high-involvement categories, while consumers may still give local brands preference in purchasing everyday products.

What Is a Global Brand?

There is no real agreement on what a global brand is. A typical definition would be "a brand that is marketed under the same name in multiple countries with similar and centrally coordinated marketing strategies" (Czinkota & Ronkainen, 2006). There are, however, some selected global brands that don't have the same name but share some marketing program elements (e.g., Mr. Clean also sells under the Mr. Proper and Maestro Limpio names among others). A number of studies have attempted to quantify the definition of a global brand. Typically, sales need to exceed $1 billion a year with a minimum amount generated outside of the marketer's home region or country (varying from 5 to 20%). Presence is also required in all of the megamarkets of the world. These definitions restrict the number of brands to be considered global to a few dozen (e.g., ACNielsen's study found only 43 brands that satisfied their narrow criteria). What's common in these definitions is the multimarket reach of products that are perceived as the same brand worldwide both by consumers and by internal constituents.

To assess brand realities on the global/local continuum, data from Young & Rubicam's Brand Asset Valuator (BAV) were used. This database is the most exhaustive of its kind covering 20,000 brands across 40 countries. Data have been collected since 1993 across a wide range of industry sectors to measure brand perceptions of more than 100,000 consumers. The U.S. study in 1999, for example, included 9,000 interviewees. The 64 measures obtained are combined to measure brand strength (uniqueness of the brand promise and perceived relevance to meet consumer demands) as well as brand stature (the depth of consumers' familiarity with the brand and the level of esteem in which they hold that brand). The subset of data used here includes the top 150 brands in 12 product categories across eight major markets in terms of brand strength. This resulted in a total of 727 individual brands. Of the 727 total brands listed, most were on the list in one country only.

Although these brands are available in one market only, not all of them are domestic brands. In nearly 25% of the cases, the brands are from another market as is the case with British Burberry in Spain. A total of 35 brands were among the top 150 in all of the three megamarkets of the world (Americas, Asia, and Europe), while only 13 brands were present in all of the eight countries studied. The inevitable conclusion is that, from a perspective of pure relevance and uniqueness, local brands are still dominant. The reason may quite possibly be that these brands are more in line with local expectations and requirements. In addition, research has uncovered the existence of strongly ethnocentric segments in the world, especially in Asia.

It is important to assess how global brands fare in terms of stature against the more local brands. The top five brands in each of the eight countries both in terms of familiarity and esteem feature a mixture of global and local brands. For example, Coca-Cola was the most familiar in each of the eight countries except for the United Kingdom, where it was eclipsed by Heinz for the top spot. In terms of esteem, the top ranked brands are often local but with a twist: They are also global players. Examples are Volvo in Sweden, Ferrari in Italy, and Danone in France. These brands may thus reap the benefits that local brands have for their fit, as well as benefits that global brands have for their perceived quality. Overall, local brands exhibit higher familiarity among consumers, but when familiarity levels are similar, global brands enjoy higher levels of esteem.

An interesting observation from the data is that nearly all of the global brands (those with a presence in at least two of the megamarkets) hail from the countries included in this study. The only exception is Denmark-based Lego, which is in the top 50 for esteem in seven of the eight markets.

Global branding will arguably face different challenges by product category. Certain categories, such as automobiles and computers, are deemed more global in terms of the similarity in consumer preferences. Of the brands in these two industries, the majority were present in more than one market. The results corroborate the perception that sectors such as food and drink are more multidomestic and do, therefore, require a "local" presence. Even in soft drinks, the percentage of brands in more than one market was only 35%. This doesn't mean that global brands don't have an opportunity, but marketers may have to tread more carefully in imposing global brand names especially at the expense of well-established local ones. Global marketers may be better advised to leverage global technology platforms to the benefit of an existing local brand.

The issue with global brands is not so much whether to globalize or to localize, but how much of each to do. The fact that brands do get a consistent lift from being present in multiple markets, coupled with the need to exploit economies of scale, creates a powerful argument for marketers when they make choices on brand portfolios. But to be the best of global while being best of local, the same marketers need to factor in uniqueness and relevance of a local brand as well as the level of "globalness" in the product category.

Note

This research was sponsored by Honda Motor Co. and the McDonough School of Business. Thanks are due to Landor and Young & Rubicam for providing data and advice. Cipriano de Leon provided data analysis and research assistance.

Reference

Czinkota, M. R., & Ronkainen, I. A. (2010). *International marketing* (9th ed.). Mason, OH: South-Western, Cengage Learning.

CHAPTER 18

Spanning the Globe

Winning Over the Antiglobals

Claudiu V. Dimofte, Johny K. Johansson,
and Ilkka A. Ronkainen

The tremendous visibility of global brands has made them successful—
but they are also vulnerable as symbols of the ills of globalization. While
the militant actions against global brands prominent in the early years
of the 21st century (such as the dismantling of a McDonald's in France,
May Day violence against Gap and Starbucks locations in Britain, or
attempts to burn down a Nike store in Minnesota) might have decreased,
the skepticism among some consumers concerning the behavior of global
companies is likely to have survived. As a matter of fact, the extremism
may have concealed the extent and true nature of the disenchantment.

The easiest approach is to dismiss those with unfavorable attitudes
toward global brands as marginal and unmanageable. The size of this
segment varies by geography, but is generally estimated to be between
10 and 20% of the population—making it clearly too large to ignore.
What is not clearly established, except through anecdotal evidence, is the
connection between these unfavorable attitudes and behavior. Several of
these anecdotes point to a surprising and paradoxical disconnect between
antiglobal attitudes and behaviors. For example, in reference to McDonald's, a French reporter commented, "We hate it and we go to it. If you
are going to the movies and have to eat in 10 minutes, you eat at McDonald's." Regardless of attitudes, consumers seem to favor availability, recognition and convenience.

To identify how American consumers feel about global brands, a random sample of 1,000 respondents over age 18 was used, drawn sequentially from an online panel of more than 3 million people. After eliminating incomplete questionnaires, the sample size was 719. The sample consisted of 51% men and 49% women, with 60% younger than 35 years old and 40% older; their ethnicity was 80% white and 20% non-white (mainly African American and Hispanic); and their education level was 74% with at least some college. Antiglobal brands consumers were identified as those scoring less than 4 on a 7-point favorableness measure (the mean of antiglobals was a full three points lower than for those with favorable attitudes toward global brands). The share of the antiglobals in the entire sample was 10%, suggesting acceptable representation (in a previous study of 3,300 consumers in 41 countries, the antiglobals' share was 13%.) There were no significant differences in basic demographics between the two groups. They included the same age groups, the same gender proportions, and the same ethnicity makeup. The only significant difference observed was in terms of education: the less educated (high school only) were more antiglobal. Although the antiglobal brands' respondents were significantly more negative toward globalization in general, there was no anti-Americanism evident. Both groups were in favor of choosing American global brands if given a choice. The experimental studies involved up to 120 participants. With antiglobal consumers making up about 10% of the marketplace and growing, they cannot be ignored by global brand managers. But antiglobals are an elusive target—openly denigrating global brands, but still occasionally buying them. Short of changing their negative mindsets, the logical strategy is to combine the safe convenience of strong brands with the aspirational element that even antiglobals find in global brands.

Global Brand Dimensions

From the survey, five factors emerged to describe the dimensionality of the global brand construct. The first reflected the reach of the brand in terms of both availability and visibility. The second factor captured an aspiration component, as global brands were seen as exciting and as symbols of achievement. Consumers also perceived global brands as being a safer choice and as timesavers, making the third factor a convenience dimension. The fourth factor represented the recognition of environmental and social responsibility, while the fifth described global brands as standardized (i.e., not adapted to local custom).

The perceptual differences between the anti- and proglobal groups were striking. On virtually all dimensions, proglobals scored significantly higher than antiglobals. Respondents with favorable attitudes found global brands to have higher quality than other brands, to be more innovative and ahead of market trends. The antiglobals disagreed. Proglobals found global brands to be exciting and prestigious, but antiglobals did not. Even on items showing basic agreement between pro- and antiglobals, the former scored consistently higher. Thus, proglobals found more cosmopolitanism and ethical responsibilities in global brands, as well as that they offered safer and more timesaving choices. The antiglobals agreed, but less emphatically. Even for relatively objective items like wider reach and availability, where both groups were in agreement, proglobals scored higher than the antiglobals. The only dimensions showing complete agreement between the two groups were the lack of adaptation to local markets and competitive dominance; both groups agreed that global brands are basically the same everywhere, and tend to be dominant brands.

Brand Globality Importance

As one would expect, these differing perceptions of global brands translated directly into distinct preferences and behaviors toward global brands. Thus, the antiglobals' negative evaluations of global brands meant that they also had lower preferences for global over local brands, and reported lower purchasing frequency of global brands. Since antiglobals also perceive global brands to have positive benefits in terms of availability, recognition, and overall convenience, they could be perfectly rational buying a global brand. Relative to the proglobals, however, they did report buying fewer global brands and were more likely to prefer local brands. These results suggest that it is important for global brand managers to combat the antiglobal attitudes; these attitudes do, in fact, bias what consumers think about and how they behave toward a brand.

But the survey responses also showed that this apparently rational behavior was not related to the globality of the brand per se. When asked, respondents generally told us that they did not care if a brand was global or not. In fact, both pro- and antiglobals suggested that brand globality was not important in their choices. We found this apparent lack of cognitive consistency puzzling. It is well known that many consumers deny marketing influences in their choices, despite evidence to the contrary. As consumers, we claim that advertising has no influence on us, but has more influence on our peers—a doubtful proposition. Similarly, brands are not usually volunteered in self-reports as critical determinants of choice, but Apple managers know better. Country of origin is presumably of no consequence either, but Korean or Indian exporters (Hyundai or Tata Motors) will beg to differ. We do not want to take all consumer responses at face value.

There could be at least two reasons why the impact of globality might not be acknowledged explicitly by consumers. Some consumers might have a fear of appearing superficial and seeming to rely on irrelevant cues. Buying a "reliable brand" is more acceptable than choosing a "global brand." This would suggest that consumers consciously suppress the real reason for their choice. But there is another possible explanation. The individual could be simply unaware of the reason. The consumer reaction to a global brand could be automatic.

Automatic Associations

To evaluate these alternative explanations, we turned to an experimental approach. First, a study using the Implicit Association Test (IAT) was used to test whether the global brand effect is unconscious. IAT is an experimental method designed to measure the strength of automatic association between mental representations of concepts in memory. The IAT requires the rapid categorization of various stimulus objects, such that easier pairings (and faster responses) are interpreted as being more strongly associated in memory than more difficult pairings (slower responses).

The results showed that, compared to local brands, global brands were more closely associated with adjectives such as "ideal" and "desirable." Global brands had an idealistic and dream quality automatically associated with them. Local brands, by contrast, were seen as more concrete and mundane and more specific and relevant—with much less of an idealistic, dream, or myth quality. This is consistent with the notion that global brands are inherently (i.e., automatically) associated with an affective, aspirational dimension lacking in local brands. This could help explain the anecdotal evidence that antiglobals seem to sometimes favor global brands as well.

To assess the relationship between explicit attitude and automatic response, the IAT responses were tested against self-reported explicit attitudes toward global brands. On the average, there was no significant difference between these two groups' automatic reactions. Even antiglobal respondents showed an equally strong positive association between global brands and "ideal" and "desirable." This paradoxical finding suggests that any direct globality effect is—at least partly—automatic. It also helps explain why some antiglobals don't feel hypocritical about some of their marketplace choices featuring (despised) global brands—they simply are unconscious of this influence, and attribute their behavior to specific benefits provided by global brands.

All consumers, regardless of self-reported explicit attitudes and despite claims that globality does not matter, show an automatic preference for global brands. They fail to explicitly acknowledge this globality impact for two different reasons. Proglobals are basically favorable toward global brands, but tend to underplay the importance of globality—because they are simply not cognizant of the extent to which they positively value global brands and how this influences their choice. As with brands in general, they simply do not recognize their own biases. Antiglobals, who have more at stake, consciously suppress any positive attitudes toward global brands over and above convenience in order to be consistent with their openly negative stand. Nevertheless, their actual behavior reflects both the convenience and the automatic attractiveness of global brands.

Incorporating Antiglobals

Consumers with reservations about global brands are a group of sufficient size, not to be dismissed. Responses to win them over will call for pragmatism and creativity. Given their real and perceived size, global brands are automatically associated with sheer, hard power (i.e., exploiting scale to gain acceptance and access). Antiglobals are not convinced that this means higher quality or more innovativeness, but instead raise questions about fairness and foster feelings of resentment. The convenience of global brands sometimes overcomes this resentment. However, a global brand marketer has an inherent ability to use the soft power of global brands, and win over constituents through the use of cultural values and aspirational ideals. Co-opting is by its nature as effective as using reward or coercive power, and even more powerful in terms of its long-term effects. Global brand marketers have the resources to develop products or communications that offer consumers both cultural and aspirational resonance.

Having global brands with the convenience and attractiveness of local attributes is the first half of the new winning formula. Through their association with global, regional, and local philanthropy, global brands cater to consumers' aspirations and expectations of corporate social responsibility. Thus, global brands as part of local cultures provide the ingredients for the second half of the new strategic thinking.

Many, if not all, of the strategies mentioned here are pertinent to the general consumer population, not merely to the antiglobals. But if these refined features of global strategy ensured the incorporation of the 10% of the population whose disenchantment with global brands made them avoid or reconsider certain purchases, it should be recorded as a significant long-term achievement.

Additional Reading

Holt, D. B, Quelch, J. A., & Taylor, E. L. (2004). How global brands compete. *Harvard Business Review, 82*(9), 68–81.

Johansson, J. K., & Ronkainen, I. A. (2005). The esteem of global brands. *Journal of Brand Management, 12*(5), 339–54.

Nye, J. S., Jr. (2004). *Soft Power: The Means to Success in World Politics.* New York, NY: PublicAffairs.

CHAPTER 19

The Effects of Terrorism on International Marketing

Michael R. Czinkota and Gary Knight

Introduction

We define international terrorism as "the systematic threat or use of violence across national borders to attain a political goal or communicate a political message through fear, coercion or intimidation of non-combatant persons or the general public" (Alexander, Valton, & Wilkinson, 1979, p. 4). Terrorism is a human imposed disaster which purposefully aims at maximum random destruction and which is planned to systematically circumvent preventive measures. The potential targets for terrorism are far too numerous to be consistently protected. Even small terrorist groups with minimal resources have the ability to achieve major effects. Typically, the cost-effectiveness equation is asymmetric: in favor of the terrorist and against the target. The cost of protecting ourselves and averting terrorist acts is many billions of dollars, while the terrorists' costs are in the millions or less (Czinkota, Knight, & Liesch, 2003).

Terrorists direct their attacks against business far more than any other target. In addition, the need for businesses to remain easily accessible to the outside and to conduct transactions with many persons with whom no prior interaction had taken place, introduces a level of vulnerability which is not typically encountered by government offices or individuals (U.S. Department of State, 2004).

Terrorists intend to affect supply and demand in order to precipitate deleterious effects on existing economic systems. The results are two key types of effects: direct and indirect (Czinkota, Knight, & Liesch, 2003; Knight & Czinkota, 2006). The direct effects of terrorism comprise the immediate business consequences as experienced by individual firms. For example, some firms located in the World Trade Center lost most of their employees and operations. While the harm is clearly tragic for individually affected people and firms, from a societal perspective the direct effects of terrorism tend to be smaller than the indirect effects. The latter accumulate and often become recognizable only over time and include long term changes such as a decline in buyer demand; shifts or interruptions in value and supply chains; new policies, regulations, and laws which have intended and unintended effects; as well as changes in international relations and perceptions that affect trade and investment. These indirect effects pose the greatest potential threat to the activities of firms. For example, interruptions in the supply of needed inputs to one industry can lead to shortages of parts and components which serve as crucial input for other economic sectors (e.g., Council on Foreign Relations, 2002). Policy measures intended to increase security may lessen the efficiency of global transportation and logistical systems. The unintended consequences of such actions may increase market imperfections and raise business costs further, and may alter the environment in ways more harmful to business interests than the terrorist events that provoked them.

From a global perspective, these effects are present for many firms, even those who see themselves as quite remote from any location affected by terrorism. Today's climate of global commerce involves extensive interaction with countless distributors and customers. Producers and marketers rely on suppliers and suppliers' suppliers to obtain goods and components. Such extensive networks increase the exposure of firms to events that take place at a far distance. Even firms perceived as having little international involvement may depend on the receipt of imported goods and are therefore subject to shortages or delays of inputs and the disruption of company operations (Steen et al., 2006).

The assessment of individual vulnerability differs based on the information, experience, and perception of an event. Over time these impressions shift, which can result in faulty managerial decisions. For example, during the days following a terrorist event, there is typically the feeling of "but for the grace of God, it could have been me." However, over time, this feeling is likely to give way to a perception of "this was an aberration and cannot happen to me." Such a shift is instrumental to restore human confidence and encourage the resumption of "normal" activities, but may underestimate the likelihood of future exposures to new risks and terrorism (National Capital Region, 2005). Therefore, success in preventing terrorist acts is likely to reduce corporate concern about terrorism. Ignorance and apathy may lead to managers resting comfortably on the belief that any future attack will not affect their firm or lead to personal repercussions (Knight & Czinkota, 2006).

It is also important to understand that in today's business climate of global competition and rapid response, firms no longer have the luxury of just aiming for "survival" in case of a terror attack. Instead, firms need to be flexible in order to be able to withstand shocks (Sheffi, 2005). They must offer assured continuity to their suppliers, their clients, their employees, and other stakeholders in order to inspire confidence in the relationship. Flexible firms will recover more quickly and can more readily sustain performance in the aftermath of terrorism's direct and indirect consequences. Firms need to develop continuity plans to deal with crises. Such plans may, for example, facilitate a shift of production to different regions of the world in the wake of unanticipated disruptive events. Particularly for firms that engage in massive outsourcing, the reliance on a single or even limited number of suppliers, or on suppliers concentrated in a limited range of locations, is quite risky. Renewed and ongoing business relationships need to be a principal goal of any firm following a terrorist attack. Apart from the importance of such an achievement for the viability of the firm, business continuity also denies terrorists their achievements.

Particular attention needs to be paid to the marketing function within corporations when it comes to a response to terrorism. Even though all corporate areas are likely to be affected by sudden shifts triggered by terrorist activity, the marketing field, which constitutes the key corporate liaison with the world outside of the firm, is likely to be under most pressure. When properly prepared, marketers can be the most capable in delivering corporate responses to such an event. Key reasons are that the field of marketing deals most closely with consumers and markets, in direct linkage to the activities of supply and demand, which terrorists aim to destroy. This proximity makes marketers the first responders to business disruption. Within industry, marketers deal with imports and exports, as well as distribution and logistics. Marketers tend to have the clearest understanding of the mutual corporate dependence so critical for effective planning. For example, when determining the need for specific emergency inputs, marketers will be able to analyze the existing relationships and networks and devise incentives to ensure that the supplier will actually provide goods and services to the firm. Dry runs and simulations can then be used by marketers to develop expectations about long-term effects and to see whether the system works as planned. Without such considerations, a plan for input contingency is akin to identifying the location of gas stations as the principal remedy for a fuel shortage, without keeping in mind that the station needs to be resupplied itself, be open, and be willing to provide the gasoline needed to the car pulling into the station.

On the supply side, marketers deal with communication with customers and suppliers, devise campaigns to present information, provide direction and alter any misperceptions. Marketers are the experts who implement steps to address imbalances and create new incentives by changing corporate pricing, packaging, or sizing. Goods or services whose price is strongly affected by changing information flows and perceptions of risk are highly susceptible to the indirect consequences of terrorism. Insurance coverage is an example. Actual or perceived terrorist threats tend to create upward pressure on the pricing of particularly vulnerable offerings. Prices may also experience a certain "stickiness," that is, once raised, prices may not be decreased. Conversely, firms in certain industries may feel pressure to lower prices in order to induce reluctant buyers to maintain or increase their buying activities. Through their actions, marketers can reverse an emerging softness in demand, rally joint responses, and avoid the occurrence of unintended consequences. With their understanding of the long term repercussions of terrorism, marketers can also be instrumental in formulating alternative corporate strategies—say a shift from an investment based foreign market expansion to an export based one (Lutz & Lutz, 2006).

The continuing efforts of marketers to understand cultural issues are also highly useful for devising terminology and persuasive encouragement. There are major cultural differences between, and even within, nations. International marketing, through its linkages via goods, services, ideas, and communications, can achieve important assimilations of value systems. Marketers know that culture and values are learned, not genetically implanted. As life's experiences grow more international and more similar, so do values. Therefore, every time international marketing forges a new linkage in thinking and provides for new exchanges of goods or services, new progress is made in shaping a greater global commonality in values. It may well be that international marketing's ability to align global values and the subsequent greater ease of countries, companies, and individuals to build bridges between themselves, may eventually become the field's greatest gift to the world.

The General Benefit of Preparedness

In most instances, corporate preparedness is of key importance to any firm. Major disasters can have a devastating impact, but even relatively small and local events can cause important dislocations for firms. For a corporation to simply assume that it never will be exposed to disruptions and substantial sudden shifts in supply or demand is a high risk strategy. For example, suppliers can go out of business or have their facilities burn to the ground; employees may be struck by illness; a labor dispute may ground shipments; rumors about product quality may dissuade loyal customers from buying.

If managers intend to safeguard the investment of shareholders and assure the viability of their firm, it is of utmost importance to prepare contingency plans and operational alternatives that respond to a sudden shock or dislocation. Firms which have not devoted efforts and resources to respond flexibly to changes risk falling drastically behind their competitors who have engaged in such thinking and planning (Crisis Management, 2000). We therefore believe that corporate preparation for the repercussions of terrorism is likely to be of general value to society and of use to the operations of the firm. Preparation reduces the risk, surprise, and punch of the system shock exerted by sudden change.

A Model of Corporate Preparedness for Terrorism

We propose a model which captures the different levels of corporate read-iness for international terrorism. This model, which is shown in Exhibit 19.1, indicates the interrelationship among conditions, activities, and people, and identifies leverage points which policy makers can use to ini-tiate improvement and change. The model might also be of assistance in evaluating policy approaches to emergency preparedness in general.

Our model starts with the trigger of either terrorist threats or inci-dents. The consequences are both direct and indirect effects. The direct effects are most keenly felt by those closest to the terrorist activity, while the indirect effects are more likely to cause a severe domino effect over time. These effects in turn trigger the actions of responders who can be either internal or external to the firm and are typically marketing managers or government officials. These responders interact with and affect directly the information, experience, and perception of society and the firm. This linkage is reinforced by the media, which has the capability to immediately transmit and magnify deleterious news. The consequence is the creation of friction that can reduce the transactional freedom of international busi-ness, be it through new regulations, more inspections, or a greater hesita-tion to become involved in international ventures. Such friction becomes

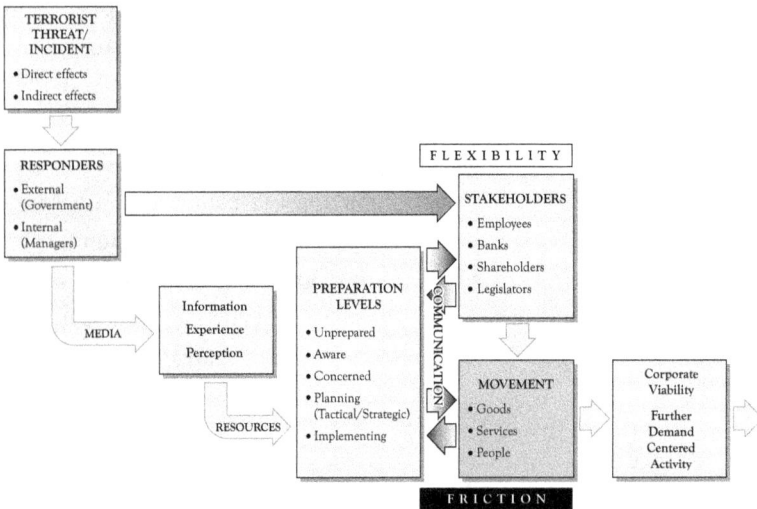

Exhibit 19.1. A model of corporate preparedness for terrorism.

particularly notable when it comes to interaction with stakeholders or the movement of goods, services, and people (Knight & Czinkota, 2006).

Within the firm, the prevailing information, perception, and experience of managers is constrained or assisted by the availability of resources and a corporate willingness to deploy them. The result is various levels of preparation for coping with sudden dislocations. We find a time-driven sequence of steps or stages of preparation. Managers typically start out totally unprepared for the effects of terrorism on their firms—such contingencies are simply not on the radar screen. At this stage, there is no history or willingness on the part of the firm to undertake any kind of investment or preparatory action. Over time and with sufficient input, managers change their attitude as they become aware of the issue, but are still not ready to take on any activity. The next level represents management that is concerned about terrorism. There begins a search for further input. Typically firms prepare by finding or developing checklists and conducting audits as to the preparedness status. As a further step, managers start to plan responses to terrorism—initially at a tactical level, which leads to a strategic level—based on the information gathered earlier. Here interaction begins to take place with various stakeholders of the firm, ranging from employees to suppliers, banks, and legislators. Finally, management devotes important resources to be prepared in case the firm encounters dislocations triggered by terrorism.

One can easily fathom that at each level of preparedness managers have different needs and concerns. Responding to these concerns is important if one is to move the participants up to a higher plane of preparation. Our research has shown that any outside assistance that delivers insufficient, overwhelming, or inapplicable help to firms will be seen as inappropriate and wasteful. A lack of trust in such help will then decrease its acceptance and perceived usefulness.

Depending on their level of preparation, managers and their firms are able to influence the movement inward and outward (including the shelter) of goods, services, and people. They can source from or supply multiple partners; they can bring in customers to evaluate products and buy them; and they can hire bright new employees at home or from abroad. To do so effectively, firms need ongoing communication to maintain contact within the company, with suppliers, and with the market.

Management also needs to communicate with additional stakeholders in the business process who may be affected by terrorism. For example, banks are exposed to a rising regulatory burden in international commerce, which drives up fixed costs. The need to create or expand entire departments to deal with compliance issues will influence a bank's willingness to go after new business that requires additional oversight and reporting. Managers will also need to consider the ramifications of their actions. There is the issue of their moral responsibility to protect employees by relocating staff and ensuring that they have employment and get paid when the ATMs are down. Access to data will be crucial to continue contact with and service to customers.

There are also the shareholders who may or may not be supportive of preparation for terrorism events and legislators abroad who may engage in negative reciprocity. All these components will shape the eventual viability of a corporation and determine its ability to engage in further demand centered activity. It is important to appreciate the long-term significance of corporate readiness for international terrorism. Unless firms achieve a minimum level of readiness to ensure their survival and prosperity, they may be the proverbial dead duck in the hunt: Once hit by shotgun pellets they may still be flying but they are destined to crash and perish.

The Study

To address the knowledge gap noted above, we conducted a substantive survey-based study to explore the link between firms, terrorism, and other emergencies. Initially we conducted interviews with managers at firms throughout the United States and overseas. This was done to uncover key issues and relationships in preparation for conducting a large-scale survey. Subsequently, we conducted an online survey of U.S. firms. The purpose of the survey was to isolate processes in domestic and international business that are vulnerable to terrorism and other emergencies and to understand what types of responses firms are making to these challenges. The case studies and survey were conducted to provide input for the formulation of national policy regarding these important issues.

Results were received from 219 randomly selected U.S. firms. Thirty percent of respondents are manufacturing firms and the remainders are in the service sector. This reflects the U.S. economy, which is 80% service based. Some aspects of manufacturing firms are more vulnerable to terrorism and other emergencies, because of the need to deal in potentially long supply chains, transportation systems, and other business activities characteristic of dealing in tangible products.

In the sample of respondent firms, about 65% had revenues of $2.5 million to $100 million, 20% had less than $2.5 million, and the remainder had greater than $100 million. Sixty-three percent of the respondents had been in business for over 20 years, 20% for 11 to 20 years, and the remainder for less than 11 years. Regarding international operations, 71% obtained up to 20% of their total sales from international sources, 19% derived between 20 and 39% of their sales internationally, and the remainder obtained over 39% of their sales from abroad.

Exporting was by far the most popular form of international entry (59% of firms), and about one-third of the firms shipped their international offerings by sea, while a smaller proportion (21%) shipped by air. Relatively few of the firms engaged in foreign direct investment. About one-third of respondents cited Europe as their most important international business location, and another third cited North America (Canada and Mexico); 20% cited Asia. Very few of these firms (less than 4%) cited other locations (e.g., South America, Russia and former USSR, Middle East, Africa) as their most important international targets. Very few of the firms (20% or less) did business with countries prone to terrorism, such as Colombia, Indonesia, Israel, and Yemen.

Major Results

Nearly all respondents (88%) said their businesses had not been directly threatened by terrorism. We asked the firms if they had been affected by indirect effects of terrorism. The most important effect, experienced by about one-quarter of all firms, consisted of increased insurance costs. The second greatest effect (18% of respondents) was a tendency to place greater importance on the integrity of international business partners. The third most cited effect (16%) was more delays in international business activities. This was followed by less trust in international business (15% of respondents). Five to 7% of firms reported experiencing the following:

unpredictable shifts or interruptions in supply chains, decreases in consumer demand, deteriorating international trade relations.

While nearly 50% of firms were concerned about the effects of terrorism or threats of terrorism, only one-quarter had prepared a terrorism contingency plan. Only about one-third said they were prepared to deal with the effects or threats of terrorism. Only 8% said they were considering moving critical operations or branching out into less sensitive areas due to terrorism. Less than 20% stated that they included terrorism as a factor in selecting or designing supply chains and distribution channels, or in developing and revising marketing strategy. Only 18% said antiterrorism expenditures were seriously considered in their firm. Only 12% said shareholders reward corporate efforts to prepare for terrorist threats.

In terms of international shipping of input and finished goods, since the attacks of September 11, 2001 (9/11), nearly one-third had experienced international shipping delays of 1 to 6 days. Eighteen percent had experienced international shipping delays of over 1 week. Fifty-four percent said their supply chain costs had gone up since the attacks of 9/11, but only a quarter had raised their prices in response to terrorism risks.

We also asked about the corporate response to terrorism. Fifty-seven percent of the firms had responded that they revised company operations or devised strategies to deal with the threat of terrorism. Almost half of those (27% of the total sample) had done so largely on their own, with little prodding by government mandate. One-third of the responders (19% of the total sample) replied that nearly all of their response was due to government mandate. About one-quarter of all respondents had spent over $50,000 in new technology and systems upgrades to comply with post-9/11 federal antiterrorism mandates. Eight percent had spent more than $200,000 for such upgrades. Fully 77% of the respondents had not pursued such upgrades, or had spent less than $50,000 on them. Only 7% of respondents had joined the federal government's Customs-Trade Partnership Against Terrorism (C-TPAT). About 21% stated that government policies toward terrorism had substantially slowed their international business operations and 16% claimed that their international growth had been curtailed by governmental antiterrorism policies.

Among the 219 firms surveyed in our study, the following additional findings emerged:

- The longer a firm had been engaged in international business, the more likely it was to prepare for terrorism.
- The more involved the firm was in international business, the more concerned their management was about terrorism and taking steps to deal with it.
- Importers and others engaged in extensive international sourcing were relatively more concerned about access to raw materials, fluctuating exchange rates, and the potential effects of natural disasters. They reported that their supply chain costs and prices had increased since 9/11 and that government policies toward terrorism had substantially slowed their international operations. Importers put greater emphasis on the importance of integrity in their international partners. They were more concerned about deteriorating international relations.
- Companies that experienced terrorism threats and expressed concerns about terrorism were also more likely to have spent money on dealing with terrorism, to have shareholders' support in preparing for terrorism, and to have prepared terrorism contingency plans and made other preparations. There appears to be a segment of firms that are more vulnerable to, or feel more threatened about, the risk of terrorism. These firms tend to be in the services sector.
- Among firms that believed government policies toward terrorism had substantially hampered their international business operations and international growth, the following characteristics applied. These firms

  - were often engaged in importing or licensing;
  - were more concerned about access to raw materials and rising oil prices;
  - had experienced decreases in consumer demand and unexpected interruptions in supply chains due to terrorism;
  - were not particularly concerned about the effects of terrorism, but had taken steps on their own to prepare for terrorism, including spending money on new technology and systems upgrades.

Conclusions

In summary, respondents to the survey were largely exporters that had experienced rising insurance costs, rising supply chain costs, delays in international business activities, and put greater importance on the integrity of international business partners. The majority has responded little to terrorism, or not at all, and there is relatively little stakeholder support for such responses. Most have been little affected, or not at all, by government-sponsored antiterrorism policies. A large proportion believes firms should carry terrorism insurance. They tend to be much more concerned about rising oil prices than terrorism or other possible emergencies.

Most respondents operate in the services sectors, and these firms have relatively more overseas operations (as compared to manufacturing firms). Services firms were somewhat more concerned about terrorism and had taken some steps to prepare to deal with it. Compared to manufacturers, stakeholders in service firms were more likely to reward corporate efforts to prepare for terrorism.

Results suggest that most U.S. firms are largely indifferent about and unprepared for terrorism and other major threats. This culture of indifference is somewhat understandable—the only major event in recent memory was the 9/11 attack, which occurred in 2001. Yet terrorism impact can be very substantive, particularly in terms of its indirect effects. When combined with other emergencies (e.g., hurricanes, floods, epidemics, supply shocks, macroeconomic crises), the consequences for businesses could be substantial.

A key challenge is that firms, especially small and medium-size enterprises, have both limited resources and competing priorities. Managers are disinclined to plan for contingencies that (a) may occur at some distant future time (e.g., not this quarter); (b) involve high levels of uncertainty and are therefore difficult to measure and plan for; and (c) shareholders and stakeholders view as relatively unimportant. A key challenge for policy makers, therefore, is to stimulate managers to invest time and money in dealing with the threat or possible effects of terrorism and other emergencies.

Fear may be the greatest enemy. The panic and psychological impact of disasters can be more harmful than the disasters themselves. For instance, the 9/11 attacks triggered a decline in construction of high-rise buildings and other vulnerable structures. While an influenza pandemic, such as the Avian flu, might kill far less than 1% of the U.S. population (i.e., the chances of dying are very small), the ensuing panic, psychological harm, and tendency of people to stay home and retrench, could have much more devastating effects. It is critical to restore confidence and maintain order as early as possible following catastrophic events. The federal government should take steps to ensure that businesses continue "business as usual" as quickly as possible in the wake of an event.

References

Alexander, Y., Carlton, D., & Wilkinson, P. (1979). *Terrorism: Theory and practice.* Boulder, CO: Westview Press.

Council on Foreign Relations. (2002). *America still unprepared—America still in danger.* New York: Council on Foreign Relations, Inc.

Crisis management. (2000). Boston, MA: Harvard Business School Press.

Czinkota, M. R., Knight, G., & Liesch, P. (2003). Terrorism and international business: Conceptual foundations. In G. Suder (Ed.), *Terrorism and the international business environment: The security-business nexus.* Cheltenham, England: Edward Elgar.

Knight, G. A. & Czinkota, M. R. (2006). Terrorism and international business: The corporate response. *Proceedings: 2006 Annual Conference, Academy of International Business.* Lansing, MI: SE. E.

Lutz, J. M., & Lutz, B. J. (2006) Terrorism as economic warfare. *Global Economy Journal, 6*(2), 1–20.

National capital region emergency preparedness campaign. (2005). Fairfax: Greenberg, Quinlan, Rosner Research Inc.

Sheffi, J. (2005). *The resilient enterprise: Overcoming vulnerability for competitive advantage.* Boston, MA: MIT Press.

Steen, J., Liesch, P., Knight, G., & Czinkota, M. R. (2006, November). The contagion of international terrorism and its effects on the firm in an interconnected world. *Public Money and Management,* pp. 1–8.

U.S. Department of State. (2004). *Patterns of global terrorism.* Washington, DC: Author.

CHAPTER 20

Taking a Calmer View

The Financial Sector's Prospects in the Wake of Crisis May Be Better Than You Think

Klaus-Peter Gushurst, Ivan de Souza, and Vanessa Wallace

As the current economic turmoil unfolds, it's easy to lose sight of the long-term implications. The crisis mind-set in the financial-services sector, in particular, is understandable. Some of the world's leading banking and insurance institutions are falling by the wayside. It is estimated that more than 100,000 professionals will have lost their jobs by the end of this year. Most ordinary savers around the world have lost significant portions of their pension and retirement savings. Governments are being tested, and leaders are under great pressure to intervene. The "bailouts" and other responses developed so far, however beneficial, will divert treasury and taxpayer money that might otherwise have been used to build infrastructure and support economic growth. Today's level of market volatility has not been seen since the 1987 stock market crash. The size of the U.S. financial sector, the interconnected nature of financial markets, and the lightning-fast communication of news and rumor around the world have exacerbated the speed and scale of the crisis's impact.

And yet, this is still a financial crisis, not a broad, fundamental economic meltdown. There is no sign of substantial risk of sovereign default in any of the major strong economies around the world. Moreover, the effects of this crisis will not be uniform. To be sure, many healthy banks and financial institutions are being punished by association; they are suffering from the shortage of credit and of investor confidence. But these effects will subside. As governments and central banks cordon off the problem institutions, a level of relative calm and confidence will return to the markets.

Even now, a number of financial-services organizations are surviving the crisis without major turmoil. They have a historic opportunity to capitalize on the events of the past 6 months and emerge better positioned than they have ever been before. Their next stage will be to develop new business models and revamp management practices for lasting success in the postcrisis world. The current uncertainty provides a base for their future advantage.

Thus, for those in the financial-services industry, now is not a time for knee-jerk responses. These times call for business and government leaders to take a clam look at the realities—to put in place measures that address economic fundamentals and establish a platform for success in the new era.

Remember, this crisis *was not driven by economic or geopolitical fundamentals.* It is rooted in the risk management of particular financial-services institutions. In the United States and Western European banking systems in particular, a combination of incentives and market signals— the rise of asset values, the tax deductibility of mortgage interest, the nonrecourse rules (which prevent lenders from having access to borrowers after foreclosure), and the strong sales commission incentives in real estate—had led to easy consumer credit and inflated purchasing power. Financial institutions, chasing market share in a rising market, had used securitization in ever more complex varieties to fund their lending. Insurers, rating agencies, and regulators had all played an enabling role. Authorities reacted slowly and, on occasion, acted without the information needed to be effective (for example, the German government in its response to the near-collapse of the Hypo Real Estate holding company). In some cases, structural factors had delayed effective response: U.S. Federal Reserve measures, such as the lowering of fund rates, had been weakened by the amount of money tied up in longer term instruments, such as fixed-rate mortgages.

As the denouement unfolds, three sets of opportunities are appearing: one for financial institutions in developed economies, one for the banks and financial-services industries in emerging economies (the so-called BRIC [Brazil, Russia, India, China] markets), and one for government regulators.

Developed Economies: A Smaller Winner's Circle

Perhaps the most profound and enduring effect of the crisis will be the death of the business principles and models born 75 years ago with the Glass-Steagall Act in the United States. Markets will become significantly more concentrated in deposits and assets; investment and commercial banking institutions will continue to converge. This will lead to lower reliance on leverage in investment banking business models. And it is already setting the stage for the emergence of new boutique and niche models, operating independently of "large organization" cultures, and requiring limited capital.

The financial-services survivors in developed countries seem to be largely retail banks and wealth management companies. They are gaining significant market share—by attracting customers who seek security and quality and by taking advantage of opportunities for acquisition.

Three factors have helped them. First, they avoided the excesses of fast growth. Instead, they built strong franchises. The insurance companies among them relied not on investment returns but on innovative operating models. The retail and commercial banks maintained sound risk and capital management practices. The investment banks kept their exposure in check, close to their underlying assets.

Second, these surviving institutions have maintained strong capital positions and diversified funding sources. They have high levels of deposits and strong cash flows, plus a range of short- and long-term wholesale sources of funding in different markets. Additionally, they have maintained open communication channels to other potential sources of funding, such as sovereign wealth funds or institutions from less-affected markets such as Japan and the Middle East.

Third, they have communicated effectively with their boards and the market. Even the players with solid fundamentals can suffer if they are tainted with negative perceptions. The strongest players have avoided this.

These financial-services institutions are proactively restructuring their businesses to make the most of their new opportunities. They are divesting assets to raise capital, boosting their positions in emerging markets, raising capital through rights issues, simplifying their portfolios, increasing their productivity and performance, and looking closely at their risk management practices. We expect to see further consolidation.

Emerging Economies: Rapid Opportunity

In the faster-growing BRIC economies, challenges and opportunities vary by locality. Most large banks in these markets have escaped the worst effects of the crisis. In a few countries, like Russia, financial institutions face substantial challenges because of weaknesses in their home markets. But in most emerging nations, banks have very limited direct exposure to the asset classes in crisis, and they face limited risk of contamination from the United States and Western Europe.

Moreover, most of these institutions have experienced rapid growth thanks to the real economic growth of their home countries and to the large numbers of new consumers using banking services for the first time. Of course, in the next year or two, this growth may slow down a bit. The weakened global economy could lead to lower export rates and reduced credit and liquidity. In China, a number of bank share offerings have already been postponed.

But for the first time, countries like China, India, and Brazil have strong internal markets and a robust institutional and regulatory apparatus. Financial institutions in these countries will be more resilient than in times past. Their greater economic diversification in recent years and structural competitive advantage in commodities will also help corporate risk profiles.

The strongest financial institutions in these markets will return, in the short term, to local financing, often with a focus on retail banking. As they manage their own fast credit growth environments, they will improve their risk controls and governance mechanisms. The wisest of them will partner with governments to develop new regulatory frameworks that are conducive to market growth and market security. Some of them, as they build scale and maintain market capitalization, will diversify and internationalize, taking advantage of their strong capital positions to merge with or acquire financial institutions in other parts of the world.

Governments: Rethinking Regulation

The capital markets have fundamentally changed. Globalization has not been halted; indeed, it is likely to accelerate after this crisis. New York and London will lose their preeminence to Shanghai, Dubai, and Singapore. Investors previously seen as relatively unimportant—particularly sovereign wealth funds and investors from oil-rich countries—are now critical enablers of the recapitalization of the world's companies and economies. The major financial institutions of the new economies have grown in relative strength through this crisis, and they have clear ambitions to become leading global financial players.

The financial systems of the future are changing as well. The amount of trading will decrease as the markets deleverage and the derivative-enabled speculation and hedging markets diminish. The market will be inherently less profitable; it will no longer contribute as much to overall employment and gross domestic product (GDP) in most markets. Employees will look to other industries for jobs; governments will look more to Main Street than to Wall Street for tax revenues.

The role of government will also change. Policy makers and governments will take as much interest in managing investment flows as they do in managing global trade. They will harmonize tax regimes, regulate foreign investment, and involve themselves more in foreign ownership and capital flow. Their goal: to prevent future crises and oversee the funding that they have injected into the markets. International agreements will be based more on pragmatic "rules of thumb" and less on complicated analytical models. Regulators will be open to well-formulated proposals on the design of measures that will support the building of institutions in this new world.

The crisis will ultimately create a healthy call for change and improvements in the financial world, particularly in risk control, governance, and regulation. Financial-services companies that focus on restructuring their businesses, partnering constructively with regulators, and tightening risk controls and capital strength can play an active role in the redesign of the global industry. For many of them, it will represent a natural evolution from the role they have played in this crisis. Now they must apply the same skills and capabilities as they move from short-term triage to build the next long-term platform of a sustainable global financial-services regime.

CHAPTER 21

Evolution on the Global Stage

Their Raw Potential Is Clear, but Chinese Companies Will Have to Master the Imperatives of "Soft Power" to Reach the Next Level of International Growth

Edward Tse, Andrew Cainey, and Ronald Haddock

One sign that a country has a dynamic industrial base is its ability to produce companies that lead their fields worldwide. The United States has Google and Microsoft, the United Kingdom has Virgin Group, Germany has Bayer, and Japan has Toyota. What can we expect to see out of China?

Despite achieving astonishing growth rates, few Chinese companies have developed brand names that are recognized beyond Chinese borders. The problem is that Chinese companies lack "soft power," an asset that every big international company exploits in one form or another. Hard power and soft power are concepts originally applied to countries by Joseph Nye, former dean of Harvard University's Kennedy School of Government; in that context, the former refers to countries' use of military and financial might to impose their will, whereas the latter indicates an ability to gain influence based on culture. In business, hard power refers to the use of scale, financial might, and a low-cost position to win business, secure acquisition targets, and gain distribution access.

By contrast, soft power is the capability to attract and influence customers; employees; and, indeed, stakeholders of all kinds to make them want to be part of the company's mission and business activities. It is based on a deep understanding of what different stakeholders value and how the company can fulfill those needs—whether through a seductive and aspirational brand, a heroic mission, a distinctive talent development approach and company culture, or a willingness to be a genuine part of the community.

This proposition is crucial, especially for companies that want to grow in the global marketplace. Customers, for instance, do not just buy the technologically superior or lowest cost product; they seek out brands that offer emotional or aspirational connections, such as BMW's link to the UK's swinging 1960s in the launch of its Mini (and enhanced by the option of putting the Union Jack on the roof or even the wing mirrors). Similarly, top-notch managers want more than stellar compensation; they want to work with the best people, enjoy personal development, and be part of a grander design. Regulators and governmental officials look at businesses not simply for their profit-making potential, but for the contribution they can make to national and local policy objectives, such as the development of the local economy and infrastructure, improvement of the environment, or creation of new jobs. Finally, even investors are increasingly incorporating perspectives such as corporate social responsibility into their investment decisions. In short, soft power embraces a company's values, whereas hard power deals with its market muscle.

In business, soft power has four dimensions. Companies can do the following:

- *Establish themselves as technology or innovation leaders,* as the South Korean electronics manufacturer Samsung has done with cell phones
- *Cultivate a management/leadership mystique,* as Toyota has done in manufacturing with the 14 principles of "the Toyota way"
- *Develop a reputation as a responsible and influential citizen,* such as General Electric (GE) has done in its emphasis on environmentally friendly products or as Burger King has done in it's promise to treat animals more humanely

- *Appeal to customers' aspirations and sense of themselves,* as Apple did in turning the iPod into a status symbol

Most Chinese companies are still figuring out which levers of soft power to pull—and how to pull them.

They are also in the early stages of their efforts to demonstrate *values-based leadership and management,* the platform of soft power that underpins the four dimensions and is especially critical to international expansion. As companies expand overseas, they need to manage effectively in different cultures, where, for example, the importance attached to hierarchy and to personal relationships compared to that of professional relationship varies widely. Japanese and Korean companies have found this transition especially challenging as they've expanded overseas. Toyota, for instance, has announced initiatives that focus on adapting and strengthening its values in far-flung business units, such as in the United States—where Toyota's core internal processes of continuous improvement, partnership with suppliers, and incremental design are not necessarily ingrained in the local culture. Chinese companies are just starting to face that challenge.

Values-based leadership involves finding ways to motivate and inspire workforces that are as diverse in their cultural backgrounds as they are geographically. It does not require the abandonment of the home country's culture, but it does require a fresh look at management behaviors that have worked well in the home market and a reemphasis on common human aspirations, concerns, and behaviors. Companies that don't inspire their employees will find themselves challenged to keep their staff—as Japanese companies learned, to their detriment, in the 1980s and '90s when they first expanded abroad. Nomura and Daiwa, for instance, paid high salaries to attract Western talent but suffered the cost of turnover when they couldn't keep their new employees for more than a year.

Compare those missteps to the approach taken by British bank Standard Chartered: When it purchased Korea First Bank, it declared a "Korea Day" across its network in Africa, Asia, the Middle East, and the United Kingdom; in each country, staff took time out to learn about Korean culture and welcome the new Korean employees to the organization. The company repeated the exercise when it bought Hsinchu International

Bank, a Taiwanese bank. This sort of welcome needs to be supported by the establishment of new, shared norms that take multiple cultures into consideration; these must be reinforced through senior management communication, promotion decisions, training, and incentive schemes. Companies such as Nestlé, HSBC, and GE have built this capability over decades. Chinese companies can look to such examples as models.

The Elephant's Soft Power

In their attempts to quickly establish soft power, Chinese companies might learn from their counterparts in another emerging market: India. Although the two countries and their economies have much in common, the differences are substantial. China, on the one hand, has had great success in deregulating industries at the macro level, drawing in vast sums of foreign and domestic investment. India, on the other hand, has been a leader in driving innovation, resulting in the massive growth of its software and offshoring sectors. Contrasting peer companies across the two countries indicates where Chinese companies can find sources of soft power that Indian companies have used successfully in international expansion.

For instance, consider two companies that make paint and other home decor products in emerging markets: Asian Paints in India and Huaren in China. Although not cognizant that it was applying soft power, Asian Paints, which is more than 50 years old, has been successful at exploiting every aspect of the concept. It became a *technology leader* by building information systems that let the company do in-store tinting and offer custom colors to customers. It developed a reputation as a *management leader* by adroitly addressing some difficult marketplace challenges. For instance, when the surging Indian software sector emerged as competition for its best employees, Asian Paints launched competitive compensation and performance policies.

Asian Paints addressed *customers' aspirations* by introducing a line of paint products that came in smaller packages and had lower prices. Finally, Asian Paints has shown that it understands the tenets of *values-based leadership*. Almost from the beginning, the family-run company understood the importance of giving managers assignments in foreign countries; it now routinely brings in nonfamily members to serve as executives and board members. These traits have made Asian Paints the number one seller of paints in India and the second most recognized brand in that country, after Tata Steel. Furthermore, it has been able to apply this formula across 28 countries in various regions, including the Middle East, South Asia, and Australia, taking into consideration their diverse market needs.

Huaren, by contrast, has made few strides on the soft-power front. In its 15-year history, it has made several preliminary moves toward management leadership by recruiting foreign technology experts and sending some workers abroad for training. And it has produced its share of innovations, including a paint that is heatproof and environmentally friendly. However, the company has not considered how those innovations might be applied to markets outside the mainland and has not made the effort to sell these products globally. As the number three paint company in China (behind two foreign competitors) and a new player on the international stage, Huaren could benefit from the lessons that Asian Paints can impart.

If history is any guide, China's up-and-coming companies won't remain unknown forever. The best Chinese companies will do what American and European companies have long done and what Japanese and South Korean companies have done in more recent decades: use their strengths in the homeland to expand internationally.

For instance, companies can leverage the positive reputation that their home countries have developed as a consequence of their economic success. For U.S. consumer product companies, this has often meant international associations with the "good life" of affluent Americans that has been reinforced by Hollywood. In recent years, many Asians, especially younger ones, have started to look to Korea as a fashionable, leading-edge country, based on its technical leadership in mobile communication and its soap operas and movies.

Similarly, China's continued growth has already started to attract attention. In Africa and Latin America, China is becoming a major foreign investor and alternative source of financing for governments and is sending many Chinese employees to work overseas. As the global community's focus turns to helping drive economic growth for the people at the bottom of the pyramid, China offers an alternative to the traditional

Western model of economic success. If they act wisely, Chinese companies have a strong base from which to build soft power, combining an empathy with consumers across emerging markets, technological sophistication inspired by the world's largest mobile phone population, and cultural attraction based on a many centuries-old civilization.

References

Hampden-Turner, C., & Trompenaars, F. (1997). *Riding the waves of culture: Understanding diversity in global business.* McGraw-Hill.

Liker, J. (2003). *The Toyota way.* McGraw-Hill.

MacNealy, J. (2007, April 9). GE: Making money, making a difference. *The Motley Fool.* Retrieved from http://www.fool.com/investing/value/2007/04/09/ge-making-money-making-a-difference.aspx

Nocera, J. (2007, June 9). Running G.E., comfortable in his skin. *New York Times.* Retrieved from http://select.nytimes.com/gst/abstract.html?res=FAFC3D5B0C7A8CDDAF0894DF404482

Nye, J. S., Jr. (2004, Spring). Soft power and leadership. *Compass: A Journal of Leadership.* Retrieved from http://www.ksg.harvard.edu/leadership/Pdf/SoftPowerandLeadership.pdf

Tse, E., & Cainey, A. (2007, August). Attracting global interest: How Chinese companies can leverage "soft power" in the international marketplace. Booz Allen Hamilton white paper. Retrieved from http://www.boozallen.cn/media/file/AttractingGlobalInterest.pdf

CHAPTER 22

Going From Global Trends to Corporate Strategy

Will Your Business Catch Them Before They Catch It?

Wendy M. Becker and Vanessa M. Freeman

An executive's ability to read trends accurately in a rapidly changing business environment can make all the difference between riding the currents of opportunity and paddling upstream against them. But even when you have a good feel for broad emerging macroeconomic, social, environmental, and business developments, how do you assess their impact on the profitability of your own company? And what should you do about them?

The need to evaluate these developments should not be underestimated. In a recent McKinsey survey, executives around the world weighed in on the forces shaping the global business environment. ("An executive take on the top business trends," 2006)[1] Asked which three trends will be the most important ones for global business during the next 5 years, these executives chose two macroeconomic trends (the growing number of consumers in emerging economies and the shift of economic activity between and within regions) and a business trend (the greater ease of obtaining information and developing knowledge; Davis & Stephenson, 2006). But it is worth noting that executives think most of the 10 trends we asked them to assess will be substantially more important for global business overall than for the profitability of their own companies.

That distinction calls for deeper analysis and reflection. For starters, executives shouldn't view even the most powerful trends in isolation.

Beneath each lies a multitude of subtrends that interact to affect not only the obvious industries but also many others, to varying degrees and in different ways. In our experience, a scan of global trends too often proves superficial or simplifies the complexity of interacting subtrends, thus putting strategies and operations at risk.

Trends to Watch

In this chapter, our survey findings are accompanied by a series of reflections exploring some of the steps that top managers can take to understand trends and use them in a company's strategy. How should executives go about the difficult task of analyzing the impact of a complex global trend (see Exhibit 22.1)? Why do growth and profits depend on a company's ability to shift the corporate portfolio continually so that it is aligned with favorable trends? What role can the strategic-planning process play in identifying growth opportunities and assessing the portfolio mix? And how can large companies use their scale to drive the innovations that could put them in front of a trend before it passes them by? (See sidebar "Analyzing a Global Trend.")

Competing With Portfolios

As global trends shape the business landscape, they will inevitably affect competition among companies. And just as companies often fail to analyze global trends in detail, they can also fall short in their analysis of the competitive factors those trends create.

The executives polled in our survey agree that competition is becoming more intense: 85% of them describe the business environment of their companies as more competitive (45%) or much more competitive (40%) than it was 5 years ago. Opinions about specific competitive challenges—low-cost competitors, the improved capabilities of competitors in general, regulatory changes—vary by industry, appropriately enough. More than a third of the representatives of heavy industry, for example, single out low-cost rivals as the most important competitive factor, as opposed to just 1 in 10 in financial services. And telecom executives are almost twice as likely as those from other industries to be concerned about innovative market entrants (Exhibit 22.2).

Analyzing a Global Trend

The complex nature of long-term global trends and the way they interact make it challenging for executives to analyze their impact on a company's profitability over the long term. But that complexity makes it all the more important for companies to get to grips with their business environment.

Take, for instance, one of our 10 trends: increasingly tight constraints on the supply and use of natural resources, or as your morning newspaper might put it for a particular resource, "Oil price hits new all-time high." Not surprisingly, fully 88% of the executives at energy companies and 69% of those at manufacturing ones expect this trend to be important or very important for the profitability of their businesses. But across industries, only 40% of our respondents agree, though 71% view this trend as important to global business overall. Fewer still—30%—say that their companies are preparing for shortages or steep increases in the price of raw materials.

We believe that many companies have yet to consider the full range of this trend's subtrends: for instance, water is increasingly scare, global fisheries are reaching a crisis point, and deforestation threatens to cause more than just economic harm. Moreover, as these ripples spread, even companies that don't seem to be affected in the near term must analyze each development's real impact on their industries, geographies, and business units. The analysis should include the effect on products, processes, customers, competitors, and employees.

Executives should consider the opportunities and risks these subtrends pose. Can companies that know all about the demand for and supply of minerals use these insights in the trading markets? Will the large-scale shipping of water become economically viable for the cargo industry? Will biotechnology companies change the game with crops that require less water or trees that grow much faster than today's?

Corporate leaders must understand how trends interact as well. Auto manufacturers, for instance, should view the trend of booming markets in developing economies through the lens of another: constrained energy resources and increasing concern about pollution. What are the likely implications when hundreds of millions of Indian and Chinese consumers buy cars for the first time? Automakers face a series of challenges: designing energy-efficient cars that are cheap to buy and drive and don't put intolerable pressure on the environment.

To ride the coming waves of global forces, a company must prepare by undertaking a comprehensive longer-range analysis of the external environment. The analysis should go well beyond a superficial scan of global issues not only to build a detailed understanding of the trends and how they will affect the company but also to facilitate open dialogue within the top team about what the future will bring. In addition, the company should regularly review and update this aligned view of the future; only then can it identify growth opportunities, plan for economic discontinuities and risks, and make the big bets necessary to capture the most rewarding opportunities.

—Wendy M. Becker and Vanessa M. Freeman

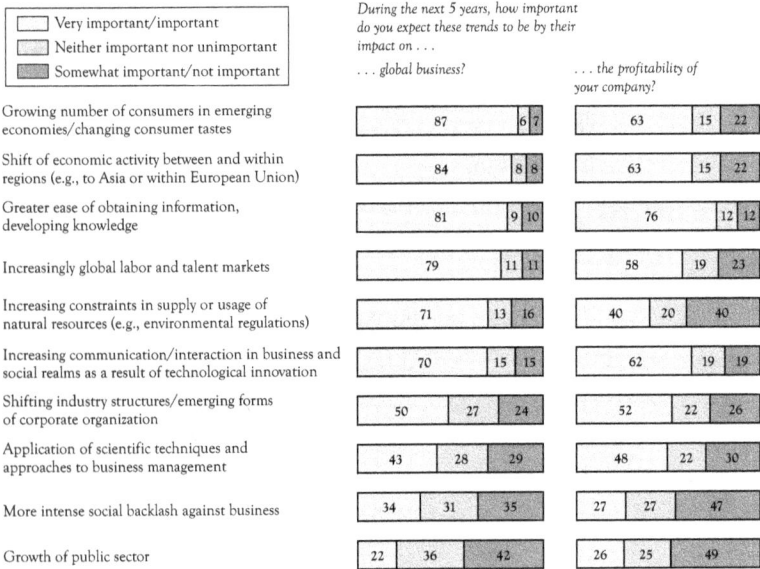

Exhibit 22.1. The Impact of 10 Trends

What single factor contributes most to the increasing competitive intensity in your industry today?

Industry[2] of respondent's company

	Business services	Consumer	Banking, finance	Health care	Heavy industry	IT	Telecom	Other
Improved capabilities of competitors (e.g., better knowledge or better talent)	27	21	27	18	25	30	18	20
More low-cost competitors	25	25	11	18	36	24	27	14
More competitors	18	13	15	10	9	11	9	18
Growing size of competitors	7	13	14	10	8	10	9	8
Growing size of innovative market entrants	10	9	9	9	3	10	17	10
Regulatory changes (e.g., market or industry deregulation, trade agreements)	4	4	12	22	8	3	17	10
Rising consumer awareness and activism	3	5	5	9	3	4	1	14
Growing number of attractive, accessible markets	3	4	5	1	6	5	2	2

Exhibit 22.2. Competitive Intensity by Industry

In our view, companies should push the analysis even further, the better to shift the business mix of their portfolios in response to the competitive dynamics of their industries. According to new research, companies that tweak portfolios to align them with favorable competitive factors are quite likely to grow faster and offer higher returns to shareholders than companies that don't (see sidebar "Keep Shifting Portfolios").

Keep Shifting Portfolios

To determine the financial impact of broad global trends, a company must sift through their second and third-order effects even as unanticipated new business models and other hybrid species sprout up and change the competitive landscape. Our research on growth in large companies highlights the importance of analyzing changing competitive factors at the most detailed level (industry, subindustry, geography) and in their most elemental form (the specific trends and subtrends that not only create opportunities and risks but also drive competition at each level). Only in this way can companies obtain insights into the way these factors will affect their future growth and profitability. By unearthing the follow-on effects of trends such as consolidation, regulatory change, the rise of attacker business models, and specific shifts in the needs or power of customers, executives can better move the portfolios of their companies toward segments and markets with favorable prospects.

Our research bears out this point. We analyzed the top-line growth of more than 150 large companies from 1999 to 2004 and tested how closely their organic growth correlated with their mix of businesses. The broadest classifications of portfolios, such as "consumer discretionary," weren't at all useful in explaining the different growth rates of companies. Classifying business portfolios more tightly into 140 subsectors (such as beverages and packaged foods) made it possible to explain about 35% of the variance in organic growth across companies. Finally, when we went as far as the reported data allowed—analyzing business segments by geography (for example, ice cream and frozen desserts in Asia)—we explained 60% of the variance. Similar results hold for differences in profitability.

What can companies do if they aren't lucky enough to hold legacy portfolios aligned with favorable trends? Quite a lot, it turns out. Our research suggests that strong growth and profits often result from intensive changes in the portfolio mix through mergers and acquisitions (M&A), the creation of new businesses, or the radical reallocation of budgets. In fact, significant changes to the portfolio occurred in two out of three companies that, over 5 years, increased their revenues at a pace faster than the growth of gross domestic product (GDP) and gave their shareholders total returns that outperformed global stock indexes. (We define a significant change as one of at least 15% in the distribution of total revenues over a company's business segments and geographies.) In contrast, almost two out of three companies that failed to expand at a pace faster than the growth of GDP hadn't shifted their portfolios in this way.

So it seems that many profitable growth companies not only know about the trends in their markets but also act on the way those trends play out at the microlevel.

—Martijn Allessie and Carrie Thompson

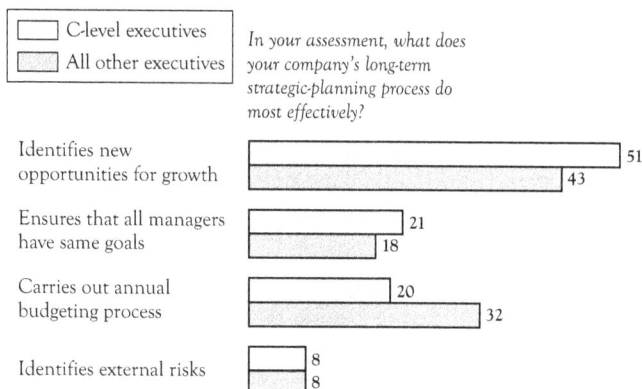

Exhibit 22.3. A Disconnect

The Role of Strategic Planning

Strategic-planning processes can play a vital role in identifying new growth areas and assessing corporate portfolios to determine the optimal mix of businesses. Indeed, in this respect the top executives in our survey emphasize the effectiveness of their companies' strategic planning. Interestingly, however, lower-echelon executives instead underline its role in the annual budgeting process (Exhibit 22.3). This seeming disconnect in perceptions about what strategic planning should and does achieve suggests that ancillary processes, removed from the plans of the core business, might better serve companies looking to grow and to develop their portfolios (see sidebar "Planning for Change").

Innovation and the Pace of Change

Innovation is high on the minds of executives around the world. In fact, they see it as the main reason the pace of change in the global business environment is accelerating so greatly (see Exhibit 22.4).

Unfortunately, a quickly changing business environment driven by a constant flow of new ideas can be daunting for executives of large companies. These executives know that speed, good execution, and incremental innovation are essential to keep a core business competitive with its peers. Furthermore, large corporations must innovate to build new businesses for themselves so that their portfolios stay in line with changing consumer preferences, budding demand in emerging markets, and other global trends.

Planning for Change

Few executives would deny that good strategic planning can help companies find new growth opportunities and evaluate what they should add to or subtract from the corporate portfolio of businesses. Yet when we talked with managers at a score of major companies, most of these people ruefully admitted that the formal strategic-planning process was optimized to maintain and develop the core business through activities such as budgeting, driving incremental growth, and aligning management with short-term financial targets. Other strategic objectives received haphazard treatment, if any.

This kind of strategic-planning process usually drives the performance of the core business effectively. Yet it isn't very efficient. Often, a 9-month planning cycle involving a huge amount of work merely generates a budget that more or less reflects the size of each business unit, with incremental growth expectations layered on top.

We believe that companies can shorten and streamline this formal planning process and thereby allow executives to focus on developing strategies. Companies should reach for these goals through tailored ancillary processes removed from the annual planning exercise and its immersion in the financial and operational details of current businesses. To design such processes, a company should determine which strategic objectives are the most important ones for its own purposes, given the composition of its portfolio and the specific attributes of its industry. One important goal should be to develop and review corporate strategies in a regular rhythm—the better to combat the tendency, revealed by our research, to make most decisions involving major mergers, acquisitions, and divestures in an ad hoc or opportunistic way.

Companies can make a good start by studying what some of them already do. One pharmaceutical company, for instance, established a new function for strategic initiatives to pursue growth beyond the core business. Planners generated a portfolio of ideas in a series of off-site meetings and vetted them with the company's top 100 managers. A strategic-initiative team then explored in detail the business viability of each idea in the queue—typically looking at two or three in parallel—and gave the appropriate business units the best ones to commercialize.

A large multibusiness company implemented a biannual corporate-portfolio review process to ascertain which businesses had an upside for growth and which should be divested to free capital for investment in new growth areas. To help liberate corporate managers from the business-as-usual mind-set of financial and operational planning, the company decoupled this portfolio review from the annual planning process.

—Renee Dye and Olivier Sibony

In the mobile-phone business, for example, leading manufacturers dance a constant minuet of brinkmanship: each must prepare near-term responses to the moves of the others while building a long-term competitive advantage through the next design or feature breakthrough in handsets. Doing all these things takes a huge amount of innovation. Although scale can be a problem for big companies undertaking this kind of effort, they can turn it to their advantage as well (see sidebar "Innovating at Scale").

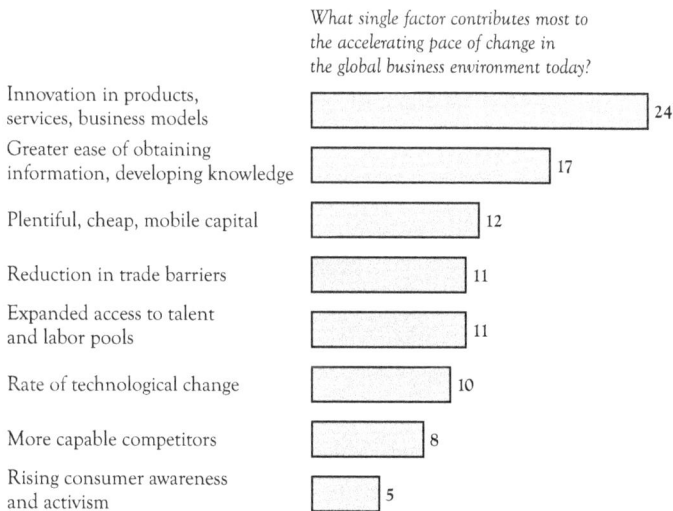

What single factor contributes most to the accelerating pace of change in the global business environment today?

Innovation in products, services, business models	24
Greater ease of obtaining information, developing knowledge	17
Plentiful, cheap, mobile capital	12
Reduction in trade barriers	11
Expanded access to talent and labor pools	11
Rate of technological change	10
More capable competitors	8
Rising consumer awareness and activism	5

Exhibit 22.4. Why So Fast?

Innovating at Scale

For a $20 billion company the required scale of any innovation and the impact it must achieve are staggering. Top managers know that unlike the leaders of a start-up, they can't bet the company on a single breakthrough. What's more, a large company's need to produce near-term results in its core business often seems to be in conflict with its need to innovate for tomorrow.

Yet there is also an upside. Many big corporations haven't yet fully used scale to transform promising ideas into innovations whose value can be amplified by their diffusion among a number of customer and product segments. To seize this opportunity, large companies must overcome two prevalent beliefs: that innovation takes resources away from the core business and that it requires an entrepreneurial culture, which flourishes only in smaller and younger companies. In fact, we would argue that far from being in conflict with innovation, a large company's core business and assets can be used as stepping-stones to innovate with an impact that smaller companies can only dream of.

Innovating at this level begins with an understanding of a large organization's scale advantages. Substantial tangible assets such as technology and human and financial capital can serve as powerful complements to the diversity and reach of brands, knowledge, and other intangibles. Large companies can also bear and manage risk as well as place a number of different bets. Companies should evaluate such assets and identify those that can collectively amplify the value of innovation and, at times, both serve the core business and provide new growth opportunities.

Scale assets can, for example, extend the reach of an innovation beyond immediately addressable core segments. Consider Motorola's successful RAZR mobile phone, which set a new standard in ultrathin handsets. This breakthrough parlays corporate engineering and design assets that can be reapplied under the Motorola brand in other market segments (such as smartphones, which handle a number of applications) where design is a key competitive factor.

Large companies can also use their assets to broaden their sources of innovation. Procter and Gamble (P&G), for example, realized that it couldn't meet its growth objectives solely through internal product development. The company therefore decided to draw on resources (such as global brands, patents, and relationships with suppliers, retailers, consumers, and regulators) in order to set up and widely publicize "open-innovation" networks, where scientists share intellectual-property agreements. Along the same lines, it has also encouraged start-ups with ideas for new products to bring them to P&G. It then uses its brand, marketing skills, supplier networks, and other relationships to diffuse these innovations through various market segments and new products. Each participant benefits as the network grows.

Identifying scale advantages and applying them to innovation isn't easy. But for companies that overcome the obstacles, innovation can be worth more than just the sum of its parts.

—Marla M. Capozzi and Bhaskar Chakravorti

Global trends form tangled webs that can catch a company's strategy unawares. Companies that refine their understanding of the way trends will filter down into their own industries, subindustries, and geographical markets can shift their portfolios and gracefully ride future trends as they emerge.

Note

1. *The McKinsey Quarterly* conducted the survey in March 2006 and received 3,470 responses from a worldwide representative sample of business executives, 44% of whom are CEOs or other C-level executives.

References

Davis, I., & Stephenson, E. (2006, January). Ten trends to watch in 2006. *The McKinsey Quarterly*, Web exclusive. Retrieved from http://www.mckinseyquarterly.com/links/22698

An executive take on the top business trends: A McKinsey global survey. (2006, April). *The McKinsey Quarterly*, Web exclusive. Retrieved from http://www.mckinseyquarterly.com/links/22697

Permissions

Chapter 2, "A Forecast of Globalization, International Business, and Trade: Report From a Delphi Study," is reprinted with permission from *Journal of World Business,* published by Elsevier, Michael R. Czinkota and Ilkka A. Ronkainen, 40(2), 2005: 111–123.

Chapter 3, "The Policy Gap in International Marketing," is reprinted with permission from *Journal of International Marketing,* published by the American Marketing Association, Michael R. Czinkota, 8(1), 2000: 99–111.

Chapter 6, "Have Lunch or Be Lunch," is reprinted with permission from *Marketing Management,* published by the American Marketing Association, Michael R. Czinkota and Ilkka A. Ronkainen, March/April 2004: 48–50.

Chapter 8, "Strategic Alliances in Emerging Latin America: A View from Brazilian, Chilean, and Mexican Companies," is reprinted with permission from *Journal of World Business,* published by Elsevier, Masaaki Kotabe, Preet S. Aulakh, Roberto J. Santillán-Salgado, Hildy Teegen, Maria Cecilia Coutinho de Arruda, and Walter Greene, 35(2), 2000: 114–132.

Chapter 10, "Three Dimensional: The Markets of Japan, Korea, and China Are Far From Homogeneous," is reprinted with permission from *Marketing Management,* published by the American Marketing Association, Masaaki Kotabe and Crystal Jiang, 15(2), 2006: 38–43.

Chapter 11, "Global Sourcing Strategy and Sustainable Competitive Advantage," is reprinted with permission from *Industrial Marketing Management,* published by Elsevier, Masaaki Kotabe and Janet Y. Murray, 33, January 2004: 7–14.

Chapter 12, Outsourcing, Performance, and the Role of E-Commerce): A Dynamic Perspective," is reprinted with permission from *Industrial Marketing Management,* published by Elsevier, Masaaki Kotabe, Michael J. Mol, and Janet Y. Murray, 37(1), 2008: 37–45.

Chapter 13, "Outsourcing Service Activities: Gaining Access to New Ideas and Flexibility Will Allow Service-Buying Firms to Remain Competitive," is reprinted with permission from *Marketing Management*, published by the American Marketing Association, Masaaki Kotabe and Janet Y. Murray, 10, Spring 2001: 40–45.

Chapter 14, "An Evolutionary-Stage Model of Outsourcing and Competence Destruction: A Triad Comparison of the Consumer Electronics Industry," is reprinted with permission from *Management International Review*, Masaaki Kotabe, Michael J. Mol, and Sonia Ketkar, 48(1), 2008: 65–93. With kind permission of Springer Science+Business Media.

Chapter 15, "The Overlooked Potential for Outsourcing in Eastern Europe," is reprinted with permission from *The McKinsey Quarterly*, Detlev Hoch, Michal Kwiecinski, and Peter Peters, Winter 2006: 19–21.

Chapter 16, "How to Be an Outsourcing Virtuoso," is reprinted with permission from **strategy+business**, published by Booz & Company. www.strategy-business.com.

Chapter 17, "The Brand Challenge: Are Global Brands the Right Choice for Your Company?" is reprinted with permission from *Marketing Management*, published by the American Marketing Association, Johny K. Johansson and Ilkka A. Ronkainen, 13(2), March/April 2004: 54–55.

Chapter 18, "Spanning the Globe: Winning Over the Antiglobals," is reprinted with permission from *Marketing Management*, published by the American Marketing Association, Claudiu V. Dimofte, Johny K. Johansson, and Ilkka A. Ronkainen, 17(5), September/October 2008: 40–43.

Chapter 19, "The Effects of Terrorism on International Marketing," is reprinted with permission from Andersson, S., & Svensson, G. (Eds.). (2009). *Glocal Marketing: Think Globally and Act Locally*. Lund, Sweden: Studentlitteratur AB.

Chapter 20, "Taking a Calmer View," is reprinted with permission from **strategy+business**, published by Booz & Company. www.strategy-business.com.

Chapter 21, "Evolution on the Global Stage," is reprinted with permission from **strategy+business**, published by Booz & Company. www.strategy -business.com.

Chapter 22, "Going From Global Trends to Corporate Strategy: Will Your Business Catch Them Before They Catch It?" is reprinted with per-mission from *The McKinsey Quarterly*, Wendy M. Becker and Vanessa M. Freeman, 3, August 2006: 16–27.

Index

Note: The italicized *e* or *t* following a page number refers to an exhibit or a table, respectively.

www.ingramcontent.com/pod-product-compliance
Lightning Source LLC
Chambersburg PA
CBHW060316200326
41519CB00011BA/1746